KEVIN SHEEDY

STAND YOUR GROUND

Life & Football

MACMILLAN
Pan Macmillan Australia

Material from the *Herald Sun*, *The Australian* and *The Age* appearing on
pp 163–4, 249–5, 257–7, 335–41 reprinted with kind permission.
Photographs courtesy of the *Herald Sun* newspaper.

Letter written by Michael Long appearing on pp 331–2 reprinted with kind permission.

First published 2008 in Macmillan by Pan Macmillan Australia Pty Limited
1 Market Street, Sydney

National Library of Australia
Cataloguing-in-Publication data:

Sheedy, Kevin, 1947–
Stand your ground: life and football / Kevin Sheedy.

978 1 4050 3895 9 (hbk.)

Sheedy, Kevin, 1947–
Australian football players—Victoria—Biography.
Australian football coaches—Biography.

796.336092

Typeset in Sabon 11.5/16.5pt by Midland Typesetters, Australia
Printed in Australia by McPherson's Printing Group
Papers used by Pan Macmillan Australia Pty Limited are natural, recyclable products made
from wood grown in sustainable forests. The manufacturing processes conform to the
environmental regulations of the country of origin.

Acknowledgements

A major project like this doesn't get done without the input of a lot of wonderful people.

I would like to thank Tom Gilliatt and Kylie Mason from Pan Macmillan and copy editor Robyn Fleming.

I am grateful to Marc Fiddian for his input into the chapter on the early days of football in Melbourne.

To Tom Hafey, thanks for agreeing to write the foreword. This is just one of the many things that Tom has done to help me over the years.

There are many, many people who have supported me through my days as player and coach. Some are mentioned in this book, some inevitably are not.

To everyone — from my first days in South Yarra to the great moments I am still enjoying, travelling the world promoting Australian football — who has stopped to say hello, have a chat, offered a bit of wisdom or an idea, my heartfelt thanks.

To my family: my wife, Geraldine; our fabulous children, Renee, Chelsea, Sam and Jessica; my brothers and sisters; my mum and dad — thanks for everything that I could ever have wished for, and more, in my private life.

My persevering assistant, Jeanette Curwood, has done a mighty job organising my diary so that I could find the time to reflect on my six decades on earth.

Finally, my deep gratitude to Warwick Hadfield. We have worked together on three books now, *Follow Your Dreams*, *The 500 Club* and now this memoir. I tried to convince him we should not use the word 'I' as often as we have this time, but he insisted you can't be asked to write a memoir and not talk about yourself. He is usually right on things like that. He also once told me that nostalgia is the most powerful drug in the universe. There is no doubt that while writing this book, reflecting on 60 years of enormous social change in our country as well as in our game, there were plenty of 'highs'.

Warwick, you have done just the most fantastic job trying to make sense out of my thoughts, my sentences, and my whole life. Here's that very important word again — thanks.

Kevin Sheedy
2008

Contents

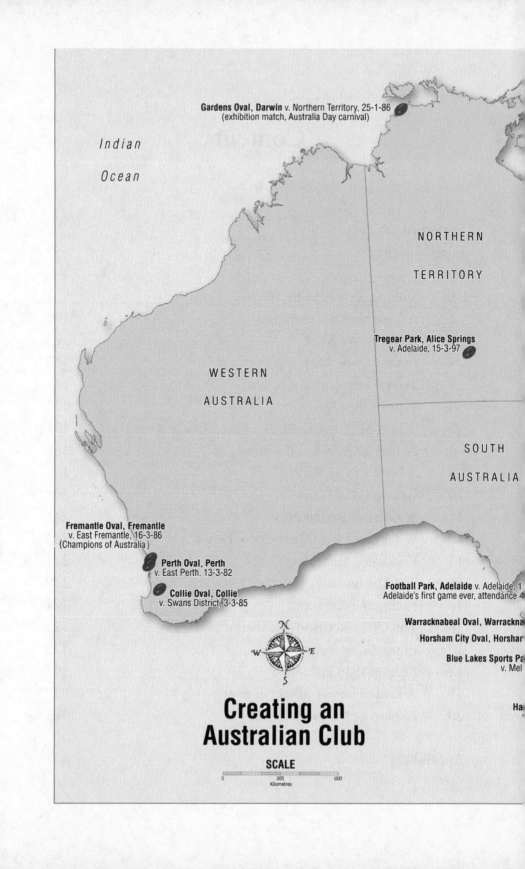

Gardens Oval, Darwin v. Northern Territory, 25-1-86
(exhibition match, Australia Day carnival)

Indian

Ocean

NORTHERN

TERRITORY

Tregear Park, Alice Springs
v. Adelaide, 15-3-97

WESTERN

AUSTRALIA

SOUTH

AUSTRALIA

Fremantle Oval, Fremantle
v. East Fremantle, 16-3-86
(Champions of Australia)

Perth Oval, Perth
v. East Perth, 13-3-82

Collie Oval, Collie
v. Swans District, 3-3-85

Football Park, Adelaide v. Adelaide, 1
Adelaide's first game ever, attendance 4

Warracknabeal Oval, Warrackna

Horsham City Oval, Horshar

Blue Lakes Sports Pa
v. Mel

N
W E
S

Ha

Creating an
Australian Club

SCALE

0   300   600
Kilometres

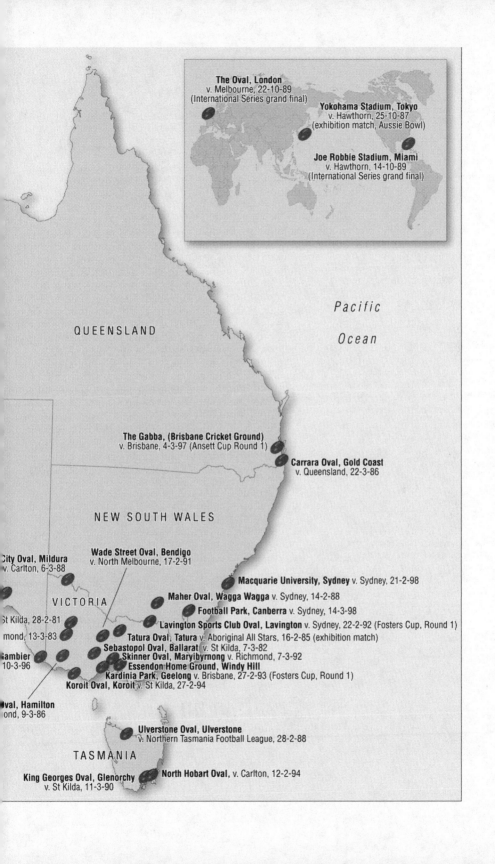

The Oval, London
v. Melbourne, 22-10-89
(International Series grand final)

Yokohama Stadium, Tokyo
v. Hawthorn, 25-10-87
(exhibition match, Aussie Bowl)

Joe Robbie Stadium, Miami
v. Hawthorn, 14-10-89
(International Series grand final)

Pacific

Ocean

QUEENSLAND

The Gabba, (Brisbane Cricket Ground)
v. Brisbane, 4-3-97 (Ansett Cup Round 1)

Carrara Oval, Gold Coast
v. Queensland, 22-3-86

NEW SOUTH WALES

City Oval, Mildura
v. Carlton, 6-3-88

Wade Street Oval, Bendigo
v. North Melbourne, 17-2-91

Macquarie University, Sydney v. Sydney, 21-2-98

Maher Oval, Wagga Wagga v. Sydney, 14-2-88

VICTORIA

Football Park, Canberra v. Sydney, 14-3-98

St Kilda, 28-2-81

Lavington Sports Club Oval, Lavington v. Sydney, 22-2-92 (Fosters Cup, Round 1)

mond, 13-3-83

Tatura Oval, Tatura v. Aboriginal All Stars, 16-2-85 (exhibition match)

Sebastopol Oval, Ballarat v. St Kilda, 7-3-82

Gambier

Skinner Oval, Maryibyrnong v. Richmond, 7-3-92

10-3-96

Essendon Home Ground, Windy Hill

Kardinia Park, Geelong v. Brisbane, 27-2-93 (Fosters Cup, Round 1)

Koroit Oval, Koroit v. St Kilda, 27-2-94

Oval, Hamilton
ond, 9-3-86

Ulverstone Oval, Ulverstone
v. Northern Tasmania Football League, 28-2-88

TASMANIA

King Georges Oval, Glenorchy
v. St Kilda, 11-3-90

North Hobart Oval, v. Carlton, 12-2-94

Foreword

Whenever I am asked my opinion on Kevin Sheedy, which happens quite a lot, my reply is simply: 'He has done everything he could to get the absolute best out of himself.' You can say that about him as a player, as a coach and as a person.

I first heard about Kevin Sheedy when I was coach at Richmond. We were told there was a skinny kid down at Prahran, in the Victorian Football Asociation (VFA), who might have a bit of potential as a Victorian Football League (VFL) player at Richmond. When I got to know Kevin better after he came to the Tigers, I discovered this young bloke with a terrific passion to improve his game. I wouldn't be giving away any secrets if I said that when Kevin came to Punt Road, he had a lot to learn — a *real* lot. The thing about Kevin that made us decide to persevere with him was his unbelievable eagerness to learn. Kevin is a great talker, but he was also then — and still is now — a great listener.

He realised very early on that football would give him opportunities in life way beyond what his qualifications as a plumber offered. But he knew that would happen only if he worked not as hard as everyone else, but harder. In many ways, he probably saw me as an example of that. I was hardly the greatest footballer in the history of the game, but I worked hard to get my 67 games with Richmond. Like Kevin, I had a trade I could always fall back on — printing. However, it was football that was my real passion and which could take me places that printing wouldn't.

When Kevin was injured so early in his time at Richmond, he could have given up. Instead, he went out of his way to make sure that when he got over his knee operation, he would be fitter and stronger than before. I watched him pretty closely through that process. He went out and learned as much as he could about the injury, then about what he needed to do to ensure a proper rehabilitation. That's Kevin — whenever he's confronted with an issue, he learns as much as he can about it.

It was, as he relates in this book, the same when he was in the army. He reckoned that if he was going to be sent to Vietnam, he should know as much as possible about the people he would be fighting against.

When Kevin became a coach, I know he always wanted to do well against me. It was also the same when he coached against other long-term coaches such as David Parkin, Allan Jeans or Ron Barassi. The challenge of matching his wits with these names was always a tough one for Kevin in his early days. It is one of the reasons why he waited until he had finished playing to become a coach — and not just *a* coach, but the first full-time coach in the history of our sport. An innovator from the start, he also wanted to make sure he was absolutely ready.

I am proud that in his early days as a coach he used a lot of the things he had learned from me and others at Richmond. Some of the people at Richmond reckoned that Kevin took anything that wasn't nailed down from Punt Road to Windy Hill!

As he developed as a coach, though, soon other clubs were taking *his* ideas, and not just on the field. He is one of the best thinkers about football we have ever seen, and one of the game's greatest promoters, helping the game develop in places as diverse as the Tiwi Islands and Sydney. I don't think Kevin will be satisfied until every town and suburb in Australia has its own Australian footy team.

I note that he takes credit for getting me the job as coach of the Sydney Swans in the 1980s. Thanks, Kevin, it was a wonderful experience for Maureen and me; living close to the beach, having club functions at the Bourbon and Beefsteak in the Cross, trying to educate the people of Sydney about our game. I reckon we did a pretty good job, too. I know they really enjoyed the time at the Sydney Cricket Ground in 1987 when we thrashed the Bombers by 163 points.

I doubt the national competition would be anywhere near as successful as it is today without the creative input of Kevin Sheedy — ideas like the Anzac Day blockbuster, the Dreamtime Game, and now the Eureka Game. That ability to think outside the square is why, when Essendon no longer wanted him, the AFL was keen to make him an official ambassador for the game.

Kevin has a fantastic family. His mother Irene was a lovely lady. He talks about his brother Pat at length in this book. I have found that Kevin was very close to all his brothers and sisters. He has been married to his wife Geraldine for longer than he coached at Essendon! That's saying something. He has four wonderful children.

When we were recruiting people to Richmond in the 1960s, Graeme Richmond and I weren't just looking for good players;

we wanted good people, too. Talent is only part of the mix for a successful team. You want people who are prepared to work hard, stick to the team rules, and be really loyal to what you are trying to achieve. That pretty much sums up Kevin in his playing days — along with his passion to learn, which I have already mentioned.

I have known Kevin for more than 40 years. We have worked together closely on any number of projects, we have coached against each other, we have chatted for hours over endless cups of tea. I reckon I know him as well as just about anyone.

Kevin Sheedy is a sensational person. And, like all of us, he keeps getting better with age.

Tom Hafey

Introduction

Q: Do you think that the perception of what the media have created around you over these years has been an accurate one?

Kevin Sheedy: What, that you don't know who I am?

Q: Do we know who you are?

Kevin Sheedy: No, and I don't want you to know. We can talk about that when my career is over.

I'm not entirely convinced that my coaching career *is* over, but I guess it's not too soon to write about myself and my life … so far. A lot of my friends have died around the age of 60. At least I've put some thought into my life, and so I've accepted the chance this book offers to write about it for my friends and family.

The young boy growing up in the inner suburbs of Melbourne in the 1950s had read only one book, and that was the Catechism. It was a very small book in which you learned about Catholicism and prayers. In the end, though, football became my religion. It helped me with my thinking and my education on the great island of Australia. It's taken me all over this great nation and enabled me to meet some magnificent people.

In my first seven months as the AFL's ambassador, following the end of my coaching contract with Essendon, football took me overseas to the Americas, to Africa and to Europe. Australian football is still building my life, showing me different ways of thinking while creating a vision for the game's future.

Writing my memoirs while travelling, I have looked back over the years and discovered that it's not all about Essendon, even though I barracked for the Bombers as a child and coached the club for 27 years. It's also about meeting lots of people in the game. The people *are* the game. They are fantastic, even when they might be your arch enemy. Having someone dislike you makes you stop to think about why they think the way they do.

Football is an unbelievable pathway that brings together people from all walks of life. There are a lot of people who avoid the spotlight, but who are essential to the game. I hope that from time to time I have stopped and said 'hello', or 'thanks', to them. It's these people who are making football the one sport in Australia that soccer will always struggle to overcome.

In the 60 years I have been on the planet so far — and my plan is that there will be a lot more to come — I have learned a lot of things that have changed and enriched that young boy from South Yarra. Yet I have always remained aware of him, and of the loving people who surrounded him, sometimes to protect him from himself, other times to protect him from a world that he was only slowly learning about.

There was a wonderful father, a beautiful mother, aunts and uncles, brothers and sisters. My father didn't get to join me on my journey as much as I would have wanted. However, he left a big impression and I still feel his spiritual influence today. When he died, I was lucky to find other people who could advise me, point me in the right direction. No one gets anywhere in life on their own. You have to have people around you whom you can trust, people with whom you can be honest and who will be honest with you in return.

I have been fortunate to have had so many of those sorts of people in my life. Some of their stories and contributions are contained in this book. They have protected me and my privacy. They have allowed me to be the public Kevin Sheedy who loves nothing better than striding out confidently to promote this great game of Australian football. They have done this whenever I have needed support, advice, friendship, or just a cup of tea, a biscuit and a chat.

Through football, the sport I chose at a very young age by a process of elimination that is described in this book, I have been given a lot of opportunities to discover so much more in life than you would expect from being able to kick and catch a piece of inflated leather. In Melbourne, football has opened doors since just about the start of the colony. It is now doing it all over Australia, which is really fantastic.

I have been given access to premiers and prime ministers. I have also been given a great gift that enables me to walk up to people in the street and say 'g'day' and learn something from them. 'Hello' is my favourite word. It's an invitation to meet. I also like 'thank you'.

The best ways to say 'thank you' include some of the things that I have helped to promote in football — the Anzac Day blockbuster between Essendon and Collingwood, the Dreamtime Game between Essendon and Richmond, and the

Eureka Game — for the working-class people in this country. This is the next big one on the agenda, with a couple more to come in the future. Every club should have an icon game.

Football has also enabled me to earn a comfortable living. I have had a long and wonderful marriage to Geraldine. I have four sensational, healthy children — Renee, Chelsea, Sam and Jessica.

That's not to say the journey hasn't been one without setbacks. One message I hope that comes through in this book is that in life, you should use setbacks to your advantage, by making them the motivation to succeed next time. The worst thing you can do when you hit a hurdle is to become bitter.

On 25 July 2007, when it was announced that Essendon would not be renewing my contract, I was disappointed that I wouldn't be able to coach all the terrific young kids I had recruited to the club in recent times. But I couldn't be bitter at the club's decision: how *could* I, after all that I had been blessed with over 27 years — four premierships, and the chance to work with an amazing array of young men and women as we developed Essendon from a suburban club into a nationally recognised one?

While this book is an autobiography and the story in it's mostly about me, it's also about showing gratitude to all the people who helped the boy from South Yarra, the plumber from Prahran, the back-pocket from Richmond, the record-breaking coach for Essendon, get to where he is today, on the cusp of another wonderful period in his life.

When Essendon said 'no', a whole lot of other people said 'yes'. The fun continues.

Kevin Sheedy
2008

1

Sinking Slowly in the West

It's late evening, 1 September 2007, Subiaco Oval, Perth, Western Australia. As the sun begins to dip into the Indian Ocean, 42,000 people rise from their seats, twirling their coats in a stirring, standing ovation. What a gracious moment these West Australians — and the few Victorians alongside them — are providing; what a stirring end to my 27-year career as coach of the team that I grew up supporting: Essendon, the black and red; the colours, too, of my first school team — a big part of my life in almost any bit of it you might choose to look.

The warmth of the send-off is welcome. It's been a chilling time at Essendon Football Club since the board decided in late July, and apparently by a vote of 10–1, not to renew my contract (or, as some people keep insisting, to sack me). Yes, 10–1; not quite unanimous, but hardly a vote of confidence that I had been doing a good job. Since that moment — when the board guys couldn't quite get their script right on the Monday evening, but let me know of their decision on the Tuesday — I have discovered, like so many other coaches before me, how hard it is to do your job when you don't have the full support of your board. They don't have an intimate knowledge of the game — in some cases, they have no knowledge of it at all — but board members are charged with making the tough decisions about the future of the team and the club. Like coaching, it's a job that comes with a lot of pressure: pressure that can break you if you're not the right kind of person to get involved in footy, which — as this send-off going on around me is proving yet again — is a completely unique beast. A lot of people who are very successful in business, or in some other area of life, think they can just move into the world of football as a board member. If they were being honest, every one of them would have to tell you that, when they got there, it was nothing like they had expected.

Right now, some people are saying the Essendon board members have been handling it all well, but others are not so certain. There are lots of stories of dissension — some private, some embarrassingly public — from which I have been working hard to shield the players during the last weeks of my tenure. But footballers don't live in a vacuum, and I haven't been able to do it all the time, especially when I'm being told by a lot of people about how unhappy some of the board members look when, against the odds, we produce the miracle and win the game against Adelaide the weekend after the public announcement that my contract won't be renewed. Of course, I can't see that from the coaching box, but digital cameras in the hands of people who can are a wonderful invention.

Anyway, all the whispers in corridors, the little leaks to the media, the innuendoes, are irrelevant now. It's game over, final siren, all clear at Subiaco Oval, and the West Australians are standing up to applaud not just me, but James Hird. Via an amazing array of circumstances, it's his last match, too. Jimmy's got tears streaming down his face. So, too, I notice through all the sound and movement, the whacks on the back, the firm handshakes and the hugs, have a lot of the other Essendon players. Up in the media boxes, the commentators are talking about the end of an era — it's the end of a couple of eras, actually.

That's why I allow myself a few seconds to think how it could easily have been the end of just one. At the end of the 2006 season, some people in management at Essendon Football Club had wanted James Hird to retire. It had nothing to do with his ability to still play the game, as the events of 2007 proved beyond any reasonable doubt. As the next few weeks after these Subiaco festivities would reveal, he wins the club's best and fairest award in 2007, so he *can* still play, especially when the performance that clinched the award for him was in this last game.

When news of the announcement of the win at the traditional best and fairest dinner reaches me in Toronto, where I'm opening the Canadian Stock Exchange, I will be more surprised than anyone that he has won it. I thought the medal would go to Dustin Fletcher who, with the spectacular arrival of Mal Michael to help him out down back, had a wonderful season: his best in years. Getting Mal from Brisbane via a delightful recruiting coup gave Dustin the freedom to play more creative football. (And if you're wondering, *Why Toronto?*, it was important for me to get out of the way and let the new coach have his moment once the AFL grand final and the official Sheedy farewell lunch the following day were over.)

Anyway, the rationale behind tip-toeing James Hird into

retirement in 2006 had to do with the salary cap and some concerns among the blokes in suits about whether his body could cope with another season. In essence, though, it was about taking the easy way out. James had been all but persuaded to quit before Matthew Lloyd, our captain, and I sat him down at separate meetings and talked him out of it. What a moment — a priceless one, compared to the few dollars the administrators might have saved in their salary cap — would have been lost, not just for James, but for the game of Australian football, if we hadn't intervened! Heroes, people who fulfil their childhood dreams while sharing with us all of the tough times as well as the good ones, are precious. They deserve to be sent off in style, not cut off while still in their prime.

So, on this golden day at Subi, I appreciate and celebrate the fact that the applause is for James Hird as much as for me. He is the best player — and one of the best people — I have ever coached. And when I say 'coached', I use that word advisedly. I only ever guided James through his career. There are some players who have to be directed on an almost daily basis. Then there are some uniquely talented individuals with whom the job of coaching comes down to the simple matter of making sure they get to the game on time. Of course, that can be a bit more of a challenge than you might think. Just ask Geelong coach Billy Goggin, who couldn't get Garry Sidebottom on the bus to Waverley Park for the preliminary final in 1981. But then it might have been Garry's fault for not turning up on time. Whatever happened, it was unbelievable.

If I was still guiding James Hird, I would have been saying 'play on' in 2008. There has been this thinking at Essendon that somehow Sheedy and Hird should go together. It's not necessarily clever thinking. Gee, if you're good enough to win the best and fairest, you should be good enough to play the next year. What if Lance Armstrong hadn't tried for a seventh Tour de France after winning six? Or even a second after winning the first? What if Layne Beachley had quit surfing at six world titles? Sometimes being in an individual sport is an advantage. You have greater control over your destiny. People who make these decisions about the future of players in a team situation should be aware of what Armstrong's and Beachley's stories mean.

Apparently, Shane Warne was too old to keep playing for Australia at 38. But the demise of spin bowling in the Australian team since his retirement in January 2007 suggests we could have done a lot worse than to ask Warnie to keep on playing. After all, Clarrie Grimmett, an old Prahran leg-spinner for a while, didn't make his Test debut for Australia until he was 34. He played for another 11 years. See, we leg-spinners know these things. If I can delve into the territory of our brother slowies — the off-spinners — for a while, Bertie Ironmonger and Don 'Rock' Blackie were closer to 50 than 40 when they played their first games beneath the baggy green cap. We've got to be careful when we say someone isn't good enough just because of a date on their birth certificate. That piece of paper from the Registry of Births, Deaths and Marriages doesn't, for instance, take into account the fact that James Hird missed three seasons, so — in football terms — he is not that old.

We need to get a bit creative about keeping the likes of James Hird playing the game for as long as possible. The fans would love it, so why not have a contract that says 'play two games, have one off'? You don't get so many James Hirds that you can end their contributions to the game prematurely. And once they're gone, they're gone forever.

This is a great part of the reason why so many people have turned out at Subi this day in September 2007, or are watching the game on the telly all over Australia. They want to see this great player just one more time. And he doesn't disappoint; his best game of the season is this one against the Eagles and, in one of those twists that sport always loves to throw up, at the venue where he had suffered one of the greatest setbacks to his career, a serious facial injury.

Anyway, from this day on, James Hird will never again run out on to a footy field in anger — with or without words of guidance from K. Sheedy ringing in his ears. Knowing how much he loved his two hours of happiness every winter weekend, chasing the ball like his very existence depended on it, I appreciate the great sense of loss that is descending on him, threatening to crush him. No wonder he's holding on to his family for dear life. Until he finds new reasons to keep on being James Hird, wife Tania, their daughter Stephanie and two sons Thomas and Alexander will be his anchors.

As well as James's family, mine is here too — the first time in 27 years they have been in the coach's box. It's the first time they have ever seen just what it is we do when we are away coaching. We're up against the team that was the premiership side the year before and is still a pretty good outfit, and we're struggling. So, there's a fair bit of hectic talk going on about what we need to do. We make a few moves and suddenly Scottie Lucas bursts into the game and kicks seven goals. We reduce a 51-point deficit to two points, but West Coast gets a late goal and we just lose.

So, here it is: the end. After almost three decades, I will never again be putting on a black and red tracksuit, climbing up into the coach's box, roaring orders to the runners, shifting the magnets, dealing with the bruised bodies and egos of this cherished club. And people are rising as one to say goodbye.

I guess there had been some warning of the type of farewell that was coming. The Freo crowd and players had clapped us when we played them at Subi a few weeks earlier. I didn't know whether to smile or shake my head. Here we are trying to get the Dockers to be a hard club like Port Adelaide, and there they are giving us a sentimental round of applause, even before the game. I had never seen that before in the 1000 games I had played or coached in the VFA, the VFL or the AFL.

The West Coast Eagles are already a hard-nosed club. But again on 1 September, the people of Western Australia with whom, apart from a couple of incidents — think 1993 and the twirling jacket, think Mitchell White in 2000 — I have had a pretty good relationship, are giving James, myself and our families this fantastic send-off. I suppose they can afford to be generous: they've got the four points. I smile to myself and wonder if it would have been the same if Essendon had won by a goal. Probably. As it turns out, we have already robbed them of a home final. Anyway, Australians, no matter on which side of the Nullarbor they live, are pretty smart people. These ones here inside the Subi coliseum would understand that, when it comes to football, I have never really been concerned about state barriers. Yes, as coach of Essendon I have always put my club first but despite still having its headquarters in Melbourne, by 1 September 2007 the Essendon Football Club is much like the game itself — a national entity. We have supporters in every nook and cranny of the country, from the Tiwi Islands Bombers in the far tropical north to Bruny Island in the cool, temperate south — where a Tasmanian bloke painted his roof black and red and called himself the Bruny Island Bomber.

I've been visiting Western Australia since 1970, helping to develop the game here in whatever way I can. The locals know I have worked with John Todd and Barry Cable — two of their legends even before there was such a thing as the West Coast Eagles. More recently, I had been involved in supporting their newest team, the Peel Thunder, by attending functions when asked to do so. One time was when Barry Cable's son was coaching, and the other was a fantastic day in the clubrooms with the new young players in that area. Essendon later picked up one of those players, Scott Gumbleton, but we didn't tell anyone that day we were after him.

Among everything else that is going on, and there is plenty, this day at Subi is a wonderful sign that the game of Australian football has become so genuinely Australian that so far from home, so far from the places where so many years ago schoolyard dreams began to become something more substantial, a boy from the inner suburbs of Melbourne, and another one from Canberra — rugby territory — can get a farewell like this. Where else in the world could something like this happen? Would supporters of an Athens-based soccer team give a stirring send-off to a coach and player from an English club? I think not, though the flying time between those two places is roughly the same as the trip from Melbourne to Perth. What we've got in Australia is unique and very, very special.

Life, especially life in football, never stops throwing up challenges, surprises and occasionally, just occasionally, moments of great pleasure and satisfaction. That's why I have never become tired of the game, not just during the 27 years I have been at Essendon, but through all those years as a player at Richmond, at Prahran, right from the time I played my first ever game of football in the black and red jumper of the St Ignatius team.

It's why I'm not sad now. Yes, Essendon is over, but there is so much life still to be lived, so much more football to be involved in.

Way back when I was a kid in shorts and sandshoes, I knew I was never going to be a musician, never going to be someone who got their thrills from literature, from reading the classics. From the moment I looked out through the school windows and saw all the activity surrounding the preparations for the 1956 Olympics at the Melbourne Cricket Ground, I knew the thing that would attract my attention the most was always going to be sport. The question was: *which* sport?

How the answer to that question became Australian football is to me part of the magic of this wonderful life I have been given, one that started out when Tom and Irene Sheedy's baby son entered the world on 24 December — Christmas Eve — 1947. Now aged 60, my journey is far from over: Tommy Hafey, my old coach at Richmond and one of my closest friends, is still contributing to the world in his mid-seventies. Tommy still gets invited to go out and speak at schools and other places. I think his message about combating obesity through fitness and health, no matter how old you are, is one that deserves an even wider audience than that. If I was in government, state *or* federal, I would appoint Tommy as the roving ambassador for good health. When he takes his famous t-shirt off, Tommy still has a magnificent build. His message is that just because you're getting older, it doesn't mean you should just waste away in a retirement villa. I want to be around for at least another 17 years like Tommy. I want to be there for his 94th birthday, and plenty more. Who knows what I will be doing then, but I want it to be a worthwhile contribution to football and the community. It might still be through coaching — I haven't for a moment given up on that yet — but it might be something even better!

Maybe, I'm thinking as this marvellous day at Subi comes to an end, it's time I coached myself again. The sun is sinking now into the Indian Ocean, but it will come up again tomorrow.

2

A Disciplined Upbringing

Like all mums should be, mine was a wonderful figure in my life. She always knew when it was time to pat Kevin on the head, or the backside. From what she used to say, it was more the former. Mum always reckoned I was a quiet youngster, one who always knew what he wanted to do in life and got on with it.

Mum also showed the same awareness with her other children, my six brothers and sisters. I was third in line; Barbara and Patrick were older than me, and Kathleen, Bernard, John and Anne-Maree came after 24 December 1947. It was kind of nice being younger than Barbara and Patrick, who really ran the family as the eldest brother and sister. I have always quite enjoyed just sitting off the pace.

We lost our Dad in early 1966 when I was 18, just as I was starting my football career at Richmond. The official cause of death was motor neurone disease. There was a lot of speculation within our family about whether this had been caused by an incident involving another person at Dad's work; whether an assault had led to the illness. We've never been able to find out any more details.

What I *have* found out over the years is how much I would have loved to have been able to sit down with him and ask, 'What do you reckon, Dad? How am I going?' Dad didn't know much about football at all; he was a racing man. His hero wasn't a Jack Dyer or a Dick Reynolds; it was a horse by the name of Tulloch. I don't remember going to the football with Dad, but he did take us to the races a lot, and to lots of other places. One of his favourite places — and mine — was the bush, where we would meet the real Australian farmer, the man on the land with tractors, fishing rods and a gun. Those were fun days for me as a young person. It helped that Dad had grown up in the bush.

Despite Dad's lack of interest in footy, I believe he would have appreciated the importance to me of those premierships at Richmond during my 251 games as a player there, or the four at Essendon as coach.

When, early this century, I became the proud part-owner of a lovely little champion colt by the name of Bel Esprit, I could just feel my father shining down on me. I think Mum, too, felt that there was a deep family connection through this lovely little horse that for a short but thrilling moment was one of the best sprinters in Australia and is already emerging as something of a champion sire. I recall one early morning — it was about six o'clock — out at track work at Caulfield. It was freezing. The wind was one of those lazy ones that go through you, rather than around. The rain was horizontal and there was hardly a soul there to watch the horses.

Through the drips and from under the hood of my rain jacket, I noticed a figure, an older woman, watching from under her umbrella. I wondered who it might be and I thought I would go up and say 'g'day' and keep her company — because that's what Sheedys do. I took a few steps closer and could see it was Mum, still keeping a weather-eye on her son — but more likely on Bel Esprit.

Mum loved the races. It gave me so much joy when, just after she died, they named a race at the annual Warrnambool Racing Carnival after her. Mum had been going to the carnival each autumn for more than 25 years. I could just imagine the two of them, Tom and Irene, up there in heaven, having a quiet chuckle about that.

When I get a good colt one day from Bel Esprit, it's a fair chance it's going to be called Tommy Esprit. Being the son of Tom Sheedy has been fantastic for me, as has being a friend of Tom Hafey.

Dad was a labourer. He worked on the railroad, and he drove trucks. He also worked as a nurse at the Kew Mental Hospital. We didn't have a lot of money when I was growing up, but we didn't notice. Anyway, dreams don't cost you anything, and I had plenty of those, especially when it came to sport.

One thing Dad taught me — something that is both a wonderful asset and a liability that to this day still gets me into trouble — was the practice of always stopping to say 'hello' to people. Dad was always interested in what other people had to say. Everyone has an interesting story to tell, so why not stop and hear it? was his attitude. Okay, I know that I can stay listening for much longer than I should, and that this habit upsets people waiting for me to keep appointments with them. But gee, I reckon that over all my years as a player and coach, all those chats on the way to somewhere else have given me more insights into football and life than any scheduled meeting I've ever been to. It was a better education than school or university.

Dad was a pretty strict Catholic. In fact, he didn't want me to play with Prahran when I first went there because in those days the VFA played its matches on Sunday. I have since learned, though, from some of his old work-mates, that they covered for him a few times so that he could come and watch me play.

He was fiercely proud of his Irish heritage, something that seems a bit strange given the amount of trouble I have got into with Ireland in recent times. If you're reading this at the Gaelic Football Association, hey, I'm one of you! Dad's parents had come out from Ireland, first to Yarrawonga, then to Bairnsdale. I remember we had some great holidays up around there — in Bruthen, Wiseleigh and Mossiface. Dad took us to meet every farmer in the region. He told us about snakes, frogs, cattle, the Tambo River. It was all about his early days, which he wanted to share with his own kids. It was a long way in the 1950s in a little Standard Eight car, up through the haunted hills outside Moe on the way to a fantastic fishing trip with our uncles, or whatever else was planned. Anything in the country, city kids loved; even the smell of the fresh air. It was just sensational. I still love going around the country and meeting people. If I owe anything to my father, it's my love of horses and my love of the country and its hard-working people.

Whenever we went up to see the grandparents, we would be put to work picking corn, cauliflowers, pumpkins and potatoes.

Mum was from Sunbury. While her religious views weren't as strict as Dad's, religion played a role in her life, too. While Dad was at church, Mum would stay at home and count the money. There was a bit of Scottish on Mum's side. Her maiden name was Nixon.

Both Mum and Dad had firm views about manners, so from very early on, I was learning all sorts of discipline.

You will go to church.
You will look a person in the eye when you shake their hand.
You won't turn your head away from me when I'm speaking to you.
You will get a haircut every second week.

Now that last one got me into serious trouble with my father. It was about the only time he ever got really cross with me. I asked him why I needed a haircut every second week.

'What business is it of yours?' he said.

'Because I keep praying to this bloke who has long hair,' I said.

'Just do as you're told,' he said.

His tone said everything. I did as I was told. It was a different time, a different generation — certainly not the 'Why?' one or the Y one!

Then, suddenly all this other discipline came into my life:

You will pick up your man.
You will play in front.
And: *Don't be late for training.*

Thanks to the inherited and ingrained Sheedy practice of stopping for a chat, I have been late for a lot of things in my life, but never for training and never for a game of football. On match days, I hardly spoke to anyone at all. I was concentrating so hard on what was ahead, preparing myself physically and mentally for my opponent.

I didn't learn those last disciplines from Dad. As I've already said, he didn't have that big an interest in footy — well, that he ever showed me. Nor was it from Mum, but I *did* learn them from a woman. Well, a couple of women, probably: Sister Rupert at St Joseph's School in South Yarra, and a bit later a young lady by the name of Veronica Nolan.

Sister Rupert came from County Clare in Ireland (the same part of the country as the Sheedys, by the way), so she didn't know much about Australian football. However, she knew that young boys needed to burn up a lot of energy if they were ever going to sit still and learn in the classroom. Because the school's grounds weren't really big enough, she would take us, or arrange for someone else to take us, to nearby Fawkner Park and let us play footy there.

Sister Rupert was a fantastic person to have in my life at about this age, because she had this attitude that she just wanted to see kids be happy. We couldn't understand the way she spoke, with her Irish accent, and she couldn't always understand us with our 'g'days' and our Australian accents. But she understood that you could get people's attention, especially the grade two kids, by allowing them to play football. There were 38 kids in our street alone, so there would often be quite a few games going on at one time. She would divvy us up into teams of nine or so. The nominated captains would pick one player each until there was no one left. These days we would call it modified football. Back then we just called it fun.

After a while, we graduated to some under-age teams. In the late 1950s — the dates are all a bit blurred now — our school team from St Joseph's turned up at Toorak Park to play in a tournament. We didn't have a coach. The role went to the big sister of a couple of boys in the team, Veronica Nolan, who did the job for two years. Her story even ended up in the papers, while one of her brothers became a VFL umpire. One of the things I really worked hard on later in life, especially in my time at Essendon, was promoting the valuable roles that women play in football. It all began for me with Sister Rupert and Veronica Nolan.

I played a lot of footy in my childhood — in the schoolyard, in the local parks, in the streets. There just always seemed to be plenty of time to do it, just as there always seemed to be plenty of decent weather. Isn't it funny how, in your childhood memories, the sun always seems to be shining, the days warm and clear? Yet, this was a *Melbourne* childhood — well, a Melbourne childhood before climate change and water restrictions. There must have been at least some grey days, some rainy ones, but not in my memory — just lots of sun. This probably explains my red nose. Back then, we didn't have zinc cream either — no slip, slop, slap — which is probably why so many people of my age have noses the colour of mine.

Life was generally pretty simple: you played outside on the streets or in the parks, and you slept and ate indoors. Our house was in Fitzgerald Street, South Yarra. It wasn't the South Yarra of today, with expensive boutiques and five-star hotels at which rock stars stay. Back then the Jam Factory was just that, a jam and fruit factory. Now it's a highly fashionable shopping centre and theatre complex on Chapel Street, surrounded by one of the most densely populated parts of Melbourne. It was more working class when I was growing up there.

Toorak was the only posh suburb at that time. If you had to put a label on us, it was probably that we were working people.

That's a group I still identify with so easily, even though footy has given me a pretty good living over the years and opened up all sorts of doors in what they call the top end of town. It's great to be able to meet people of influence, people of wealth, people of talent in music and the arts, and so on. But I still love being Kevin Sheedy, or 'Sheeds', the grown-up version of the boy from South Yarra, the son of a labourer who got himself a trade as a plumber, just hanging about with other similar sorts of people, having a bet, maybe doing a bit of fishing and a lot of talking.

Mum and Dad had only just moved to South Yarra when I was born. Before that, they lived at 81 Richardson Street in Essendon, just a decent drop punt from Windy Hill. So, I was conceived in Bomber territory. Essendon was different from South Yarra. There were some beautiful large homes. And, of course, it had its own VFL team. Other family members still lived in Essendon, so I spent a lot of time in and around Union Road, Maribyrnong Road and Mt Alexander Road right from my early days, visiting grandparents and aunts and uncles, and learning all about the myths and legends of Windy Hill.

Footy was different in South Yarra and Prahran, more earthy and grassroots. However, crowds numbering in the thousands would turn up to watch local teams representing pubs like the Royal Exchange, Max Hotel and College Lawn play each other. A lot of former VFL players would turn out in these, trying to prove they were still worth a go in the VFA and so get a game for Prahran.

If you asked me what it was like growing up at that time, I'd have to give you a one-word answer: brilliant. In 2007, I discovered I wasn't the only person from that era who had the same view. I did an interview on ABC Radio National with Phillip Adams, presenter of the *Late Night Live* program. Phillip was the creator of the *Life, Be In It* advertisements in the 1970s that tried to get people up off the couch and out being active. I can tell you we never needed anything like that in South Yarra. We knew what life was, and we were in it just about every minute we were awake.

The funny thing about doing this interview with Phillip — who has done so much to promote the arts, the Australian film industry, and much, much more — was that it was his first-ever interview with a sportsperson. As a youngster, he had barracked for Richmond, and even somehow ended up in the change rooms at Punt Road with people like Jack Dyer. But Phillip became pretty disenchanted with football and helped Keith Dunstan, the famous Melbourne journalist, set up the Anti-Football League. The Anti-Football League really upset Tom Hafey, my coach at Richmond. He used to say, 'Kevvie, how can they think like that?' In fact, and I wonder if Phillip and Keith realised this, they were doing football a favour, providing another reason for people to talk about it. Whatever, Phillip Adams has always been a stirrer. At the end of our interview, he asked me to convert him back to football and I think I might have achieved that because he wanted a list of other sporting people to interview. Welcome back, Phillip!

During the hour-long interview, it turned out that although he was seven years older than I was and our adult lives had gone in vastly different directions, we pretty well shared the same childhood: selling newspapers for a few extra bob, learning to leap on and off trams, racing our billycarts down Punt Road Hill. Just like Phillip did, as kids, the ever-growing Sheedy clan always had all sorts of simple things to keep us entertained.

My brother Patrick and I used to play football with a ball

made of rolled-up paper. You got a goal by kicking the 'ball' through the door of the outside toilet. My memory is a bit hazy on this, but I think that during my childhood we were part of the changeover to sewerage from the days of the dunny man, or the pan man. He was the fellow who took away the full pan and replaced it with an empty one. We had a narrow laneway — just wide enough for one person — at the back of our house which gave him access to our toilet, so I don't recall there being an incident at our house like the one Clive James describes in his book *Unreliable Memoirs*. Somewhere in South Yarra, though, I'm sure there would have been plenty of occasions over the years when the contents of the full pan were up-ended as the dunny man tripped on an old rake, or maybe a pushbike left lying in his path.

If you had a tennis ball, you were the richest kid in the street. You could hone your hand-eye coordination by throwing the ball at a wall and catching it, or by tossing it back and forth with a couple of mates. There was in all this an echo of Don Bradman, who practised as a youngster with a golf ball and a stump against the water tank, an echo thankfully we can still hear in Australia today.

In the streets, we all wanted to be Bradman, or Richie Benaud, or Jack Dyer or Dick Reynolds, depending on whether we were playing cricket or footy. Then a man with the strange name of Barassi came along and we all wanted to be him.

These days in footy clubs, a lot of attention is placed on the players' core; the deep abdominal muscles that help improve balance. I got my first early lessons in balance from jumping on and off trams, sometimes to sell newspapers, sometimes just for the heck of it. While selling papers on the road you could feel the wind from the passing trams, trucks and cars. For me it was a wonderful feeling of dicing with them, like a matador with a bull, with the bundle of newspapers as the cape. Every now and then, though, I'd be brought from Spain back to South Yarra when a driver would call out, 'Get off the road, you bloody idiot!'

It was probably horribly dangerous and would get you a fine these days, but we just did it without thinking about it. It was all part of a life that was much freer than the one my own children experienced.

I also got some pretty valuable lessons from dodging the trams and traffic to sell my newspapers. If you didn't get out of the way, if you didn't see them coming while concentrating on getting to a customer, you'd get a pretty serious bump. It was a good lesson for footy, where you have to focus on the ball, but also need to know who and what is around you. All those games in the park organised by Sister Rupert were also good training. The playing areas would overlap, so while you were concentrating on your game and your ball, you had to keep looking around to make sure some other kid keeping his eye on another ball and another game didn't crash into you. It's amazing the things you do as a carefree kid that end up being helpful to you as an adult!

People today who buy their milk and bread from the supermarket may not know that 60 years ago, they used to be delivered to your front door — by horse and cart. My mate was Robbie Brown. His dad was our milkman and a marvellous character. He would let us jump on to his cart and hold on to the horse's reins. We used to think it was us who got the horse to stop, but of course the horse knew the whole route and halted automatically outside each house where Bobby had to deliver his milk. We had two bakers, Gawith's and Stockdale's. Alan Stockdale, the Victorian treasurer and a committee member at

Melbourne, came from this family. We also had an iceman and a bottleman. Can you imagine the tram on Chapel Street being held up by a milk cart or baker's cart today? No, the world wasn't as fast then as it is now.

I'm not the sort of person to say the good old days are better than today. It's great that we have generational change. It's important, though, that we remember the times that we had, just to remind us of where we came from and the things that have made us what we are today.

The population of Australia grew rapidly, by 25 per cent, between 1950 and 1960 with both the baby boom, of which I was a tiny, pink part, and postwar immigration. But in 1950 it was still less than half of what it is now, so even places like South Yarra, which were so close to the centre of Melbourne, were a mix of country and inner-city life. For instance, you didn't have to go to the nursery to get manure for your cottage garden; you just followed Bobby Brown's cart. Traffic jams were pretty well unknown because car ownership wasn't as universal as it is now, when some families have three or four cars parked in the driveway — Mum's, Dad's, the kids'. In a lot of instances in our street, women didn't even drive, let alone have cars.

I found the arrival of Greeks, Italians, Czechs, Poles and other people from Europe fascinating. I was learning about places outside South Yarra, about places I would never otherwise have thought about too much. It's interesting that I was exposed to these people from overseas before I met my first real Australian, an Aboriginal. You just didn't find many indigenous people on the streets of South Yarra, even though I have since learned the

Wurundjeri tribe, from the Kulin Aboriginal nation, had been the original inhabitants of the area. After the first white settlers arrived in the 1830s, their lives were altered forever in a way that went way beyond mere generational change.

I guess the first Aboriginal person I was aware of was the boxer George Bracken, who turned up on the television when I was about 13. He was 20 and an Australian champion with an amazing build. This century, I was able to invite him to come to watch Essendon play Sydney. I discovered that, after leaving boxing, he had become a youth worker in inner-city Sydney. He works with the police. I asked him to lunch as a bit of a 'thank you' for the work he was doing then — aged well into his seventies and still in great shape. I think I was also saying 'thanks' for being one of my first idols. Often, when you meet your idols, they don't live up to your expectations. George did. He was softly spoken; a real gentleman.

It wasn't until Richmond recruited Derek Peardon from Launceston in Tasmania that I met an indigenous Australian for the first time. He had been signed by the club from an orphanage. The club had to get permission from his guardians. That was in 1966. Meeting Derek, I began to learn more about these other people living in my country, Australia, who looked different from the people I was used to seeing in the streets of South Yarra. Over the years, those people have made a wonderful contribution to Australian football, and the Dreamtime Game we now play each year between Essendon and Richmond is one way of saying 'thank you' to them.

There were a few reasons for creating the Dreamtime Game. A lot of Richmond people were upset that they hadn't been asked to be involved in the Anzac Day blockbuster. They wondered why we asked Collingwood. Well, Bruce Ruxton, the head of the RSL in Victoria, was a Collingwood supporter, and we needed him to be a supporter of this game. Initially, the RSL hadn't been keen on football being played on their sacred day but we all believe now that a huge crowd at the MCG is a good way to say 'thank you' to the people who sacrificed their lives, or their youth, to make Australia the sort of place it is today — mostly a good one.

Anyway, Richmond has now got the Dreamtime Game, which is a pretty obvious call since the colours of the Tigers and the Bombers — black, red, yellow — are those of the Aboriginal flag. We also wanted to create a blockbuster, high-pressure game in honour of Aboriginals because for a long while there had been a sort of slur that they couldn't perform in the big matches. There is a lot of blindness in people when it comes to race. They couldn't see Polly Farmer winning a grand final for Geelong, or Sydney Jackson, who won two flags with Carlton.

Eventually, a Richmond player from the Tiwi Islands, Maurice Rioli, turned that belief — that Aboriginals couldn't play in big games — on its head when he won the Norm Smith Medal in the 1982 Grand Final. His side, Richmond, lost, but Maurice showed grit and courage right to the end. How wonderful it was that in 1993, Maurice was able to award the Norm Smith Medal to another Tiwi Islander, this time from Essendon, Michael Long. And how wonderful for Michael Long, his team-mates — and his coach — that this was a grand final-winning performance!

Of course, the immigrants from Europe were already making their contribution — Barassi, Silvagni, Jesaulenko, right through to Koutoufides and most recently Bachar Houli, our first Muslim player, who made his debut in 2007. Interesting name that, because a basher is one thing he isn't. Very polite and thoughtful: a credit to his family and his people, as well as to the Essendon Football Club.

When the Europeans first started arriving after the end of the Second World War, there was a fair bit of tension. There were Germans and Italians; and Australians had fought against their soldiers in the war. There were nine or ten Italians living across the road from us and I know my dad struggled with that a real lot. Not everyone understood then that a lot of Italians, even a lot of Germans, hadn't wanted the war. News of the world was limited in those days.

Over the years, I think we have become better as a country at welcoming newcomers, and sport has had a role to play in that. There are many things I love about Australian football, but the one thing that shines through all the time is the way it keeps bringing together people from all sorts of backgrounds in a large and mostly happy family. Like any family, there are squabbles, but when it gets down to it, we are all united by this great game that we invented right here in Australia that embraces Aboriginals, Muslims, Italians, Greeks, Ukrainians, Albanians, the Irish and, hopefully, people from the Horn of Africa who are arriving here from war-torn nations in need of help. It's terrific that Australia is providing that help.

I know that the Western Bulldogs are doing their bit to make African refugees feel welcome. We all should, both for community-spirited reasons, and also from the football slant. Some people smile when I say these things, but some of those young, tall, loose-hipped Africans have playing in the ruck stamped all over them. And there are wins all around. Of course, Australian football finds a new recruiting pool, but if people are made to feel part of our community more quickly, they are less likely to set up their own isolated enclaves. Researchers at Deakin University are finding that sport, along with music and other activities, is a way to get not just children involved in the broader Australian community, but their parents, too.

Back in the early days after the war, though, you could understand why people were wary of some of the 'New Australians' from countries that had fought against us. Ron Barassi is actually Ron Barassi Junior. His father, Ron Senior, died as one of the Rats of Tobruk, serving his country and paying the ultimate price. Ron never got to meet his dad. At least I had 18 precious years with mine.

My years as a Nasho, or National Serviceman — a later part of my life about which I am very proud — enhanced my appreciation of the serving soldier. Our country has had quite a few generations of fighting men and women who have given us the freedoms and quality of life we have today.

While I was in the army, I learned that one of our great generals, Sir John Monash, was Jewish. That worried some people. I don't know why; surely if you're a good leader, a good strategist, that's all that matters? The older I got, the more I discovered that there were so many things to learn, and so many ways to learn them.

As well as saying 'hello', my parents always taught me to say 'thank you'. It's a word we don't hear often enough today. That's why I'm such a huge supporter of things that do say 'thank you'; why I put a huge emotional effort into promoting the Anzac Day game with Collingwood, the Dreamtime Game, and now the Eureka match. This will be played between Richmond and North Melbourne, the Kangaroos (or the 'Shinboners' as they were originally known, because many of their players worked in the abattoir). The Eureka flag, blue and white like the Kangaroos' colours, will feature, too. The Eureka incident on the gold fields of Ballarat in 1854 was one of just two civil uprisings in the history of Australia. It is said by many to be the fountain of democracy in Australia, where working people insisted on having a voice. So the Eureka Game says 'thank you' to working people.

But I'm getting way ahead of myself. I still had to become Kevin Sheedy, VFA and VFL footballer, before I could start any of this big-picture stuff.

Boy, weren't there a lot of people trying to get in the way of that back in the 1960s. Of course, when you've got a dream, you don't take much notice of the naysayers; you find a way around them, through them, over them — something I was going to discover I needed to be very good at. Something I have had to remain very good at right up until today. Along with kicking and catching a piece of inflated leather, it's one of the most important skills I've ever learned — that and developing a deep knowledge of not just *what* is happening, but *why* it is happening.

3

The History Man

History tells you we never learn from history. I say that quite a lot, mostly because every day, whether it's in football or in life generally, I see all sorts of mistakes get repeated. I make a lot of them myself, but the less often I repeat them, the better.

None of this has stopped me wanting to learn as much history as I can — one, because it can help stop me from making the same mistakes again; and two, because it can help me put things in context. I'm a huge fan of the Chinese proverb that goes: *When you drink from the well, know who built it.*

When I was doing National Service and there was a chance I would be going to Vietnam to take part in the war there, I went to night school to learn all I could about Vietnam's geography, economics and politics. If I was going to be in the jungles of Southeast Asia fighting these people, I wanted to know everything about them I could, in order to understand the context that had taken Australia into a war in a far-off country that didn't seem to be threatening us directly. I was very fortunate that the Australian government changed its politics, but many other young Australians weren't so lucky.

When, as a teenager, I was at war with the Victorian Football Association over my wanting to leave Prahran and play in the Victorian Football League with Richmond, I was still pretty wet behind the ears when it came to the politics and history of football. As far as I was concerned, they were just people who were trying to stop me from fulfilling my dream of playing with the VFL. All these years on, with the benefit of hindsight, experience, context and history, I'm able to see things a little less narrowly. The VFA wasn't taking a personal set against me; I was in fact just a small player in a rivalry with the VFL that was much, much older than me.

By the time I had coached and played 600 games in the VFL, I had grown much wiser about all these things. I even invited Alec Gillon, who as the head of the VFA in the 1960s refused to agree to my transfer from Prahran to Richmond, to come to the function celebrating my milestone. He came, with his son, and we shook hands. History had flown ... it didn't matter anymore.

A lot of people in Sydney and Brisbane, where there have been two rugby codes for the past hundred years, have a view that Australia football in Melbourne has always been a pretty homogenous thing. When you study the history of the game, though, you discover that nothing is further from the truth. For more than a hundred years, there was a strong, occasionally even bitter, rivalry between the VFA and the VFL. It wasn't a case of professional versus amateur, which was the cause of the split in the rugby codes. It was more about pride and prejudice, some parts of Melbourne looking down on other parts and their football teams.

It was Sir Neville Cardus who said that cricket reflects the society in which it is played. He described Victor Trumper as the bird in flight, and Don Bradman as the aeroplane. I'm not sure what that makes Ricky Ponting — a rocket scientist? While cricket is a vital part of Melbourne's history, the story of the journey from John Batman's 'fine place for a village' to the world's most liveable and lovable city is probably better told in a sporting context through the prism of the VFA and the VFL. Football is the universal language of Melbourne. Get into a taxi and the driver might come from just about anywhere in the world. Straightaway, though, you can strike up a conversation with him or her, simply by asking: 'Who do you barrack for?'

Until you've lived in Melbourne, it's probably hard to fully understand the way football permeates everything. At their funerals, great men and women are remembered for two things — their achievements in public life and who they barracked for in the footy. It was the case with John Wren, one of the most powerful people in Australian politics even though he never officially held high office. In fact, many would argue it was football that killed him. A passionate supporter of Collingwood, he died shortly after the 1953 Grand Final. Even though his beloved Magpies had won, the stress of Geelong's fight back late in the game proved too much for his heart.

Interestingly, the same was said about Jock McHale, Collingwood's legendary coach from another era. He, too, died shortly after that game, the last moments of which he and Wren had watched together.

At his funeral, B.A. (Bob) Santamaria, a familiar face from the days of black-and-white television for people my age growing up in Australia, was remembered for two things — splitting the Labor Party and barracking for Carlton. It's simply the way of Melbourne.

So, to really understand my city and to better understand the modern game of Australian football with its tentacles spreading out all over the country, even internationally, we need to understand where this game has come from. Who was it that built the well?

I invited the remarkable Marc Fiddian to my 'office' at the Hilton Hotel in Melbourne. What Marc doesn't know about the VFA hasn't happened yet — and probably never will, now that the VFA has been absorbed into the VFL and AFL structure. He isn't just interested in football, though. He is one of those outstanding people who take a great interest in histories big and small. He has written more than 50 books, including a history of the Victorian Railways and one called *A Miscellany of Left-Handers*.

The books of his that really interest me, though, are *The Blue Boys*, the story of the Prahran Football Club, and his history of the VFA, a copy of which he brought along to give to me at our meeting.

I hold a lot of my meetings at the Hilton, over a club sandwich and a cup of coffee or tea. I feel pretty comfortable in this leafy bit of Melbourne. It's just across the road from Jolimont Station and the MCG, and just a decent Polly Farmer handpass away from the old hotel where, in 1859, Tom Wills and a few of his cronies drew up the first rules of the game — Melbourne rules, as they were first called. There is no better place to write about Australian football than the MCG precinct, particularly if, like me, it's where you've pretty much 'lived' most of your life, ever since those days of St Ignatius on the hill.

It was there the wonderful coach John Kennedy came and spoke to the whole school. I can still remember the seriously steely voice with the strong message to kids who wanted to make something of their lives. No one dared take their eyes off him. You could feel for the next three or four or five weeks that everyone was on the right road to get the best out of themselves. I didn't actually meet him until decades later, but I never forgot him.

The game that's regarded as the birth of Australian football was played between two school teams, Melbourne Grammar and Scotch College, in 1858. Of course, various forms of football had been played before then. There is a theory that the game was actually brought across from Tasmania by the original settlers of Melbourne, John Batman and John Pascoe Fawkner. Some amateur Tasmanian historians claim the little village of Perth was the venue for a game of football even before Melbourne was settled.

The AFL's view is that the match between the two colleges was the first game; hence, the 150th anniversary celebrations, in which I have been involved, are in 2008. That decision has its critics in New South Wales, where some rugby league supporters claim the 150th anniversary was created to compete with their game's 100th anniversary celebration. I was reminded of this by Gillon McLachlan, from the AFL, when we were in New York in 2007. The news had even reached the Big Apple that the rugby league people weren't happy. I thought, 'Gee, Sydney and Melbourne are still upsetting each other over compressed air in a footy.' Of course, there's more now than just the rugby games and our code. Soccer, or 'football' as they want to call it, is in there too. By the way, I reckon they should get rid of the name 'Socceroos' if they want to call their game 'football'. They can't have both. We will stand our ground on football. Though you have to ask yourself why they would even want to do that in the first place. It's been simple up until now — soccer, rugby league, rugby union and Aussie rules. I can't see why they would want to shaft us and say they are the only game that can be called 'football'. Having said that, this country is the only one in the world that gives all four codes a fair go — another great testimony to the Australian people.

As ever with great moments like this match between the colleges in 1858, there are lots of myths and mysteries, and some terrific stories like that of Dr John Macadam. Tom Wills was nominated by Melbourne Grammar as their umpire. Scotch's nomination was Dr Macadam, a medical practitioner from Scotland who was a science master at the school. In 1858, Dr Macadam also had the honour of having the macadamia nut named after him. So, there were apparently nutty people involved in football well before me.

For a long time it was said that Wills and his cousin Henry Harrison were the driving forces behind the establishment of the game. There is now even some contention about that. A historian commissioned by the AFL as part of the 150th anniversary celebrations says that two journalists, William Hammersley and James Thompson, deserve far more recognition for their efforts in setting up Australian rules in the late 1850s. Whatever the strengths of that new thesis, I have always thought it amazing that this game which so grips Melbourne was first promoted by two people born in New South Wales. Thomas Wentworth Spencer Wills was born at Molonglo Plains, not far from Canberra, while Henry Colden

Antill Harrison was born at Picton, between Canberra and Sydney. By 1858, both men were living in Melbourne. That year, Tom Wills, a highly proficient cricketer both as hard-hitting batsman and bowler, wrote a letter to the editor of *Bell's Life in Victoria and Sporting Chronicle*. It was published on Saturday, 10 July and I have included this 'strong letter of history', as I call it, here:

SIR, — Now that cricket has been put aside for some few months to come, and cricketers have assumed somewhat of the chrysalis nature (for a time only 'tis true), but at length will again burst forth in all their varied hues, rather than allow this state of torpor to creep over them, and stifle their new supple limbs, why can they not, I say, form a foot-ball club, and form a committee of three or four to draw up a code of laws?

If a club of this sort were got up, it would be of a vast benefit to any cricket-ground to be trampled upon, and would make the turf quite firm and durable; besides which it would keep those who are inclined to become stout from having their joints encased in useless superabundant flesh.

If it is not possible to form a foot-ball club, why should not these young men who have adopted this new-born country for their motherland, why I say, do they not form themselves into a rifle club, so as at any rate they may be some day called to aid their adopted land against a tyrant's band, that may some day 'pop' upon us when we least expect a foe at our very doors. Surely our young cricketers are not afraid of the crack of the rifle, when they face so courageously the leather sphere, and it would disgrace no one to learn in time how to defend his country and his hearth. A firm heart, a steady hand, and a quick eye, are all that are requisite, and, with practice, all these may be attained.

Trusting that some one will take up the matter, and form either of the above clubs, or, at any rate, some athletic games, I remain, yours truly,

Beautiful words, aren't they? A game to keep cricketers fit. Years on, that letter has had an echo in Denmark where there was an ad in the paper from an Australian ... wanting a kick. The Danes now have a ten-team comp and a great junior development program that sends kids to Australia each year to play against Victorian schools.

Tom Wills might have got the idea of a football team to keep cricketers fit from something he had seen in England, where he also spent a lot of time. A similar plea to keep cricketers fit led to the setting up of the Sheffield Football Club (let's call it 'soccer') which these days is regarded as the oldest football club in the world.

The Melbourne Football Club is the second oldest and Geelong the third. Wills played for both Melbourne and Geelong, occasionally in the same season, and in the early days the application of the rules was pretty haphazard.

The game was different from rugby football, but the differences only became really discernible as it progressed and the bouncing of the ball and the high mark were formalised. (The rule about bouncing the ball was introduced so that slower players could catch the faster ones.)

Matters became more coordinated in 1877, when the Victorian Football Association was formed. That was also the year that the first-ever cricket Test match between England and Australia was played at the MCG, so it was a significant time in the history of Australian sport.

Before then — that is, between the late 1850s and 1877 — there had been an Australian rules competition featuring teams such as Melbourne, South Melbourne, Williamstown and Geelong, but these clubs organised the games among themselves. There was no such thing as a draw, like we have today. For example, South Melbourne would say, 'We're the best side in it, so we had better play Geelong twice.' The lesser clubs, who at various times might be Williamstown, North Melbourne, Footscray or Richmond, would only get to play South Melbourne once.

There were no finals or a grand final; the premiership was decided by the club finishing on top of the ladder. There was one occasion, though — in 1896 — when two clubs had the same number of wins and draws: South Melbourne and Collingwood. They actually played off, Collingwood scoring 6.9 to 5.10. The venue was the East Melbourne Cricket Ground, for many years the home venue for Essendon, or the 'Same Olds' as they were known in those sepia days. This ground no longer exists. In 1921, it was taken over by the railways and used for stabling yards.

After its formation in 1877, the VFA developed into a competition of 18 teams. But within a decade or so it had become unwieldy and the administrators decided to get rid of three Ballarat clubs. That made a fair bit of sense. To get to Ballarat, the Melbourne clubs had to take what Marc Fiddian called 'the haunting refrain', the train. At that time there was no direct train service to Ballarat from Melbourne. The line went via Geelong, so it was quite an effort just to get to the goldfields town, let alone play a game of football and then get back home.

Other reductions in the number of clubs were made through amalgamations — University and Melbourne became one entity, as did St Kilda and Prahran. That amalgamation took place because Prahran, which had played in just two seasons, 1886 and 1887, didn't have a home ground. The club had one season at the Albert Ground, the other at Wesley College, which when you think about it, makes sense. The school's oval was down the end of Greville Street.

Those amalgamations brought the number of clubs down to 13 before Williamstown was forced to merge with South Williamstown. That had ramifications that echo right through the history of the game up to today. South Williamstown had the Williamstown Cricket Ground, a top-class venue, while Williamstown had the Gardens Reserve, closer to Williamstown Beach. The Williamstown club in the VFL today still plays on the cricket ground at Willy!

Another sidebar to this amalgamation will resonate with the Richmond supporters of today. The Williamstown jumper had been black and gold, and South Williamstown was blue and white, so they took the blue from South and the gold from Williamstown to create the modern colours. That opened the way for Richmond to have the black with the yellow sash the Tigers still wear today. It wasn't always that style, though — and this is what I love about studying the history of things, you find out all these little interesting stories — in its first year in the VFL, in 1908, Richmond had black and yellow stripes.

By the 1890s, the VFA was fairly rigid about keeping the number of clubs to 12. The rules could be bent, though, if a junior club was deemed worthy of the municipality it represented. So, who was the junior club for whom the rules were bent? You guessed it — Collingwood. So, bending the rules is hereditary for the Magpies and it's been happening ever since — certainly for the half-century I've been alive. Collingwood is the only club that would have the gall to put their headquarters in Swan Street, in the heart of Melbourne Football Club's territory. The Melbourne power brokers should have been moving into Swan Street, way before the Magpies.

As I read more and more about the history of our game, it becomes clearer that the most successful clubs are those that see change coming before it arrives, and adapt to it quickly. I think that's why St Kilda keeps heading south along the waterways every 20 years. They're heading to Tasmania. Rest assured, there won't be ten AFL sides in Melbourne in 20 years' time. Tasmania is going to be the last bastion for a Melbourne club that's going broke. The (Van) Demons or St Kilda should have nailed Tasmania before Hawthorn got there. Playing games in Tasmania is a brilliant strategic move by the Hawks, and not their first one. They had already planted themselves into the eastern corridor of Melbourne, out around Waverley, before getting themselves sponsored by Tasmania for half a million dollars a year.

By the way, there is no reason why Tasmania, which has half a million people, can't have a team in the AFL. How many people are there in Port Adelaide?

When I look at Melbourne, the Demons, I sometimes worry about the people at the club who are in charge of making decisions about the future. Sometimes I think the only thing that's saving the club is its name and its status as the first Australian football club. If Melbourne had been called Fitzroy, would it still be in existence? I guess while they are still around, they have a chance of surviving. As Ken Barrington, the great English cricketer, used to say, 'So long as you're still at the crease, you have the chance to make runs.' Melbourne needs some runs. They didn't need to let the Tasmanian opportunity slip, or to have allowed Collingwood to set up headquarters under their noses.

The Lexus Centre is a long way from Collingwood's humble beginnings. Dight's Paddock in Collingwood was the club's home ground, near the waterfalls just below the junction of the Yarra River and Merri Creek. The paddock and the falls were named after John Dight, one of Victoria's first settlers who, in 1840, had established Melbourne's first water-driven flour mill. The flour mill has recently been restored but the ground, it must be said, still looks like a paddock.

At the same time as Collingwood was coming into the VFA there was a lot of discontent among the stronger clubs who wanted to break away and form their own competition, the Victorian Football League. Those clubs, the instigators, were Essendon, Geelong, Fitzroy, South Melbourne and Melbourne. Carlton was allowed to join this group because, even though in the 1890s it wasn't that successful, it had a good record before that. Even though St Kilda wasn't one of the top sides at that time, it was brought in so as to have a club south of the Yarra River. Guess who was the eighth side? Collingwood! Straight into the VFA, straight into the VFL … yep, the Pies always take the dream run.

When the VFL broke away in 1897, there wasn't the hostility that we saw, say, between the Establishment and Kerry Packer's commercial World Series Cricket in 1977. It was more a case of the strong clubs just becoming contemptuous of the weaker ones. Geography came into it a bit, too. It was a long way from Collingwood to Williamstown. This was, of course, well before the era of the car, the revolution inspired by Henry Ford and the Model T production line. Of course, the Collingwood players could get the ferry, something I used to do 65 years later when I was working as a plumber and had to go and do a job at Williamstown.

By the 1960s Williamstown was pretty much a suburb of Melbourne, rather than the village it was in the 1890s. Apart from Essendon, which was made up of former pupils of the private schools, the whole VFA competition in its formative days was essentially a competition between villages. That village concept continued in the VFA for a long time, even though it was pretty much dead in the VFL by the 1940s. Many would argue that Port Melbourne still has it. A lot of those villages have been absorbed into larger municipalities. At one time, Prahran had its own council; it doesn't anymore. Villages have become suburbs that have become cities, with names that seem to come out of nowhere.

The end for most of the old Melbourne villages, their being absorbed into suburbia, arrived just after the Second World War. The parents of the baby boomers, more mobile than any generation before them thanks to Ford cars and our very own Holden, began moving out to places that previously had been the province of sheep, cattle and fruit growers — Burwood, Blackburn. It was the beginning of the suburban sprawl.

One interesting aspect of the growth spurt was the lack of what many would call a soul in areas such as Box Hill and Camberwell. Some would say that while you could get your soul saved at the many churches, the lack of grog made them otherwise pretty unexciting places to live; even now, they are part of the Golden Real Estate Package.

There was no hotel between Bourke Road and Blackburn. That was the result of a quaint little bit of democracy called a local option poll. The people in those suburbs got to vote on three options:

They could remain wet.
They could reduce the number of hotels.
They could go completely dry.

To achieve the last option, they needed to get 60 per cent of the vote. That this was achieved in some areas, but not in others, was largely due to religion — the Catholics voted for pubs, the Baptists voted to be dry. On a trip to America with Mal Brown I stayed at a friend's home in a little town in Texas called Friendswood. There was no grog allowed in that city at all. Then Mal and I said, 'Where are they racing today?' and we were astonished to hear there was no horse racing in Texas. That was a shock to two Aussies on tour in Texas: no drinking in Friendswood, no racing in Texas. But doesn't everyone in Texas ride a horse? Amazing!

I never drank until I was 35. When I did take up alcohol, I kept looking around for a pub between Bourke Road and Blackburn. In the end, they finally got a pub in Springvale Road, Burwood.

After the withdrawal of the VFL clubs in 1897, there were just five clubs left in the VFA — Port Melbourne, Footscray, North Melbourne, Williamstown and Richmond. To make a balanced competition, Brunswick was brought in. John Curtin, a future Australian prime minister who led Australia through the dark days of the Second World War before dying in office just six weeks before the Japanese surrender, played for Brunswick. Curtin was never a leading player at the club, but his association with its president, Frank Anstey, was to have a huge impact on his politics.

Anstey had stowed away on a sailing ship as an 11 year old to escape the poverty of his life in London. He ended up in Australia where he became a high profile, left-wing politician, representing his community through football and in both the Victorian and then the federal parliaments.

In 1901, Australia had gone from being a bunch of colonies to being a federation of states; a country. With the arrival of the new nation and the new century, the VFA had begun to recover from the loss of clubs to the VFL in 1897. A decade after the split, the recovery had become so potent that the VFA was threatening the VFL's status as the premier competition. The easy way for the VFL to keep its advantage was to take a strong club from the VFA and so, in 1908, Richmond changed competitions. The VFL was keen to keep a balanced competition, so a tenth club was sought.

North Melbourne amalgamated with West Melbourne, thinking their combined might would impress the VFL. However, this partnership was passed over, which meant the end of the West Melbourne club even though it had won the VFA premiership in 1906. The reason for the knock-back was probably North Melbourne's poor reputation when it came to crowd behaviour — all those tough wharfies and abattoir workers. Whatever, a chastened North Melbourne went back to the VFA and the tenth spot went to University, a club that has the dubious honour of being the shortest-lived team in VFL history.

In turn, in 1908, the VFA brought in two new clubs — Northcote and Brighton — as the football vine began moving out into the suburbs. (Brighton became Brighton-Caulfield in 1962.) With these new sides, the ten-team VFA competition continued on its merry way until the early 1920s when the VFL administrators began considering more expansion plans.

With the demise of University in 1915, the debate within the VFL had been about the need to get back to ten teams, but that grew into a push for 12 teams. We're having the same sorts of debates today over expansion, but instead of talking about villages and towns in Melbourne, rather it's places like the Gold Coast and the western suburbs of Sydney.

Another significant event at the time was the shifting of the Essendon club from the East Melbourne Cricket Ground out into the suburbs. How indicative is it of the fact that you never know where the future will take you, that many years later the club — under that most wonderful of presidents, Ron Evans — would find itself voting to move back to the Melbourne Cricket Ground.

The three clubs brought into the expanded VFL were Footscray (the most powerful of the VFA clubs at the time), North Melbourne and Hawthorn. North Melbourne's first game in the VFL was against Geelong, and the Shinboners won it. Geelong's supporters were so furious that their club, with its proud record, had been beaten by the upstarts, they tore up their tickets in protest. There were a lot of shamefaced people later in the year arriving at Kardinia Park with all sorts of excuses for 'losing' the ticket they needed to present to get a ticket to the grand final.

After a slowish start, 1925 was a Geelong premiership year — a bit like 2007. It's probably a poor reflection on the game nowadays that having a membership ticket doesn't guarantee you a place at the grand final. But then again, we have a lot more members than we used to have. I doubt there will ever be a long-term resolution of the annual controversy over people missing out on tickets. A system should be developed, though, to ensure that long-term members, people who have invested money in their club, get to attend the grand final.

If you don't have a membership, you are a barracker. But if you buy a membership, you have helped to develop your club. Each year, I buy a membership for each club. Why? Well, in the first instance, I can afford it. I like to support all the Melbourne clubs and if I disagree with the policy of a club, I like to be able to say so. I can say to Eddie McGuire, the president of Collingwood, 'I don't like that decision.' If he criticises me, I can say back: 'Hey, don't speak to your members like that!' I can ring up Frank Costa as a member and say, 'Gee, you're tough on Mark Thompson.' Maybe I should ring up Ray Horsburgh as an Essendon member and say, 'Gee, you were tough on your last coach!' You can have a lot of fun being a member of a club.

But back to the Roaring Twenties. The inclusion of Hawthorn (the 'Mayblooms' as they were known then) in 1922, had been contentious. The Mayblooms — I just love saying that and thinking of Allan Jeans, David Parkin, Dermie Brereton, John Kennedy and Leigh Matthews as sweet little flowers — hadn't been a major force in the VFA. However, because Glenferrie Oval was controlled by the Hawthorn Council, they got priority over Prahran which by now was playing at Toorak Park. That venue was controlled by the local cricket club and the VFA didn't like sharing gate-takings with cricket clubs if it could avoid it. This was before 'the law of the land' was signed off in 1968 by the Victorian Parliament, which said that football clubs could have grounds for six months and cricket clubs the other six months.

Things were going along pretty smoothly in the VFA until

the arrival of the Depression at the start of the 1930s. The worldwide economic downturn hit the Association much harder than it did the VFL. VFA supporters were working-class people, those who had become unemployed as the depression took hold. In many cases, the only income a lot of VFA players had was from playing football, so they would often conceal their injuries in order to keep playing. Another way to get some money was by playing in mid-week competitions for companies such as Yellow Cabs. It was all pretty hard on the body, but if it put food on the table, then the players just had to do it. Tough times, tough people.

No sooner was everyone getting over the Depression than they were plunged into a war. In 1938, just before the outbreak of the Second World War, the VFA made a number of watershed decisions. Administrators decided to break the permit agreement with the VFL. Up until then, if a player wanted to cross from one competition to the other, he had to get a clearance. Breaking the agreement was advantageous to the VFA because one of its clubs could go and get a peripheral player from the VFL to make their team stronger and more attractive to supporters. Except in the most exceptional circumstances, players going from the VFA to the stronger VFL competition had little impact on the performance of the team.

The other important change was the adoption of the throw pass. A player could throw the ball from above the knee and below the shoulder, not unlike a pass in rugby, except that it could go forward. It was mainly used to get play going after a free kick or a mark. It was quicker than a handball and tended to be used by smaller players like rovers, wingers and centre men. The throw pass might have been a good thing to introduce into the VFL to make it easier for Kevin Bartlett. He certainly couldn't handball!

The most important aspect of the throw pass, however, was the fact that it gave the VFA an identity; it set it aside from the VFL. And people liked it, and liked it enough to stay and watch their local Association game rather than, say, follow their VFL side all the way to Geelong.

From the 1930s, probably right up until the 1960s, it was the normal practice for people to follow two teams, their League club and their Association club. There were the hardened, rusted-on followers of Association teams, but they were in the minority. The throw pass made the game more attractive to the swinging supporter, providing a golden time for the VFA. The throw pass lasted until the end of 1949 when the VFA made another decision that was to have a big impact on its future. It voted to join the Australian National Football Council. To do that, it had to comply with the rules of the game about the handball, and also about transfers — which didn't help me much, or the VFA for that matter. In one moment, two of the VFA's major selling points were lost. At the time, it seemed like a good idea to be part of the ANFC, but officials were later to rue the decision.

This is one skill, other than tackling, that kept us close to rugby, and not everyone was happy about it. When I started playing in the VFA as a baby boomer, there was still one difference between the two competitions: the VFA only had 16 men a side. There were no wings, and so there was a lot of open football. That's worth remembering, because it provides an opportunity in the future for the AFL if we all get sick and tired of flooding. They could simply reduce the number of players allowed on the field to 16. Put the other two on the bench. It's something that could be trialled in the pre-season cup, if only to teach the coaches a lesson. That would also make it easier to play AFL game on small overseas cricket grounds.

In 1949, all the VFA got in return for joining the ANFC was the invitation to play in interstate games, where it was no match for most of the teams with the exception of Tasmania. The VFA representative sides might occasionally beat South Australia; however, they never beat Western Australia or the VFL.

During the 1950s the VFA went back to its old tricks from the 1880s and admitted more clubs. By 1960 the number of clubs had risen to 17 and, again, the competition had become unwieldy. History tells us, we never learn from history.

This time, rather than amalgamations, the VFA went in a vastly different direction — two divisions. There were ten clubs in the first and initially eight in the second division, though that eventually became ten clubs. Divisional football bounced off in 1961.

There was another problem facing not just the Association, but the League too, in the early 1960s — the postwar population boom meant that crowds had grown, so much so that some clubs were finding their old grounds were too small. In 1965, Richmond moved from Punt Road to the MCG. It was a momentous decision but the right one. Eventually, all the Melbourne clubs were playing at either the 'G or Telstra Dome. It was a great move and it took a long time for other clubs to catch on! There is a lovely story of football politics attached to the Richmond move. To make it happen, Richmond needed the approval of the VFL. At that stage, the Tigers under Graeme Richmond were involved in a very aggressive recruiting campaign. Dick Clay had already been wooed from North Melbourne, and Richmond was chasing Essendon's Alan

Noonan who, at times, was staying at Graeme's home. Allan Hird played a trump card as president of Essendon and vice president of the VFL. He told Richmond that if they wanted his vote to go to the MCG, they had to back off Noonan. The rest is history.

St Kilda was another club on the move in the 1960s, taking a fancy to the facilities at Moorabbin, which had a VFA club. They formed a partnership, but the VFA thought it was treason for one of its clubs to help a VFL club, so Moorabbin, the premier club, was kicked out of the competition. With the demise of Moorabbin, which at that stage was still a market gardening area with an airport, a lot of very good players suddenly had to find new clubs. One of those players was the now trucking magnate, airport owner and much more, Lindsay Fox, who went to Brighton-Caulfield where I had the pleasure of playing on him in my Prahran days. I'm not sure which of us felt like we had been hit by a truck by game's end — probably me.

Graeme Dunscombe was a coach at Moorabbin in their final year in the VFA, a man ahead of his time in many respects. He played motivational music to the players long before it became accustomed practice to have 'Eye of the Tiger' booming through change rooms. His choice of music could be interesting. Sometimes he even played Russian music. Certainly, the selection of tunes was always upbeat. He was fond of quoting Winston Churchill and other great statesmen in his speeches to the players. In the off-season, his idea of an end-of-season footy trip was to go trekking in the Himalayas.

Even with characters like Graeme, in the early 1960s the VFA was struggling to hold its place against the VFL which, of course, had already teamed up with the phenomenon that has changed sport probably more than anything else in history — television. In 1967, Channel 0, what is now the Ten Network, came into being and began televising VFA games on Sundays. This gave the Association enormous exposure because it had the whole audience to itself. The VFL didn't play on Sundays. Calling these matches was where the young Eddie McGuire, the boy from Broadmeadows who is now the man from Everywhere, got his start.

With television bolstering interest in the VFA, the rivalry with the VFL again became pretty intense, the more so as players sought to switch from one competition to the other. This is where I fell foul of the VFA when, after winning the second division premiership with Prahran in my 50th game, I decided to accept an invitation to go to Richmond.

I wasn't the only player who was supposed to be the subject of a $3000 transfer fee. Peter Bedford, the cricketer/footballer, was another with a price on his head when he shifted to South Melbourne. He went in 1968, and also without a clearance. Bedford was a wonderful athlete, a natural at most sports. Of course, it was still possible to have careers in both football and cricket then, something else that has changed dramatically in recent times, mostly in favour of Australian football. That might change, however, as young people skilled at both games see the money that can be earned from the new Twenty20 cricket competitions in India.

Rex Hunt, the policeman, was another good cricketer/footballer. I remember one day he hit Bedford out of the ground at Punt Road, right up to where the Tiger is now on the grandstand. I can just imagine him staring down the wicket at the dumbstruck bowler and going, 'Yibbity yibba!'

Transfer fees also applied if players went from the VFL to

the VFA, and that happened a lot with fringe players. If a player thought he was likely to be cut from a VFL side, he would throw in his lot with the VFA. Probably the most notable player to go to the VFL from the VFA was Max Papley. He played in a premiership in the VFA with Moorabbin before joining South Melbourne, where he won the best and fairest award in 1966. In 1968 he went to Williamstown, mainly because of a better financial offer, something that was important in the days when footballers also had jobs. He was the absolute superstar of the VFA competition. In 1969 the VFA was such a strong competition that about half a dozen former players were in the VFL state side for the ANFC carnival in Adelaide — players like Terry Waters, Bob Murray at full-back, Peter Bedford and a bloke called Sheedy.

Thanks to the Channel 0 broadcasts, the 1970s could best be described as halcyon days for the VFA. There were plenty of good players, as blokes who weren't quite good enough for the VFL slipped back across to the Association — happier to be big fish in a small pond and to be paid pretty generously.

As money came into the game through television broadcasts and sponsorships, the payments got better.

One side effect of this was that the flow of players back to the bush started to dry up. It's worth remembering that in the 1950s, Collingwood let their favourite son, Bobby Rose, go to Wangaratta when he was still a relatively young man because he could earn more as a captain–coach in the bush than the Magpies could pay him. Sending your players back to the bush had been a great way of recruiting future stars. No sooner had a former player become set up in his pub and his new bush club than he would be on the phone back to his old club saying, 'You should have a look at this kid', and so on.

The bush also became a great recruiting ground for senior coaches. Richmond brought Tommy Hafey back from Shepparton to deliver the club one of the most glorious eras in its history. These days, coaches are expected to undertake an apprenticeship as an assistant coach with an AFL club before being allowed the reins as a senior coach. The last senior coach to come from the bush was Grant Thomas at St Kilda. He did pretty well; his winning percentage is one of the best of any to come out of the country. In the end his confrontation with his president, Rod Butterss, stifled his career. He did remarkably well in the time he was there. St Kilda have now let go two coaches who have taken the team to the top four — Thomas and Stan Alves. When Thomas was sacked, the club went to the tried-and-trusted modern method, a former assistant coach with Sydney — Ross Lyon.

Times change, and the successful clubs have to change with them. In the 1970s the VFL thought it was time for a change, too — to Sunday football. It was a huge social shift, one furiously resisted in a lot of places, particularly by the churches, but it began to happen nevertheless.

Reserve-grade games were played on Sunday. Senior matches were played in Sydney and Brisbane and broadcast live back into Melbourne. In the mid-1970s, Richmond played North Melbourne at the Gabba in Brisbane in an exhibition game.

In 1981, the VFL, by now run by the visionary expansionists Alan Schwab and Jack Hamilton, sent Essendon and Hawthorn to play at the Gabba for premiership points, a match in which Ron Andrews got reported and was suspended. Soon after, the blood-letting that changed the Bloods, South Melbourne, into the Sydney Swans took place. The landscapes were changed forever — landscapes plural, because this move was to have an impact way beyond Melbourne. The VFL was becoming the massive, national corporate entity that would grow into the AFL.

Sponsorship and television rights became the main income stream, pushing aside chook raffles and beer sales and pleasant Sunday mornings. As it expanded to include Brisbane and the West Coast, the VFL needed more players, so instead of going to the VFA or even back to the bush, many good players were traded between VFL clubs. Essendon traded seven players to Brisbane, apparently to balance the books at Windy Hill. Carlton was less generous in its contribution to helping set up the Brisbane Bears, offering a player who had moved to England, Ian Aitken.

More players required in the expanded VFL meant fewer good ones available to the VFA. Combine that with the lack of television after the Channel 0 days finished, and the voracious growth of the VFL and the VFA was about to enter a fatal decline. First, clubs started dropping out of the second division as they could no longer pay their way; even sides like Dandenong, which had a huge area from which to attract support and had won a premiership in 1991.

Alec Gillon, my old nemesis who had run the VFA so fiercely for 27 years — good number, that — was no longer in charge. He had lost out to a challenge from Alan Wicks from Frankston. Alec lived into his nineties and it must have saddened him deeply to see the end of his competition. The last year of the VFA was in 1995. With the AFL now in full cry, the new secondary competition in Victoria was to be called the VFL.

Unbelievably, in that last season, Williamstown didn't win a game. That was a strange thing to watch happening. Willy was the personification of the VFA and if *they* had run out of steam, it wasn't surprising the competition had. I had barracked for Williamstown since 1956, following their scores in the paper, especially when they played Port Melbourne. Prahran didn't have much of a team back then — the Two Blues were lucky to avoid winning the spoon — and I felt an affinity with the people of Williamstown. Some good people have come out of the place over the years: Joan Kirner, Steve Bracks — two Victorian premiers. It seems to attract a certain good Labor sort of person.

Larry Floyd was another of these — and a person remembered at the time of his death as much for his achievements in football as in public life. He represented Williamstown in the state parliament from 1955 until 1973. Larry moved to Williamstown as a young man and managed a few games in the seconds. His greater contribution to the club came as an administrator. It is even said that he only got into politics in the first place — getting elected to the local council — to ensure that the Williamstown Football Club could get a better deal at the local government level. He was a fantastic football administrator, ending up at Carlton — a good Labor man at Carlton, unbelievable — where he was the Blues' first full-time secretary.

Larry's minutes of meetings were meticulous, as was his writing of a history of the VFA which he set out as a social history of Melbourne as much as a story about games of football. From 1877 until 1995, the two had been inextricable, and some of that continues in the modern-day VFL when, occasionally, you can still get a whiff of the old village atmosphere. Or maybe I have been listening for too long to Phil Cleary, another politician from the Left whose life has been intertwined with the VFA.

The new competition even gets a bit of television coverage — on the ABC on Saturday afternoons, with Phil telling us breathlessly to get down and support this wonderful competition where you can still go out on to the field at quarter and three-quarter time and listen to the coach talk to the players.

These days the VFL is a mix of AFL reserve sides, stand-alone Victorian clubs and a team from Tasmania. It's a good competition in its own way and might one day have its own history like that of the VFA. But it's highly unlikely, overshadowed by the towering figure of the AFL, that it will ever develop the deep sense of tradition, the great stories of social history, that the VFA in its battles with the original VFL has given us.

History is telling me that a great era has passed, but it's one that we all need to be thankful for, especially a young man by the name of Kevin John Sheedy who discovered, through the VFA, the beginnings of the pathway that allowed him to follow his dreams through more than 1000 games in the VFL and the AFL, and then into moving the game into international development — the playing of Australian football overseas.

4

From Boy to Man, via Prahran

By my mid-teens, when I was going to Prahran Technical College, it was a pretty interesting time to be alive. A lot of the certainties that I had grown up with were being challenged, and a lot of those challenges were coming through a new form of music — rock-and-roll. The Beatles were still to burst on to the transistor radios and record players of those people who could afford them, but Elvis already had. He was The Man, taking over from Bill Haley and the Comets.

There were also these two singers called Johnny I can recall listening to. Johnny Ray, an American, sang a song called 'Cry'. It was such a great tear-jerker that he used to shed a tear himself while performing it. They don't write them like that anymore.

Television also brought us closer to Afro-America and the great talents of Dionne Warwick, Little Richard and the Platters.

The other Johnny was JOK, Johnny O'Keefe, our own home-grown Wild One. I thought it was great that an Australian could sound as good as any of the superstars from overseas. He was up there with Elvis for me. It gave a lot of us confidence back then to know that Australians could be up there alongside the best in the world. At that stage, I wasn't aware of anything like publicity machines. I just formed my own judgment about what sounded good to me. I also enjoyed it when Helen Reddy and Diana Trask did well overseas, and then a bit later on, Peter Allen. How smart was Peter Allen to write a song called 'I Still Call Australia Home'? Australians love that, to see their people doing well overseas but still loving where they came from. You see it in sport as well, and in business.

I admire Rupert Murdoch for a couple of things. The first is that he is still working, still making good use of his talents despite being in his seventies. The second is that he has managed to turn an Australian company into one of the biggest in the world. I don't think anyone in Australia cares that he has an American passport these days; we all know he's an Australian kid out of Adelaide. I think everyone agrees that it's a good thing for the confidence of all Australians to know that we can take our big ideas and make them happen.

Back in the early 1960s, not everyone agreed that rock-and-roll was a good thing. My parents were filthy on it. The churches, too, weren't very impressed. There was some justification for this. Suddenly, there were all these kids wearing pointy-toed shoes, fluorescent-coloured socks, pin-striped hats and skin-tight jeans. But it wasn't so much the dress of these rockers that was of concern; it was more their attitude that they owned the streets.

In the other camp, you had the kids who listened to jazz and wore duffle coats and desert boots. After every dance, there would be a fight, and most of the time the rockers would have started it.

Moving through my teenage years, with all these rebellious images and sounds around me, I found myself being challenged to choose between dedication and dances. Did I want to keep working towards becoming a VFL footballer, or did I want to go out dancing? (I had already come to the conclusion, using a unique Sheedy algorithm, that if I was to be a successful sportsperson, it would have to be in football. I will explain that algorithm a bit later.)

I had to decide what was more important to me: football, or the good life? We were moving into more affluent times. In the early 1960s, for many of us, 'watching television' meant standing outside a shop window in Chapel Street. However, that was beginning to change: more people were getting televisions in their homes; more and more chimneys had aerials attached to them. If you had a transistor radio you were considered wealthy, but more and more people were starting to get transistors. If you had a camera, things were *really* looking up. In my really early days, when people gave me a photo, sepia, with a neat white border, gee, that was pretty damn impressive. But more and more people were getting cameras. Millions of the famous Box Brownie 127 model cameras — made out of Bakelite — were sold around the world between 1952 and 1967.

There were lots of things, then, in my Dreamtime, to lure me away from football. I believe that your teenage years are your dreaming years. It's the time when you start to think about the sort of life you might want, and how you might achieve it, using all the things you've already learned. It's like looking at a map of the world and working out which route you're going to take to see all the places you want to see.

It's a time when you come to crossroads and have to make decisions about which paths to take and which ones to bypass, about what's right and what's wrong. All around you there are lots of different opinions on what's right and wrong, and on many occasions you won't make the best decision. No one is at fault. We can all make wrong decisions; we all stumble. It's the smart people who can pick themselves up and start over who will be the winners, and I hope I have done that more often than not. So, these days I always encourage young people to keep going when times get tough.

What I also started to learn as a teenager is that so much of my education happened after the school bell — and in later life, after the final siren. If you can combine all that with what you have learned at school, and blend it with your upbringing at home, you've got a chance to have a fairly good life because you will be blessed with a great deal of commonsense. It should all be pretty easy. However, time and again in society we see decisions made without commonsense entering the equation.

I was 15 when I made what I believe was my first, very own commonsense decision. The thought process, the conversation with the Kevin inside my head, went like this:

'Well, Kevin, you love cricket, and you love spin bowling ... However, they usually only pick one spinner for Australia. The chances are it won't be you. Anyway, Richie Benaud is captain ... he's a leg-spinner, and a legend, and they won't drop the captain for you. So next sport!

'I love tennis, the Davis Cup. Neale Fraser, the captain of the Australian Davis Cup team, lives up the road.

'Once again, they pick them from all over Australia and they have so many to choose from — Lew Hoad, Ken Rosewall, Roy Emerson, Fred Stolle, Rod Laver, Tony Roche. But this is even more difficult since you can't afford a tennis racquet, even if you do have a tennis ball. Plus, they don't get paid.

'Boxing? Even though Dad often goes to the fights with Mum, he says there will definitely never be any boxing. "Don't even think about it," he says when Pat and I say "But *Dad*".

'Kevin, you know your dad is working at the mental institution and he has seen too many brain-damaged souls.

'On top of that, Dad will just say, "Do what you're told".

'So, time to look at other opportunities. There seem to be a lot more in football. There are 12 teams in the VFL, and they all need 20 players. So, there are 240 needed to play every week at the top level of Victorian football. Six of them in every team are tall.

'That means 72 are taller than you.

'But that still leaves 168 spots. It looks like footy is the way to go!'

I'm still very good at maths — *my* maths, that is. I didn't believe I would have any need for algebra until I came across the AFL draft. Up until then, I thought algebra should be the capital of Algeria.

Anyway, my sport of choice became football, the game I had been encouraged to play by my brother Pat. He has always been supportive of me — in a uniquely Pat Sheedy sort of way. Whenever Dad told me to do something, I would say: 'Fair enough!' Pat would say: 'Get stuffed. I'll do what I like.' And he had then, and still has, this marvellous ability to do that and get away with it. Everybody loves Pat; I have never met a person who didn't. All my life I have been Patrick Sheedy's brother. He is like Paul Hogan on the baker's cart. On second thoughts, maybe he is Strop — or maybe both.

When I played at Richmond, when I coached at Essendon, I would keep hearing stories about Pat and his escapades around Melbourne. He is the best trader I have ever seen. He can trade *anything*. And he has always been very kind to his little brother and, as time has progressed, to his little brother's family. Often I would go out early in the morning to discover that on his bread run around Melbourne, he had left some fresh rolls, still warm, for Gerri (my wife Geraldine) and the children.

My kids laugh with delight every time they meet up with Uncle Pat. When *I* walk in, they just say: 'Dad's home.'

Pat knows every suburb in Melbourne, and he knows everyone in them ... nightclub owners, bookies, publicans. He's the original 'I've been everywhere man' — born under a Lucky Starr, so to speak. While I'd be slugging away through another cold winter at Essendon, he'd be heading off to America, or to see someone in England, or I'd get a phone call: 'I hope you have a good time this season. I'm off to the West Indies.'

Even recently when I've been going through a tough period, I got a phone call from him offering support. At the end, he said: 'Good luck. I'm heading off on a bit of a cruise up to Alaska.'

Lots of times he'll leave a message on my phone: 'When you've got time, pop in!' But he's the one who's never got time. That's the sort of sense of humour he has, though.

Pat was, and is still, a big influence on me — in everything in life, but especially in football. He was very good about keeping my feet on the ground. He'd say things like: 'Listen, Bighead, do you actually think before you open your mouth sometimes?'

Or: 'Have you come back to earth yet?'

Or: 'Can you actually explain some of these outlandish comments you make, because the people out there aren't sure what you're doing?'

Or: 'What tribe are you talking to this week?'

There's another favourite comment of Pat's that I really like: 'Does anybody down there at the AFL understand?'

He can be pretty incisive about what needs to be done to promote the game, even if he has never been as intimately involved in it as I am. I have felt guilty many times over the years for 'borrowing' some of his ideas for my newspaper columns. Well, I call it 'borrowing'. He says I 'stole' them.

I have been writing columns for a long time, from way back in 1974 when I began with *Inside Football*. I have written them for *The Age*, the *Sunday Herald Sun* and also, for a few years, *The Australian*. I really enjoyed that newspaper because it allowed me — and Pat — to speak to all of Australia, to get people in Sydney and Brisbane used to some of the issues that we were talking about in Melbourne.

Pat is always right on the money when it comes down to how people feel: real people, those who are on a weekly wage, who have to struggle to bring up a family. Patrick is a very good barometer of public opinion.

One of the best websites that politicians and others policy-makers could go to is the one that will never exist — the Pat Sheedy website. He's too busy to set it up, but if he ever did, it would be a fantastic way to find out what real people are thinking. His great skill is that he makes people connect.

*

Back in the Swinging Sixties — and sometimes the swinging was the music, sometimes it was the rockers connecting with their punches — Patrick, with his big brother words of encouragement and commonsense, was helping me to connect with the path to VFL football, as was another person by the name of Bill Maxwell.

I am a Melbourne person. I don't mean the city in which I have lived all my life (so far), but the football club, the oldest one in the AFL. This is because, in the 1960s, South Yarra was in what was known then as Melbourne's 'recruiting zone'. The national draft has changed that; today the whole country is essentially every club's recruiting zone. Back then, when I was getting ready to try out for the VFL, the state was divided up among all the Melbourne clubs who, with Geelong, constituted the whole competition. There was no Brisbane, no Sydney, no teams from Adelaide and the West Coast. It was just we Victorians.

I had no problems about playing for Melbourne, even though my family background had made me an Essendon supporter. The red and blue influence was all around me in South Yarra. Melbourne players lived in boarding houses close by, and if you actually got to see one of them, to say 'G'day', it was like talking to a god.

Bill Maxwell was the maths and science teacher at Prahran Technical College when I was there in 1963. Every year he would get some of his students a trial with Melbourne. I became one of those young hopefuls. Of course, the trial came with absolutely no guarantees. The mathematical equation was pretty basic:

There were 100 kids trying out.
They all looked good.

I probably looked just like most of them, so standing out was a real challenge. I did my best to at least *look* like a footballer, something I was helped with by my dad who would polish my boots for me. I always made sure I had my socks pulled up and that my jumper was tucked in. You didn't want to stand out for being untidy, not at Melbourne, the club of the Establishment.

Jim Cardwell was the manager of Melbourne at the time, and was also in charge of recruiting for the under-19s and under-17s. Getting into that under-17s side was the way to reach the senior side via an almost infinite number of training games that would go on right throughout the day. In a way, they were little different from racing trials at Cranbourne, where the young horses are tried out to see if they are sprinters, stayers or something less glamorous. There used to be an old saying in Melbourne about slow horses: *Watch them go around at Cranbourne this week, and Olympic Park next week*. This meant they had been turned into dog food and given to the greyhounds.

I knew I was never going to be a greyhound on the footy field, but I always tried to keep a measure on how I was developing by looking at the other players around me of my vintage, cross-checking between myself and the school champions, the local superstars. At our school, it was Kevin Bartlett, the captain of Prahran Tech's footy team. We're a bit like the Keith Richards and Mick Jagger of football, we two Kevins. Mick and Keef, the engine room of the Rolling Stones, go back to a sandpit in a kindergarten in East London. Kevin Bartlett and Kevin Sheedy go back not just to the schoolyard, but to the Try Boys teams as well. That was up in Cromwell Road, South Yarra. If I had known back then about Oliver Cromwell, and what he did to the Irish, I probably would never have taken part, in protest!

Even given his obvious abilities in those formative years, I don't think anyone could have predicted what Kevin Bartlett would achieve in football. He is *the* absolute superstar of my time at Richmond — five best and fairests. He played for Victoria 20 times, and then became the first person to play more than 400 games. Even when in 1980 he was 'retired' to the half-forward flank by the Richmond coach, Tony Jewell, he still kicked more than 80 goals ... no one does that, unless they're Kevvie Bartlett.

At his best, Royce Hart, the greatest centre-half forward of the 20th century, kicked 80 goals in a season. Yet, some people will say Royce was a better player than KB. I don't know if that is really the case.

Anyway, I looked at what Kevin was doing, and at what the other recognised good players were doing. I then looked at myself and I guess what I saw was a skinny runt of a kid, really. This is what they were thinking at Melbourne, too, and that I was only five foot ten in the imperial measurements (or 178 centimetres) and half the country was that height. So there was this theory that there were hundreds of people out there like me — too small, too slow and not all that skilful, either.

Also, Melbourne was the club that went for amateurs and boys from the colleges — Wesley, Melbourne Grammar and Scotch. I'm not really sure who the decision-makers were at Melbourne back then, but I do know they weren't measuring the right things when it came to me — my determined spirit, and my willingness to learn. As coaches, we all have to learn to tell the difference between those with talent and not much else, and those with the other ingredients needed to get the absolute best out of themselves.

Wayne Bennett, the wonderful coach of the successful National Rugby League side, the Brisbane Broncos, describes one of the turning points in his career as happening in 1984, when his team of that time, Souths, lost a grand final to Wynnum-Manly 44–4. He says a bloke walked up to him after the game and said: 'Wayne, if you were a racehorse trainer, you'd train a lot of second and third places. You keep picking the wrong guys; you keep putting your belief in the wrong people.'

Wayne says he went away and thought long and hard about that comment and realised he had to start mixing players with talent with players who were committed to being successful and were also dedicated to his coaching plans. In 1985, Souths won the grand final, beating Wynnum-Manly 10–8.

Over many years of playing and coaching, I have heard a lot of remarks about players, and I've seen judgments made based solely on the cover of the book, not on what's inside it — 'too small', 'too slow', 'too fat'. Now, 'too fat'; *there's* a category to work with. In the back of my recruiting book, I've got a list of blokes who were too fat. It reads like this:

Tony 'Plugger' Lockett: 1360 goals.
Jason 'Piggy' Dunstall: 1254 goals.
Doug 'Fat Cat' Wade: 1057 goals.

All I know is that fat people kick goals, so when you take a commonsense approach, a blend of all the things you have learned, rather than just basing your decisions on crude measurements, it's amazing what can be achieved.

Tony Lockett kicked 4.84 goals a game for St Kilda and Sydney. Jason Dunstall's ratio for Hawthorn was 4.66. Doug Wade would return 3.96 goals a match for Geelong and North

Melbourne. The one with the best ratio of all time was another player with a big backside, Peter Hudson, a bloke from Tasmania via Hawthorn with no pace who still managed to kick 725 goals at an average of 5.64 per game. Obviously, if you want to be a good goal-kicker, it helps to have a barge arse.

Talking about backsides and goal-kickers, Mark Jackson averaged 3.3 goals a game in a career best described as 'colourful'. This was the fellow who, while playing for Melbourne and after having been told by the Hawthorn full-back Kelvin Moore that he would never be a full-forward while his backside pointed to the ground, did a handstand in the middle of the ground. Jacko might have made life difficult for a lot of people, including plenty of coaches, but he was an amazing character and a monster of a man.

I wasn't a monster, I didn't have a big bum, and I would never have been game to do a handstand on any footy field, let alone a VFL ground. I was just another kid who apparently looked like so many others. Melbourne said 'no'.

It was a decision that, rather than discouraging me actually inspired me: 'They might think I can't play football, but *I* know I can. I'll show them.' But *how*, and where?

A couple of my local mates, Ken and Noel Bosch, suggested I try out for the Prahran side which played in the VFA. At 16, I was now too old for the Try Boys, and perhaps pretty young to be trying out for the Prahran under-19s, but I thought: 'Why not?' I hadn't given up on the VFL; I just had to be a bit cleverer about getting there. I still thought I could make it if I could just find the right shop window to show off my skills, in the same way that Kevin Bartlett, who had shifted into Richmond's recruiting zone, had been picked up by the Tigers. So, I went to play for Prahran.

*

One of the first people I met at Prahran was the under-19's coach, Bert Fritzlaff. He was very welcoming, saying: 'Look, just start training on Mondays and Wednesdays and we'll see how you go.' Suddenly I found myself playing against blokes who, if not entirely fully grown, at 19 were a lot further along the road to manhood than I was. It was a rude awakening. Thank goodness the VFA was 16-a-side and I had somewhere to hide. I got out on the wings and watched the game, and learned how to read it without always getting my senses knocked out of me by these bigger players.

I was the youngest kid in the team, something that produced more than its share of nerve-wracking moments both on and off the field; like turning up at a street corner and hoping my lift would arrive to take me to the game. We were playing teams like Sunshine out in the emerging outer-suburbs of Melbourne.

To the amazement of a young bloke from South Yarra who thought he was lucky to have a pushbike, a lot of the players rocked up on motorbikes, or in their Ford Customlines or FJ Holdens. And they were huge; absolute monsters. Some of the ruckmen and the centre-half backs were six foot four (193 centimetres) and built like brick dunnies. They were hard people. I'd be warming up and having a look at the other team and wondering if I was going to get home safely that night. I wasn't ever frightened as such, but because I was the smallest, I had to be concerned about my physical ability to handle some of the knocks.

There was another reason to be worried about personal safety. In 1963, Melbourne was a tough city in which to be growing up. Football was a brutal game played between suburbs that didn't necessarily like each other much. The western side of Melbourne was like it is today. A lot of the people were immigrants, and they were trying to prove themselves in their new country — through hard work and even harder footy. People from Preston and Mordialloc were different again.

Football was actually teaching me about my city. I went to suburbs called Northcote and Westgarth, Box Hill and Springvale. There were cattle, horses and orchards along Springvale Road instead of the endless mass of suburbia we have today.

The president of Prahran, and a person who was very generous to me, was Charles Lux. On meeting him, I immediately thought he owned the Lux soap company. He actually owned a menswear store in Chapel Street, Prahran, near the corner as you head into Windsor. He is one of the best people I have ever met in football. In the change rooms, people would say that, too, but then add that he was Jewish. I didn't know what they meant by that and asked them to explain. They'd reply that he was committed and strong, but also (wink) very thrifty with money. I said, 'That's okay, I've been praying to a Jewish guy all my life.' Nothing else was said to me about Charles and his religion after that.

Charles would do really generous and thoughtful things. Like, he'd say, 'Pop into my shop. If you're going to be a Prahran footballer, I need you to dress well. I'm going to give you a couple of pairs of trousers, some shirts. You can pay me over the next year or so, and I won't charge you interest if you play for the team.' When you're 16 and you've never had anyone do anything like that before, it's pretty special.

The most impressive thing about this guy was he was that genuine. He really cared about the youth of the day. He also cared more about his honesty than his wealth. They say of Generation X and Y people nowadays that they don't care what you know until they know that you care. Charles Lux would have been an outstanding person to young people today.

It was Charles who eventually signed my clearance to leave Prahran to go to Richmond, despite opposition from many other people in the VFA. When we talked about that clearance, and my determination to go to Richmond, he said he wanted to be sure I was making the move for the right reasons. Once I had convinced him my reasons were genuine, that was it. He gave me his full support.

I always look back on my Prahran and VFA days with great warmth and affection. The club had had an interesting history in the VFA. It was first formed in 1886. It disappeared for a while, having amalgamated with St Kilda, but then the royal and sky blue jumper re-emerged in 1899.

In 1909, the club finished top of the ladder, then lost the semi-final to Brunswick. Shortly after that game, four players were sacked 'in mysterious circumstances'. The Two Blues regrouped to win the preliminary final, but lost the grand final that year. In 1959, the club was kicked out of the VFA after losing sole use of Toorak Park, but it was readmitted in 1960. When the two divisions came into the VFA a year later, Prahran went into Division Two, which was where it was when I arrived there.

Most of the people at Prahran were generous and caring, something that, I'm delighted to say, went right through to the women's committee. Imagine this scenario, almost an alien one, today: we would go to Geelong West to play, then we would drive all the way back to the Prahran social club for a barn dance. The women on the committee were probably aged somewhere between 40 and 50 and they made it their business not only to do all the catering, but also to show young people like me how to barn dance. And woe betide you if you didn't want to get up and dance, if you tried to be a wallflower, as was the case with plenty of 16-year-olds back then who were too embarrassed to admit they couldn't dance. I think of those women now and smile — wonderful people like Mrs Pearson, Mrs Seedy, Mrs Simmons; good people from life-member families at Prahran who never stopped teaching me social skills, and about life, through their involvement in football. It was all pretty amazing. One minute, as a kid from South Yarra, I had never heard of these people; the next, as a Prahran footballer, they were providing me with a rich education.

That is what football can do, even when you're 60. This is what I love about the game — it intertwines with your life and it doesn't let you drop off when you stop playing. Many people in the arts or music scene would love to have that sense of community spirit, of a soul.

Which begs the question: Where does that spirit and soul come from? Can it just be switched on like a light? I don't think so. Rather, it's the accumulation of all the things that people learn as they grow.

So long as we keep providing people with positive experiences, we will retain our spirit and soul. In the 21st century, we will have to do it in different ways to the 1960s — you don't find too many barn dances in the era of the iPod — but we must still find ways for young people to have wisdom passed on to them, remembering the Charles Lux method of showing them first that you care, so that they will start to care about what you know.

Another aspect of a trip to Geelong West also shows how much the world has changed in the past 50 years or so (or as Richmond legend Jack Dyer put it once: 'Footscray isn't as far away as it used to be!'). It was a big decision for us whether we stopped off at Werribee to have a toilet break, stretch the legs, and get something to eat. It was the same when I was at Richmond. Tommy Hafey used to spend a lot of time deciding how we would get to Kardinia Park. Would we take the bus, would we go in private cars, would we have a stopover at Werribee? One year, the Tigers went by train and Tommy reckoned the players lost concentration on the short walk from South Geelong Station to the ground, so we never went by train again. These days when I drive to Geelong, I just sail right through on the new freeway — between the speed cameras.

The Geelong West ground, just off Church Street, remains a fascinating one for me. It's not often you play on an arena where they have a bike track to keep you in. Funny thing is, not that long ago I met the bloke who put in that track. Little did I know on my first visits that this ground was where the legendary Australian cyclist Russell Mockbridge started his career, one cut short by a road accident in 1958. According to one of the myths about Mockbridge, who won two Olympic gold medals, the first time he turned up at the Geelong West Cycling Club wearing his trademark spectacles and looking anything like a potential world champion athlete, he went out for a ride with the regulars. About halfway through, he asked if it was okay to go out in front. When the answer came back 'yes', they didn't see him again until they got back to the clubrooms. A legend had been born.

I have always enjoyed the way that different sports can blend together, such as the way cycling, football and cricket still do at Geelong West, or football and netball are now doing all over Victoria. It's something that is a bit harder to do these days at the elite level because of all the specialisation that goes along with professionalism. I played football against Peter Bedford who also played cricket for Victoria. Dick Reynolds, the King of Windy Hill, played a lot of good cricket as well as footy for Essendon. Ron Evans, the Essendon footballer who became head of the AFL Commission, also played cricket for North Melbourne.

By his time, though, Craig Bradley had to make the choice between cricket for South Australia and football for Carlton. James Bartel, who won the Brownlow Medal in 2007, made the decision to play football after playing junior representative cricket for Victoria. I wonder what the Indian Premier League will mean to our sport? If someone like Andrew Symonds can get $1.47 million on top of his Australian contract for 40 days of Twenty20 cricket, then a lot of potential footballers — especially in rugby league and Australian football, where the money is nowhere near that — might start choosing cricket: another challenge for our game, particularly when there are two new franchises coming in, voted for by the AFL and the club presidents. We'll just have to assume that a hundred more players can be found, and around a hundred more people per club to help look after them.

When kids are growing up, *all* sport should be important. I advise young people to try them all. Even when you are no longer a youngster, you should try to enjoy them all, either as a player, a spectator or an administrator.

Over the last five decades, I have seen four codes — Australian football, rugby union, rugby league and soccer — grow together. It has been done in a spirit of both reasonable cooperation and competition. We have all put each other under pressure, so we have all had to get better. I reckon one day there will be a time when the boffins of sport in Europe and America will ask how Australia, with its relatively small population, managed to grow four codes together. I'm still not entirely sure we know what we're doing, but we're doing it and we must keep on doing it.

About ten years ago, I was in the office of the Victorian Premier of Victoria, Jeff Kennett, now the president of the Hawthorn Football Club. I suggested that we hold a grand prix of football — all four, even five, codes. Australia would play New Zealand in rugby union. The Kangaroos would play Great Britain in rugby league. Australia could play Italy in soccer.

We could ask the Americans to play a game of their football, maybe Notre Dame against Stanford. And if the Irish keep talking to us this time, we can have a game of International rules. If not, a blockbuster AFL game would do, or the Best versus the Rest.

Sometimes, big picture ideas have to just sit there for a while until people get used to them. They have to be placed at the right time. Rush them and you can lose the impact. I believe this grand prix of football will happen one day. We have to keep coming up with ideas that excite people. Five big nights, five big games on a couple of pieces of real estate that often lie empty — the MCG and Telstra Dome. Gee, you'd have to be a pretty sad sort of person if that didn't excite you.

That's the future. Let's go back to those days of the fragile but ever-willing-to-learn Kevin Sheedy at Prahran and the people who were so generously helping to develop me.

I played my first senior game with Prahran in 1964. Then the big moment came in 1966. Prahran finished third after the home-and-away season. We beat Sunshine in the first semi-final, 11.15 (81) to 2.7 (19). That got us into the preliminary final where we beat Northcote in a nail-biter by a point. So we were into the grand final, against Geelong West. It was going to be my 50th game for the club. We ensured it was a memorable occasion all round, winning 17.12 (114) to 5.15 (45).

The Prahran on-ballers that day were Graeme McMahon, a future president of Essendon, and Kevin Sheedy — future coach. Isn't it amazing that, 34 years later, we both had another premiership cup — the first AFL premiership of the new millennium? How could we even have imagined sharing that sort of achievement, so many years apart, and the second premiership in a competition that didn't exist when we won the first one? As Ken Barrington says, you have to stay at the crease to score runs. Graeme and I had that second opportunity because we stayed in footy.

There have been many other interesting personal journeys over the years that began in the VFA. That first game in the seniors at Prahran was against Camberwell. The opposition captain–coach was Bert Gaudion. In his day job, he was a detective-sergeant, a highly respected one, at the Malvern Police Station. The game was barely a few minutes old when I felt a sharp pain across my eyebrows. Bert had given me a clip just to let me know what senior football was all about. The cut required four stitches. I couldn't believe a policeman would do such a thing.

Many years later, we two dags, Gaudion and Sheedy, turned up at the AFL Tribunal together, but not for belting each other. Bert was the advocate when for the only time in my career I was up before the beaks … as a 55-year-old. My reporting followed the infamous Mitchell White incident — or the seagull incident, depending on who you believe — and my running a finger across my throat in a slitting motion. Someone at the AFL thought it had brought the game into disrepute, probably because the little league kids were just in front of me. I must admit it wasn't just the AFL that wasn't happy. My mother wasn't — and when Irene wasn't happy, you knew you were in trouble.

Bert must have been a better copper than an AFL Tribunal advocate. He lost the case and cost me $7500. Actually, I didn't help his cause much, as I pleaded guilty. We laugh about it all now.

The tribunal is one of those quirky organisations you find in football. It has a job to do, particularly in the modern era when the market research done by the AFL clearly shows that people, especially mothers, don't like all the old-fashioned biffo stuff that used to be part of the game. Mostly I think the AFL gets it right, though not in the case that cost Chris Grant, the wonderful Footscray player, a Brownlow Medal. I wasn't particularly happy that the AFL reported me following the seagull business with Mitchell White, but I reckon the decision by Ian Collins to report Grant was bordering on being un-Australian. The umpires had seen the incident, either live or on the video review, and didn't think the clash involving Hawthorn's Nick Holland was worthy of a report. However, Collins, the Football Operations Manager — and, it must be said, in his day a pretty rough-and-tumble sort of a footballer — did. Grant has never really forgiven 'Collo', and I think a lot of other people in football haven't either.

People wonder why I use the term Martians when I talk about the AFL and other authorities but ... geez, unearthly decisions from the top have dotted this country for a long time, and continue to do so.

My first matches at Prahran were under a former Melbourne player called Dennis Jones. Dennis was a strapping centre-half back; fairly physical, very strong-minded. Through his mother he is related to Vin and Jarrad Waite, the father–son combination at Carlton. Dennis had been pretty unlucky not to have played in more premierships for the Demons than the one he achieved in 1959. The Melbourne backline at that time was Geoff Case, Ian Thorogood, Tassie Johnson and the best back-pocket in the comp, John Beckwith, who ended up as a captain and coach. Dennis just couldn't break into the side, so he ended up back at Prahran.

When Dennis had taken over coaching Prahran he was serious about embedding some young players into the team. Three of those players were Kerry Ryan, Terry Hogan and Kevin Sheedy. Ryan, a fantastic, mobile full forward, was pretty much like all the Melbourne types who played in that position. I always thought he had the ability to play a lot of VFL football, but in the end he played just one game, in 1966. Melbourne had so many good players at that time, the opportunities were always limited.

In 1964, when Melbourne won the premiership, the full-forward was Barry Bourke, a very good player. He was quite versatile, too, playing a lot of his 175 games in the back-pocket and as ruck rover. The centre-half forward in that grand final was Graeme Jacobs. He was later to help me recruit Darren Williams to Essendon from Vermont. He said to me, 'This boy will play league football. You'd better go and get him.' The thing about Graeme Jacobs pushing Darren towards us was that it would weaken the club he was involved in now that he was out of VFL football, but he still did it because he didn't want to stand in the way of a young man making the most of his talent. And 'Daisy' pretty well did that, playing in two premierships for Essendon and representing Victoria. Graeme Jacobs' son Trent is now the marketing manager at the Richmond Football Club. Footy just loves throwing up these nice little twists.

Terry Hogan was a brilliant young centre-half forward, six foot two or three (188 centimetres) with a prodigious kick and the ability to take a classic mark. He took up a business opportunity rather than those presented him by football. We all grew together at Prahran, all using Kevin Bartlett as part of our inspiration. He was still only on the fringes at Richmond. Peter Hogan and Frank Dimattina kept him out, but only for a while. Talent soon got its reward and, when it did, we thought: 'If Kevin can make it, we can, too.'

The VFA premiership in 1966 marked the end of one period of my footballing life and the need to start a new one, to keep that date with destiny I had promised myself with the VFL. Some significant things had happened during my four-year stint at Prahran. I wasn't quite the skinny little kid anymore.

5

Tiger Tiger Burning Bright

My parents had by now shifted to Armadale, which meant we had crossed the Kooyong Road and were out of the Melbourne metropolitan zone and in Richmond's. And Richmond had been made aware of some of the things I had been doing at Prahran as a player. A wonderful person by the name of Kevin Healy, who was the captain–coach of a Mornington Peninsula club, had rung Graeme Richmond, the guru of all things recruiting and more at Richmond. Healy was an ex-Prahran person and a plumber, both good qualifications for football and for life. He worked in one of the plumbing companies I started with called Vincent's Hardware, on the corner of Palermo Street in South Yarra. Paul Vincent, who owned the business, had also been a very important person to me because he had said 'yes' and given me a job. Boy, doesn't that give you a lot of confidence when someone says 'yes' to you!

Paul ended up as president of one of Hawthorn's main coterie groups, the Confreres, and he was very good at giving opportunities to footballers. Brian Taylor and John Kennedy Junior also worked at Vincent's Hardware.

Plumbing mightn't seem like the most appealing occupation, but one of my first jobs had been pulling the guts out of chickens. Cleaning out sewage pipes for people around Toorak felt like a real step up. And anyway, digging ditches got you fit!

I believe Kevin Healy had watched me as a player and as a person, and thought I was worth recommending to Richmond. I am forever grateful for that recommendation, because it also led to my first meeting with Tom Hafey. On Kevin's recommendation, he came to watch me play for Prahran. Then along came Graeme Richmond, followed by another Richmond recruiting expert, Jack Titus, and then vice captain Paddy Guinane, all running their cold, all-knowing footballing eyes over me.

Graeme Richmond is one of the most amazing people I have ever met in my life. I dedicated one of my books, *Follow Your Dreams*, to his memory. He was tough, ruthless, because that's what you had to be in football if you wanted to make your club a great one. But he was also a provider of opportunities to people who were willing to take them. He had a great knowledge of football. When people think about Graeme Richmond the administrator, who turned the Tigers into a powerhouse, they forget that he was also a coach.

As coach of the Richmond under-19s he had a great grasp of what was happening in grassroots football. What a remarkable position that was to take on, coach of an under-19s team at a working-class club when he had been to Geelong Grammar, the school attended by the Prince of Wales, Rupert Murdoch and Kerry Packer.

I think Graeme couldn't resist the chance to work at a club that shared his name. Ron Barassi did so much for his clubs, but he would never be called 'Ron Melbourne' or 'Ron Carlton'. Eddie McGuire has made Collingwood into a national — even international — brand, but even though a lot of people call him 'Eddie Everywhere', he can never be 'Eddie Collingwood'. That's what Graeme Richmond had, and I think that was his main motivating force; simply: 'If this club is going to have my name, then it must be the best.'

He was a character, a bloke with a voice that could cut concrete and a way about him that said, 'If there's a tough decision to be made, well — look out, Cocko — I'll be the one to make it.' Graeme liked to take senior players on his recruiting trips with the famous Form 4s, the recruiting documents, in his briefcase. I went on one of these trips to Tasmania with him, partly to learn a few things about recruiting as my non-playing role at Richmond was moving from promotions and development to development and recruiting.

I was 28, and getting towards the end of my own playing days. I was a premiership player, and the sort of person Graeme thought might be able to impress the family of a talented young player and convince them to allow Richmond to sign up their much-loved son. Parents were often the key to getting the players you wanted. If you impressed *them*, you were almost over the line. Graeme knew that in spades.

When we arrived at Hobart Airport, we were picked up by Harry Jenkins, the Tigers' recruiting manager in Tasmania and a top fellow. We all went to the house in Hobart where the prospective recruit lived and Graeme knocked on the front door. A woman answered, obviously the lad's mother. We had noticed on approaching the house that someone had put a lot of work into the garden. It was lovely. Graeme immediately started talking about the garden, asked to be shown around and admired all the plants. Until then, I had never known Graeme Richmond to take an interest in anything even vaguely horticultural. I doubt if he even knew the meaning of the word.

The father, we learned from the mother as we toured the garden, was out running. When she took us inside the house, she introduced us to her son, a giant beanpole who was lying on the couch watching a 'Sylvester and Tweetie Pie' cartoon on television. I was watching Graeme intently. Here was the opportunity to learn from the master. Graeme kept talking to the mother, and I could see him observing the young man. Then the father came back from his jog. He was red-faced from his exertions, his body covered in sweat. The youngster was still on the couch. He hadn't moved. He had hair down to his shoulders. He looked a bit like Jesus Christ. He had a strong, athletic body, not bad for a young man of, say, 16 turning 17.

More pleasantries were exchanged; a cup of tea was offered and accepted, along with scones and biscuits. In my mind, they were a lovely family. All up, we stayed for about an hour.

When we left I was anxious to know what Graeme thought. I was then, and probably still am, impetuous in these sorts of areas. My view was that the boy was perfect. He had the build of an athlete. Today he'd be someone you would seriously consider for the draft. 'Well, Graeme, what do you think?' I blurted out.

His reply absolutely gobsmacked me. 'Jesus, Kevin, I'm so embarrassed,' he said. 'I can't believe we've wasted our supporters' money coming down here for such an absolute stuff-up like today.'

I said, 'Why, Graeme?'

'Well, we're here too late, by about 20 years. The *father* is the person we should be recruiting; the son is a lounge lizard. He'll never make it. We've wasted a day and our supporters' money!'

He then added: 'Anyway, let's go and see Royce Hart's mum and dad and thank them again for their wonderful son.'

And we did. They were two of the most genuine people I have ever met in my life. Royce's dad, a farmer, disappeared for about ten minutes and left Royce's mum running around preparing tea and making these people from Melbourne feel welcome. Hart Senior then came back into the room washed, shaven, and wearing a collar and tie.

As we drove back to the airport, Graeme spoke very highly of the Harts. We didn't pick the other kid; he never made it anywhere. Graeme's judgment was impeccable.

When Graeme had made the decision to recruit Royce Hart, he had also relied heavily on the assessment of the Tigers' Tasmanian recruiting agent, Harry Jenkins. Harry had watched Royce playing in the under-19s for Clarence when he was still eligible to play under-17s. Despite the age difference, Royce won the best and fairest. On Harry's recommendation, Graeme flew to Hobart to meet the Harts. When Mrs Hart heard Graeme offer Royce the chance to come to Melbourne, she said he would first need some appropriate clothes. Graeme quickly offered to buy Royce a suit and half a dozen shirts. Royce was signed, sealed, and duly delivered another shirt, the famous number '4' in which he made his senior debut in 1967 … all part of a wonderful journey that saw him named in the AFL Team of the Century at centre-half forward.

When you hear that story, you probably don't wonder so much why football followers today think players get paid too much — a legend recruited with a suit and six shirts.

After a couple of years of weights work while playing in the under-19s at Richmond, Royce had the body to match his talents. In his first seniors game, against Essendon, he was a revelation. Playing at full-forward, he kicked three goals for the Tigers in their first game on the way to the 1967 Grand Final, in which they beat Geelong.

Graeme had not only pulled off one of the recruiting coups of the century, he had made a great personal investment in Royce, allowing him to board with him when he first moved across from Tasmania. This is the level of commitment that Graeme had to the club that bears his name.

Everyone who knew Graeme would have a thousand stories about him. He was larger than life. He called everyone 'Cocko'. He had this thing about getting good people to Richmond. He would come back from a recruiting trip and say, 'They're just the sort of people we want at this club.' He meant highly moral, honest, committed people. Surprisingly, in his own life, Graeme was fascinated by the criminal element of Melbourne. I think he almost hero-worshipped them. All up he was a man of many, many parts and he had a profound influence on my life, right from the moment he invited me to join his club. I often wish he were alive today so that I could ask him about some of the other decisions he made, especially the one not to support Tom Hafey as coach of Richmond in 1976. Without that support, Tom resigned.

'Graeme, with the benefit of hindsight, and given what has happened to Richmond since then, would you still have made that decision?' is what I would ask. I'd then, just as I had in Hobart all those years ago, sit back and wait for the answer.

Tom Hafey was 46 years of age when Richmond dumped him. That's the age Vince Lombardi was when he got his first coaching gig in American football for the Green Bay Packers. Tom had won four premierships, been to five grand finals, and taken his team to the finals 80 per cent of the time before Vince Lombardi got his first job. Everybody talks about Lombardi and what a great coach he was with the Green Bay Packers. I wouldn't deny any of that. However, he coached only around 140 games during his whole Green Bay Packers career. After getting the sack from Richmond, Tom Hafey went on to take Collingwood to another five grand finals and to coach another 200 or so games of VFL/AFL football. That smacks of a singular greatness, too — a greatness Richmond denied itself.

'So, Graeme, did you underestimate the spirit and the soul and the dedication of a legend called Tom Hafey?' I would ask him.

Up until then, Tom and Graeme had been inseparable at Richmond. They complemented each other. Tom was great for young people in terms of all sorts of guidance, but particularly in regards to fitness and health. Graeme, on the other hand, was a bit of an amateur sports psychologist. If a player wasn't playing that well, he could leak to the media that so and so was in danger of being dropped. After the headlines duly appeared, invariably, that person would play their best game of the season the next Saturday.

When Graeme was dying of cancer, I know that Tom went to his bedside and held his hand, but I think the great bond between the two men that made Richmond such an irresistible force was never restored.

Todd Shelton, who was for many years Graeme's business partner and this year becomes a sprightly 80-year-old, visited him two days before he died. They talked about how successful Graeme had been in his life. However, Graeme was upset because, as he told Todd, he had hurt a lot of good people. But, to achieve success, he said, you had to do that; you had to get rid of people who might not be up to the job, even though they were decent human beings.

Ah, administrative decisions in football. You can carry the scar from some of them for a long time. It was an administrative decision that had stood in the way of my move from Prahran to Richmond, but I had been determined it wouldn't prevent me achieving my ambition to play in the VFL.

In 1966, when I received my invitation to train at Punt Road, it said 'Richmond' on the top of the letter and 'Richmond' on the bottom, just under Graeme's signature. I remember being very impressed by that, and by the wording in between. The introduction was quite quaint, a pleasant letter recognising 'fine performances over the years at your club at Prahran'. Graeme then went on to say that, in case I didn't know, I'd moved into the Richmond zone and could become a Richmond player if I wished to. *If I wished to!*

I was excited. I guess it was like being invited on to *Australian Idol* today, if you're a singer, or being invited to join the ABC Sports Department if you wanted to be a commentator. Then I heard of the deflating decision handed down by the VFA that I would be disqualified for five years if I went without a clearance, which the board members, led by Alec Gillon, were in no mood to give me.

My dad had died by that time, at the far too young age of 50, and I asked my mother Irene what she thought I should do. Mum was pretty annoyed with the VFA officials because she felt they shouldn't be standing in the way of young people wanting to make something of their lives. Most times Mum was this caring, friendly person who treated people the way she liked to be treated herself. However, it was never smart to get on her wrong side, because she could be pretty ruthless. So, her advice?

'Go!' she said. 'If you believe in yourself and feel that you're good enough, just go. You don't want to be sitting around for the rest of your life, asking yourself should you have gone.'

It was great advice, even though my decision meant I wouldn't be allowed to play in any National Australian Football Council (ANFC) competition anywhere in Australia for half a decade. If I failed at Richmond, football would be pretty much over for me.

However, there was a league called the Federal League that had a club called Glenhuntly. They played at the oval behind the Caulfield Racecourse. It was tougher than the VFA; it was ruthless football and guess who played in it — my brother Pat. So, there would have been some satisfaction if I had been forced down that path. Apart from some trial games at Prahran, I hadn't really ever played serious football with Pat.

Mention of my brother reminds me of the decision I made, many years after I first joined Richmond, to recruit the next two Daniher boys to Essendon. Terry and Neale Daniher were already there when I went after Anthony and Chris. Whatever else happens to them in life, at least they all got to play together once — the final round in 1990. Getting them all to Windy Hill nearly cost me my life, though — literally. Through Kevin Egan, our football manager at the time who was training to be a pilot, the club had hired a plane to fly up to Ungarie to meet with Chris Daniher and his parents, Jim and Edna. Chris was the last brother still at home on the family farm.

The landing on a private runway wasn't too bad. I think all the other brothers were there when we arrived. We played a bit of cricket, had lunch and were ready to leave at around 4.30. We then noticed that the pilot was looking a bit perplexed. Without a windsock (I should have brought the one from Windy Hill, but apparently it was tied up that day), he didn't know which way the wind was blowing.

Jim Daniher wet his finger, held it up to the breeze and said it's coming from whichever direction he reckoned it was. When we did get airborne, the pilot said that Jim had been spot on. The next thing, the door I was sitting against flew open. As much as I tried for the next half-hour, I couldn't get it closed. If I was taking it pretty seriously, no one else was. All the pilot said was: 'You're all right. You won't blow out. The wind's coming from the other side of the plane.' And club director Neville Gay, bless him, kept on saying: 'The coach always goes first, Kev, not the committee!' A prescient observation? In fact, both he and Brian ended up going way before me.

Neville recalls another plane trip back from Ungarie when the pilot informed us that we would have to make an unscheduled landing to get fuel. He duly landed the plane, but didn't purchase any fuel saying it was too expensive. He reckoned he had just enough to get us back to Melbourne. He got on the radio to arrange a priority landing and, as all these other planes circled around, we whisked down the runway with the fuel gauge well and truly on empty.

Anyway, risking everything, and with my mum's advice ringing loudly in my ears, I made the decision to leave Prahran and go to Richmond.

I'll never forget my first few days and weeks there. I was very nervous. I still didn't know Tommy Hafey all that well, but I had heard a lot about him. He was the bloke who killed you out on the training track, though there was — I was happy to discover — far more to him than that. He had come from Shepparton to coach the Richmond team in 1966, taking over from Len Smith, who died not long after at just 53, not a lot older than my dad.

It's often said that footy — the stresses of being a coach — killed Len. I don't know if that's true; however, he and his brother Norm, who had been so successful with Melbourne, both died relatively young. Allan Jeans, Tom Hafey, John Kennedy and Ron Barassi are all now in their seventies and still contributing to the game, so how much did we lose when Len and Norm died before their time? The medal for the best player in the AFL grand final is named after Norm Smith.

Len's legacy is that of being credited with creating the modern game. If you read his famous *Golden Rules*, you can see how much influence he has had on certain aspects of the modern game — particularly the quick handpass and the rapid play-on.

Rule 1. Get the ball through the goals in the quickest possible manner, but remember that kicking the ball into an opponent is a football sin. (Attacks should be started from the half-back line, and the quickest route to goal employed.)
Rule 2. Two men together at all times.
Rule 3. No packs or crushes.
Rule 4. Crumbs, crumbs, crumbs.
Rule 5. Play close to opponent back men.

Rule 6. Team spirit, intelligent talking. (Call specific instructions to your team-mates.)

Rule 7. Mind your opponent.

Rule 8. Stand on the mark.

Rule 9. Stop your opponent from playing on.

Rule 10. Tackle opponent in possession of ball. (Legitimate tackling is the only way to take a ball from your opponent.)

At Essendon we were very strong on Rule 9.

Most premierships are won employing Len Smith's rules. He would be thrilled to see the way the modern game is played, especially the way Geelong performed throughout the 2007 season on the way to its first premiership in 44 years. The Cats constantly produced classic high-scoring efforts through speed of ball movement from the back half. In fact, it was twice as quick as in the 1960s when Len was trying to introduce it. What I would really love to know from Len and Norm, if they were alive today, is how they would get rid of flooding, where you end up with just about 36 players at one end of the ground.

As well as influencing the game, Len had a big influence on me. When, in Round 5 in 1967, I injured my knee, he told me to get it operated on straightaway, and not wait. Because it was Len Smith giving me advice, I followed it. I knew it had to be the right decision, even though in those days a lot of people didn't come back from a cartilage operation. That was why, for a lot of people like me, the efforts of John Townsend, the Melbourne player, would be very inspirational. He was one of the first players to make a really successful comeback from a full knee reconstruction, one carried out by the surgeon and long-serving North Melbourne club doctor, John Grant. Townsend won a best and fairest award before the injury and operation in 1965, and another one after it in 1969.

That surgery, and the football John Townsend played subsequently, have become landmarks in the medical history of Australian football. In 2006, the Coaches Association gave their annual award to Dr John Grant for the opportunities he has given to so many sportspeople to continue their careers. The words 'he's done his ACL' still send shocks through footy clubs. But there is hope these days, whereas 50 or more years ago there was none. An untreated Anterior Cruciate Ligament (ACL) injury makes it difficult, if not impossible, to continue playing sports that require players to twist and turn — as John Coleman, the Essendon champion, found out in 1954.

In 1964, Grant began using the ground-breaking method of treating the injury that had been developed by an American surgeon. Essentially, a graft of tissues, including the patella tendon or hamstring, is used as a substitute for the ACL. According to a report I read in *The Age* in Melbourne, Grant's operation was a breakthrough because it protected the graft from being dissolved by an enzyme (hyaluronidase) contained in the fluid of the knee joint. 'The ACL has a protective coating, like a sausage skin, so fluid can't get at it,' Grant said. 'But the first operations didn't put a covering on the graft, so the hyaluronidase made it disappear.'

Grant had used the method pioneered by the US surgeon Kenneth Jones, which involved drilling a hole into the thigh bone and inserting the graft between the thigh bone and the shin bone, where it was protected. 'The only difficulty he had was that he was putting a ⅜-inch drill from the front through the knee. Technically, that was going to be difficult, and also all the crumbs finished up in the knee,' Grant said. 'I changed and got a (hollow) drill and came from the other side, so that overcame that technical problem.'

According to *The Age*, the drill used — a modified version of what you'd find in a hardware shop — is a little more high-tech today. Rather than cutting open the knee, surgeons operate using arthroscopy, meaning the patient doesn't spend weeks in plaster and can move around within a day. Otherwise, the operation remains largely unchanged.

There have to be awards for people like John Grant because the success of football depends on more than just the players. The Coaches Association has also honoured Noel Judkins for his efforts in recruiting. Noel was a fantastic person, the first full-time recruiting manager for the Bombers, there for three premierships and five grand finals.

If I were to give an annual Kevin Sheedy Award, Tommy Hafey would have won it many times over the past 40 years. I had just lost my own father named Tom when this other man called Tom came into my life and helped to shape it in a positive, fatherly way. When I injured my knee during my first year at Richmond, after taking a huge risk to move to Richmond from Prahran, the person who was most supportive of me during that time was Tom Hafey.

In life, you have a lot of people who are your 'coaches'. They come in all shapes and sizes. And there's a fair bit of advice out there. The trick is to know who to listen to. I learned pretty quickly that Tom Hafey was a good person to listen to. He remains that today. I love our phone conversations.

'How're you going, Tom?'

'Sensational, Kevvie, and getting better!' He is so totally positive about life, even now at 77 years of age. His great strengths are that he is personable and approachable, and he communicates in a way that everyone can understand.

When I first got to Richmond in 1966, although I'd had the years at Prahran, I really had no idea what it would be like in the VFL — the big league, with those extra four players and the ramped-up training. I did know Kevin Bartlett, who when I joined, was hovering between the firsts and the seconds. There were still some people saying he wouldn't make it because he was too skinny. Obviously, they were too blind to see his calf muscles.

Overall, I got a pretty good welcome to Richmond when I first arrived at Punt Road, the club's fabled home that began life as a cricket ground in 1856 — it's older than Australian football. The importance of a warm greeting is something I have remembered throughout my career as a coach: you need to make the new young person coming through the door feel as welcome as possible. And his family, too!

There were a lot of tradesmen at Richmond, people with whom I had an immediate affinity. There were a few blokes like Michael Green, Trevor Gowers and Barry Richardson who were going to university. There was also a good mixture of city and country people.

The experienced players of the time were Neville Crowe, 'Bull' Richardson, the great Roger Dean, Billy Barrot, Paddy Guinane, Barry Cameron, Billy Brown and John Northey. There were a couple of real characters in Brown the rover/wingman and Michael Patterson, who had one of the best nicknames I've ever heard — 'Swampfox'. He was named after the character in a television program that was popular at the time because of his ability to hit and run, just like it said in the theme song to the show.

John Northey also had a good nickname, 'Swooper'. He wasn't named after a television show, though. He got his nickname for the way he would just swoop on to the ball.

The new kids on the block were blokes who were to become part of not just Richmond's folklore, but the whole game of Australian football: Kevin Bartlett, Royce Hart, Francis Bourke, Dick Clay. Could they play footy? You bet they could. All of them were motivated to do well. For Francis Bourke, it was a case of if he didn't make it in footy, he would be back on the farm — up around Nathalia somewhere — milking cows. 'Saint' Francis hated milking cows. In 1980, he came up with one of the best lines I had heard in footy: 'I have always said the best way to have a tight defence is to have the ball on your forward line!'

Sometimes in life, you can just be so lucky. I had fronted up at a club that was absolutely ready to peak after a couple of decades of being down, and all because my parents had moved from South Yarra to Armadale, and because a person by the name of Kevin Healy had been kind enough to make a phone call.

It was funny getting changed in the Richmond locker rooms. This was in the days when players worked at jobs for 40 hours a week. I would look over to Michael Green, who'd just come in from university, nicely dressed. He was in locker 37. Two lockers along was Tony Jewell; like me, he was a plumber, which meant he had dust and cobwebs all over his overalls, the pockets of which contained rulers and other tools.

Roger Dean, another plumber, was at number 3, just down

from my locker, number 10. He worked for the railways and always had his hair spot-on. There wasn't a lot of trench digging to be done by plumbers on the railways, not a lot of dust to be gathered. I think he had pretty well got his work organised so that he could get to training right on time, and not too tired.

Kevin Shinners, also a plumber, from the Dandenongs via Prahran, was in number 18. Big Johnny Ronaldson, whose son Tony went on to play basketball for Australia, was yet another plumber. I don't think anything ever went wrong with the plumbing at Punt Road — or if it did, it wasn't hard to find someone to fix it.

As I reflect on that Richmond change room, I can still recall the tenants of those lockers, like it was yesterday:

Locker 1: Paddy Guinane (son of Danny), a science teacher
Locker 2: John Ronaldson (whose son Tony played basketball for Australia — genes!)
Locker 3: Roger Dean
Locker 4: The great Royce Hart
Locker 5: Rex Hunt, policeman-turned-commentator
Locker 6: Trevor Gowers
Locker 7: Eric Moorebank
Locker 8: Dick Clay
Locker 9: John Northey, who ended up coaching in 300 games and running pubs
Locker 10: Kevin Sheedy, who ended up coaching and then, who knows what else?

On my right in locker 11 was a bloke we called 'Father Bowden' because he had left the priesthood to become a VFL footballer.

Michael Bowden retired after the 1969 premiership. He had a big family, including two sons, Sean and Joel, who both played for Richmond. Michael was also a foster parent to young people with problem backgrounds; all in all, a very good sort of person, one of the best at Punt Road.

'Bull' Richardson was in locker 12, so in the first dozen numbers at Richmond, there were people from all walks of life. And from all sorts of places — the inner suburbs, the country, Tasmania — a rich mix of experiences in life that could be moulded into one of the strongest teams in the history of Australian football.

In fact, in 1969, the name 'Tigers' became the strongest in football all over the country. That year the Claremont Tigers won the flag in the West Australian Football League. In Adelaide, Glenelg was the premier side. In Victoria, it was us. Up in Sydney, the Balmain Tigers beat South Sydney to win the rugby league premiership. *Tiger tiger burning bright!*

At Punt Road, it was part of a remarkable run of success. From 1967 to 1982, the club won five flags from seven grand finals. That's just about a premiership every two years! So, what a period to have lobbed at Richmond, after Melbourne had said I wasn't tall enough, wasn't quick enough and didn't have enough skills. I wonder who it is I should ring up at Melbourne and say 'thank you' to for knocking me back all those years ago, because they gave me the opportunity of a lifetime — the opportunity to be part of one of the most successful eras in Richmond history, and to play in three premierships.

What all this told me, is that you should always take knock-backs as opportunities. I ought to know that, I've just had another one — from Essendon! But when I look at all the opportunities that have already opened up, I can't help but be excited, rather than despondent. I could move to the Gold

Coast, or to the Western Suburbs of Sydney. All you have to do is readjust your thinking, replace emotion with a bit of intelligence, and — in this great country of opportunities — things will quickly start to happen for you.

Opportunity certainly presented itself early for me at Richmond. I hadn't played a reserves game before I went straight into the seniors, up against Darren Peoples from Fitzroy. He was quick and skilful enough to play 77 games for the Lions, so it was a real challenge in my first game.

Soon after I was on Dennis Marshall, the Geelong Team of the Century player. So it was a tough baptism in those early days, but it was also the fulfilment of a dream. My first game was on the MCG. Can you imagine what it feels like to run out there for the first time as a player and hear the crowd, knowing that all those people would see me if I was outplayed by my opponent, knowing that I could be banned from playing for five years if I failed. Thank goodness for adrenaline.

I was pretty happy to have these quality opponents early on, though, because I've always tried to measure my own performances against the best. I would also have been thinking that if I can just get past Peoples, if I can hold my own against Marshall, then I'm justified in developing a bit more confidence in my own game.

I played a few games, and then I was sent back to the seconds to 'get a few touches', as we coaches like to say to players when we drop them. Ian Wilson, who went on to become the president of the club, was then the manager of the reserves. It was while I was playing in the seconds that I did my knee, an injury that meant I would be out for the season.

It was an amazing year to be sitting out. Richmond won its first premiership in 24 years in 1967. I got to watch the euphoria from inside the club, but still on the outer in the sense that I wasn't in the team. We had only lost three games all year and had beaten Geelong — our grand final opponents — in both home and away games. The Cats were pretty inconsistent in 1967, but at their best they were capable of upsetting anyone, including the minor premiers.

Neville Crowe was missing from the Richmond side after being suspended for striking Carlton's John Nicholls during the second semi-final. Geelong was without John 'Sammy' Newman, the back-up ruckman to Polly Farmer. Newman had part of a kidney removed after being injured in the first semi-final. Over the years, Sam has had a fair bit removed.

Geelong was at its most mercurial from the first bounce and was soon up by 15 points. Richmond responded to lead by a goal at quarter-time and by 16 points at half-time. Geelong then kicked four goals in seven minutes in the third quarter before Billy Barrot, a great big game player, sparked a Richmond revival. At three-quarter time, Richmond was in front by two points. I really respected what Barrot did in that game. He was electric. At times he did things that were so against the basic rules of the game they would have riled junior coaches. But this was Billy, and when he hit the adrenaline rush button in a big match, he was unstoppable. He was why the Tigers believed they could win in this era. He gave life to the likes of Roger Dean, who had been around in the poor years. This is where Graeme Richmond had the timing right. A lot of clubs have good players but don't have the timing right with senior players, so they don't combine them with the next generation of talent. We still retire older players too quickly.

I guess this game was also the first time where we really saw the benefit of Tommy Hafey's hard-training program in a big game. The scores were level four times in the final quarter. There was a dubious moment when the Richmond captain, Fred Swift, marked a long kick between the main uprights and right on the boundary line. Geelong supporters claim the ball had in fact crossed the line and was a goal. In the end, the Tigers got home 16.18 (114) to 15.15 (105).

Royce Hart kicked three goals to finish his first senior year in style. He also took one of a couple of great marks. The other was awarded to Ken Newland, an absolute screamer. If you go into the Geelong clubrooms, there is a huge picture of it on the wall between the football department and the rest of the administrative buildings. When he was chairman of selectors at Geelong, Barry Richardson used to hate to have to walk past it on the way from Mark Thompson's office back to the car park. There he was, both feet firmly on the ground, being used as a stepladder by Newland.

It was pretty tough not being able to play football with all this going on around me, but Tom Hafey remained very supportive. 'Keep going, Kevvie. Keep working,' he'd say.

I started to do a lot of weights training under Stan Nicholls, who had worked with a lot of great tennis players and footballers. I also had a personal fitness trainer, Bill Boromeo, who was also the club's summer fitness coach. Bill was highly regarded in athletics for his training programs. I wanted to get that little extra three or four per cent I felt I needed to get there in the VFL. Stan's programs also worked on those bits of the Sheedy frame that my work as a plumber didn't exercise naturally.

Plumbing, with a few exceptions — Roger Dean, for instance — was a pretty demanding occupation. But whether you were sitting in an office at the railways, studying at university or digging ditches made no difference to Tommy. He trained us all the same: hard. It says everything about Tommy's belief in the importance of supreme fitness above all else that he brought in Percy Cerutty to work with us. Cerutty is a legend in the world of athletics, or a madman, depending on who you're talking to.

'I would sooner die than be beaten,' Cerutty once said. 'I'm extremely hostile about defeat. I hate the person that's beaten me, and I hate myself worse for being beaten.' You can see why he and Tommy got on so well, and why Tommy wanted him around Punt Road.

How would those comments go down today? They would be absolutely smashed on talk-back radio, in the papers — front *and* back page. All the sports stations would run the story, and parents would be ringing up complaining about this sort of attitude. Though when you go to the grand final and your team is competing, you probably do hope they've got a bit of Percy in them.

Percy's views weren't universally endorsed. Some people thought he was a charlatan but others revered him, particularly for the work he did turning Herb Elliott into an Olympic gold medallist.

Cerutty's own personal fitness story is an inspiration. At 43, he suffered an almost complete mental and physical breakdown. His doctors told him he wouldn't live much beyond another couple of years. Percy became convinced that the only person who could save him was himself. In the days of steak and three veggies, he became a vegetarian. He took up weight-lifting, and as his strength returned he began walking and then running.

There was a growing touch of the Renaissance man about Percy. He began listening to the works of the great composers. He also adopted the postural technique of Frederick Mathias

Alexander — the Alexander Technique — and, in the pursuit of an ever faster and fitter body, turned for help to a racehorse. Cerutty was out for a jog one day that took him through Caulfield Racecourse where he came upon the great sprinter of the day, Ajax, at track work. He reckoned that something passed from the horse to him that morning. He began to study the way horses moved, then spent time looking at antelopes and chimpanzees at the Melbourne Zoo. He then came up with what he called his 'naturalistic theory of movement'.

As well as his love of Italian opera, Cerutty worshipped the Greek philosophers. In 1946, he invented his own version by combining the words 'Spartan' and 'stoic' to create his Stotan Philosophy. It entailed diet, philosophy, cultivation of the intellect, and openness to artistic endeavours. He began training runners, who would visit his camp at Portsea, on the tip of the Mornington Peninsula. Some of them turned out to be pretty successful.

Cerruty realised that his methods and philosophy could be translated into the business world, so he became a personal trainer to businesspeople. 'I admit that the only god I worship or know is success,' he once said. 'And I try to put that into the minds, the personalities, of others. But I never impose anything. They choose. They don't even have to come here, but if they are I'm going to talk on that level. I feel that it's far better to know you've tried and perhaps not succeeded, than to look back and wonder whether you should have really tried hard.'

As word spread of Cerutty's methods, particularly following the success of athletes like Les Perry, who represented Australia at the 1952 Helsinki Olympics, more and more people began knocking on the door of his South Yarra flat, seeking his guidance. They were all told that the accepted practices of the athletics coaches of the day were absolute rubbish, and that all they had to do was just get out there and 'stress the organism' by running further and harder than anyone else. And if they put in the greatest effort possible, this would not just affect their results on the track but could also impact on other areas of their lives as well, in very powerful and positive ways.

Cerutty had an unsteady relationship with the legendary John Landy, the second man in history to run a sub-four-minute mile. In the 1950s, running those sorts of times was, in the mind of the public, up there with climbing Mt Everest or a man going to the moon. Landy, who went on to become governor of Victoria, is also remembered for one of the greatest acts of sportsmanship in Australian history. It took place during the Australian Athletics Championships in March 1956, the year of the Melbourne Olympics. Ron Clarke, brother of the wonderful Essendon footballer Jack Clarke, tripped and fell during the race. Landy thought he might have put his spikes into Clarke, so he went back to check that he was all right. He then looked up, saw the field was now about 30 metres ahead of him, and turned in an amazing performance to catch them and win the race. Even the hard-nosed types in the press box applauded Landy, but not Cerutty. Landy had got to the Helsinki Olympics on the strength of public subscriptions, particularly from the people of Geelong. He didn't do as well there as he might have, but on his return he began to train harder and to achieve more outstanding results. Landy, to this day, remembers the kindness of the people who raised the money to send him to Helsinki. He was upset by Cerutty's suggestion that they had wasted their money.

Cerutty also fell out with Ron Clarke. In 1964 at the Tokyo Olympics, after winning a bronze medal in the 10,000 metres,

Clarke was getting ready for the 5000 metres when he heard a voice say: 'Ah, you've got no hope, Clarke. You always were a weak bastard.' It was Percy's way of goading athletes, to make them get out on the track and prove him wrong; but in Clarke's case, all it did was upset him and he finished ninth.

Herb Elliott, winner of the gold medal for the 1500 metres at the Rome Olympics in 1960, was Cerutty's greatest success story. Just as Percy suggested, Herb has also been very successful in his business life and, when it comes to fit septuagenarians, is up there with Tommy Hafey.

This is how Percy summed up Elliott: 'I've got a good dictionary up there, and the words "fail" and "failure" have been ruled out for years. I don't know what people are talking about who use that word. All I do know is "temporary non-success", even if I've got to wait another 20 years for what I'm after. I try to put that into people, no matter what their objective in life. Athletics, I always say, is only a start, but you prove on the track something, beating others and getting somewhere, that you can use as an experience in after life. As I told Elliot, "Beat 'em on the track and you'll beat 'em in business". And he's getting on, see?'

Herb Elliott also came to Punt Road to speak with the young players at Richmond. He encouraged us to train at our utmost level every time we went out on to the track.

Cerutty and Elliott weren't the only superstars from other sports who came to speak with us. World champion boxers Lionel Rose and Johnny Famechon also came to Punt Road. One of the best speakers we ever had was Harry Beitzel, the umpire, who delivered a talk called 'Up There on Cloud Nine'. Basically, it was about getting yourself ready for a big game; dreaming of what you can create by putting your mind into another realm from ordinary life. He encouraged us to think that yes, it could be us up there on the dais, and that we could get there by being totally committed to ourselves and to our team-mates.

We had a different speaker come to the club every couple of months. Graeme Richmond, Tom Hafey or Alan Schwab would just keep putting them in front of us. The thing that impressed me was that, most of the time, they were people who were very good at getting their message across. Over the years, I have listened to many speakers and some just don't press their point home at all. I reckon Graeme, Tom and Alan got it right about 90 per cent of time. They were excellent judges. Who would have thought an umpire could have something so positive to say?

It was a privilege to be at a club where everyone was just so committed to getting the very best out of themselves, whether it was through psychology, or by reaching the fitness levels that Percy Cerutty demanded. During Richmond's glory days, that Hafey fitness training was pivotal to the club's success. If the game was close at three-quarter time, we always believed we had the legs to beat the opposition. Most times we did.

As well as general fitness, rehab training was very important, especially for me as I tried to overcome my knee injury. I can only thank the surgeon who performed my operation, Bill Doig, for the great job he did as I joined a select group of players I am very proud to be part of, Tom Hafey's Second Efforts, players given a second chance.

Hafey and Graeme Richmond, as their partnership and experience in running the club grew, took on players that others thought weren't good enough. Paul Sproule was recruited from Essendon, a three-for-one trade deal, because they believed he had more than he had shown at Windy Hill. Another Hafey classic was Robert McGhie. He had to leave Footscray for disciplinary reasons. Tommy grabbed him, knocked the rebel into shape, and McGhie played in successive premiership sides. It's experiences like these that make coaching special: when you take somebody and give them an opportunity, and they reward both you and themselves by taking it.

There's also the other side of coaching, the side that makes you really wonder sometimes if you want the job: cutting players. It's never pretty, it's never easy; but as a coach, your first loyalty is to your client, the club. And if you want your club to remain strong, then you have to be forever refreshing the player list. Tom Hafey found that out at Richmond. During the time of his first two premierships there were no changes; no players from other clubs. That's when Tommy discovered that a few people were walking around with haloes, thinking they were living in heaven.

I felt for a short while that *I* was in heaven, when in 1969, I not only got my career back on track, but I also got to play in a successful grand final side. You never forget the people you win premierships with. After the final siren goes, as you hug your team-mates, as the cup is being presented, it's like you're in this moment where the rest of the world doesn't matter. You have slogged your guts out for probably nine months, endured all sorts of setbacks and now you have this precious moment that you want to last forever. Of course, it doesn't, so you spend the rest of your life trying to get it again. Some people only have it once; some achieve it more than a few times. Look at Martin Pike, a misfit, who went on to win four — one at North Melbourne and three at Brisbane. I wanted to recruit

Pike to Essendon, but was advised against it. I said to my three advisers, 'If *he* makes it, *you're* gone.' By the time Pikie was wearing his fourth premiership medal, all three were no longer at Windy Hill.

In the 1969 Grand Final, I was in the back-pocket, pretending I could play a bit, overcoming my deficiencies by learning to read the other players better — the little things that I had to keep doing all the time because of all the talented people we had at Richmond at the time. In the back-pocket, the refuge of all slow centre men, things were pretty basic; easy for me to understand. There was only one way to go, and that was forward. It's amazing to recall now what a year that was, both personally and for the club, especially the coach. I knew that, whatever the outcome of the grand final, come the Monday, I was off to join the army. Now, that's a real Mad Monday. As for the coach, even though we had won a premiership in 1967, Richmond's first in 24 years, at the start of 1969 there were people calling for Tom Hafey to be sacked. It wasn't entirely based on football knowledge, something that is still the case when it comes to sacking coaches these days.

At most levels the players thought Tommy was fantastic. He hated losing, but he taught us to respect winning and to cope with defeat — or 'temporary unsuccess', as Percy Cerutty called it. His training regimen was very, very hard. True, some of the players bitched about that, but it was more a case of letting off steam than a real issue with most of us, because we knew what the benefits of that hard training were: the ability to win when it mattered in the final moments of a tight game.

But some of the whingeing reached the ears of the board, particularly the president, Ray Dunn, who had another axe to grind with Tommy. Cerutty had come to training one day and given Dunn, a Queen's Counsel who was accustomed to being deferred to, a fearful pasting about being overweight. It got to the point where Richmond was getting ready to sack Tommy in the middle of the year. I believe that Graeme Richmond stood the line and defended his coach, and the rest is history — we won the flag from fourth. Back in the days when there were only four teams in the finals, not many sides did that. In some ways the political battles over Tommy were a good thing, because they galvanised the players.

Nineteen sixty-nine was an amazing year — one during which a man first walked upon the moon. We could watch it live on television, too — grainy, in black-and-white, but still a miracle, especially for those of us whose first experience of the box was watching it through shopfront windows in Chapel Street.

Back on earth, it was a significant year in Australian football, too. There must have been a full moon around the time of the Anzac Day weekend match between Carlton and Collingwood because the umpires threatened to go on strike. They were angry that four players reported during the game — Peter Jones, Ricky McLean, Ted Potter and Len Thompson — were let off on a technicality: the reports had been filed incorrectly.

There was more threatened strike action later on — from the cheer squads. This came as the VFL sought to ban confetti and floggers — no, not Hafey and Cerutty, who flogged us on the training track. Now *that* would have been nice. Rather, these floggers were the things made out of crepe paper that supporters thrashed around every time their team kicked a goal.

A new rule was also introduced which penalised the side that kicked the ball over the boundary line on the full. With a free kick replacing the throw-in, the game became faster, the football more direct. Sides with great full-forwards looked set to dominate. Peter Hudson kicked 16 goals for Hawthorn in May. When Hawthorn played Geelong at Kardinia Park, Hudson kicked six of the Mayblooms' 14 goals, but at the other end, Doug Wade kicked eight of the Cats' 16. On the same afternoon in Melbourne, Peter McKenna kicked 16 of Collingwood's 19 goals in the game against South Melbourne. McKenna kicked four points in the final quarter, missing the chance to break Fred Fanning's grand old record of 18 goals.

Hudson ended up with 120 goals for the season, but most notably, was kept goal-less against Richmond by Barry Richardson. 'Bones' Richardson was a great defender in an era when there were many great full-forwards. One thing I can never understand, though, is why a physiotherapist would get called 'Bones'. Shouldn't he be 'Muscles' and the chiropractor 'Bones'? But no ... when he first came down from Barnawartha, in northeast Victoria, there wasn't much skin or muscle on him, but plenty of bones. Talking of skin and bones, at full-forward we had Rex Hunt, then a gangly, enthusiastic 20-year-old whose left foot couldn't be relied on in front of goal. Under Tommy, we were trying to play the new, fast, direct football, but between Rounds 7 and 12, we won just one game.

The knives were well and truly out for Tommy by the time we came to play Collingwood — unbeaten for seven rounds. We won by two points. We only lost one more game that season.

We went into the semi-final against Geelong with the critics still predicting that Tommy's harsh training sessions would cause us to tire. We won by 118 points. Arriving at the MCG that day, I would never have predicted that result. Geelong had made the finals in 1968, and had finished a good third in 1969. We had been close during the season — we had 13 wins, they had 13 wins and a draw — and I had expected it to be close on this day. It's funny what finals pressure can do to you.

In the preliminary final, we kicked seven goals in the third quarter — bye bye, Magpie.

Just under 120,000 people packed into the MCG for the grand final where Carlton, the Blues, were to be our opponents. They were supposedly refreshed after their week off, while there were still people out there chirping that Richmond would be sore and tired after our tough run into the finals, and the floggings Tommy was giving us on the training track.

If we were going to be tired at the finish, we'd better get cracking at the start then. Eric Moore kicked a goal within seconds of the opening bounce, then Royce Hart kicked another soon after. Mike Green, who had been inspirational in the ruck against Geelong and Collingwood, continued his good form against John Nicholls and Percy Jones. A four-point lead at quarter-time had grown to 22 points at half-time.

In the third quarter, gee, it looked like the critics were right: we *were* tired. We conceded four goals before Brent Croswell put the Blues in front with a brilliant solo goal. We were trailing by four points at three-quarter time.

What happened in the final quarter was magic. We knew that in the tight games, because of all our hard training under Tom, we would never be beaten on fitness. Armed with that knowledge, we went out and played superb football. Bill Barrot took the sort of mark that lifts a side when it most needs to be lifted, and then kicked the goal. Kevin Bartlett took control of the game at his end, while down back, we kept Carlton to just two behinds.

After the game, the Carlton coach, Ron Barassi, lamented the loss. 'I felt, and I always will, that we should have won that game. We had our four fixed forwards — Alex Jesaulenko, Robert Walls, Brent Croswell and Syd Jackson — who played their worst games for the year, maybe for even two or three, in that one grand final. What a time for it to happen.'

I was proud to be part of the Richmond defence that helped those champions have that bad day. It was all a wonderful moment, and a wonderful continuation of my education in life. First, you never know the future, no matter how hard you might plan for it. Second, I saw up really close for the first time how politics can wreck a footy club if you let it.

Just a few months before, if politics had prevailed over commonsense, Tommy Hafey would have been sacked. It takes a strong person to keep going in those circumstances thankfully for Richmond, and for me, Tom was that sort of person. He stood his ground. In the end, the politics had become our inspiration. The Tigers had their second flag in three years; I had my first after all the dramas of leaving Prahran followed by the anxieties caused by my knee injury. It was a moment to savour.

The celebrations were short and sweet for me, though. On the Monday, I went off to join the army.

6

Sapper Sheedy

I didn't get to celebrate the 1969 Grand Final victory as enthusiastically or for as long as some of my team-mates. For a start, I didn't drink when I was 21. It took until I was 35 to acquire a taste for alcohol, no doubt because of the powerful influence of Tom Hafey, who as he will tell you, has never let alcohol pass his lips. Barry Richardson does claim, though, that I had a glass of wine with him after the grand final and that it was he who introduced me to what remains to this day one of my favourite tipples — a glass of chardonnay.

There was another reason for the shortened post-match festivities. My number had come out of the barrel, to use the common term of the time. That meant I had been conscripted to undertake two years of mandatory military service, or National Service; hence becoming a 'Nasho'.

A lot of young people today might not know about National Service. It hasn't been a part of the Australian landscape since Gough Whitlam, the incoming prime minister, abolished it after winning the 1972 federal election. Before that, conscription had been around in various forms since Federation. Between 1905 and 1909, there was a form of conscription for boys aged 12 to 14, and for youths aged 18 to 20.

In 1911, the federal government made it compulsory for all males aged between 12 and 26 to undertake military training. It wasn't a popular move — particularly the conscription of young boys — and by 1915 there had been about 34,000 prosecutions and 7000 detentions of trainees, parents, employers and other people who had disobeyed the new law.

During the First World War the Labor prime minister Billy Hughes tried to introduce full conscription in order to help Australia's war effort. He attempted to do this through two highly controversial plebiscites. The first one narrowly rejected conscription by a vote of 51 per cent to 49 per cent. A second plebiscite on 20 December 1917 was also lost, and this time by a bigger margin.

The issue was so contentious that it split the Labor Party, with Hughes crossing the floor and becoming prime minister of a Nationalist government, which would have been a bit like Kevin Rudd joining the Liberal Party today. A number of people were arrested for protesting against conscription, something that would have an echo in the late 1960s and early 1970s when I was called up. One of those taken into custody was John Curtin, the former Brunswick footballer in the VFA who went on to become a war-time prime minister almost 20 years later. At that time of his life, Curtin was a member of the Socialist Party. Trade unions also actively opposed conscription, as did the Catholic Church via the towering figure of Archbishop Daniel Mannix. He was accused of being a traitor. At that time in Australia — really, right up to the time I was going to school — Catholics and Protestants didn't get on all that well.

I can remember insults being traded back and forth on the way to school. Thankfully, in recent times we've realised we need to be a bit more tolerant of each other, even to actually start to like each other. I think we've realised that, because there are so many other religions out there, we Christians need to stick together. After all, we were all worshipping the same guy who got crucified on the Cross.

Those who supported conscription did so on the basis that it was a sign of loyalty to Great Britain, and also to the many young men who had volunteered to go off to places like Gallipoli and the Somme, many of them making the ultimate sacrifice.

In the Second World War, all men aged between 18 and 35 and all single men aged between 35 and 45 had to join the CMF, the Citizens' Military Forces. They were known not as 'Nashos', but as 'Chockos' — short for 'chocolate soldiers' — because regular servicemen felt they melted in the heat of battle. That was proven to be wrong on a number of occasions, especially in New Guinea, where they could be sent to serve because at that time it was an Australian territory, not an independent nation as it is today.

After the Japanese bombed Darwin, most Australians came to support the use of the CMF outside Australia and its territories and they found themselves in all the major war zones of the Pacific area, fighting alongside those who had volunteered for the war effort. In 1945, after the Japanese surrendered, conscription was suspended. It was revived again in the early 1950s during the Korean War.

In 1964, another war had broken out in Asia, this time in Vietnam, and compulsory National Service for 20-year-old males was again introduced. Selection was based on date of birth — your number coming out of the barrel — and you served full time for two years.

In March 1966 the government, led by Sir Robert Menzies, announced that Nashos would be sent to Vietnam to fight in units of the Australian Regular Army, and even under secondment to American forces. Initially, the decision was reasonably popular, but it soon fell out of favour in Australia in the most controversial way. We began to have demonstrations against the war, and to use terms like 'draft dodgers' and 'conscientious objectors'.

When the president of the United States, Lyndon Baines Johnson, visited Australia in 1966, protestors chanted: 'LBJ, LBJ, how many kids did you kill today?' In Sydney, a group of women set up an organisation called Save Our Sons. In 1970, five members of that organisation — they came to be known as 'The Fairlea Five' — spent time at Fairlea Prison in Melbourne for handing out anti-conscription brochures while on government property.

By the time I was getting fitted out in jungle greens, surveys were showing that about 55 per cent of Australians wanted our soldiers brought home from Vietnam. Gough Whitlam promised to do that if Labor was elected in 1969, the famous *Don's Party* election. He lost that election and it wasn't until December 1972 that he finally came to power and National Service was abolished.

On the Monday after the 1969 Grand Final, there I was in Swan Street, ready to serve my country, going from football hero one minute to short back and sides, 'yes sir, no sir, three bags full sir' the next. I don't remember thinking a lot about the rights and wrongs of conscription then. I respected the rights of those people who felt strongly against it to make their protest. That's what a democracy is all about. In the past, we had fought hard to protect Australia's democratic rights. As far as I was concerned, though, Australia had called me and I answered 'yes'.

I know that for a lot of people losing those two years from their life proved incredibly difficult. Normie Rowe's career as the King of Pop in Australia never quite recovered. There was never another string of hits like 'Shakin' All Over' or 'Que Sera Sera'. How weird now that, in 2008, he has discovered that his birth date wasn't among the numbers drawn from the barrel. He learned this after he was recently pulled over for speeding by a policeman who shared his birth date, but hadn't done national service. There's a mystery in there somewhere to be sorted out.

Another Nasho was Doug Walters. Many will say he was never the same cricketer after his two years in the army. As a 19-year-old he had made centuries in his first two Tests, which were against England. There were a few commentators who used to argue that while in the army Dougie had learned a new shot: a flick behind square-leg, during the playing of which his feet came to attention. Probably a bit fanciful. Peter Brock, the champion racing car driver, was another one called up for National Service. As a medical orderly, he actually gave Doug Walters his various inoculations. Peter was serving at Bathurst, in the central west of New South Wales, way before he became king of the famous Mount Panorama there.

Royce Hart, also a Nasho, had a novel way of celebrating our 1969 Grand Final win. He signed up to play for Glenelg in the SANFL grand final, an attempt to become the first player to win two senior premierships in the one year. He was knocked unconscious in the early minutes of that game.

For many, many people, their two years with the army altered their lives dramatically and in some instances tragically. They were asked to serve in Vietnam, an experience from which a lot of them have never recovered.

I believe there are many good reasons to return to having National Service in Australia. However, Nashos should never be sent overseas to serve in conflicts like Iraq or Afghanistan. That should be the job of the professional, volunteer soldier. When they join up, they know full well they could be sent to a theatre of war. It's what they train so hard for, especially the people in some of the Special Forces regiments who have been doing a remarkable job in Afghanistan.

Certainly, people who do National Service could, if they wanted to, go on to join the regular army. They might find they like the career opportunities the army has to offer, but it should remain a clear matter of choice. For me, being in the army as a sapper — an engineer — was about building bridges, not blowing them up.

I have already said how disappointing I find it that the number of youth clubs has declined in recent times. These were — and are, where they do still exist — a great opportunity for people to get out from in front of the television, the computer games, and mingle with different people, learn social skills and so on.

For me, a kid from South Yarra who had hardly ever been outside Melbourne, the army provided me with opportunities to broaden my knowledge of life. Australians didn't travel very much in those days, so I had rarely met anyone from New South Wales or Queensland. Sure, I had met Tasmanians, West Australians and South Australians because they had come to

Melbourne to play footy — but actually visiting those places? Mostly, no. So, having to go to New South Wales, to Casula, as part of my early training, was a good opportunity for me to see more of my own country. Though it did nearly kill me: near Newcastle, I came off the road while driving back from Queensland and cleaned up a few guide posts. The car was a write-off. Fortunately for me, I wasn't. I caught the train and still made it to parade on time.

The other important thing the army did was to provide me with guidance. I know how lucky I was that, at the time of my father's death, this other Tom — Tom Hafey — had come into my life to help me through those difficult years where you go from being a teenager to a young man. The army was another father figure, teaching me about discipline, hard work, respect, valour and how to get on with people who had gone through difficult times.

As we know today, because of the dreadful youth suicide figures and the number of single-vehicle car accidents, the years between, say, 17 and 21-22 are a very dangerous time for males. One mistake can be very costly. So, if they have a lot of good people around them, young people might not make those mistakes.

I discovered a lot of good people in the army, including a bloke by the name of Warrant Officer Jim Ponting who was in charge of basic training. I remember thinking 'Gee, what sort of man is this?' He made training sessions with Tom Hafey and Percy Cerutty seem like a Sunday School picnic.

Eventually, I ended up at Puckapunyal, or 'Pucka', or 'Pucka-bloodypunyal' as a lot of people call it. It's an army camp a couple of hours drive north of Melbourne, just off the Hume Highway. It's one of the most famous military camps in Australia. It was opened in November 1939 for troops from the 17th Brigade and the 6th Australian Division, one of several new camps set up to train men for the Second World War.

I was pretty pleased that I ended up there, for a lot of reasons. In fact, there soon became a bit of a Richmond–Puckapunyal exchange, if you like.

When I was leaving for the army, Graeme Richmond had taken me aside to give me a bit of advice. It was typical Graeme: 'You'll have two years, Cocko. Make the best of them. You'll have the best sort of training you can have, so take advantage of it. Sure it will be tough for a few weeks, but it's nothing you wouldn't run into on a football field.' Obviously, Graeme hadn't heard of Jim Ponting either!

Graeme organised about 20 people to come up to Pucka to celebrate my first leave. Even though I wasn't allowed to leave the area, it was like a delayed grand final celebration. Fantastic!

There was another reason I was happy enough being a city boy in the country. This was 'Bluey' Shelton country, one of my first footy heroes. He and Richie Benaud were my two greatest sporting heroes as a boy.

Ian Shelton came to Essendon from Avenel in 1959. He was the reason I chose to wear the number 10 jumper when I went to both Prahran and Richmond, and why I consider ten to be my lucky number today. I retired on 10 May. I got married on 10 January. There is just something about the number ten I really like, and it all started with 'Bluey'.

He played at centre-half back for Essendon. He was a big bloke with red hair. The way he played footy, you would think he had spent a lot of time watching the tanks on manoeuvres at Puckapunyal. He was a member of the Essendon premiership sides in 1962 and 1965. When he left Essendon, he became captain–coach of Seymour and then he went back home to Avenel, just up the road from Puckapunyal. This part of Victoria isn't just Shelton territory, it's Ned Kelly territory as well. The fabled Australian bushranger roamed all over the region.

According to an article that appeared in the *AFL Record* in 2003, if it wasn't for Ned Kelly, Essendon would never have had a red-haired centre-half back playing in two premierships while wearing the number 10 jumper. Nor would that centre-half back Jack Shelton have played 28 games for St Kilda and seven for South Melbourne before being killed at Tobruk in 1941. Nor would his son William have played 12 games for Hawthorn.

The story of why Australian football should feel indebted to Ned Kelly goes like this: In 1865, 'Bluey' Shelton's grandfather, Richard, fell into the fast-flowing Hughes Creek, in Avenel, while on his way to school. Only seven, he was rescued by the ten-year-old Ned Kelly. According to reports of the time, young Ned jumped without hesitation into the creek while fully clothed and dragged young Dick to safety. The pair, cold and wet, made their way to the nearby Royal Mail Hotel which was owned by Dick's parents, Esau and Elizabeth Shelton. The boys dried themselves by the fireplace and Esau lent Ned some clothes.

The Sheltons rewarded Ned for his bravery with an elaborate green silk sash complete with gold fringes. About 15 years later, he was wearing the sash under his famous suit of armour in the shootout with police at Glenrowan. Ned was captured after receiving 28 bullet wounds and was executed less than five months later, on 11 November 1880. The frayed, blood-stained sash still survives today and is on display in a museum in Benalla.

'If Ned Kelly didn't do what he did,' 'Bluey' Shelton told the *AFL Record* from his Avenel farm, 'who knows? My grandfather might still have been able to get out [of the water] by himself. But then again, he might not have. It's a big part of our family history because my grandfather ended up having 12 kids (eight sons and four daughters), including my father.'

The story doesn't stop there, though, because there is a link between Kelly and my family. My maternal great-grandfather, Michael Cusack, saw the Kelly Gang on their way to rob the bank at Euroa. Michael, who was only a boy at the time, was trying to catch water rats in Faithfull's Creek on the outskirts of Euroa when he saw the four gang members — Ned Kelly, his younger brother Dan, Joe Byrne and Steve Hart — ride by. At the time, the Kellys had £500 on each of their heads after having killed three plainclothes policemen just six weeks earlier. They held 22 people hostage at a nearby sheep station which they used as a base for the £2260 bank heist.

Well that's the story that's been passed down through the family ... and I'm sticking to it.

I really enjoyed helping Ben Collins, who runs a Ned Kelly website, for a number of reasons. As I said, 'Bluey' Shelton was one of my first heroes. And it was fantastic to be able to tell the story of my family's connection to this famous Australian.

There are a couple of important elements to the Ned Kelly story — mateship and battling the odds. That's why I have had another Ned Kelly expert, Brendan Pearse, address the players at Essendon from time to time.

Ben Collins pointed out another connection between footy and the Kelly legend that tickled my fancy. The late Carlton premiership captain, Bob Chitty, starred as Ned Kelly in the 1951 film *The Glenrowan Affair*. Like Kelly, Chitty was a top horseman who grew up in Corryong, a town in northeast Victoria that is part of the legend of *The Man from Snowy River*.

Ned Kelly was, as Ben described him, a phenomenally tough bushman with a high tolerance for pain, a peerless bare-knuckle fighter and a commanding leader of his gang. Chitty was his equivalent in a football sense. He led the Blues to victory against South Melbourne in the infamous 'bloodbath' grand final of 1945, after which he received an eight-match suspension for elbowing a South player.

When the film came out, Richmond great Jack Dyer, who had tangled with Chitty on several occasions, was moved to say: 'Chitty never needed armour.'

While the film was criticised for being 'dreary' and 'unimaginative', and the acting was described as 'petrified', Chitty at least resembled Ned with his high cheekbones and piercing eyes. He was paid £25 a week for the part — he got only £4 a week as captain at Carlton — but he was too embarrassed to let his former team-mates see him while he grew a beard for the role.

In another twist, one of the founding members of Chitty's beloved Carlton Football Club — long-time enemy of the Kelly family, Sir Redmond Barry — was the judge who condemned Ned Kelly to death for murder. According to John Phillips, chief justice of the Victorian Supreme Court, Barry didn't give Ned Kelly a fair trial.

Kelly and Barry had a remarkable exchange in the courtroom in which the primary school-educated bushman held his own against the learned judge. When Barry passed the death sentence upon him, Ned famously responded with: 'I will see you there, where I go.' Ironically, Barry suffered blood poisoning from a carbuncle on his neck and died 12 days after the outlaw was executed.

Also helping to keep the legend alive are VFL clubs Essendon and Williamstown, who battle each year for the Game As Ned Kelly Trophy. Essendon's Shelton–Sheedy link is obvious, while Williamstown lays claim to Ned serving about six months there: three aboard the prison hulk *Sacramento* and another three ashore in an artillery battery.

These are all great stories and a reminder of the European history of the region around Puckapunyal. The name of the military camp is a valuable reminder of the people who lived in this part of Victoria before the Kellys, Sheltons and Cusacks arrived. The word 'Puckapunyal' is an Aboriginal one, but its meaning isn't entirely clear. Some say it means 'death to the eagle', while other variations are: 'the middle hill', 'place of exile' and 'valley of the winds'.

Puckapunyal is still used by the Australian Army today and is probably best known as the home of the Royal Australian Armoured Corps and the Army Tank Museum.

When I got to Puckapunyal I was installed in the 21 Construction Company, under Major General Arthur Fittock. I am forever grateful to Major General Fittock because, after some friendly banter and negotiations, he gave me my first opportunity to coach and to prove to myself and others that I had the ability to lead. It was then that I really began to think about coaching. I thought I'd like to try it and see how I went. So, if anyone at Essendon is looking for someone to blame for the past 27 years, they can blame him!

It all came about like this. Richmond went to Major General Fittock to ask him if I could continue to train and play for the club. This was in the days when the Barassi Line was firmly in place. Those north of where it passed through the NSW Riverina area played rugby, either union or league. Those south of it played Australian football. Major General Fittock was a rugby union man. He hadn't heard of me, though a few of his junior officers had mentioned just before my arrival that I might make a likely coach for Puckapunyal's footy team. This impressed Major General Fittock because, while his rugby union team had been pretty successful, that wasn't the case with the Australian football side.

'I was always getting a bit cross with them about their lack of success,' Fittock said. 'Then, late in 1969, I remember them coming to me and asking who would be coach next year. I asked them who they thought it should be and they said "Sapper Sheedy". When I said there was no one by that name on the books at Puckapunyal, they told me he would be soon, though, and that he played in the VFL for Richmond.'

When the request came from Richmond to allow me to keep playing and training, Fittock was happy to agree, so long as I coached for the army side, the Red Roosters. It was just the most amazing experience. There I was at 21 to 22, coaching men older than myself. I could yell at them for not staying on their man or get angry with the ruckman for not contesting, but it was still dangerous if I didn't handle things well. They were my superiors and, once the siren went, they could put me on canteen duties, having to peel spuds for days on end. It would be like Wayne Swann telling Kevin Rudd to lift his game during question time. Not politically correct, and not real smart, either.

Some of these people had been to Vietnam; they had carried their wounded or dead mates out of the jungle. You can't just tell them to go out and show a bit of courage. They have already done that in an arena far more demanding than football. I realised quickly as a coach that you can't separate the human side from the rest of it. I learned all that in the army, and I left it a different bloke from the one who went in.

Playing footy for the army, I even got to play on some of 'Bluey' Shelton's childhood grounds. I used to look around the boundary to see if he had come down from the farm to watch us play. I never saw him and, at that time, I didn't have the confidence to ring him up and ask him to come. Since then, I have gone on the public record as saying that 'Bluey' Shelton has an open invitation to come into the dressing room of any team I am coaching.

Another thing I learned was how hard it is to have split loyalties, trying to serve two masters: the army *and* Richmond.

We won the flag the first year I was coach of the Red Roosters, and we played in the grand final again the second year. Richmond asked me not to play in that game because I had been carrying a few injuries. That was pretty tough. I had really bonded with my army mates. However, I chose to do the right thing by Richmond.

At three-quarter-time, though, we were behind, so I quietly slipped on my footy gear, ran on for the final quarter and we got there. You can understand why I'm still pretty angry about missing the chance to play in a cricket premiership with Richmond. I would have had one of the most unique collections of flags in the history of sport — Prahran, the Australian Army, Richmond and Essendon in football, and Richmond in cricket.

Left: Great to go to where Tom Wills and the indigenous people connected up at Moyston. Good to see young people learning their history while having fun with a football as well. Kids should always remember their best friend is a footy. Mine was.

Left: Kevin Sheedy, age 4. Kids should be encouraged to follow their dreams.

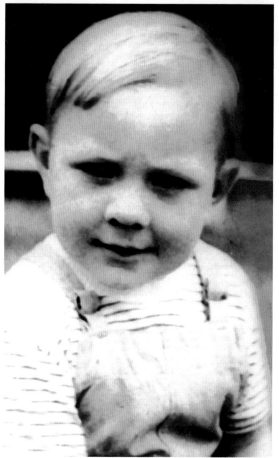

Left: When you're caught behind, just punch ... discipline is so important in football.

Left: If you are going to hit anyone hit the big fella, in this case, Carl Ditterich.

Left: I really enjoyed my cricket and learned so much at Richmond from my coach George Tribe who played VFL and Test cricket. The wicketkeeper was David Cowper and he taught me a lot too. I got my chance to play First XI when Jim Higgs was away playing for Australia.

Left: Me and Ronnie Ward from Richmond. Ron was wishing me all the best as I left Richmond to go to Essendon.

Above: Phil Carman didn't listen, so he left. Early days as coach of Essendon.

Left: Who wears short shorts? Getting Brian Wood was great for Essendon; young Mark Harvey and Mark Thompson are in the background. You need kids, but you need experience, so we recruited former Tiger captain Brian Wood to help us win a premiership.

Above: Time out with Jess, dressed for a party with her friends.

Right: Back-pockets get used to having high-flying forwards on their backs in games. It even happened at home, too. Chelsea and Renee (with the long hair at the back). There ain't no rest at home even when you go home for a rest.

Above: It is 1981, my first year at Essendon and everyone is a bit anxious. Bernie Shea, the assistant coach is on the far right, Brian Donohoe, finger to mouth, is next to me and on the left, Graeme Johnson, a former premiership player.

Below: 'Kevvie, get the ball to Royce and get out of the way.' Tom Hafey in the T-shirt, Royce Hart and umpire Bill Deller. Note Tommy's cup of tea. It was either a T-shirt, or a cup of tea — or both — with Tommy.

Above: Renee and me at the 1985 Grand Final parade.

Left: Back-to-back premierships ... Simon Madden, me and Terry Daniher and a couple of impressive trophies. These two players are absolute legends.

Above: Talking to Michael Long. This picture reminds you that they turn up skinny and then we turn them into machines. Longie looks like a bantamweight fighter from Mexico.

Left: The shorts just keep getting shorter ... Billy Duckworth, one of Essendon's best ever recruits. He helped turn the 1984 Grand Final in our favour.

Left: Terry Daniher and me enjoying a Bombers' premiership in the 1980s.

Below: Taking the game to the world ... Footy Records *(left)* in Japan and *(right)* Miami. Developing the game world-wide is as important as in Australia.

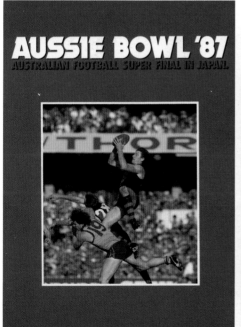

AUSSIE BOWL '87
AUSTRALIAN FOOTBALL SUPER FINAL IN JAPAN

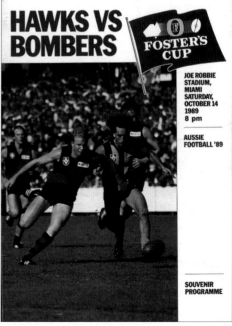

HAWKS VS BOMBERS

FOSTER'S CUP

JOE ROBBIE STADIUM, MIAMI
SATURDAY, OCTOBER 14 1989
8 pm

AUSSIE FOOTBALL '89

SOUVENIR PROGRAMME

Above: Team photos are wonderful things. Look at Dean Bailey with a beard, moustache and a head full of hair. He is in the middle row, second from the left. More importantly, this photo has all four Danihers in it. They all played in the one team in 1990. Funny how things work out, Dean Bailey replaced Neale Daniher at Melbourne.

Below: Draft day with Roger Hampson and legendary recruiting officer Noel Judkins picking the team for the 1993 premiership. Stephen Wells, who put the mighty Geelong team together, is in the background. This photo is 15 years old, and Stephen's still at Kardinia Park.

Above: Matthew Drain and Robert Shaw, terrific assistants along with Mark Harvey in the 2000 premiership. Always appreciate the people who work with you!

Below: My great friend Bruce Reid *(left)*, one of the finest carers for AFL players for just about all his life. Played for Hawthorn and Preston, then worked as a doctor at Richmond and Essendon.

Above: John Barnes and me at Windy Hill. It was terrific to get him back from Geelong for the premiership year in 2000. Thank you, Geelong. But now Geelong has gone on to win its own premierships.

Below: Dr Ian Reynolds attending to one of our players. The care of players by the medical staff has been proven as important to the game. Ian had been with me for over 30 years at Richmond and Essendon.

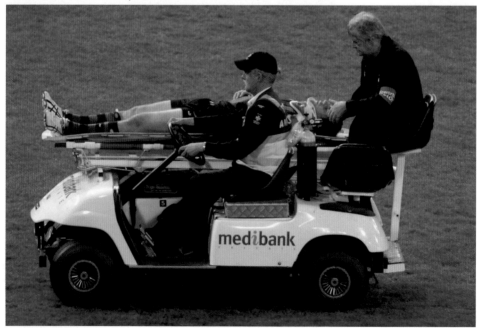

Above: Some real characters ... this would be a decent rat pack. From left: Bruce McAvaney, Andrew Demetriou, Charlie Sutton, Gerard Healy, Ron Barassi, Kevin Bartlett, Sam Newman, Neil Kerley, me, John Elliott (with his mouth open) Mike Sheahan (with his mouth open, too), Eddie McGuire and Mal Brown. Any ego would struggle in this room. It was a great lunch celebrating Neil Kerley's birthday.

Right: Me, Brenton Sanderson and Mark Thompson getting the Victorian team up to beat the rest of Australia. It was a great game to be involved in, in my first year off in 44 years.

Left: Me and Mick Malthouse at the Shrine of Remembrance in Melbourne. Mick was always terrific about promoting the Anzac Day game.

Below: Not just the AFL, but my mum didn't like this gesture aimed at the West Coast's Mitchell White that eventually cost me $10,000, just for touching my throat. But you just do silly things at times.

Left: Bel Esprit was a bolt of lightning in my life and after winning premierships it was great to win a Group 1 Race.

Below: Tossing the coin before the game in which I broke Jock McHale's record ... Brad Johnson is captain of the Western Bulldogs and Mattie Lloyd captain of Essendon. Also on the ground my children, Renee on the left, Sam and Chelsea. Jessica was away overseas.

Above: Kepler Bradley and me. He should still be at Essendon. It was a poor decision to let him go. Tall players need time and patience.

Below: Sam Sheedy lands one on Muhammad Ali at the Beverly Wilshire in Hollywood. Ali grabbed Sam's fist and put it on his nose. Ali didn't know us at all, but he did that for Sam and that's what you have to do if you want to be well known around the world, look after the fans.

Mixing Richmond and army duties was tough for other reasons, too, mostly to do with the trip from Puckapunyal to Punt Road and back. On Thursdays, I had to leave the camp at about 3 pm for the trip, around 150 kilometres, and I wouldn't arrive at training until about 5.30, so I had to do extra work after the others had left. After waiting around for selection, I'd be lucky to get back to Pucka before midnight, and I would have to be up and on duty at 8 am, take training with the Roosters in the afternoon, then drive back to Melbourne again for the game on Saturday. And no matter the result on Saturday or whether or not I got injured, I had to be back for parade on Monday mornings.

It was hard work, and pretty dangerous driving through winter fog and sleet, but I shouldn't really complain too much. I didn't get sent to Vietnam. Things were pretty much winding up over there for the Australians, although it was always in the back of my mind and that of my fellow soldiers: 'What if?'

All up, I was given opportunities in the army — not just by Major General Fittock, but by a lot of people — for which I remain extremely grateful. They saw something in this bloke from South Yarra, something more than a plumber or a footballer. They gave me the confidence to believe in myself as someone who could lead other people. I have a lot of respect for the army and for what it can help you to achieve. It's part of the reason I have been such a big supporter of the Anzac Day match between Essendon and Collingwood. To me it's a way of saying 'thank you' to the serving soldiers of many generations who have given us the chance to live in a great place called Australia.

Some people think that celebrating Anzac Day glorifies war. I don't think it does that, because there isn't anything glorious about war. But celebrating Anzac Day gives young people a chance to learn about their history, and I think that *is* important.

When I was in France in 2006 after the International Rules series against Ireland, I stayed with a good friend of mine, the philanthropist Basil Sellers. He took me to a little cemetery that contained the graves of Belgian soldiers who had died defending the town of St Jean on the Cap-Ferrat peninsula. The cemetery was spotless; there were fresh flowers delivered every day — it was like a florist's. Every day, all these years on. The marvellous people of this little town were saying 'thanks', and that was pretty special to me. I don't think we say 'thanks' enough these days. By tending the graves, the town's young people also learned their local history, and perhaps will learn not to repeat the mistakes that led to the creation of that little garden of headstones.

Another recent highlight for me that reminded me of my army days was receiving my National Service Medal. Established in 2001 to commemorate the 50th anniversary of National Service, it is available to the 300,000 Nashos who were conscripted between 1951 and 1972.

The reception took place at the Noble Park RSL Club. The room was packed, mostly with a lot of men who had gone to Vietnam. David Gibson, from the Central Army Records Office, presented the medal. He gently took the mickey out of me a bit, too, reminding everyone in the room that I had listed my hobbies as swimming, squash and football — in that order — during one of my first interviews. The person who had taken the interview later wrote that I was a 'good type with a friendly manner and realistic'. Obviously, another New South Welshman who had never seen me playing football.

My mother, the bushranger-spotting Michael Cusack's grand-daughter, had come with me to the club for the presentation and Mr Gibson noted her attendance. As he mentioned her name some of the blokes yelled out, 'She's better known than you are, and better looking.' So I wasn't just Pat Sheedy's little brother, but also Irene Sheedy's little boy.

There was more heckling when it was revealed that I had risen to the rank of corporal with the 21st Construction Squadron. 'Social climber,' someone called out.

That day at Noble Park RSL was a great one. I was very proud to receive my medal. It said 'thank you' for serving my country; it was something I'd done gladly, but it was nice to be acknowledged. In return I had some of the most rewarding experiences of my life. The army taught me to be proud of Australia and to enjoy my country and the freedom that our defence forces have fought to give us.

7

'Kevin Sheedy Could be a Good Coach One Day'

The whiff of complacency that followed our 1969 Grand Final win had turned into a bit of a stench during my time in the army, and Tommy Hafey and Graeme Richmond began bringing in players from outside the club. Ricky McLean came from Carlton and played in the 1972 Grand Final. Ian Stewart was brought across from St Kilda, Wayne Walsh back from South Melbourne, Paul Sproule from Essendon and Steven Ray from St Kilda. Rex Hunt was traded for Gareth Andrews after the 1973 premiership win — a straight swap between Geelong and Richmond.

Changes in the playing list, even the senior team sheet, were constant. There were nine players in the 1973 grand-final winning side that weren't in the 1972 side. It could nearly have been ten. Graeme Richmond had been quietly arranging for me to coach at Subiaco in Perth. Graeme, as we have already established, was pretty ruthless when it came to recruiting, and also when the time came to get rid of players. Tony Jewell used to reckon that Graeme had a trapdoor in his office because if you were a player and you were called in, you were never seen again. Over the years, Graeme fielded a lot of calls from clubs looking for their next coach. He would handle them in his unique way. I can well imagine the conversation about me:

'Now listen here, Cocko. This is not for the boy's ears himself, but we think [which meant Graeme thought] that this player's career is over. There is nothing more embarrassing than to be standing at the MCG listening to all the Richmond supporters screaming for another premiership and knowing we're letting them down with dumb, slow players who can't perform on the big day. We have to eradicate these people from the club. If I was you, looking for a coach, Kevin Sheedy could be a good coach one day. But listen here, I'm telling you now, it hasn't come from my lips.'

Tommy Hafey had no idea this was happening. In fact, he still can't believe that it *did* happen. I learned many things while in the army doing my two years of National Service. One of them was: always consider the opposition. I learned you had to fight a different war in Vietnam than had been fought in Europe. I worked out what was going on: after having not played so well in the first half of 1972, my opponent had become Graeme Richmond.

The Subiaco president, a solicitor, Brian Singleton, and the club's general manager, Basil Fuller, came to visit me where I was working on a building site. Dressed in suits, they looked like a couple of detectives.

'Who's in trouble with the police?' I asked.

No one, but K. Sheedy is in trouble at Richmond. I wasn't ready either to coach, or to leave the Tigers, even though I had just had my first coaching interview. I said 'thanks, but no thanks' to these good gentlemen, told Graeme Richmond in no uncertain terms that I wouldn't be going anywhere, and made sure I re-doubled my efforts at training and out on the field.

When I kicked the first three goals in the 1973 Grand Final, I thought that was a pretty good way to show Graeme that I had the skills, the speed — well, quick thinking — and anything else he needed for me to keep playing for the Tigers.

The only other time I nearly left Richmond while a player was when Dennis Jones went across to coach Central Districts in 1967. He asked me to come over if I felt I needed a year out of the VFL to settle back into the game in 1968 after my knee operation.

I went to meet two fine people — Charlie Pyatt, the president, and Norm Russell, a committee member and Adelaide pharmacist. I spent two or three days looking around to see if I thought I could enjoy Adelaide. It was a pleasant experience, but it was all brought to an abrupt halt when we finally remembered I had been disqualified from playing for any club in the ANFC for five years. These days, a ban like that wouldn't last five minutes. It would be restraint of trade. But I had to wait until 1970, the year the Queen visited Australia, for the monkey to be lifted off my back. It wasn't a royal pardon, but one brought about by some more clear-thinking sporting administrators outside of the ANFC who could see it was wrong.

Not all my dealings with the ANFC were unpleasant ones. I have many reasons to be very grateful to Bruce Andrews, who was in charge of the organisation in the 1960s. He gave me my first real chance as a development officer, my first professional job in football, when he asked me in 1968 to do some development work on the northwest coast of Tasmania. I had to get permission to leave Richmond, and my job as a plumber, for a week.

Bruce just had this hunch that I might be good with kids. I had been doing a lot of speaking at what were called 'pie nights', back in those days, and there had been some positive feedback to him about those, from people like Graeme Richmond, John Nix and Ray 'Slug' Jordon, who coached footy at both Richmond and North Melbourne, while also wicket-keeping for Victoria. I am very thankful now that they were such willing referees.

Bruce sent me to Cooee and to Penguin. On the way I got to meet up with Darrel Baldock, the St Kilda champion, 'Bull' Richardson and Fred Wooller, who were all coaching there. I never got to Scottsdale where Brian Donohoe was coaching; the bloke who would play such a significant role in my own coaching days at Essendon.

In Devonport, I had one of the more surreal experiences of my life. I had got into town late in the evening and gone straight to my motel. At 7 am, I pulled open the blinds and there was a huge ship parked right outside my bedroom. It was the cross-channel ferry, the *Princess of Tasmania*, which had pulled into the Mersey River. These days, the tallest building in Devonport is still the *Spirit of Tasmania* — when it's in port. At 21, I had no knowledge that Devonport was even a port. I just thought I was unwell.

That week in Tasmania would eventually lead to my first full-time job in football.

When I came out of the army in 1971, I worked for 18 months at Forrest Hills Plumbing. It was about that time that Jack Hamilton and Alan Schwab, now in control of the VFL, were looking at ways of ensuring that football remained a strong sport among schoolchildren. That was partly in response to the work of Rale Rasic, who was already doing a great job of promoting soccer.

Rale is one of the great characters not just of Australian soccer, but of sport generally in Australia. He had come out here from Croatia in his mid-twenties, his head full of images of sunshine and beaches. He arrived at Melbourne Airport in July dressed in short sleeves and shorts — and froze. If we Australians didn't know a lot about the people coming here from Europe after the Second World War, there were plenty of people from Europe who didn't know much about Australia, either!

After 18 months, he went back home to fulfil a commitment to serve in the army. It was at that time he learned one of his most important lessons as a future coach — what the human body is capable of enduring. Rale would have to march for nine hours over mountains in temperatures five below freezing. It gave him an exceptional mental toughness. He realised when the mind had to take over from the body.

On his return to Australia, he began a revolution in soccer and coached Australia to the World Cup in 1974. Then, just to prove that this sort of thing doesn't happen only in Australian football, he was sacked and replaced by an Englishman, Brian Green. No, I've never heard of him, either. It took Australia another 32 years to get back to the World Cup finals! Were the people who made the decision to sack the coach ever held accountable? Probably not.

Anyway, if what Rale had created wasn't appreciated in soccer, it certainly was at the VFL. The Australian game's monopoly on the hearts and minds of young kids was over.

Alan had decided to establish a new position, that of a full-time development officer. It would be advertised, but he gave me a heads-up before the advertisement was made public and suggested I apply. I had by now learned to listen to anything Alan suggested. He was about seven years older than I was, a graduate of Camberwell High School where he had played in both the top cricket and football teams. Football was his real passion. After leaving school, he had joined the VFL as a junior clerk. He worked at St Kilda as assistant secretary; then, in 1969, he came to Melbourne to replace Graeme Richmond as secretary. They were huge boots to fill, but he did the job and did it well. He stayed at Richmond until 1976 before returning to the VFL as administration manager. In 1985 he became executive director of VFL, then, when an independent commission was set up to run the game, he became executive commissioner, with Jack Hamilton the head commissioner. The setting up of that commission was one of the best things that happened to our game. It was also one of the toughest decisions ever to be pushed through against all sorts of opposition, mostly from Melbourne-based clubs that didn't want to lose control of the game. Thankfully, the skill of people like Alan and Jack prevailed and we have the modern, national code we have today.

This job as a full-time development manager was among the first of many changes that Alan would set in place. It sounded fascinating. One: it was the chance to work full-time in football, something that I had long dreamt about. Two: it carried with it a pretty heavy burden. They wanted me to go out and find out what football was doing right and what it was doing wrong in the broader community. I quickly found out that a lot of people were mightily peeved about what football wasn't doing to nurture the next generations. Basically, for a long time people at the grassroots thought they had been taken for granted. What a wonderful turnaround to today, when you see the energy invested in AusKick — all those games on the ground at half-time.

Once I had found out what the problems were, Alan Schwab wanted me to come up with plans to improve the game in the eyes of the public. That meant writing reports and preparing other documents. All this meant a considerable shift away from the work practices of a plumber. At that time, I hardly shaved more than once a week, and that was to go out to a dance — probably to The Powerhouse, the venue in Albert Park where I first met my wife, Geraldine. I had come to enjoy dancing after those wonderful lessons from the ladies at Prahran.

As for writing reports, in the seven years I had been a plumber and soldier, the only time I had anything to do with paperwork was when I needed a few more materials — the odd requisition form, in triplicate, so long as I remembered the carbon paper.

I could see this job had enormous possibilities, particularly in an area I had discovered I really enjoyed — helping to develop young people. I loved going to the pie nights at local clubs and talking to the kids, hearing about their ideas on footy and on life, what their dreams were and how they thought they might fulfil them. So that was one tick on the CV for this job — but, gee, there were a few empty boxes, too. But while I didn't have formal training as a teacher, I had been to school a lot, and I had learned a few things from the nuns about how to keep young people engaged with what you had to say.

I'd also had coaches who said 'Don't give up,' and a couple of caring parents who had always encouraged me in new ventures by saying, 'Just keep your head down and work hard.' At about 24, with all these bits of advice starting to take on new meaning, I felt I was maturing as a person. I reckoned if I could draw on all that learning, and if I really wanted this job, I could do it. It was a simple case of 'where there's a will, there's a way', or 'nothing ventured, nothing gained'. I often heard people whom I admired for their thinking say things like that. I used to write sayings down in a little exercise book. Another one was, 'Son, don't light fires under your enemy; you'll get burnt!' And: 'Be careful how to treat people on the way up, because they're the people you will meet on the way down!' I reckon Todd Shelton, Graeme Richmond's business partner, would have told me that a hundred times.

I suppose it was unusual for a plumber — any tradesperson, really — to hit the right chord when they go into a school environment. But I also had some other wonderful assistance. I have nothing but admiration for the teachers who embraced what I was trying to do when I visited their schools. I found out something very important very quickly — only 25 per cent of school teachers were males. So, I had to factor that into how footy could be taught in schools. There were other things I needed to know before I could write my reports and develop my plans.

Principals had to make decisions about whether to spend funds on science books or sport. Sport was expensive, with the biggest expenditure being bus hire to take the kids to sportsgrounds. Sometimes, I would give a school half a dozen footballs. That school would then use the money saved on footballs to buy basketballs. There was no real win there for football, the thing I was supposed to be developing. So, I set about trying to develop an understanding of what the schools and teachers needed, what we could do to help them, and how they in turn would help us in an ongoing way with encouraging kids to play footy. It was no use if once I left the school, nothing else was done.

We agreed that winning at all costs wasn't necessary, so long as everyone had fun, intermingled and learned a few social skills as well as footy ones. I don't think we have enough places in Australia now where young people can intermingle. A lot of the youth clubs have gone, and that is disappointing. I'd often go down to my local youth club after tea. Those youth clubs, and the experiences I have had in them are one reason why I have always believed that no matter where people come from, whether it be Aboriginal communities in the outback or high-rise flats in the city, if you give them the opportunity to learn both sport and social skills, then you are giving them the chance to prosper in life.

Once, I went to Richmond to see if I could have some funds, approximately $4000 to $5000, so I could start an eight-team competition among the high-rise flats in the inner suburbs. The officials of the time said they didn't have the money for the things that were needed at the club, let alone to spend on one-parent families whose kids might not even be in the Richmond recruiting zone. Undaunted, I went to the Richmond women's auxiliary, led by Alice Wills, and asked if they could do some fundraising to help get these kids a game of footy. The ladies were fantastic. We booked the Camberwell Civic Centre for four nights and played videos of the 1967, 1969, 1973 and 1974 premierships. All four nights sold out quickly. We made $10,000, about half of which was profit.

I learned another valuable lesson through that project. If you've got an idea, then that's great; but if you've got an idea of how to pay for it as well, you'll get a much better reception.

When I finally took over the development job, I was able to implement a lot more of my ideas. We appointed coaches to develop the skills of young people living in the eastern suburbs of Melbourne as far out as Croydon. Each coach had 25 kids they worked with in an indoor gymnasium. Players like Ian Owen, a premiership player, and Ron Thomas, later manager of the Swans, were employed to take these squads.

I did the same thing at Essendon when I went there, promoting these extra skills sessions in dry, warm conditions rather than outside in the slush, wind and rain. The hope was that some of these young people would eventually make it to the club's senior list. Of course, the standard comment was that if you were training indoors, you were soft; but I had well and truly learned by now that whatever you did in football, you always had to overcome some sort of criticism. I had seen that so clearly in 1969 when we won the premiership despite the critics we had even inside our own club.

If those critics went quiet for a while amid all the back-slapping in 1969, they were back in force in 1970, when we missed the finals. After that disappointment, Graeme Richmond stated: 'Cocko, we're going to shake the place up. We're going out to recruit players from all over Australia, and we're going to make sure that everybody feels their place in the club is under pressure.' It was probably similar to what Peter Jackson is doing at Essendon at the moment.

If any proof was ever needed that Graeme meant what he said, it came when the club swapped Billy Barrot for Ian Stewart, who by that time was a dual Brownlow Medallist and premiership player at St Kilda. Certainly players had been traded in the past, but there had never been a straight 'superstar swap' quite like this one. I was stunned by it. My relationship with Billy hadn't been without some strain. When I got to the club, I was the young buck centre-man trying to take over from the old buck. Billy was a very proud man. Sometimes in the intra-club practice matches, our clashes got a bit heated.

It got even worse than that one day in the change rooms when I asked Billy to sign an autograph for a young kid. He signed away and as I was taking the autograph book back to the fan, I looked at what Billy had written. It was along the lines of 'get effed'. I lost my cool at that moment and punched him. It wasn't a smart thing to do, but I was just furious that he could treat a supporter that way. We didn't understand depression so well then. In modern football, Billy and his problem behaviour would have been dealt with in a much more sensible and sensitive way than just by dumping him.

Although I have well and truly forgiven Billy for that incident now, I'm still not in favour of giving half-baked autographs with spaghetti signatures to fans. It must be terribly disappointing for a youngster to go home to show off the signature he got from his favourite player, and no one can really read it. Whenever I sign a book, or a serviette, or whatever it is someone asks me to sign, I always try to personalise it, to give them some sort of positive message. 'Have a good life,' is one of those.

Recently, I met a young English cricketer by the name of Jaik Mickleburgh; he's just 17 but is already on the books at Essex. When I signed an autograph for him, I used a line I had got from Ken Barrington: 'You can't make runs sitting in the pavilion, you have got to be at the crease.' Even though he was an emerging English cricketer, Jaik had never heard of Barrington, one of England's finest in the days of Benaud and co., so he learned a little bit about the cricket history of his own country that day. Hopefully, he will also learn to take Barrington's advice — because, boy, could he play cricket.

Just as Ian Stewart could play footy! Ever since he had been an ambitious youngster in Hobart, Stewart had known how to work the system. The Saints hadn't wanted to recruit him as early as they did, but he hinted that other clubs were interested and forced their hand. When it came to leaving the Saints after playing in the famous 1966 Grand Final in which Barry Breen kicked his legendary point, he had to move pretty carefully. Schwabbie had worked for a short time at St Kilda and so knew Ian. At this time, the Richmond hierarchy were having some doubts about Billy's worth, even though he had been a dominant figure in a couple of premierships. They thought he was undisciplined and quietly let St Kilda think it might be able to recruit him. At the same time, Stewart was indicating to St Kilda that he would be heading for Perth, so the Saints needed a replacement centre-man of class. Once St Kilda had signed Barrot, Stewart asked for a transfer to Richmond, something that, though a bit of a shock, would at least save the Saints a transfer fee. Robert Redford and Paul Newman would have been proud of this sting, though a lot of Richmond supporters weren't at all happy.

Barrot was popular, he was still a gun-player, and he wasn't happy either when he worked out he had effectively been sacked by the club. There were pretty unpleasant scenes when a large number of supporters made their feelings known at the annual general meeting that year.

Ian Stewart's efforts in 1971, however, quickly showed the wisdom of the trade from a Richmond perspective. In contrast, things went really badly for Billy. He played just a couple of games and was cleared to Carlton mid-season. There he and Ron Barassi had a dust-up and his VFL career was over. He ended up at North Melbourne but didn't play a senior game there. You just can't believe that. A player of his class not getting a game at North Melbourne.

In contrast, Stewart went on to win his third Brownlow, starring in a semi-final against Collingwood that propelled the Tigers into the preliminary final. Barrot and the Saints might have felt there was some karma in the result of that game — Richmond lost by five goals.

In 1972, Richmond's mix of old and new players made the grand final, but lost to Carlton. I was gutted by the loss. Before each of the grand finals I played in for Richmond, I would go to the MCG the day before and sit in the empty stadium and try to imagine what the next day would bring. I could never have imagined what Carlton did to us. That loss, and Graeme Richmond's attempts to send me off to Subiaco, really fired me up.

The next year, the scheming, the clever deals and the hard work under Tommy Hafey on the training track paid off for Richmond. Ian Stewart carved out his name even further in footy history, winning Brownlows and premierships with separate clubs — the only player ever to do so.

He played pretty well in the grand final, kicking a couple of goals late in the game despite a leg injury. He and I had made a pact before the game to get five goals between us because we felt if we did, that would provide that important little bit extra to get the team over the line. It was something we achieved.

Ian retired halfway through the 1974 premiership year. Just to show you how funny football can be, the fans that had been against the trade deal involving Stewart and Barrot now signed a petition asking Ian to withdraw from his retirement plans. One of his final games was the 'Battle of Windy Hill' on 18 May in which he kicked five goals. That was the game that nearly cost me any chance of coaching at Essendon ... ever. Sharing its name with a famous battle in the American War of Independence, our war at Windy Hill didn't kill anyone — but, gee, it might have come pretty close. The police had to step in, as an absolute donnybrook broke out between players and officials from both sides.

I wasn't part of it, but I did come down to have a look. Kevin Bartlett didn't even want to look. He said, 'No way.' He said that we could stay and watch if we wanted, but that he was getting off the ground and into the rooms to get all the orange juice before the rest of us. It made sense to get off the ground. For a start, there were so many people on it. I had this thought that if you're out there when you're not supposed to be, then you deserve to come off second best. That's why there was little or no sympathy for the bloke who streaked on to the Gabba during the recent summer, only to be bowled over by Andrew Symonds. You don't ever expect to see a cricketer drop anyone the way 'Roy' did that day.

I had certainly never seen anything like this day at Windy Hill before, though maybe the brawl in the 1990 Grand Final would come close. After the dust settled, Ron Andrews was suspended for six weeks, though Brian 'The Whale' Roberts scored a few points with Essendon supporters for declining to name the villain when called before the tribunal. Roberts said he thought it might have been a kick from one of the police horses that busted his cheekbone. Cheeky!

Essendon runner Laurie Ashley was disqualified for 'conduct unbecoming and prejudicial to the VFL'. The Bombers' fitness coach, Jim Bradley, was outed for six matches for assaulting Mal Brown. In turn, 'Big Mad Mal' got a week for thumping Ashley. Stephen Parsons from the Tigers got a week for hitting Bradley.

Graeme Richmond was in the thick of it, too. This was a bloke who, as many who had seen him acting as bouncer at some of his drinking establishments would know, would rather have a fight than a feed. 'Cocko' jumped on Bradley and apparently punched him, and was then 'arrested' by the Essendon player, Barry Grinter, who in his day job was a police constable.

Other police were later to bring charges against Graeme Richmond, one of assault causing actual bodily harm and one of unlawful assault. The VFL banned Richmond from any involvement with the club for the rest of the season; however, that ban was lifted when at the City Court, in circumstances that raised a lot of eyebrows about the place, both cases were dismissed.

If you used boxing terms to describe the game, you'd have to say Richmond won on points — ten, to be exact.

We also won the grand final, beating North Melbourne. This game wasn't just a case of two good sets of players going up against each other, but two good football departments. The Kangaroos had the brilliant administrative skills of Allen Aylett, David Robb and Ron Joseph and had recruited Doug Wade from Geelong, John Rantall from South Melbourne and Barry Davis, the man I would ultimately replace as coach there, from Essendon. Another prize gain was their coach, Ron Barassi. So, it was two legends in the coach's box, too — Hafey against Barassi.

It was a challenging time for both clubs and a thrilling one for Melbourne's footy supporters. This suburban game in Melbourne, while slowly starting to realise it needed to look to further horizons, could still fill grand finals stands to capacity. The 1972 Grand Final crowd was 112,393. In 1973, it was 116,956; a year later, 113,839.

There can't be many other cities in the world where, from an area the size of that around Richmond, Carlton, Collingwood and North Melbourne, you could generate so much interest in games of football. London could get close, perhaps, with teams like Arsenal, Tottenham Hotspur, Chelsea and Crystal Palace.

I don't think, by the way, when it has gone to London, the AFL has made enough of the fact that there are places in England called Richmond and Essendon. I believe the people who live in those places should always be invited to matches in London. Mick Jagger has a big house on the edge of the Thames in Richmond, and he's a real sports nut. Imagine if you could get him interested in Australian football? What sort of exposure would that create?

Essendon is a small village north of London in Hertfordshire. I don't know of any famous rock stars that might live there, but British writers Barbara Cartland and Beatrix Potter both have an association with the place.

Apart from the premiership, something else happened to me in 1974 that was the biggest eye-opener of my life to that point. I was given the opportunity to go to America with Malcolm Brown and Todd Shelton. Todd was a great travelling companion to someone who had never been overseas before (if you didn't count a visit to Devonport). He was a magnificent student of commonsense, a person who kept his feet — and mine — on the ground.

The trip was about six weeks long and I used the money I'd been paid from football that year to develop my coaching skills and to touch base with professional sport, especially American gridiron.

People who know Mal Brown might not believe it, but his planning of the itinerary was perfect. We went to a lot of unbelievable places and each time, I think my wonderment about what existed outside of Australia just grew and grew. I thought, 'Gee, haven't I been living in the backblocks?' The airports were bigger, the buildings were taller. I was hypnotised by the spaghetti junctions of all the freeways.

It was a shock to my system, but it also developed in me this highly adventurous thought — that if I ever became a coach, it had to be as a professional one, full-time. What I saw in America, and what I believed could be achieved in Australia, really whetted my appetite for coaching.

In 1975, Richmond lost the preliminary final to North Melbourne. The end of the winter of 1976 brought two of the biggest surprises in my career. The first: I won the best and fairest. Everyone said that there had to have been some sort of awful mistake because, for a lot of people, 'Sheedy' and 'fairest' didn't fit in the same sentence, unless it also contained 'least'.

I guess for many opposition supporters I was the sort of dirty player they could easily hate. Football was a different world back then in regards to what you might get away with on the field. There was only one umpire, only a few television cameras. A lot of things used to go on behind play. Sometimes they were deliberate illegal hits to try and literally knock someone out of the game. Other times they were genuine contests that would leave people seriously injured, and these would develop a mythology of their own about so-and-so taking out a player.

I did a lot of terrible things on the footy field, and I did a lot of not-so-terrible things on the footy field. A lot of things I did were payback for hits on what we called our 'fair' players at Richmond. So, if something hit Bartlett or Hart, we had to measure up against their players. We had to make sure we weren't rail-roaded by other clubs and coaches who set out to nail our players. That was the team mechanism, and we had enough of the right sort of people in our side to work that way — Neil Balme, Kevin Morris, Ricky McLean, Robert McGhie and probably me.

In more recent times, I have often had people come up to me — amazingly, a lot of them women — who would say, 'Kevin, how did you change your ways?'

When I would ask them what they meant, they would say: 'I used to hate your guts barracking against Richmond, but never while you've been at Essendon.'

Somewhere between the ages of 30 and 60 I hope I learned something.

At Punt Road, Graeme Richmond made you feel that you were playing combative football. We were taught to smash our opponents, physically and mentally. Tommy would be there to bring the team together, to make sure we were fit and had an enthusiastic attitude. That's why we won so many last quarters. Graeme wanted to make sure not only that we won, but that we destroyed the opposition in a way that left them scarred for the rest of their lives: 'If you play against Richmond, you will never forget it.'

He would send you out to get an opposition player who might be playing well, and you did it. Whether it was an illegal clash, or just a powerful legal one — well, sometimes there was only the smallest difference in it. You've got to be careful when you line somebody up. I once lined up Darrel Baldock, thinking I would knock him all the way back to Tasmania. He was too quick for me and I ended up crashing into Roger Dean — a mightily *unimpressed* Roger Dean.

Looking at all the fuss over the behaviour of the Australian and Indian cricket teams recently, there's no doubt that we got away with murder. If the same standards that apply now had been applied to us then, the media — society generally — would have been tearing us apart.

I don't blame Graeme Richmond — or anyone else — for some of the less pleasant things I did on a football field. It was a case of no one can make you do something if you don't want to do it. If it got you a game, you considered doing it. Players of that era did it unashamedly for that reason. A lot of us had come from tough upbringings from which footy had given us a way out. You would do everything possible to hang on to that opportunity. Since then, though, I have tried to put a bit of fun in my life — as a father, as a coach, as a leader in the AFL.

The second shock came when Richmond forced Tommy Hafey to resign. The end of the Hafey era absolutely stunned both me and Kevin Bartlett, in particular, but generally the whole team. It was as big a shock as Barrot going, only more so because this was the coach being given his marching orders.

It could be said that Bartlett and I had the blinkers on when it came to Tom: we thought he could do no wrong. Obviously, he wasn't perfect — but gee, just look at his record. In his time at Punt Road, the worst the Tigers had done was finish seventh. He finished first four times, second once, third twice, never fourth, fifth on two occasions, sixth on one occasion and then the seventh in 1976. That was all in the space of 11 years. Richmond finished in the top four just five times in the next 30 years.

If Tommy was sacked just because he had been there a decade, well, that was a joke. In the book *A Touch of Cunning*, I said that Essendon wouldn't do anything like that with me. I was right; the Bombers waited 27 years. I have been very fortunate.

The people who took over from Tom were Barry Richardson and Tony Jewell, grand final mates of mine. But they just weren't Tommy Hafey: they certainly didn't create a record of achievement like his. 'Bones' Richardson took us to fourth and seventh. He's a pretty smart guy. He'd been to uni and was a bit of an intellectual, I suppose, in the eyes of a guy from Prahran Tech. He was, and still is, a great student of the game of football and he thought the game was changing — and changing away from the Tom Hafey style. One comment he made about Tommy, whom he respected greatly for his achievements, was that he had the same experience every year for 15 years. The new world of football was about growing, thinking outside the square and trying new things all the time.

I probably didn't know quite enough then to understand that he might have been right. I was terrifically loyal to Tommy, but I also tried always to be loyal to Barry. If I had an issue, I spoke to him about it and to him alone. I know he understood that. I think he also knew that Graeme Richmond was still talking to me quietly as well. Barry really tried to bring a lot of changes to Richmond, many of which have now been adopted by a lot of clubs in the past 20 years or so. He also picked young players and gave them their chance.

When he took over from Barry, Tony Jewell made those young players ruthless. His time produced a premiership — when I was an assistant coach — in between finishing eighth and seventh. He was then replaced by another legendary player, Francis Bourke. Obviously finishing seventh was the telling number for Tommy, Barry and Tony. So much for lucky number seven.

These days, Richmond seems pretty good at always finishing ninth! The people who made the decision to let Tommy Hafey go have visited a lot of failure on the club. Ian Wilson was the president at the time. Has anyone tried to make him and his fellow board members accountable for the years of failure they have visited on the club? When you look back at the great coaches, men who created eras attached to their names, and then at the way they were sacked, there is a recurring pattern. Soon after, the club goes into decline, and the people who made the decision seem to get off scot-free.

Norm Smith got sacked in the middle of the year after six premierships. Who made that decision, and why? A pretty good question when you consider Melbourne hasn't won a premiership since.

Bobby Davis — or B.b.b.b.b.b.obbbbby Davis, to give him his proper name — is another example. Why did he go as coach after taking the Cats to the grand final in 1963? It was a long time before they won another premiership ... 2007.

I wonder what goes on within a club when they sack a coach, or agree to them leaving, after he has delivered a premiership. What made Carlton get rid of David Parkin when he had a record of two premierships in five years and never finished lower than fifth in the other seasons? With decision-making like that happening, why would you ever want to coach at Carlton again?

Parkin left Carlton for a second time in 2000 and since then the Blues have won three wooden spoons and nearly had a fourth, coming 15th.

There is no certainty about Carlton now, even though Brett Ratten, the new coach, has been a marvellous player, winning three best and fairest medals. Bartlett won five at Richmond, but you should never think about the player's career — best and fairests, Brownlow Medals or number of goals — when rating them as a potential coach. It's a recipe for disaster.

A lot of people think that players like me make better coaches than superstars like Royce Hart and Wayne Schimmelbusch because we had to do it all the hard way — really learn to play the game, rather than just achieve success naturally. I think that's partly true. It explains, say, Denis Pagan, Tom Hafey, Mick Malthouse and even Kevin Sheedy. But it doesn't explain Leigh Matthews, rated among the best three players ever. What coaches have to be are better thinkers than is ever necessary as a player. That's because they're not thinking for one person anymore, but for a whole club, and not just for four quarters, but for four or five years ahead — or, hopefully, ten or even 27.

Some clubs get a top coach just once every 20 years. History tells you that when you do get one, you should try and keep them. That must have been a big part of the thinking at Geelong, by 2007 the only Victorian side to win a premiership since Essendon in 2000. No other Melbourne club had won a premiership since the Bombers, but a lot of coaches have lost their jobs. That's something to think about.

*

After my experience overseas with Mal Brown and Todd Shelton, I had a real taste for travel, so when I was asked to be part of the Galahs' trip to Ireland in 1978, led by Harry Beitzel, I couldn't say 'yes' fast enough.

When I look back now ... gee, the Irish have got me into trouble. Don't they understand I'm one of them?

It didn't go down all that well at Richmond that, while I was involved in that tour, I broke my ankle. I needed a fair bit of extra time to recover before the 1979 season.

Even though I didn't break a leg, I don't think coaching against Ireland during the last couple of years while I was at Windy Hill did me any favours with the Essendon board. For me, though, it was possibly the last chance to coach my country, something I had always desperately wanted to do. When you look at people like Wayne Bennett and Bobby Fulton in rugby league, they have wonderful careers with their clubs, but they also have the opportunity to coach their country on an annual basis. The series between Australia and Ireland was back, but there were no guarantees, as we have seen, that it would be permanent. If I was going to coach my country, I had to take the opportunity when it presented itself. But, as I said, it came at a cost at Windy Hill.

At the time of the Australia–Ireland series, Peter Jackson, the Essendon CEO, went away on a leadership course to Japan with some of the young players. I don't think it went down well that he was there and not me. Maybe I took my eye off the ball, especially with Matthew Knights also going on that trip. So, the Irish might be able to claim to have finished both my playing and coaching careers.

*

Anyway, back to Richmond in 1979 when I think I found myself standing on Graeme Richmond's famous trapdoor. Graeme asked me to consider retiring so that the club could start to bring through some of the young players Tony Jewell wanted. I was the one singled out more than Kevin Bartlett, who nearly went on to play forever anyway, and Francis Bourke.

Graeme told me to go home and think about it for a couple of days. I had by this time, and this was one of the better common-sense decisions of my life, obtained an open clearance from Richmond. This meant that if Richmond didn't want me — and clearly they didn't, something that hurt — I could go elsewhere, to another VFL club, and show them they were wrong.

In fact, after I retired from playing in May of that year and took on the role of skills coach, I got an offer to play with Carlton, from Alex Jesaulenko. In the end, though, I didn't go to Carlton. It just wasn't what I wanted to do at that time in my life.

How I got the open clearance from Richmond is another twist in my life. I had played District Cricket for Richmond in the summer of 1977/78, and the team had made the final, to be played against Carlton. Richmond Football Club wouldn't let me play in the grand final, even though it could have given me the rare distinction, if the Tigers proved successful, of senior premierships in both cricket and football, and for essentially the one club. The cricket club also played at Punt Road and is strongly linked with football through wonderful people like Ron Reiffel, who played six games of footy for Richmond before giving cricket one of its finest contributors, and Test paceman and now umpire, young Paul.

Ron looks after both the football and cricket museum at Richmond. A couple of years ago, I saw there a photo of all the players involved in Richmond winning the Victorian Cricket Association club championship (for best performance in all grades) in 1977/78. I asked Ron for a copy of the photograph so that I could show it to my disbelieving family to prove I had been good enough to play cricket at this level, even alongside Test players such as Jim Higgs and Graham Yallop.

I have a couple of other favourite parts of Ron Reiffel's collection in the Richmond Museum. The first is the picture of me taking a mark in the 1974 Grand Final. I thank Ron for having that up there because, in the years to come, people might see that and think that I could take a speccie. Truth is, I rarely ever got off the ground. My other favourite part of the collection is the photo of Maurice Rioli — a wonderful player, wonderful man, the first indigenous player to win the Norm Smith Medal.

Ron also has a copy of my First XI figures — 13 wickets in five games, including 4–13 against Northcote and 3–31 against North Melbourne. My average was just under 16, not bad for a leg-spinner. Richmond went into the final against Carlton without a spinner. The question will remain forever, would a little bit of leg-spin have changed the result? I had got a couple of wickets when we played against Carlton earlier in the summer, a bit more expensively than against Northcote and North Melbourne. However, by the time of the final, I would have been a much better bowler.

At 30, coming late to cricket, I was soaking up as much information as I could to improve my bowling. I was lucky that George Tribe was coach. As well as playing 66 VFL games for Footscray he was a wily, left-arm spinner who had played in three Tests for Australia. He probably should have played more, but he made more of a name for himself playing in

England, first in the leagues, then in the County Championship with Northamptonshire. For eight years in a row from 1952, he achieved the fabled double, 100 wickets, 1000 runs. George and I had a lot of conversations about flight, about variation, about zip, about cunning and guile. I also learned something about coaching from George — one-on-one coaching. At that time it was done better in cricket than in Australian football. I might have been lucky having a wrist-spinner teaching me who could pass on tips about the technique in which he specialised. Whatever, it was a vast improvement on football where you had two coaches looking after a list of as many as 50 to 55 players.

I liked leg-spin bowling — Richie Benaud was one of my childhood heroes. When you got it right, leg-spin bowling was, so I read as a youngster, the most dangerous sort of bowling to face. That had really stuck with me over the years, and when I first went to Richmond to play in the 1976/77 season I wanted it to be as a leg-spinner. If you could get a leg-spinning delivery to dip just before it bounced, then turn sharply to the right-hander's slips, you were really challenging the batsman. If you could get your wrong'un in the right spot and completely baffle the batsman, that was again special. But being a slow bowler, your mistakes, your bad balls, were more easily punished. It was a challenge I really relished and the reason why I would train so enthusiastically with the footy club, then head straight across to the cricket nets at Punt Road.

I was really proud of what I had achieved in cricket that year when I managed to move quickly from the fourths to the firsts. Once again, I was travelling in the footsteps of big brother Pat. He was a very good cricketer and, for a while, had coached the young Shane Warne. Some people thought I was mad, going to Richmond, the club at which Jim Higgs, the Victorian and Australian leg-spinner, was playing after moving down from Kyabram. But the Sheedy abacus was at work again. As a first-class cricketer, Higgsie could be away a lot on tours and that is how it panned out. The cricket club saw me as a capable fill-in who wouldn't complain when Jim was available. By 1978, though, he was a long way from available for Richmond. He was in the West Indies with Bobby Simpson's team. Just after the Centenary Test Match in 1977 at the MCG, all hell had broken loose in cricket. Kerry Packer had secretly signed up most of the best players in the game for his own World Series Cricket. Suddenly gone from the Australian game were Ian and Greg Chappell, Rod Marsh, Dennis Lillee — the absolute cream. The force of television had struck cricket. I wonder what the combination of television and India will do now, 30 years after the Centenary Test? In sport, you just about get used to one revolution when the next one comes along.

In 1977, Bob Simpson came out of retirement in his forties to lead the weakened Establishment side against India at home, then to the West Indies. Jim Higgs, who had been bowling superbly for both Richmond and Victoria, got his chance to play Test cricket in the Caribbean, making his debut at Port of Spain, Trinidad, in early March 1978. Australia lost that match by an innings against the fierce fast bowling of Andy Roberts, Joel Garner and Colin Croft; but Jim didn't do too badly, taking 4–91 in the West Indies' only innings. Another Richmond player, Graham Yallop, made 81, the top score in Australia's second innings. That was a pretty tough tour for Australia. Peter Toohey, the New South Wales batsman, was put in hospital during that Test, while there was a riot during another Test. I must one day find out if Jim would have preferred to have been playing for Richmond in the relative comfort and safety of Melbourne. Higgsie went on to play Test cricket for the full-strength Australian side, appearing in his last Test in 1981. He became an Australian selector for a while, revelling in the revival of leg-spin bowling via Shane Warne, and is still involved in the Richmond Cricket Club, these days as vice president. Watching Jim, and then Warne, I know I didn't really spin the ball. I gave it a bit of a friendly tweak! Those two really ripped it so much you could hear it fizzing through the air. They were freakish.

After being told I couldn't play for Richmond in the cricket grand final, I pursued an open clearance from the Richmond Football Club. I told the club that if I wasn't given one, I would never play for the Tigers again. The president, Ian Wilson, signed that clearance, which I put away in the bottom drawer. I still have it. It is in the safe of my solicitor and long-time friend, Brian Ward. I didn't leave Richmond then, but I was strong in my view that a football club should never treat a person who had been at the club for over a decade, and had been a captain, with that sort of lack of respect.

I was pretty much a loyal Richmond Football Club servant for seven days a week. How hard could it have been to allow me to fulfil my ambition to play in that cricket grand final? I was asked once if I had any great regrets in my life and my answer was that I didn't fight harder to be allowed to play in that game. I have never been entirely sure who made the decision to stop me: it was probably Graeme Richmond or Ian Wilson, with Barry Richardson locked in to support them as coach.

The clearance did come in handy a few years later when, after serving as an assistant coach at Richmond, I got the senior job at Essendon. Ian Wilson told me that he would never clear me to Essendon, and 'if we did we would charge that mob at Windy Hill a fortune'.

It's funny how as we get older our memories can start to go. I had to remind Ian of the open clearance he had signed back in early 1978.

Leaving Richmond was a big step. It's the sort of club where you find people like Ron Reiffel who will dedicate just about their whole lives to the place. Ted Soderblom is another one of these great servants. He is still the property steward at the footy club, having joined Richmond at about the same time I did. In the early 1960s, Ray Jordon had asked Ted, the son of a Swedish immigrant, to help out with under-19s matches. He met Tom Hafey and Graeme Richmond and was part of the most successful era in the club's history. With his wife Dawn, also a Richmond person, born and raised, he has remained steadfastly loyal ever since. People like Ted and Dawn, and Ron Reiffel, are the epitome of the Richmond spirit.

Richmond was — and can still be — not just a great club, but a great football team as well. People often ask me which club I have the strongest feelings for — Richmond or Essendon. I'm a life member of both and have won premierships at both. The answer I give is that you love all your children the same. I remain a passionate supporter of Richmond. It still hurts when I see the club not doing well. My time at Punt Road was a fantastic experience. There were angry moments, testing times, but that would have been the case wherever I was. Richmond gave me the chance to put to good use so many of the things I had learned growing up in South Yarra, or while playing with Prahran.

At the same time, not only did my education continue, but I was given the wonderful opportunities to play in three premierships, win a best and fairest, even to captain the club.

I not only met, but was able to work alongside, some brilliant football people, people who would do so much to shape the adult Kevin Sheedy — Alan Schwab, Graeme Richmond, and Tom Hafey in particular.

In 1979, the more mature version of Kevin Sheedy didn't need to go away and think for too long about Graeme Richmond's words. The young bloke the club was grooming to replace me was someone I really liked. Terry Smith wouldn't be a superstar, but he wouldn't be someone to waste the opportunity.

The little Kevin to whom I often talked, and who would talk back to me with so much commonsense, knew my playing days were over. It was time to enter the new era for which I had long been quietly preparing myself pretty much from my time doing National Service at Puckapunyal — coaching.

8

Across a Crowded Room

I liked her eyes.

I liked the way she danced.

I first met Geraldine Currie in 1972 at The Powerhouse — an alcohol- and drugs-free venue in Albert Park. The place was a lot of fun, and this night it featured Allan Eaton and his Big Band. For those who might not have heard of The Powerhouse, it is a huge function centre today, with one of the biggest dance floors in Melbourne. Its floor-to-ceiling windows offer great views out over the Albert Park Lake, especially at sunset.

She was, as The Beatles sang, just 17 and working in a pharmacy in Rosanna.

I would know Geraldine for about seven years before we decided to get married. Up until then, basically I had wanted to concentrate on my career in football. When I was serving in the army at Puckapunyal, I had made a commitment to get the absolute best out of myself over the next ten years. I was single up until I was 31, but the time became right, near the end of my footy career, to think about the future. Most of the time in my playing days, I was selfish about football. Nothing was going to get in the way of that. Many of my team-mates got married and had children. When I look back, it was a selfish view, but it seemed to me at the time it was the only way I could have a decent career. If I took my eye off the ball, I would slide into mediocrity, I thought. So many young people drop off the rails because they think training is too hard, or they find a girl, or a job. It was an unwritten commandment in my life that the women I met had to realise that football came first. Most of them shunned me after a few weeks, thinking I was just a one-man band playing on the football pathway. This attitude cost me many relationships with many wonderful young women at that stage of my life.

Geraldine was a very patient person — then and now — while I have always been in a hurry to get things done, often tripping over myself but, thankfully, having my friends and family to pick me up. I hope, though, as time has gone on, I have got a bit smarter. Geraldine and I were also very compatible; we seemed to get on pretty well through thick and thin, more my thickness than hers.

So, we were married on 10 January 1979.

When people ask me how I proposed to Geraldine, I usually say flippantly: 'She trapped me!' In a funny sort of way, she did — because of the type of person she is. She is very much a person who likes to stay in the background. She made one of her very few forays into the media limelight just after Essendon announced they wouldn't be renewing my contract. She just wanted to let people to know that I was hurting. She did it in her own modest, beautiful way.

If I reproduce here what she said to the *Herald Sun*, you will perhaps get a better feel for what she has meant to me than I can say in my own words.

'He might not be showing it but he is hurting deep down — he is human,' she said yesterday in a rare interview, adding: 'It was out of the blue.'

Mrs Sheedy emerged from the background to speak up for her husband of 29 years, saying he had been upset he had not been able personally to break the news of his sacking to two of the couple's four children before they heard it from others.

'He came home late on Tuesday, about 11.30 pm, and he told me there would be a press conference the next morning at which it would be announced that he probably would not be coaching next year.

'I stood up and put my arms around him, gave him a hug, and told him how sorry I was.

'I told him life goes on, and we have our health and our children, and that no matter what he does or what happens he would always have the support of myself and our children.

'He decided he would contact all the children very early the next morning to tell them himself.'

Mrs Sheedy said she was shocked when her husband told her he was being cut from the club he coached for a record 27 years.

'Our daughter Renee, who is 27, was just a 10-month-old baby when Kevin started at Essendon. So for all the kids, Essendon has always been their second family.

'My family had always followed Essendon, so it really was a big part of all our lives.'

Daughter Renee, working in a hospital, heard the news from a patient and Jessica, 20, overseas with a faulty mobile, learned from others that her father was to leave Windy Hill at the end of the footy season.

Sheedy was able to tell Chelsea, 24, and Sam, 21, who were disappointed by the news.

Despite her shock at his axing, Mrs Sheedy said she had always known her husband's extraordinary run at Essendon would end one day.

'You know the day is going to come, but I probably believe he had four or five more coaching years left.

'I feel regret for him, because he is still keen to keep coaching and he's got the fire in the belly.

'He's so totally committed, and in whatever he does he strives to do his absolute best.

'He loves football.

'It is his life away from his family.

'But we still have family. We have each other. We have our health, and our lives will go on.

'I have nothing bad to say about Essendon — they have always been good to us and we have had a wonderful time with them.'

The family has been overwhelmed by the public support shown to Sheedy since his sacking was announced.

Mrs Sheedy said she expected her husband to return to coaching, but hoped she would be able to change one thing about their family life.

'Well, we have always had to have holidays out of the football season, so we always end up having holidays in Europe in the middle of winter.

'I love the thought of actually going on a holiday in Europe in summer,' she said.

'I'd also like to thank all our friends and Essendon supporters who have backed Kevin for 27 years.'

So you can see why I, well I guess you would call it 'suggested', rather than 'proposed', back in 1978 that we get married, just before I went overseas with the Galahs. It was a case of something like 'I'm going away on this tour and how about we get married when I get back?'

Our marriage took place on 10 January 1979 in St Ignatius Catholic Church in Church Street, Richmond. It's a special place in my life. As the years have gone by, I have wondered why our family has chosen certain schools and churches. St Ignatius is close to what used to be Vaucluse College, a school for young Catholic women. Vera Cusack, my mother's mother, had gone there for a while after it opened in 1882, so I think my mum was retracing her own roots by going to St Ignatius. I remember that the schoolgirls wore brown hats, which was unusual in Melbourne. That was in the days when in church women had to wear a hat or have a handkerchief covering their heads. It's amazing the changes that can happen in a lifetime.

Life takes us on all sorts of journeys. I took Geraldine on one for our honeymoon, to visit the football clubs of Adelaide. I reckoned we went to just about every one of them. She knew that I wanted to coach. I was about to become an assistant coach at Richmond. I felt that the best opportunity early on as a senior coach might be in South Australia. If we were going to move to Adelaide, to bring up a young family there, I wanted her to be comfortable about the place. Dennis Jones, my coach at Prahran, told me Adelaide was a good place to bring up kids.

A lot of Melbourne people have gone to Adelaide and really enjoyed it, while others — and I had two of them, Robert Shaw and Gary Ayres, at Essendon in recent times — have really been given a tough time.

As we drove along the Murray and through the Richmond recruiting zone — Kerang, Swan Hill, Boundary Bend, to Mildura and the Sunraysia district (really exciting honeymoon, eh?) — on our way to Adelaide, Geraldine and I spent a lot of time talking, me doing most of it. I talked about what had happened over the past ten years; about my time at Puckapunyal and how that had transformed my thinking about a lot of things; and about what I had seen at Richmond and why I wanted to be a coach.

Geraldine indicated she would be happy enough to go to Adelaide, but of course, things turned out differently and we ended up in Essendon.

There, she was just amazing. She's a fair bit younger than I am. In fact, when we first got to Essendon, she wasn't much older than a lot of the players' girlfriends. That also meant she was a lot younger than the board members' wives, people she would be expected to socialise with. And, of course, she had a young baby, plus a mad husband who was running around frantically trying to prove to everyone that he could be the first full-time coach in Australian football.

Geraldine coped with it all serenely, and still does. I'm very lucky I caught those fabulous eyes of hers across a crowded dance floor all those years ago at The Powerhouse, because she has been an absolute powerhouse in my life, coping with my annoying ways and deficiencies — and there have been plenty of those.

9

New Era at Windy Hill

I can remember sitting in the stands at Windy Hill, home ground of Essendon Football Club, in late 1980. There was no one else in the ground, not another soul but me, and this soul was stirring, wondering, planning ... dreaming.

Would I coach Essendon? *Could* I coach Essendon? I had already said 'no' a few times before. The first time was when the Bombers had asked me to come across in 1976 as player–coach in place of Des Tuddenham. He had been brought in as an 'outsider' from Collingwood as captain–coach. A tough, no-nonsense type, he took the club from the bottom of the ladder to the finals three years in a row, but thereafter things had gone awry and in 1976, he was shifting back to Collingwood.

The person who approached me about replacing Des was Allan Hird, the then president of Essendon who these days, particularly among the new generations of Bomber supporters, is best remembered as the grandfather of James. Allan Hird played 154 games for Essendon, included among them the grand final victory in 1942. He was a long-time administrator, serving as treasurer, vice president and, for seven years, president. He was a man to be respected, and I enjoyed very much the conversation we had. The way he spoke suggested that he believed I could be a successful VFL coach. He had obviously been talking to other people who held that view, among them Lindsay Thompson, who was then the Minister for education in Victoria — Allan was his director general. Thompson, who died in 2008, was a passionate Richmond supporter who had obviously watched me develop at Punt Road. He could see that there were a number of talented players coming through at Richmond who might one day become coaches. He provided Allan Hird with the valuable information that I might be one of them.

I said 'no' to Allan Hird at that time because I still wasn't sure about my own abilities as a coach. I also still had a deep affection for Richmond. To me, back then, you didn't leave Richmond once you had committed to it. I had done that right from the moment they picked me. I had even painted my bedroom black and gold. My brothers and sisters can vouch for it, and the fact that I probably had *too much* black. The room was meant to resemble the Richmond jumper, lots of black on three walls and the ceiling, and one wall in yellow. I think it was all part of getting the black and red out of my system after I had switched my allegiance from Essendon, my first love. I have always had this thing about not walking out on commitments. I didn't walk out on Richmond as a player. In 1979, my contract wasn't going to be renewed. In 2008, I can say to the fans at Essendon I didn't quit on them; my contract wasn't renewed.

Despite my deep sense of loyalty to Richmond, in 1976 — from the moment of my chat with Allan — the thought formed that if I could get everything I needed in terms of qualifications and experience, there could be an opportunity to coach the club that was part of my family history.

Then, in 1979, the Bombers asked me to join them as assistant skills coach to Barry Davis. At that stage, I had a similar position under Tony Jewell at Richmond and my thinking was, 'Why go to another club just to sit under someone else?' So, I stayed with the Tigers in 1980, and what a great choice that was — a premiership year. I watched and learned as Tony, Paddy Guinane and Dr Rudi Webster created a unified drive for success. I learned from Tony that whatever skills you had at handling footballers, you probably needed even better ones when it came to handling the board. Tony was very good inside the boardroom. Paddy Guinane was a sensible sounding-board to have around the club for us all to bounce ideas off. Every coach needs one of those, too.

At first impression you wouldn't think that Rudi Webster, one of the great characters of sport, was a football person. Born in Barbados, he played first-class cricket for Scotland, for Otago in New Zealand, and for Warwickshire in the English county competition. Above all that, though, he's made his mark as a sports psychologist, rather than a sportsman. He had a huge impact on developing the mentally tough West Indian sides that played under Clive Lloyd, and Greg Chappell recently asked him to get involved in toughening up the Indian side. Perhaps we can blame Rudi for Harbajhan Singh!

There's another interesting twist there all these years on. My solicitor, Brian Ward, was part of the legal team that represented Cricket Australia when the whole Harbajhan Singh case was heard in Adelaide in the summer of 2007/08. Wardie has also worked closely over the years with Malcolm Speed, the bloke who stepped down as CEO of the International Cricket Council. Malcolm had a difference of opinion with his board on what was going on in Zimbabwean cricket. Some people on the ICC like to use Zimbabwe's vote to get their way on certain issues, so they weren't prepared to upset them. One thing I have learned over the years is that politics isn't just a part of footy. It's a part of *anything* where you find people.

Back at Richmond in 1980, there was a good lesson for me that you don't necessarily have to be a football person to be successful in football. The most important thing is to be a *good* person. Rudi Webster showed me that. So, too, did the Englishman we had as a general manager, Richard Doggett. He was as different from Graeme Richmond, Schwabbie and Ian Wilson as you could be, in the sense that he didn't know anything about football. What he did know was how to make people get on together, and that was important in a club still suffering from the departure of Tommy Hafey. Hafey was forced out at Richmond, but he wasn't sacked. When he knew he didn't have the support of the full board, that he had lost Graeme Richmond's support, he resigned. To his supporters, though, and he had a lot of them, it was still a massive shock. Richmond has yet to recover.

Still, we managed to put together this amazing time in 1980. We had a Pom, and a West Indian sports psychologist. Our fitness guru, Peter Grant, was another outsider. He had a background in surfboat racing. Good ideas can come from anywhere. To be successful in surfboat racing, you have to be fit, and you all have to pull together.

There were a lot of new words and ideas going around at Richmond in 1980. One of those was 'biorhythms'. I thought it was some sort of new pen, when I first heard of it. Tony

Jewell also made the players think of themselves as winners and then reinforced it with his passion. Dennis Collins was dropped from a grand final for missing a meeting with the team psychologist. That's passion. That's ruthless. That's Tony.

When it came to the players, Tony, Paddy and Rudi had an interesting chemistry to work with. There were some great footballers in the autumns of their careers, many of them my contemporaries, including Francis Bourke, a country boy who that year won his fifth premiership. Milking cows, or not wanting to milk cows, is a mighty motivational force. It's a wonder more coaches haven't tried it — instead of doing a long training session after a bad loss, why not send the team off into the Western District for a day to help the dairy farmers!

There were some wonderful young players, some still with their milk teeth, who were being developed: Mick Malthouse, Jim Jess, Dale Weightman, Mark Lee and Emmett Dunne were among them. I had first spotted young Emmett when he was a 14 year old at a pie night at St Christopher's, in Doon Street, Syndal. With the nickname of 'Plod', he is now one of Victoria's most senior policemen and has also served on the AFL Tribunal. Right from the outset, you knew Emmett was just the right sort of good person.

One thing I had learned from Alan Schwab and Graeme Richmond was not to miss anything; to keep every option available for talented kids and for people of good character. Here was one that I had spotted myself coming through. Emmett played in that 1980 premiership side along with Terry Smith, the young bloke for whom I had retired to give him his best chance at playing senior football.

I had been responsible for a number of innovations at Punt Road as part of what I felt was keeping Richmond up to speed with changes in modern sport. I had convinced Ian Wilson and the treasurer, Brian Carson, to put in lights so that we could train at night. Hardly rocket science nowadays, but back then … well, they took some convincing. Something else I was big on was putting up nets behind the goals, but they put them at the wrong end. I was trying to prevent the balls flying out of Brunton Oval and possibly causing an accident. But they were put at the other end of the ground — to protect the possums in the park, perhaps?

All up, it was a great experience, but as an assistant coach, you don't — quite properly — get much of the kudos. That praise — like the blame when things go wrong, or even when they don't go wrong — always goes to the senior coach.

So, sitting in the empty stands at Windy Hill, I was contemplating whether I would ever have the same precious moments that Tony Jewell and Tommy Hafey had known as premiership coaches.

I had walked away from Essendon the first time, in 1976, thinking I may not have been talented enough to do the job. Now, I was quietly asking myself: 'Are you good enough to be in the top 12 coaches in Victoria? Can you move into the realms of people who are legends in the game? Can you successfully pit your mind against Barassi, Jeans, Hafey, Parkin? Can you think and plan well enough to lead a club? Do you have the courage to risk failure?'

I was in this mindset because Essendon was by now looking for a replacement for Barry Davis. He had done the job in 1978, 1979 and 1980. If I thought my Essendon pedigree was a bit special because of my family links to the area and my knowledge of the club, well his was just about absolutely impeccable. He was recruited to the club from Essendon High

School and became one of the best half-back flankers in the history of the game. He was a premiership player in 1962 and 1965 and had been senior captain in 1971 and 1972. If there was a blemish on his black-and-red record, it was that he left the club under the ten-year open transfer rule in 1975 to go to North Melbourne. There, he led the Kangaroos to the premiership. Even though he hadn't had a lot of success as coach of Essendon — his resignation came when he kept a promise to quit if the side didn't make the finals — he was still highly regarded by many at Windy Hill, including Colin Stubbs, the club president who was part of the subcommittee looking for his replacement. Often when a new coach goes in, the old one has been sacked and is hardly the flavour of the month, so you don't have to worry too much about people saying, 'Well, last year we did it this way', and so on. Because Essendon had handled the transition away from Barry so well, he was still this highly respected figure. I think that had to come into the calculations for the incoming coach. Barry wouldn't be looking over my shoulder, but others still close to him might be.

Colin felt that Essendon had developed its playing list under Barry to a stage where the club needed a full-time coach. Barry also felt the time had come for a full-time coach, but his work for the Education Department meant he couldn't make that commitment. Why give up that job security for the uncertain lifestyle of a football coach?

The other members of that coaching subcommittee were Neville Gay and Brian Donohoe, two other solid servants of Essendon, and the club's general manager, Roy McConnell. Roy was highly respected as a general manager because he had also played the game, winning two flags in 1949 and 1950. From what I have gathered over the years, this committee went over a lot of very highly qualified candidates with a very, very fine-toothed comb. Names like John Nicholls, Len Thompson, Neil Kerley, Ron Barassi, David Parkin, Allan Jeans and, thankfully, Kevin John Sheedy, were part of the mix.

Barassi, however, was very quickly out of it. He made it clear he was going back to Melbourne after his successful times at Carlton and North Melbourne. Eventually, it came down to a choice between Allan Jeans and me, with John Nicholls apparently an unlucky third. Allan's and mine were the two names the coaching subcommittee took to the executive and finance committee.

There had been two interviews along the way, both held at Colin Stubbs's house. I prepared for them both, but particularly the second one, like I had never prepared for anything in my life. At about this time, I think I got a precious piece of advice from Jan Richmond, wife of Graeme: 'Kevin, you've got to get rid of the tracksuit!' She was right. If I was going to make a decent impression, I had to show them I could look like a leader, as well as talk like one.

I had barracked for Essendon ever since I was a kid. As a player I had won three premierships, gained a best and fairest and captained a VFL side. However, none of these qualifications would count for much if I couldn't convince Colin Stubbs, Brian Donohoe, Neville Gay and Roy McConnell that I had the knowledge, the vision, the insights, the feel for what was happening in 'the modern game' needed to coach an ambitious club that was working towards another era of success.

I learned everything I could about these people who were interviewing me, especially about their roles at Essendon. And I learned as much as possible about everyone else there, not just the players. As a coach, you have to try and know everything about your club; that way, you can put out bushfires even before they have started. You'd be surprised how many people there are in football clubs running around with boxes of matches.

I gathered later that they felt I was a bit cocky about the way I knew what everyone, especially the coaching subcommittee, did within the club. I prefer to think that, rather than being cocky, I was expressing my confidence that, after years of preparing myself, I was ready to become a senior coach — and not just *any* senior coach, but the first full-time coach in the history of the game.

There was also probably one of the strangest questions ever asked at a job interview for a coaching position: Did I mind if people smoked in the change rooms after a game? Roy McConnell was a heavy smoker. In those days, both smoking and drinking were a part of the culture even on match day. Neville Gay and Brian Donohoe and I have often laughed at Bob Syme's practice of taking out hip flasks of brandy at half-time when he was coach of the reserves. Purely for medicinal purposes, of course, as in keeping the players warm!

I was very honest in what I had to say when we came to more standard questions, such as: 'What do you think of our playing list?' They put forward some names and said they were young, skilful players on the way up. I think I heard the sound of a few jaws hitting the floor when I told them that Essendon had no skilled players. What they had, I said, was a lot of *potentially* skilful players. I also suggested that a lot of the Essendon players were a bit short on discipline. I don't think they'd expected that response, either.

I was adamant that the players had to learn to play in all positions; that there was no reason why a centre-half forward shouldn't play at centre-half back. I had learned enough from

Barry Richardson and Tony Jewell, and from my own observations, to know that Australian football was about to enter a great era of change. To succeed, both Essendon and I had not just to embrace that revolution, but to lead it. Having players that could perform all over the field was part of the revolution.

Like them, I was insistent that the role had to be full-time. After what I had seen in America, I knew that this was the only way to go.

Apparently, after the interviews the subcommittee came to the view that I was more a man of the 1980s than Allan Jeans, though both Allan and I did win a few premierships in that decade. On their recommendation, the full committee voted 14–1 in my favour, the one actually abstaining from voting rather than being against me. There is always one, isn't there? Sometimes in your favour, sometimes not. Thanks, Daryl Jackson, for standing your ground in July 2007.

Mention of the person who abstained back in 1980 still brings a smile to the faces of Neville Gay and Brian Donohoe. This bloke had a habit of not being able to make up his mind on a lot of issues, not just the coach. Brian describes him as a bit of a St Thomas, the doubting Apostle.

Neville and Brian also like to recount some of the things that were said about me when they checked out my bona fides from other footballing people. Graeme Richmond said I might be a good coach so long as they could stop me talking. Tony Jewell apparently dismissed the back-spinning handpass I had been working on as a bit of nonsense.

However, there was a tradition at Essendon of giving untried coaches a go and in the end Colin, Brian, Neville and Roy were prepared to take that risk with me and make their recommendation.

Once the full committee had confirmed that decision, we still had to negotiate a contract. I had a wife and young baby to think about as well as a career in coaching. Brian Ward handled all the legal matters beautifully. Wardie and I have more than just a solicitor/client relationship. We are mates who go back a long way; in fact, there are many parallels in our lives. We are the same age. He lost his father when he was young. We share a love of gardening. He played in the VFA, for Sandringham. He was a handy little back-pocket at a time when Melbourne had plenty of those, all trying to get a spot in a premiership side, so his chance of playing in the VFL never eventuated. However, his association with Sandringham, both as player and administrator, brought us into contact for the first time. Because of a constitutional quirk at Sandringham, a player had to serve on the club's committee. Because he was both a popular sort of fellow and a law student, Brian was elected to that position.

There were a few Richmond players transferring to Sandringham in those days, where they could get more money than they could make in the VFL. Brian's legal expertise was also used in drawing up some of their contracts. That brought him to Graeme Richmond's attention. Early in the 1979 season, when my future at Punt Road was well and truly in doubt, Graeme asked Brian to meet me and to look after me, because 'this bloke is really going to go places; he has a real lot to offer football and you should be part of that too'. It was actually from Brian's office, after we'd had one of the first of the many long chats we've had over the years, that I rang Graeme Richmond to say that I would be retiring.

Brian and I had talked about how Graeme thought that of the ageing brigade at Richmond — Hart, Bartlett, Sheedy and Bourke — I was the slowest. Brian's advice was that if that's what Graeme thinks, then it's pretty much over. He remembers the moment when I made that call as a highly poignant one for both us. 'There was just this breathtaking silence, the moment of overwhelming grief that this playing career that he had worked so hard for had come to an end. For me, it was one of the most poignant moments in sport.'

Brian also recalls that after Graeme Richmond said, 'Good decision, Cocko,' we quickly got back to focusing on the future — in the short term, staying on at Richmond as the skills coach; in the long term, becoming a senior coach in my own right.

By the time we had got to drawing up that Essendon contract in 1980, Brian was pretty much *the* expert on a lot of sport's legal matters, including restraint of trade. He had seen what had happened in Sydney, in the case involving the high-profile Balmain rugby league player, Dennis Tutty.

In 1971, Tutty won a landmark High Court ruling against the NSW Rugby League's player transfer rules. To achieve that, he had to spend two seasons out of the game. That meant he wasn't part of the Balmain side that won the 1969 Grand Final. It cost him more than that, though, including his place in the Australian side. It's little wonder that Arthur Beetson, a member of the Rugby League Team of the Century announced in 2008, called Tutty 'the Cassius Clay' of that sport. 'He was the bloke who dared to buck the system,' Beetson said. 'He fought the league on principle.'

Tutty, who these days lives on the pension, believes his stance has 'made more millionaires than Harry M. Miller' because it opened the way for players to transfer beween clubs for better pay packets.

A cousin of another Rugby League Team of the Century member, Reg Gasnier, Tutty was graded by the Balmain Tigers at 17. In 1964, he was the youngest player ever to appear in a grand final, when the Tigers were beaten by St George, Gasnier's team. By 1967, he was a Test player. Because of a pay dispute, he decided to leave Balmain for Penrith but Kevin Humphreys, then the boss of the Tigers, wouldn't grant him a release. So, the matter went to court where Tutty won and the reverberations were felt around the country. The VFL had its own similar case in the early 1980s when Silvio Foschini didn't want to go to Sydney. He went to court and was allowed to play with St Kilda. Brian Ward played a prominent role in that case.

It's pleasing to know that in 2008, the Centenary Year of Rugby League, the National Rugby League players' association is going to honour Dennis Tutty for the stand he made, which has made a lot of today's players in all football codes much better off financially. And I really admire Tutty for sitting out of the game for those two years. It wasn't unlike the threat from the VFA that hung over me in my early days at Richmond. There must be something about being a Tiger that makes a bloke want to do what he believes is right, no matter what the risks.

When Brian Ward told Graeme Richmond about the Tutty case, and about what it could mean in the VFL if the Tigers wanted to bring a player to Punt Road from another club, the response was typical: 'Is that right?' Together they used the implied threat of a legal battle — the fact that a player couldn't really be stopped from going from one club to another — to bring quite a few players to Richmond, including Paul Sproule, Robert McGhie and, famously, John Pitura, who was the subject of a huge fight between the Tigers and the VFL over the clearance rules. Richmond was fined, but Pitura eventually came to the club.

Never one to seek the limelight, Brian is still today one of the most influential sports lawyers in Australia. His list of clients has included the Australian Rowing Council, Cricket Australia and the International Cricket Council. It gives me a laugh to go into his office and see included among the logos of his clients on the wall a caricature of me twirling a jacket above my head.

Brian also achieved something really marvellous when he first began representing me at Windy Hill: he won over Allan Hird. Allan had a complete disregard for lawyers; he simply refused to deal with them. But he made a special exception for Brian. 'Brian Ward, you say? Mary Ward's boy?' Allan said, when told who my lawyer was. Allan and Mary were first cousins and he had introduced Brian's parents to each other. Allan no doubt had to make another exception when his grandson, James, married Tania, a lawyer.

As Brian recalls it, because of his experience, Essendon pretty well left the drafting of the contract to him. He still has the neatly typewritten document, along with the clearance I had obtained from Ian Wilson, which I used to leave Richmond.

Not everyone at Punt Road was supportive of my move when I offered my resignation as assistant coach. Graeme Richmond told me that, as a Catholic, I wouldn't last more than five minutes with the 'Masons over there'. There was this thing about Essendon that it was a bit of a closed shop, especially in that group of players that had been coached by John Coleman in the 1960s when the club won two premierships. However, I had been brought in to do a job, with a vote of 14–1 by the committee, and I was going to do it. As time went on, I was even able to joke that at Essendon the Protestants raised the money, and the Catholics — the football department — spent it.

One of the great things about those interviews for the position of full-time coach was the chance to meet Brian Donohoe. Every coach needs a Brian Donohoe, a confidante, a sounding board, a friend. Brian is Essendon to the core, despite going to a Catholic school — the famous footballing school, Assumption College at Kilmore. According to Brian, 'You had to be a bloody good footballer to be a Catholic in the Essendon team in the early days'. Brian was good enough to have played 34 senior games with the club, but his greatest contribution came as chairman of selectors. He had — and still has — a lot of wisdom. He also has a quiet strength. He needed that pretty quickly when I decided after our win in the first night series game in 1981 that I would play in the second. I was pretty keen to play, but Brian won the argument — a good result all round. He showed that while he respected me enough as a potential coach to appoint me, he could also be forthright in making decisions that were best for the club. He also had coaching experience, which helped. In 1961, he had shifted to Tasmania and coached Scottsdale to two premierships. He had also coached at Daylesford in Victoria.

Over time, as is inevitable, we had our differences over selection. One night, I stormed out of a selection meeting. He rang me the next day and said: 'You're the coach. It's your decision, but make sure you get it right.' You should have seen the look he gave me when about 18 minutes into the game, I had to change the player. He had been right.

Brian had another great skill: he could see trouble coming long before it arrived, and that could be very helpful. There is always a lot of politics in a football club. I don't like playing politics, but I do like coaching, so sometimes you had to be political — or as I would rather put it, diplomatic. Tom Hafey and I have argued about this for years. He believes that the coach is 100 per cent always right and the board members should stay right out of running the team. I have always said to Tom, 'Just give the board *something*; agree to do a little thing their way.'

'No way!' was always his reply.

When Essendon won the grand final in 2000 there was one board member going around town acting like he'd personally kicked five goals and won the Norm Smith Medal. If that's what he needed to do, why worry about it? I've often helped board members with their businesses, too. I never thought of that as a big deal, either. We were all part of one club, so why shouldn't we all help each other? Sometimes, however, that spirit of co-operation wasn't totally reciprocal and Brian was very good at telling me when I needed to be diplomatic.

I know that something he was really keen to do in the early days was to keep me away from the committee as much as possible. His view was that yes, he and the rest of the panel believed I could coach, but I needed the space to develop my own coaching style. There had also been a suggestion at one time that Jack Clarke be brought back to the club to assist with my development, but again Brian thought it would be better to let me grow in my own way. One thing that really helped in that regard was the day I spent with Jack Hale, the former Hawthorn coach, who had done so much to turn that club around — so much so that legendary Hawks mentor John Kennedy always gives him a lot of credit for the Hawks' flag in 1961.

When I did go to committee meetings, Brian would ask me a few Dorothy Dixers and then get me out of there as quickly as he could. In those early days, Brian took so many knives in the back for me he would have needed a lot of blood transfusions. I really enjoyed helping him celebrate his 70th birthday. He is a freak and a genius, and proof you don't have to play 200 games to know a lot about football.

I often wonder about the relationship between coaches and boards. I think the good boards get the level of delegation right. They appoint the coach and leave him to get on with the job of coaching. Sometimes I think it is probably the CEO who is the one the boards should be keeping a close eye on, not the coach.

A new issue in the modern game is the amount of energy coaches need to have. If you look at what coaches were asked to do when I had my first contract drawn up and at what is required of them now ... well, you almost need to be Superman. I know clubs are committed to getting 40,000 members and all those sorts of things, but perhaps they are asking too much of the coach to look after the team *and* be involved in so much of the marketing side. Perhaps boards need to let coaches get on with doing what they know, and the success that comes from that will get their club the 40,000 members they want.

Neville Gay, another solicitor, was also very supportive when I first came on board at Essendon. He explained to me that there was no need to worry just because the president, Colin Stubbs, and the general manager, Roy McConnell, had both up and quit the club shortly after I had arrived. When that happened, I had bowled up to him to find out why. Neville is one of those people with a soothing way of telling you things. 'It's all okay, Kevin, all part of the plan,' he said, and he was right.

Neville is also the sort of person who only ever got involved in Essendon because he thought he could do some good for the club. It has never been about Neville, something I really admire.

I was so pleased that Brian, Neville and Colin Stubbs could come to my final farewell function at Essendon the day after the 2007 Grand Final. What a journey it had been since those two meetings in Colin's house almost 30 years ago when we were younger, thinner and had more hair, but no real idea of what we were getting ourselves into. Thanks, Brian. Thanks, Neville. Thanks, Colin. Thanks, Roy — for believing. Thanks for saying 'yes'.

One of the first things I did when I became coach at Essendon was to make sure every player had his own ball. We had already done that at Richmond when I was the assistant skills coach to Tony Jewell. That caused a bit of a stir at the time at Windy Hill, a few raised eyebrows, maybe a whisper in a corridor among the Masons. I know that the treasurer, Noel Allanson, wasn't happy. Balls weren't cheap, but handling a football had to become second nature to every player if we were to get our skill levels up. As premiership coach David Parkin puts it, we expect our players to be able to handle an oval ball — to kick it, catch it and bounce it — as if it were a round ball.

Then there was the fitness of the players. A lot of people loved to call me 'Kevin Hafey' because of the way I endorsed and admired Tom's coaching methods. I knew from my own exhilarating experiences at Richmond the joy of winning important games in the final quarter just because we were fitter than our opponents. We had to have that ability at Essendon as part of our armoury.

The other important thing we had to develop in our play was a presence. We had to make the opposition wary of us. They had to know that every time they went to contest the ball, there would almost certainly be a collision. Des Tuddenham, who was inducted into the AFL Hall of Fame with me in 2008, had introduced that into the club during his time there. In fact, people like Essendon stalwart Ken Fraser, who only really knew me by reputation as a Richmond player, thought that was what I was doing, taking Essendon back to the Tuddenham style. Instead, I was taking us towards the new Essendon style. We had to have presence, but we had to be very skilful, too.

At a personal level, something else I tried to introduce was the coach wearing an all-black tracksuit and footy boots on match day. After the slow start to the 1981 season, I decided that the idea wasn't working. I know Brian and Neville were happy to see it disappear. I just didn't like the idea of coaches wearing suits. Now they wear tailored AFL gear with sponsors' logos, even on the collar.

Early in the 1981 season, when we were losing games, there were rumblings on the sidelines about the players being trained too hard. The complaints weren't from the players, though — well, at least not from Terry Daniher, who would come up and tell me I wasn't training them hard *enough*. There are critics everywhere in football!

We had won the night grand final, the Escort Cup, named after a brand of cigarettes. Back then, as Roy McConnell's question at my job interview more than hinted, sport and cigarettes were pretty much inseparable. Just about every sporting club would have its own rep from a tobacco company keeping the shelves stocked, although that was about to change. Melbourne is regarded as the birthplace of the fight against sponsorship by cigarette companies of sporting clubs and competitions. It was led by Professor David Hill, who went to Harry Beitzel, who, as well as being a top umpire, had his own

PR firm. Harry told Professor Hill that he could get a bunch of footballers to come out in support of anti-smoking campaigns.

'And lo and behold, he delivered us about 25 names; top players from every league club,' Hill said. 'There was Peter Hudson, Stan Alves — all the big names of the time. We used to produce little swap cards for kids with a league footballer's picture — an action picture — and "I don't smoke because it's not good for my health".'

That was followed by the passing of the Victorian *Tobacco Act* in 1987 which allowed funds raised from tobacco licensing to be used in health promotion. A lot of those funds were used to buy out tobacco sponsorships and replace them with the Quit campaign as a major sponsor. According to Professor Hill, that Act and the system that went with it was a world first, one that has since been copied all over the world. So, we should never think that even though we're down here at the bottom of the world, we can't have an influence way outside our country, even when it comes to marketing our home-grown game overseas. If the idea, or the product, is good enough, it will sell itself. And I believe our product *is* good enough. American football — gridiron — can't hold a candle to Australian football. If we can get a decent toehold in the United States, the quality of our game will do the rest. I love David Parkin's description of gridiron: 'When the team that has the ball loses it, they don't even trust the players who lost it to get it back. They send out a whole new group of players to win the ball back. When they win it back, they don't trust them to play with it. They send out the same bunch of blokes who lost it!'

The soon-to-be-doomed Escort Cup was Essendon's first cup since 1965. Tim Watson, the boy from Dimboola, kicked an inspirational goal after leapfrogging the pack. He was only 20, so you could put that sort of inventiveness down to youth. Everyone else was doing that. We had become known as the 'Baby Bombers'. I remember thinking then, watching Tim at 20, that a decade earlier he and a lot of his young team-mates could have been called up into the army.

As the season progressed, we built up our momentum in the day premiership, too. Thanks to Neville and one or two others, we had changed a few things at committee level, such as the decision to play in black shorts instead of red, which had to be passed twice because someone had unpassed it. We won 15 games in a row. Some people at Essendon, Neville Gay and Brian Donohoe high among them, still believe that if Neale Daniher hadn't been injured in the second-last home-and-away game, we could have won the premiership in our first year. As it turned out, we lost the elimination final to Fitzroy.

In 1982, we again lost an elimination final, this time to North Melbourne. By the time 1983 came around, losing another elimination final was likely to be regarded as a failure, a sign that we could improve, but only so far. We beat Carlton to get over that mental barrier, cleared another hurdle by beating Fitzroy, then North Melbourne, and suddenly we were in the grand final against Hawthorn, coached by Allan Jeans.

So many things happened in that match that would become pivotal to the future of the Essendon Football Club. Tim Watson was knocked out by Colin Robertson, who went on to win the Norm Smith Medal. Russell Greene also did a tight marking job on Tim, something that didn't go unnoticed, especially by Brian Donohoe. Robertson's hit on Watson was a pretty interesting turn of events, since a week before the finals series, Don Scott, the former Hawthorn captain, had accused

Essendon of using Roger Merrett as a hitman. Well, he didn't name Roger, but it was pretty obvious that's who he meant. Roger had been working extremely hard on his game to create a presence when he was on the footy field.

Scott, who was reported 15 times during his career, didn't mention Roger by name when he wrote in the *Sun News-Pictorial*: 'There's a hitman operating in the League's final five and unless one of his pursuers captures him on Saturday, he will be sniping in September. This guy is doing it frequently. If he is being encouraged to carry out these sniping acts by his coach then it's a giant slur on his club and the game. Most players know who I am talking about, but the football public can't be told. I can tell you that he has claimed five victims, one of them a mate of mine.'

Don continued on in the same vein in this column and was joined in his criticisms of Roger, me and Essendon by Ron Barassi. 'I know who Don is referring to,' Barassi said in a newspaper interview. 'He got one of our players during the year. Don't expect the club president to call in this player and don't expect the VFL to stop him. Apart from the umpires, the only person who can bring him into line is his coach. And that's if he wants to because he must know what is going on.'

Derryn Hinch, the radio broadcaster, went a lot further than Scott and Barassi, actually naming Roger. Neville Gay acted for him in the defamation action that was settled out of court. Ask Neville if the settlement was in Roger's favour and he smiles and nods, then adds: 'But Roger didn't think it was enough!'

I can only assume that Essendon must have been starting to worry everyone else — that they recognised the Bombers as potential flag winners even that far out from the grand final — because Bill Deller, the umpires' boss, was reported as saying there hadn't been any complaints brought against any players. Bill said: 'The first thing I knew about it was when I read it in the paper this morning. It's all brand new to me.'

Essendon rallied around Roger. Greg Sewell, a highly respected former player, made the formal response. He said the club was appalled at the scurrilous campaign against Roger and believed that he played the game hard, but fair.

Barry Capuano, another former player and now our general manager, summed the whole thing up brilliantly: 'We doubt the issues would have been raised if Essendon was out of the finals. The club takes heart that we are regarded as strong premiership contenders, sufficient for others to engage in psychological warfare at this time.'

Merrett's transformation from peripheral player to game-breaker wasn't noticed just by worried outsiders. Tim Watson said of Roger: 'He has a presence that not many other guys possess. Opposition players fear him. He's intimidating to them and when you've got someone on your team that can have that effect on the opposition, then you're halfway there.'

You might wonder who put Don Scott up to writing the claims in his ghosted column. Was it his idea? Was it the tackle Roger made on Kelvin Moore that had irked the hierarchy at Hawthorn enough to suggest to Don that he should write something? We'll probably never know. Over the years, Don has always travelled to the beat of a different drum. He's always been a colourful personality who has made a good living out of being outspoken.

Whatever, Roger had the final say in all this when he very cleverly noted that, when I first became his coach, I had advised him to model his game on, yes, Don Scott! That was true. And Roger had responded by working really hard on his game. If nothing else, the controversy stirred up by Don Scott was a wonderful endorsement of Roger's dedication over the previous two or three years. He certainly played a tremendous role in getting us to the 1983 Grand Final, which we then lost — to Hawthorn — by 83 points, a record losing margin in a grand final.

There was a lot of criticism of me because I had left Ronnie Andrews out of the team for the grand final. Hawthorn officials said the sight of him playing in the reserves grand final had been a real boost to their players. I dropped Ronnie because I didn't believe he was committed enough to our cause, and perhaps because he wasn't fit enough. Earlier in the final series, he had been suspended for yelling abuse at an umpire. That showed a lack of discipline.

I was devastated at losing the grand final. It hurt as much as I thought it would. I knew how much losing the 1974 Grand Final at North Melbourne had cut into Ron Barassi. I was impressed by his post-match performances, where his disappointment was so apparent. I actually kept newspaper clippings about that game because of all the things he said.

In 2001, when we lost to Brisbane, I wrote a column in *The Australian* about what it means to lose a grand final. I noted the positives from the season, for our club and for the game in general. Having a flag flying from the Brisbane Town Hall was a great step towards turning the national league into the national game. But all those words I wrote were just like putting a bandaid on a broken heart.

At Essendon in 1983, however, there were people who didn't feel the need for a bandaid — mainly because they didn't have a broken heart. They were probably the ones who celebrated beating North Melbourne in the preliminary final like it was a grand final victory.

I didn't say much out on the field as the Hawthorn players got their medals, or in the change rooms, except maybe for asking the players to promise themselves they would be back here next year. But by the time I got to the grand final dinner, and saw people not hurting enough, I couldn't hold my tongue any longer. I simply let fly. I took the microphone and said that any player who didn't feel sick inside didn't deserve to play for the club again.

'If it doesn't hurt tonight, then Essendon will never win another premiership,' I said. 'To put it mildly, it was the most disappointing day of my life. I don't want you to enjoy tonight. I hope you all watch the game again. For me, that's what it's all about. That's why I came here.

'I hope the honest, football-loving people of Essendon realise our hurt and shame because of our shocking and unaccountable grand final performance. That's the way I believe we should feel about today.

'There is no room for excuses when we play games like we did, whether it's during the year or in a grand final — particularly in a grand final ... Winning premierships is what football is all about. Winning is the only way to have a really great time. I know it's hard, and you may feel it's hard on your ears, but I don't want you to enjoy yourselves tonight. Not at all!'

I reminded the players, too, that some of the people who had smiled after losing the preliminary final in 1981 hadn't reappeared in 1982. Then I congratulated the reserve side, which, coached by my old Richmond team-mate Kevin Morris, had won its premiership.

I don't think a lot of players at Essendon at that time had ever been spoken to like that before. The speech also upset a lot of people at the board, corporate and coterie level, as well as a lot of women members of the club. If we hadn't gone on to win the premiership in 1984, there was probably a fair chance I would have been sacked. My speech was covered by the media and there was a lot of anger and criticism around the place.

But that's what happens in footy when you lose. In Australia, we have a habit of really kicking people when they are down. It's something that, if we really want to succeed at a new level as a nation, whether in football or commerce, we need to get rid of. Criticism needs to be constructive, not destructive. One of the things that Mark Thompson and his senior playing group did so well in 2007 was to learn to talk honestly to each other. No one was to take umbrage at criticism, so long as it was constructive. Look how well that worked.

I'm prepared to accept that at the 1983 Grand Final dinner, I might have said some things that I shouldn't have, but I probably said a lot of things that night that helped us to win the next two grand finals. In football, as in life, you can't always be 100 per cent right or 100 per cent wrong. At football clubs, some of the things you do make you a lot of friends. The same things can also make you a lot of enemies. Would we have won the next year, and the year after, if I had accepted that losing a grand final was acceptable on the basis that second best is a lot better than finishing with the wooden spoon? I don't think so.

Those two premiership seasons in 1984 and 1985 were great times to be around the Essendon Football Club. Not only did we win the two flags, we also won the ABC Sports Team of the Year award. Terry Daniher accepted the award on the club's behalf. I remember Norman May, he of the famous 'Gold! Gold to Australia! Gold!' call at the 1980 Moscow Olympics, asking

Terry how a person from New South Wales ended up playing in the VFL. Norman May was a very good rugby union man, and no doubt would have liked to have seen all four Daniher brothers playing for the Wallabies.

In the 1984 Grand Final, we — and, not least, Roger Merrett — got revenge for the events of September 1983. But we hadn't got there without a fair bit of controversy. As most people know, these days I like to muse a lot about things, sometimes to myself, sometimes out-loud. One of those out-loud musings was a flippant response to a question about why Hawthorn was such a powerful side. I replied: 'Whatever they're sniffing, we would like some of that, too!'

The blokes flying the *Enola Gay* wouldn't have seen a bigger mushroom cloud than the one that went up over Melbourne as a result of that comment. Allan Jeans, a policeman, was furious that someone should accuse his team of taking drugs. So were a lot of other very influential people in Melbourne who just happened to be Hawthorn supporters — people like the governor and the police commissioner. To this day, I don't think Allan has forgiven me for that comment. I reckon he believes if anyone was sniffing anything strange, it was me. Really, though, those words were said not just in jest, but also out of admiration for the way he and his team played football. Hawthorn did have a magic ingredient that some of us might have been lacking, and I think it came straight from their coach. It was man management. Allan was very good at it, as all those lovely stories about him dropping players for 'team balance' attest. And when you say 'team balance', you have to imagine him saying it in that hypnotic voice of his.

There is a lovely anecdote, one probably greatly embellished by repeated telling, woven around Allan's other great sporting passion, lawn bowls. A few years ago, Allan was in line to play for his club in an important game, but wasn't selected. When a lot of former players like Dermott Brereton found out, they couldn't get to the phone quickly enough to assure him it was all about 'team balance'.

We had great team balance by the end of the 1984 season. We had finished the home-and-away season with 18 wins. That was one more than Hawthorn, but in Round 12, they had beaten us pretty comprehensively. They beat us again in the semi-final, but this time it was getting close — just eight points — at the end of a game described as one of the greatest of that era.

We thumped Collingwood in the preliminary final to set up what was — given all that had gone before in 1983 and during 1984 — going to be an absolute blockbuster: two great clubs standing toe to toe. You might read that and wonder why only 92,685 people were there to watch it. There had been a hailstorm the night before, but it was nothing compared to the way Essendon, led by the tireless Billy Duckworth and with Tim Watson, Darren Williams, Leon Baker and Paul Weston not far behind him, stormed home in the final quarter.

Hawthorn set the early pace. They led by a goal after just 30 seconds when Dermott Brereton got a free kick at the first bounce and got the ball to Leigh Matthews. Colin Robertson — that man again — had the Hawks two goals up before the game was two minutes old. He got another goal in the fourth minute. When Richard Loveridge kicked a goal in the seventh minute, the Hawks had the first four. At the next bounce, a brawl broke out. A message had been sent out to Simon Madden to start a fight. If it wasn't so serious, it would have been funny. Simon couldn't fight his way out of a wet paper bag, but he did his best. I think there was a lot of badly bruised thin air after the game. But we hadn't come this far to lose again, so we had to do something to make our presence felt. Five minutes later, we got our first goal through Leon Baker. The relief was temporary, though. Hawthorn kicked the next two goals through Brereton and Michael Tuck. At quarter-time, it was 6.1 (37) to 2.4 (16).

There was no reason to believe things were going to get much better in the second quarter. The Hawks had the first goal after three minutes and another one eight minutes later.

The first hint of better things to come came in the 21st minute. Terry Daniher took the ball from a kick on right centre wing. He sent a handball 15 metres to Alan Ezard whose own handpass through traffic found Darren Williams, who took a bounce, then got the ball to Bill Duckworth who couldn't miss from three metres out. And didn't.

In the coach's box we knew we were playing as well as the Hawks. The scoreboard, however, begged to differ. At half-time it was still Hawthorn in front 8.6 (54) to our 3.11 (29). We began to try some different things. The wisdom of teaching players to perform all over the ground, the issue I had raised as part of my plan during my job interview at Colin Stubbs's house, now came to the fore. We pushed Billy Duckworth forward, and later Paul Weston and Peter Bradbury, and sent Leon Baker to half-forward and Darren Williams to the middle.

Hawthorn kicked the first goal of the third quarter through Leigh Matthews. A free kick against Gary Ayres gave Leon Baker our first goal of the second half in the 16th minute. In the 18th, Billy Duckworth really started to make his statement about the way he wanted this match to go — as in nothing like in 1983. He took a great mark, beating two Hawks, David O'Halloran and Ayres, in the contest for possession. Brereton —

ever the pest whether on or off the field — kicked the steadying goal for Hawthorn in the 23rd minute. At three-quarter-time, those who had put their money on the Hawks were feeling pretty comfortable, with their side four goals ahead.

As a coach you can exhort your players to do all sorts of things. The quarter-time and three-quarter-time addresses of people like Barassi and John Kennedy are a part of the game's folklore. Sometimes you get to the huddle hopping mad and words come pouring out like lava. Afterwards, you want to cut out your tongue. Other times, you might not have a clue what to say, but you say it anyway. It's a frank and honest one-way exchange and your body language is being analysed by every player and every supporter. It's partly theatre, partly an important part of the game. When I got to the three-quarter-time huddle in the 1984 Grand Final, inside I was pretty excited. I sensed Hawthorn was gone. I think Allan Jeans knew it, too; just by the way he was addressing his players who were seated around him. I wanted to get that positive message across, but at the same time, I wanted to make sure the players knew that success would only come if they played at their absolute best. So, making eye contact with as many players as I could, I reminded them that the game was in the balance. Then I remember pointing across to the Hawthorn huddle and saying something like: 'Have a look at 'em. They're gone.'

I walked around the players, repeating: 'We've got it.' And as I looked into their eyes, I could see they believed it. I think they had sensed this as much in the third quarter out in the middle as we had from up in the coach's box.

I told the players some pretty basic stuff. We needed to get off to a good start, and we needed to bloody well start kicking straight. All those behinds had killed us, but as Steve Waugh would say years later about dropped catches in a Test match, at least it shows you're creating chances. I continued going around the huddle, accentuating the positives, reinforcing what I felt the players were already thinking — we can win this — but with the caveat that we had to do it ourselves: Hawthorn weren't going to just lie down and give it to us. The Hawks were far too proud a side to do that.

Apparently, a lot of things were being said up in the stands, too. Alec Epis, a former Essendon player, was really letting fly about me and my coaching, claiming that the team was undisciplined, and so was I. What Alec didn't know at the time was that he was sitting in the same row as my sisters Barbara and Kathleen, Barbara's husband, and my brother Pat. They were fuming at what they heard, but for the time being at least, they bit their tongues.

After the game, Barbara confronted Alec and told him that a former senior player like him ought to have been more supportive. In Round 21 in 2007, after the loss to Richmond in what should have been a stirring send-off for James Hird, Barbara had another chat to Alec about his apparent lack of support for me as a coach over just about the whole 27 years I was at Essendon. She also told him that she thought there were Essendon players that day who hadn't really tried and she wondered why that might have been. You've got to love big sisters. Perhaps I should have got her to address the players a few times during the three-quarter-time breaks.

Words are one thing, but actions are what finally win a grand final, and there were plenty of those in the final quarter of the 1984 Grand Final. The first of them came after just a few seconds. Simon Madden, back to punching the ball rather than thin air, won the tap at the opening bounce. The ball fell to Williams, who kicked towards goal. There was a scramble for the ball before Leon Baker latched on to it and kicked a goal. We had got off to a good start.

Peter Bradbury, back with Essendon after a season with Port Melbourne, took a mark that Terry Daniher and three Hawthorn defenders thought was theirs. Two minutes had gone and the difference was now just two goals. On ABC Radio, Doug Bigelow, the former Essendon player and committee man turned commentator, said: 'Essendon are coming home with a wet sail.' The good start we'd made was turning into a great one.

Then came a moment I am sure Mark Thompson still savours, even with his 2007 premiership at Geelong under his belt. The final quarter was eight minutes old when Tim Watson smothered a kick from Loveridge. The Dimboola Dasher picked up the ball and kicked to Duckworth. Spying an unmarked Thompson 20 metres in-field, he played on with a deft kick. Thompson kicked the goal from about 40 metres out. 'Great gutsy comeback by the Dons,' said Doug Bigelow. In the ninth minute, we hit the front for the first time through another little Baker gem. For nine minutes, the game remained evenly balanced. Robert DiPierdomenico was reported for knocking out Kevin Walsh, who left the ground on a stretcher, accompanied by our long-serving club doctor, Bruce Reid. The Hawks were a tough outfit and we all knew they wouldn't go quietly. Peter Curran got the goal that put them back in front after Terry Daniher gave away what was then a 15-metre penalty. Thank God it wasn't a 50-metre penalty, something else I might have been responsible for bringing into the game.

Early on in my coaching stint at Essendon, we had introduced an edict that asked the players always to control the ball. So, even when it went out, they were to hang on to it for as long as possible before the boundary umpire could throw it in. If an opponent got a free kick, we'd cling on to the ball as long as possible so that our team-mates could get into position. When we kept doing this despite the occasional 15-metre penalty, the VFL introduced the 50-metre penalty.

Even without the additional 35 metres, this free kick was one of those moments when coaches — along with supporters — age visibly. Thankfully, the young men in black and red held their nerve. Roger Merrett, the alleged hitman, really hit them the best and hardest way possible. He judged the flight path of a Paul Van Der Haar kick better than everyone in line for it and kicked an easy goal.

After the close marking job Russell Greene had done on Tim Watson the year before, we had prepared our own version of it. Brian Donohoe had made a video of all the things Greene had done to Watson, the little pushes, the niggles and so on. We had shown it to Shane Heard, one of the fittest and strongest blokes at the club. He was to do exactly the same to 'The Dipper' in the grand final. Robert DiPierdomenico with his big moustache, hair and chest, was a sort of a totem for Hawthorn. The other players responded to him. But we reckoned if we could run him ragged — he wasn't their fittest player — we had a chance. When he started to cramp up, spirits rose further in the Essendon box.

Then came one of those moments that you savour as a coach or a supporter: a length-of-the-field goal. Duckworth marked a poor attempt at goal from the tiring 'Dipper'. He took play to the left half-back flank, where he kicked to Bradbury. The mark wasn't clean, but there was plenty of time and space; yet another sign, perhaps, that Hawthorn was tiring. He kicked towards Roger Merrett who brought the ball down, then handballed to Mark Harvey. His kick was aimed in the direction of Van Der Haar. The tension exploded into a roar from the black and red cheer squad as The Flying Dutchman's left mitt knocked it towards Paul Weston who kicked the goal. Poetry with a piece of pig skin. And vindication of the decision to put the youngsters, Harvey and Thompson, on the field. The recklessness of youth can empower a football team, even without the players knowing it. For a young player, your first games can be a bit like going to your first dance. You're not entirely sure what to expect, but you go out and give it your best shot and make sure you have a good time. Thompson and Harvey did just that.

Our next goal came when Weston, now at centre-half forward after starting in his customary defensive position, handballed from 50 metres out to Tim Watson. He kicked that goal and another one a minute later. 'Could be enough,' said Doug Bigelow in understatement.

Leigh Matthews got one last goal for the Hawks in time-on, but we trumped that with one of our own when Merv Neagle kicked one over the pack. This was Leigh Matthews' last game of senior football. It wasn't the way he would have wanted to go out. He has made Essendon pay at least twice since then, in the 1990 Grand Final, when he was coach of Collingwood, and again in the 2001 Grand Final as coach of Brisbane. Leigh never forgets.

When the final siren went, there was pandemonium — and not just in the stands where my sister Barbara was confronting Alec Epis. Essendon had won the grand final, the club's first since 1965. A whole bunch of young men who had learned their lessons, who had trained until they could train no more, and who believed in themselves when others didn't, had created a new era of success at Windy Hill.

Billy Duckworth won the Norm Smith Medal. My mind wandered back to the way we had brought him to Windy Hill. Essendon were telling me about some great player they had, the best available recruit in the country. I said, 'Well, I know who the second-best available recruit is. He's in Western Australia'.

'Well, let's go get him, then!'

We did. Alan McGillivray chased and hounded Duckworth to come to Essendon. I never got around to asking who Essendon's preferred number one recruit was.

As the celebrations were going on, I thought back to that lonely day at Windy Hill when I had wondered if I had what it took to be a premiership-winning coach. It was a great feeling to know I could do it. And if I could do it once …

In the week after the 1984 Grand Final, I again had good reason to be grateful to Brian Ward. Things had become a bit tight money-wise in the Sheedy household. Wardie rang his local bank manager who was an Essendon supporter, and everything was quickly put right. On the Wednesday after the grand final, I turned up at the manager's branch with the 1984 Premiership Cup. You should always remember to say 'thanks'. The bank manager hadn't done anything out of the ordinary. As Brian puts it, really all he did was 'uncork the bottleneck'. Nevertheless, he had taken a real load off the shoulders of my family by helping us to build a house. Two Essendon coterie members, Ross Larmer and Michael Northwood, designed and helped build the house for me which helped keep me at Essendon.

In 1985, we defeated Hawthorn in the grand final again, after finishing the home-and-away season as minor premiers with 19 wins — our best-ever season. The Hawks were third, behind Footscray, but won their way through to the grand final for a fourth meeting for the season. We had won all three previous clashes, including the second semi-final. The Hawks were ahead by a goal at half-time in that game, but we kicked seven goals in the third quarter to seal the match.

In the grand final we kicked the last 11 goals in the final quarter, a record. The most memorable moment in the first quarter was a mighty brawl. If it had happened in 2008, the AFL's cash register would have gone into meltdown collecting all the fines. A couple of decades ago, these mêlées weren't just inevitable in a big game; they were pretty much compulsory. They were a statement of intent, or that lovely old line from rugby union, about getting your retaliation in first. Football is now more aware of broader community concerns about wanton violence on the field, as distinct from the idea that a lot of people were wanting to see the violence.

At half-time the Hawks led by a goal. In the third quarter we kicked those crucial seven goals to set up the storming finish. Simon Madden won the Norm Smith Medal, though he must have been pushed all the way by Dermie Brereton, who kicked eight goals in a superb solo effort for the Hawks. I have always had a lot of respect for Brereton, and not just because we share an Irish heritage. He was both a great player and a very brave one.

At Essendon, a lot of people went overboard, as you would expect. The *Essendon Gazette's* headline was: 'Double Header… and now for the hat trick!' I tried to be a bit more cautious, saying that I thought we only had one more year of this sort of success ahead of us before we needed to start playing a smarter brand of football, one that included getting off to a better start in important games. I knew, too, from my experiences at Richmond, that we would need to start freshening up the playing list. That would mean some hard decisions, such as letting players go who, while still very popular with their team-mates and supporters, were reaching that stage of being past their best.

By 1985, I was a different type of coach to the one who had arrived at Windy Hill in 1980 with the attitude of 'Well, you've taken the job, you've got a young family to support — just bloody well get on and do it'. I received criticism then for not being a great planner. I still do. But there are reasons for giving that impression. Some coaches like to dominate everything; to be dictators. I probably began like that. However, I found that if you say to people 'I need help', they will open up their hearts and minds to you. It's a great way to keep getting new ideas and to keep people involved. It allows them to develop themselves as much as they help you develop your team.

My own growth in that area stems from some advice I was given very early on at Essendon by Noel Allanson, the club trea-surer and the head executive at the Victorian Country Roads Board. He said to me: 'Kevin, delegation doesn't mean abdication.'

I was really keen to develop as many people around me as I could. I was the full-time coach. A lot of them were working part-time for the club, some even as volunteers. I felt it was my responsibility to do more than just coach the footy team. There are a lot of football coaches who just want to win a premiership, and stuff what happens to the club along the way. I was discovering that I wasn't one of them. I wanted the whole club to grow. I had ideas outside the football department that I wanted to see used.

10

Growing the Game

Early in my time at Essendon I suggested to the person in charge of marketing that a way to get more sponsorship dollars would be to sell more signage on the grandstand at Windy Hill. I was told to stick to coaching. But there was the opportunity to have signage above the roof as well as below it. When you sit and watch hours of video replays of games, you see more than the mistakes on the field or clever passages of play. You see which sponsors' logos are getting the most exposure, and which parts of the ground with no sponsors' signs are being shown frequently on national television.

I went back the next day and said, 'I'll buy another seven signs.' That annoyed him.

I said, 'What's your problem?'

He said, 'There are already seven signs hanging off the roof and they have all been sold.'

I said, 'What about the seven on the top of the roof that aren't there yet?'

That year there were 14 signs, not seven, and that raised another $70,000 for the club, twice my wage. I have always considered that I coached Essendon for nothing that year!

I believe a coach should be always supporting the CEO in building sponsorships, membership numbers, the overall brand of the club. I think that, in 2008, some clubs might have taken that too far, demanding more of coaches than it's reasonable to ask. A good CEO, however, will get the balancing act right.

Wanting to see Essendon grow was one of the reasons I rejected the offer from Dr Geoffrey Edelsten to coach Sydney which came shortly after the 1985 Grand Final. I wanted to keep developing what we had started at Essendon.

The Sydney experiment, the decision at the start of the 1980s to shift South Melbourne to the harbour city as the Sydney Swans, had brought a whole new dimension to Australian football — private ownership. Dr Edelsten was what people would call flamboyant, although when I first heard that word, I said: 'What position does flamboyant play?' You've got to have your fun! You don't have to take footy seriously all the time, just most of it.

Geoffrey Edelsten owned a string of medical centres in Sydney. They would have grand pianos in the foyer, or be decked out in pink décor. His young wife, Leanne, drove a car with personalised number plates that said 'SEXY'. His love of Australian football came from his childhood spent in Melbourne, where he barracked for Carlton. After qualifying as a doctor, he began to show a lot of innovative flair, setting up Melbourne's first after-hours clinics and establishing Australia's first commercial pathology laboratories. Becoming the first person to own a sporting franchise in the VFL was just part of the extraordinarily lavish existence that Edelsten had created for himself.

A day after the 1985 Grand Final I got what you might say was an offer I couldn't refuse: $1.2 million for five years, with another $250,000 if we won a premiership. Edelsten was also on the hunt for players. Simon Madden apparently got an offer of over half a million for three years.

I would have been foolish not to consider the offer. I had a wife and a growing family. I believed in expanding the game outside of Victoria. I didn't mind the idea of living in Sydney. But there was something not quite right to me about the whole setup. Certainly, Edelsten was managing to get Australian football a profile in Sydney it had never achieved before. But beneath the glamour, there didn't appear to be a lot of substance. And after my first four or five years at Essendon, I thought I knew what substance was. It was the result of a lot of hard work that really hadn't even been started in Sydney.

The VFL had sent the Swans north without the support they really needed. It was a bit like sending Neil Armstrong to the moon and giving him a bus ticket to get home. There were plenty of people who believed that the money from the sale of the Swans should have been spent in New South Wales developing both the club and the game, not going back into the coffers of struggling clubs in Melbourne. And there were plenty of people in Melbourne who couldn't believe we were wasting any time and energy on a side in Sydney. Thankfully, as we now gaze across a national landscape with teams from Perth, Adelaide, Brisbane and Sydney, that view hasn't prevailed.

Having said that, I think I was also angry that Edelsten was throwing around huge offers to players like Gerard Healy, Jim Edmonds, Merv Neagle and Glen Hawker. They would be hard people to replace at their Melbourne clubs, who had put in a lot of hard work developing them. While I applauded expanding the game into the Sydney market, I didn't believe it should come at the expense of the Victorian clubs. It had to be done on a more even basis.

So, a fortnight after I got the offer, I told Dr Edelsten 'no'. I did recommend a very good alternative, though, a bloke by the name of Tom Hafey; and with the help of Harry Beitzel, he eventually signed with Sydney. In often difficult circumstances, and with a bizarre media circus going on around him that would have completely bemused Tommy, he did a pretty good job with the Swans, getting them to the finals and giving a lot of Sydney people something else to do on a Sunday afternoon. The Swanettes added even more glamour than Leanne and the good doctor. They were 18 professional dancers who, high on a podium above the crowd, celebrated each Sydney goal with their pom-pom waving and high kicks. According to member Vanessa Clarke, being in the Swanettes was regarded as one of the best gigs for a dancer in Sydney. They performed at the Showground end of the Sydney Cricket Ground, while at the Paddington end, there was another version called the Swantits — blokes in drag with hairier legs than Leigh Matthews. It was all pure Sydney, but it couldn't last. Dr Edelsten was gone as chairman after just 12 months and eventually the AFL had to take control of the club and send Ron Barassi to Sydney to save it. What a great sacrifice that was by Ron to lend his name to the Swans. He was prepared to have his win/loss ratio as a successful coach at Carlton, North Melbourne and the Demons reduced in order to see the game prosper in Sydney. That's another reason why, when you think of Ron Barassi, you have to think of more than the great player or the great coach. You have to think of him as this great ambassador for the game.

I can't say that I had any particular inkling that Dr Edelsten would end up having his licence to practise as a doctor taken from him, or that he would go to gaol. Probably in the end, loyalty to Essendon, this club that had given me a chance — said 'yes' — tipped the balance in the Bombers' favour more than anything else.

The whole process wasn't without some positives. Watching what was happening in Sydney, and seeing how fragile the Melbourne clubs were to outside influences, I realised the importance of expanding awareness about this wonderful club that had given me so many opportunities over the previous four or five years. Essendon had always been this tight little suburban club, with players such as Barry Davis, Ken Fraser, Jack Clarke and so on all drawn from the local area. A handful of good players had come down from the bush, especially the Wimmera, and from interstate, to augment that local talent. But the times were a'changing: when you looked at the area around Essendon there were vast tracts where no one lived among the pockets of densely populated suburbs. We had a racecourse. No one lived there. We had two airports, Essendon and Tullamarine. No one lived there. So, we were going to have to draw future members and supporters from outside the traditional Essendon area, as well as from within it, if we were going to survive. We had to make our airport the bus station. We had to get on the plane and take our game and our club to everywhere and anywhere that would have us. I smile today to think that there is now an aircraft called an Airbus. The Bombers thought of it first.

When he arrived at Essendon and saw our itineraries, Roger Hampson dubbed me 'Paladin', as in 'Have Team Will Travel'. I love fiddling with the map of Australia. I love drawing lines from where Windy Hill is in Melbourne to all

209

the places around Australia with whom we have established some sort of connection, either by visiting the place to play a game, by recruiting a player from there — just about anything that establishes a link. We looked around at all the other clubs that play in black and red — North Sydney in Sydney, Lauderdale in Tasmania — and made sure we were talking to them. And, of course, there are the Tiwi Bombers on the islands off Darwin. It's so important to reach out to people. In a country with so much professional sport — in addition to the four football codes, we also have basketball, cricket and tennis — you can't wait for the people to come to you. You have to be prepared to go to the people, wherever they are. Essendon did.

If I was to sing my own version of Lucky Starr's song, 'I've Been Everywhere, Man', it would have a place for just about every letter of the alphabet. I'm sure I went to Zeehan on the west coast of Tasmania while we were driving to Queenstown, home of the famous gravel oval. In 2007 that oval, which really is made out of gravel, was inducted into Tasmanian football's Hall of Fame. I have probably attended more than 5000 functions by now, and spoken to hundreds of thousands of people. It has never been a chore. When I give a talk, I always try to hang around for a while afterwards; not just come in, say what I have to say and leave. It's amazing how much people appreciate that. It's just one of those little things you can do to help build your club up into an organisation that doesn't have to get by on a day-to-day basis, that can find the time and space to plan ahead while sitting on a few dollars in the bank.

In the early 1980s, Essendon was off to a pretty good start at creating this whole new club. We were beginning to make money, and we had overcome this nemesis called Hawthorn.

By achieving that, however, I had annoyed a lot of people. When you're winning, you can just view that as part of life. When you're losing, those pissed-off people become a problem for the coach. They carry their grudges like hand grenades. They begin to agitate, sometimes because they are genuinely concerned about their club, sometimes just because their ego wants to see their names in the media. There were a few of those coming to the surface during the 1986 and 1987 seasons.

Compared to the grand final years, 1986 and 1987 weren't great successes. It was a bit like getting kicked out of paradise!

In 1986, we were unlucky, with a lot of injuries to Roger Merrett, Paul Van Der Haar, Tim Watson and Darren Williams. We made the finals but lost an elimination final to Fitzroy by a kick in the last 60 seconds. In 1987, we won nine games and played a draw against Geelong at Windy Hill.

Our worst result was the 163-point loss to Sydney at the SCG. Everything went wrong that day, even the blimp we planned to use to promote our sponsor Nubrik refused to fly properly. Thanks for nothing, Tom — I got you and Maureen a gig in Sydney with a house overlooking the beach, and you do *this* to me! Just shows you how things can backfire. In reality Tom got that gig because his teams were always sensationally competitive.

I knew that a view was forming that my time had come to an end at Essendon. The club was starting to look for a new coach.

By 1988, the club had a new president, Ron Evans, a softly spoken former Essendon player and a highly successful businessman. I remember watching with amazement as this new person came in and began to run the club along firm business lines. Despite my best efforts to put a sponsor's logo on everything at Windy Hill, we still weren't making the money we needed to be a successful club in the new, increasingly professional football environment.

In 1987, Essendon had cleared seven players to the Bears on the Gold Coast for more than $300,000, for the purpose of balancing the books. It was a disgrace that players of the quality of Geoff Raines and Roger Merrett — especially Roger — were let go. Both should have been kept, but the board then had the power to do anything. I don't know who made the final decisions. It might have been Greg Sewell, it might have been Barry Capuano. It might have been someone else on the finance committee, or even the whole board.

Essendon at that time had become a very political environment, not unlike it was for most of 2007. Caroline Wilson wrote an article in *The Age* titled 'An ill wind at Windy Hill'. It was a bitch of an article; Caroline at her best, ripping into us all. She always was a Richmond girl, being the daughter of Ian, the club president the year I wasn't allowed to play in that cricket grand final and the bloke from whom I had got the open transfer. Caro and I have had a few scraps over the years. She's a great one for lurking in corridors, listening to whispers and citing anonymous sources. I prefer my sauces from Rosella or IXL. At least you know what bottle they came out of.

I knew that, in 1988, there were lots of discussions about my future. How the numbers played out, I don't know. In the end, I believe that Brian Donohoe and Neville Gay might have gone to Ron Evans and said, 'We have to keep this person.' In his gentle way, Ron made that happen, too.

My staying created a lot of dissension. I had made a lot of tough decisions that didn't win me much support. It got worse, as it always does, when we didn't win. Most people in footy can't handle losing. As coaches, we can put our heads down and start working towards more success. People outside the football department, particularly board members, have to go out into the community and cop flak about their footy club.

Presidents have to be able to find a balance between supporting their employees and bowing to the pressure from supporters to make populist decisions. I doubt that Ron Evans ever made a populist decision in his life unless he also believed it was the right one.

I had had three presidents by 1988 — Colin Stubbs, who had stepped down very soon after my appointment as coach, Greg Sewell and Ron Evans. Greg Sewell had three grand finals and two premierships to show for his time. Then along came Ron. He moved Capuano aside and Roger Hampson became the new CEO. Barry and Ron probably didn't see eye-to-eye on a lot of issues, including the way Ron built his commitment to Essendon around his many other business interests. This meant a lot of early morning meetings. I don't think Barry liked those too much. Ron eventually went to the AFL after helping deliver Essendon to a preliminary final in 1989 and a grand final in 1990. He was the best leader I had worked with in VFA, VFL and AFL and I have had some of the best.

We had a wonderful year in 1989. Nobody gave us a chance and we all but got to the last Saturday in September. I'm still sad we weren't able to present Ron with a premiership either then or the next year, when we lost the grand final to Collingwood. I have never known a person who deserved one more than him. The vision — the planning — he brought to the club was simply masterful.

His night of nights was his performance at the meeting held to vote on whether Essendon should leave Windy Hill and begin playing its home games at the MCG. It was a huge issue. The traditionalists thought we were selling out. Two former presidents, Allan Hird and Greg Sewell, spoke against the move. Those in favour of it countered that the club wasn't selling out; it was buying into a more secure future by playing games at a venue with the capacity to cater for the new audiences we were beginning to attract as we went from suburban club to national entity.

That night of the vote, Ron Evans turned the slurs and insults into a calm debate. He opened up the future of Essendon for everyone to see. I had never seen that done before. This was more than delegation without abdication: it was a very important way to give Essendon people ownership of their future.

In the end — it was in around 1996, I think — I know that Allan Hird had come to believe that Essendon made the right decision to move to the MCG. Unfortunately, though, quiet people like Ron never get the applause and the credit they deserve. They move on before their genius can be seen. I believe Ron Evans *was* a genius, and his death in March 2007 was one of the greatest losses that Australian football has sustained during my time in the game. His words of wisdom behind the scenes have done a lot to keep football on track, to ensure that cool heads prevailed in times of crisis. He was an Essendon man, an AFL man — but most of all, he was an excellent person, a wonderful family man and a leader in the community.

In July 2007, on the day Essendon announced it wouldn't be renewing my contract, I had an amazing phone call from Ron's wife, Andrea. She said that she had been 'speaking' to Ron and that he wanted me to know he was thinking of me. Andrea knew I would understand what she was saying. During the media conference on 25 July, I even offered a few words up to Ron myself, knowing he would have been looking down on the proceedings having quietly done his bit, even when he was seriously ill, to ensure that I would have an exciting life in football after coaching. If truth be known, he had been encouraging me for some time to finish up at Essendon because 'we need you at the AFL'.

As I said, I was so disappointed for Ron that we lost the 1990 Grand Final. It's a match I hate to think about. It's certainly not on my list of favourite videos or DVDs to watch. We were simply thrashed by Collingwood.

I'm hopeful that the joke about who kicked five goals in the 1990 Grand Final (answer: Essendon) has become who kicked six goals in the 2007 Grand Final (answer: Port Adelaide). If so, I will have even more reason to be grateful to Mark Thompson.

Between the grand final loss in 1983 and the one in 1990, I had learned a fair bit. This time there was no bitter, public outpouring. What was required was something more concrete, a rebuild from the bottom up. It required energy, patience, calmness and, most importantly, we had to make the right decisions.

I know we made one wrong one; that was to let Tim Watson retire in 1991. He'd been playing football since he was 15, he was tired of me ... I had heard and read all the stories. And yes, I know I had driven him crazy, just like Tommy Hafey had driven his best players crazy at Richmond because they were the people you turned to when you needed something special. Tommy will forever be remembered for something he may not have even said: 'Kick the ball to Royce Hart and get out of the way!'

As a club we should have been smarter than to let a player with Tim's qualities go. We should have come up with a plan that allowed him the breaks he needed to get rid of the staleness in his system. We owed that to him as a player, as a valued employee.

I'll never forget the meeting where we decided to bring Tim back for the 1993 season. A fair bit had been going on behind the scenes. In 1991, we had come sixth, in 1992, eighth. Some people at the club, without any real official backing, had been interviewing Gary Buckenara about him taking over from me as coach. I knew they were, but they didn't know I knew. That's because Gary had told Neville Gay's brother Terry, who was at Hawthorn, that he was going to coach Essendon.

After a Christmas lunch conversation between Neville and Terry that indicated something different, it was suggested that Gary should ring Neville and find out what was really going on. According to Neville, who was then on the board at Essendon, Gary's name had never come up for discussion.

I had also been talking to Sydney again, or their people had been talking to me. I went to Sydney with Geraldine and my solicitor Brian Ward and his wife Leslie. The meeting was with one of the Swans' latest financial backers, the financier Peter Weinert. He was in a partnership that ran the Swans with Craig Kimberly, Mike Willesee and Basil Sellers. We met at his house overlooking Watsons Bay, a very desirable part of Sydney's eastern suburbs. I seem to recall you could see Doyle's seafood restaurant. Peter's wife, Janine, was also present. I have never fully revealed the size of the financial offer made to me during those negotiations. They were big numbers, way beyond anything that Essendon could match.

Again, as a father with a family to support, I was honour-bound to explore the opportunities. This offer from Sydney was carried out in the most professional manner of all the contract discussions I have been involved in. I knew then Sydney would get there in the end! I listened to what Peter had to say. He was an enthusiast for the Swans and there was plenty to like about him, and about the Sydney lifestyle that was on offer.

When I got back to Melbourne, I rang Peter and told him I had decided to stay with Essendon, even if Essendon hadn't fully decided I was staying with them. There still wasn't a final offer on the table but, in the end, we reached an agreement.

If asked what was the key ingredient in our success in 1993, I'd say it was planning for a team that could play on the MCG, our new home ground. It had to be young, it had to be fast, but it had to have some degree of experience in it, too — a few players who, when they walked into the room, well, there was an aura about them. You need that around young people.

I had a plan to get a player like that, ready-made, from the West Coast. His name was Tim Watson. After Tim retired from Essendon he was snapped up by the Eagles, who had by now grown into a very clever — some might say cunning — club. According to Brian Cook, the very successful CEO at

Geelong who was then running the Eagles: 'We saw Essendon as one of the major threats to win the flag in 1991/2/3 and the drafting ensured [last WCE pick] that he could not "return" to Essendon in the short term. There was also the feeling that, after a rest, Tim might like to come to Perth, but that was always a possibility rather than a high probability.'

Watson was, I believe, the only 300-game player ever to be on their books. The West Coast will most likely never produce a 300-game player on its own — the air travel will make sure of that.

I was also aware that there was a bit of a whisper around that Tim might go to St Kilda. The word on the street was: 'He's freshened up, he's had a year off, and all he needs in order to go to Moorabbin is a phone call.'

By now, my contract with Essendon resolved, I had moved on to a fourth president. David Shaw, an AFL life member, had taken over from Ron Evans. We had a meeting, a bit of a brainstorming about the future, the year ahead — David, Roger Hampson and me. It was at the MCG, about the same time as the AFL's annual general meeting. Roger Hampson is a real footy head, a knockabout sort of a general manager. He knew we had to get the team above eighth as soon as possible. If he liked an idea that might achieve that, he was prepared to have a gamble and run with it. He liked the idea he was about to hear.

David Shaw — well, I still didn't really know David Shaw, so I was unsure about his reaction to what I would say next.

As we were looking out over the MCG that day in late 1992, I read out the St Kilda forward line for 1993 — Winmar, Loewe, Harvey, Lockett, Watson. I will never forget the look on David Shaw's face. Tim Watson playing for St Kilda.

We all agreed: we had to get him back. But would he come back and play under me? I was now firmly of the view that you didn't have to kill senior players on the track. The challenge had become keeping them alive, vibrant, fresh. I promised Roger and David that I would get Tim a personal coach to look after him and he would only train once a week and just come and play.

I remember the moment when Tim Watson kicked the last goal in the preliminary final of 1993; Roger looked over and said, 'What an unbelievable decision this has been by the club.'

In the end, it clearly didn't matter why Tim was there or whether he liked me or not. The most important thing was the presence of a great player in and around a team that also included a great bunch of kids. Obviously, because we were such a young side, a lot of players were very nervous going into the grand final. James Hird says his legs were like jelly.

Tim was a very good influence at that time. Going up the race to run through the banner, he was telling a joke. The young blokes couldn't believe it; he was about to go out and play one of the most important games of his life and, instead of being as taut as the top string of a Stradivarius, he was joking around. These are the little things that can make a difference. In 1971, Carwyn James, the wonderful Welsh rugby union coach, sat in a corner of the change rooms writing letters to the folks back in the valleys just before the British Lions went out to play — and beat — New Zealand. That British side is the only one ever to beat the All Blacks in a series. Now *that* was something to write home about!

As for my coaching style, well, in 1993, even after 13 years as a coach, I still wasn't always sure how to get things right, but at least we did the right thing by bringing Tim back. We had righted a wrong. Instead of letting Tim retire, we should have balanced his games out. But everyone is scared to make changes that appear to completely throw out the old ways of doing things. And the norm is that when you have a contracted player, he plays every week.

Well, 1993 was the year we were going to change the rules. I was going to put a player who was in Year 12 at high school in the team: Dustin Fletcher. And I wasn't going to play him every game. In fact, we would even let him play in an important school game ahead of a match for Essendon.

We could afford to take risks — we were 50–1 to win the flag. Those sorts of odds and lack of expectation give you a lot of freedom. Freedom can be dangerously good. I wasn't under pressure to win a flag. All I was being asked to do was build a platform on which to win a flag.

I did the same thing in 2006 when Matthew Lloyd and James Hird were out of action. We whacked in a lot of kids. It was, statistically, our worst year, but philosophically it wasn't. We really trimmed the rosebush — delisted a lot of players — but I've got no doubt the flowers will come out in the next three or four years and some of them will be the rare black roses. One of them will be the smallest player since Bill Hutchison, Alwyn Davey.

The message is simple: when you're not going to win a premiership, plough development time into players and don't get too worried about wins and losses. If you do, you won't coach to the plan of developing the next chance to win a premiership.

Much of the criticism in my last years at Windy Hill was that Essendon missed the finals three times. Peter Jackson, the

CEO, made that comment at the best and fairest night in 2007 while I was away overseas. I could easily have taken offence. I haven't. Peter Jackson's great talent as a CEO is he knows how to collect money. However, he doesn't know how to develop a football team. That's the problem with some people who move out of their own fields of expertise into another area and then express their opinion to a board that also has no expertise in that area.

An example of this is the theory that if you haven't played in the finals for three years, you've got to make a decision to get rid of the coach. John Kennedy would never have got another chance of a premiership at Hawthorn if that was the case. He didn't make the finals for three years after replacing Peter O'Donohue in 1966. In 1967, the Hawks finished tenth, next year they were sixth, the next year fifth, the following year, eighth. In 1971, they won the flag, beating St Kilda in the grand final.

And what about Mark Thompson at Geelong? What a special bond there must have been between Bomber, Geelong president Frank Costa and CEO Brian Cook to work together for eight years, through thick and thin, to get a premiership. The great Leigh Matthews also missed the finals three years in a row at Brisbane.

Peter and other people at Essendon are too serious about 'the brand'. It *is* important, but footy clubs are a bit deeper than a mere brand. If you focus too much on the brand and not enough on the substance beneath it, that creates a problem if you're to take the long-term steps towards winning a premiership. Even at the start of 2007, when I knew I wouldn't be coaching Essendon again, my colleagues and I in the football department still kept applying new ideas to the team. I could have easily picked a team that would win a few more games and might allow me to hang on for a new contract. However, that's the sort of coaching that ruins clubs. I could never let that happen to Essendon.

Most board people don't know how to coach. Peter isn't a coach; he has no experience of coaching, so really he should be leaving the coaching and the planning of a team to coaches. He should stay in management and not make that mistake you see so often in footy clubs — falling in love with the players. Managers, chief executives and marketing managers in football clubs can do that: they keep telling you they need great players so they can market the club, get the brand right.

Don't worry, Peter. If you get a premiership, getting the brand right will take care of itself. You just have to be patient.

A lot of my time at Essendon was spent defending the hard-nosed men and the kids of lesser ability but with a great spirit, the other ingredients you need besides great players to create success. Dean Wallis was a classic case. People in management would say, 'What about Wallis?' I would say, 'Leave him alone. He'll be there when the time is right!'

They would snap back: 'When is that?'

'As soon as possible!'

No one understood what Dean Wallis meant within the football group. His team-mates loved him. He was the bloke who looked out for them when they were out at night. If they were having a quiet drink and someone came up and started to get a bit silly, Dean had this ability to just get that person out of the way without causing any trouble. He was a footballer's footballer: honest on the field, terrific company off it. You don't need a team of sports psychologists when you have a Dean Wallis in the change room: he keeps morale up just by being there. He was a good player, too, better than the management at Essendon thought in 1999 and 2000 when they had factored in their salary cap predictions only a handful of games for Wally. Again, football judgments should be left to football people.

I believe in the John Kennedy and Allan Jeans way of developing teams, teams that can last a while, teams that make people want to support your club. I don't believe in management interfering in that design. When that happens, and whether you've been at the club for 27 years or for 37 years, the cast has just been broken.

To their great credit, in 1993 Roger Hampson and David Shaw didn't interfere in the design — they gave it their strongest support and were rewarded with a premiership.

What a year it was. In 1992 we had lost two retirement players with more than 2000 games' worth of experience. Simon Madden hung up his boots after 378 games. What a great story he is, along with his brother Justin. The Maddens are the only family to have produced two 300-game players. Their school, St Bernard's College in Essendon, produced not only these giant 300-gamers, but a third, Essendon dual premiership player and All-Australian, Garry Foulds. Simon went back to coach St Bernard Old Boys in 2005. He's now the ruck coach at St Kilda. His brother Justin, who left us for Carlton because he didn't think he could fulfil all his ambitions vying for the same spot as his brother, is now a leading politician in Victoria. What a great family.

And speaking of great families, Terry Daniher played his last game at Essendon in 1992, the reserves grand final. Denis Pagan was the coach. Neale Daniher is going to write a book about his family, so I leave greater detail on their life and times at Essendon to him. Terry brought a lot of courage to Windy Hill when, along with Neale, he was traded from South Melbourne for Neville Fields. The Swans hadn't even looked at Neale. We did, and at the other brothers, too, Anthony and Chris. When Terry played his last game in the reserves grand final in 1992, another 313 senior games' worth of experience was lost to retirement.

But we did have Tim Watson coming back! And he had just a bit more speed than Terry and Simon.

The table opposite shows how the year unravelled statistically, but those figures just don't do the real story of a fairytale any justice.

We won the 1993 pre-season cup, beating Richmond pretty comfortably, but you're never really sure what that means. A lot of teams flatter to deceive in the pre-season cup. At least it gave the supporters hope — and the band and the fireworks weren't bad for the 75,000 who went to the game, while another 10,000 were turned away. There was the spark of the Dreamtime Game ... people like watching Essendon and Richmond play. And we grabbed the name from Ainslie Roberts' wonderful book *Echoes of Dreamtime*.

Gavin Wanganeen gave us a little preview of things to come in September by winning the Michael Tuck Medal for best on ground.

We started the home-and-away season slowly enough, losing our first game, then drawing with Carlton. What a game that was for Stephen Kernahan, who lived up to his nickname 'Sticks' by hitting the sticks — the behind post — when everything was set up for him to be the hero for the Blues. Stephen had the ball about 40 metres out, well within his range, but after floating off his boot, it refused to go between any of the bits of woodwork. The game was the highest-scoring draw in history.

Summary of 1993 Season Scores

Round	Score		Versus	Score	Gnd	Result	Marg	Lad Pos	Avg PF	Avg PA	Avg Win	Avg Loss
1	17.8 (110)	vs	West Coast	17.21 (123)	Sub	Lost	-13	9	110.0	123.0		13.0
2	20.12 (132)	vs	Carlton	19.18 (132)	MCG	Drawn	0	12	121.0	127.5		13.0
3	16.13 (109)	vs	Collingwood	21.13 (139)	MCG	Lost	-30	13	117.0	131.3		21.5
4	28.13 (181)	vs	Sydney	14.11 (95)	SCG	WON	86	10	133.0	122.3	86.0	21.5
5	11.15 (81)	vs	Footscray	20.7 (127)	WO	Lost	-46	11	122.6	123.2	86.0	29.7
6	23.18 (156)	vs	Geelong	19.18 (132)	MCG	WON	24	10	128.2	124.7	55.0	29.7
8	19.11 (125)	vs	St Kilda	9.13 (67)	Wav	WON	58	8	127.7	116.4	56.0	29.7
9	16.15 (111)	vs	Adelaide	10.5 (65)	MCG	WON	46	7	125.6	110.0	53.5	29.7
10	19.15 (129)	vs	Fitzroy	19.11 (125)	MCG	WON	4	5	126.0	111.7	43.6	29.7
11	17.14 (116)	vs	Hawthorn	12.14 (86)	Wav	WON	30	3	125.0	109.1	41.3	29.7
12	10.11 (71)	vs	Melbourne	15.15 (105)	MCG	Lost	-34	6	120.1	108.7	41.3	30.8
13	21.15 (141)	vs	Richmond	8.15 (63)	OO	WON	78	4	121.8	104.9	46.6	30.8
14	23.17 (155)	vs	Bris Bears	4.15 (39)	MCG	WON	116	3	124.4	99.8	55.3	30.8
15	13.13 (91)	vs	Nth Melb	19.15 (129)	MCG	Lost	-38	7	122.0	101.9	55.3	32.2
16	12.17 (89)	vs	West Coast	13.9 (87)	MCG	WON	2	6	119.8	100.9	49.3	32.2
17	15.14 (104)	vs	Carlton	12.11 (83)	MCG	WON	21	3	118.8	99.8	46.5	32.2
18	18.15 (123)	vs	Collingwood	7.13 (55)	MCG	WON	68	2	119.1	97.2	48.5	32.2
19	18.9 (117)	vs	Sydney	13.18 (96)	MCG	WON	21	1	118.9	97.1	46.2	32.2
20	14.14 (98)	vs	Footscray	12.13 (85)	MCG	WON	13	1	117.8	96.5	43.6	32.2
21	14.10 (94)	vs	Geelong	19.12 (126)	SS	Lost	-32	2	116.7	98.0	43.6	32.2
QF	14.14 (98)	vs	Carlton	15.10 (100)	MCG	Lost	-2		115.8	98.0	43.6	27.9
*1SF	16.12 (108)	vs	West Coast	11.10 (76)	MCG	WON	32		115.4	97.0	42.8	27.9
PF	17.9 (111)	vs	Adelaide	14.16 (100)	MCG	WON	11		115.2	97.2	40.7	27.9
GF	20.13 (133)	vs	Carlton	13.11 (89)	MCG	WON	44		116.0	96.8	40.9	27.9

*Biggest ever first semi-final crowd involving a non-Victorian club.

Happily for Stephen, he was able to redeem himself a week later, and this time from 50 metres out, against Hawthorn, to give the Blues an upset win right on the siren.

Round 6 was a day out for goal-kickers. Gary Ablett kicked 14 for Geelong, while Paul 'The Fish' Salmon hooked ten for us. The Geelong boys drank a lot of cans on the way home across the Westgate Bridge, helping Gazza celebrate his performance. Significantly, and as a sign of things to come, we were celebrating the win — on the MCG — as much as Paul's fine performance. We won 11 of the next 13 games, and during that period we got Tim Watson back on the paddock.

In Round 16, we played West Coast at the MCG. It was one of those niggling little matches that you're always bound to have when you have both teams coached by grubby little back-pockets from Richmond. I'm talking about me and Mick Malthouse.

Mick is always tough to coach against with his constant references to Confucius, always looking for that inscrutable bit extra to upset the opposing players and the opposing coach's box. This night, he was really upsetting me. Every time we sent our runner Bryan Wood out on to the field, Mick sent his runner out to hear what Brian had to say. It was close right up to the end, when we trailed by four points with only seconds left. Paul Salmon took a mark and then, bless him, kicked the goal just before the siren.

I was so excited that I ran out of the coach's box before I had time to think and was twirling my coat around my head. Of course, the television cameras caught it and replayed it, and replayed it, and replayed it. You can still find it on YouTube.

I felt a bit of a goose afterwards, the more so when my mother Irene told me she thought I looked stupid. A bit like the

226

1990 Grand Final, I tried to forget about the whole incident but then, when the Eagles and the Bombers played each other over the next few seasons, and supporters of both sides started twirling their coats and scarves, I became more relaxed about that night. It had become a symbol of a new rivalry in Australian football, Essendon versus West Coast. And of a new connection between the East and West of Australia: people on both sides of the Nullarbor relate to it.

It had also become a bit of a symbol for me, so much so that when I came to get a logo done for my business cards, it included a little caricature of me spinning a coat over my head. And of course, when we got to Subiaco in September 2007, the twirling of more coats and scarves formed a big part of that generous farewell to James Hird and me.

The week after we beat West Coast in 1993, we turned in what I think was one of our better performances of the year — again at the MCG, this time against Collingwood. The decision to build a team that could play at our new home ground was proven to be as good as the one that brought Tim Watson back to Windy Hill.

It was a dark and stormy night, but more than 87,000 people still turned up to watch us win 18.15 (123) to 7.13 (55). I think out there in pundit land, that was the moment when the talk started about Essendon, the 50–1 favourites at the start of the season, being a genuine premiership threat.

Just about the worst thing you can do in football is get ahead of yourself. I don't think the players did, but a lot of other people might have and they were all brought crashing back to earth in the final round. We were on the road at Kardinia Park, or Skilled Stadium as it is known these days. Not only did we lose by 32 points; we lost some of our best players to injury — Dustin Fletcher, Joe Misiti, Mark Thompson, Dean Wallis and James Hird. We were probably a bit lucky that the other matches that weekend fell our way and we still ended up as minor premiers. However, just getting to the grand final, let alone winning it, had suddenly become tough indeed.

We went into the first-ever night final at the MCG against second-placed Carlton with a vastly different side to the one that had been picked for the Geelong game. We also had to get used to the change of routine that night games create. You arrive later at the ground, which means you have more time during the day to think about the game. For some people that can be a good thing; for others, they can get too worked up.

In the end, we coped with all that pretty well for a young side. We lost to the Blues by just two points. There was, however, a lot to take out of the game, given that even without our best side, we had still finished close. There was no need to get too pessimistic.

The next game was against the Eagles — sudden death. We regained Hird, Fletcher and Misiti, but Mark Harvey succumbed to injury. Our first half was impressive. We shook the Eagles off our coat-tails nice and early on the way to a 32-point win.

That victory set up one of the finest moments in the history of Australian football. I know there are people who, whenever it is shown on Foxtel, still watch the replay of the second half of the preliminary final against Adelaide not completely convinced we will recover from that 42-point deficit and win.

It was the stirring sort of performance that makes you so proud to be associated with the group of young people who pulled it off. The self-belief required was absolutely phenomenal, the commitment by the players to their team-mates extraordinary. Nothing is impossible when you work as a team. Whatever it was that we had in that game, you'd love to be able to put it in a bottle and open it up time and time again. The comeback in the 1984 Grand Final had been sensational, but I think for sheer audacity, this pipped even that moment. How dare we believe we could still win when we were 42 points down at half-time?

The headline in *The Age* said we had done a Lazarus. He was a great motivator, the bloke who helped Lazarus, but I doubt that 'take up thy bed and walk' would work on a footy team. In fact, when you look back at all the great comebacks, it's hard to find one ingredient to explain them all.

Probably the greatest comeback was by Carlton in the 1970 Grand Final. The Blues trailed Collingwood by 44 points at half-time — and it should have been a lot more, except the Magpies weren't kicking straight. At half-time, Ron Barassi gave his players one of his more impassioned speeches, in which he encouraged them to 'handball, handball, handball!'. However, it had to be more than that: they sparked a 'Lazarus on steroids fight back', something Ron talked about in my book *The 500 Club*.

'At Carlton, I had taken up the Len Smith doctrine of the running game,' Ron wrote.

This emanates from Len Smith's famous notes on how he felt the game should be played. He also talked about the theoretical quick goal … take the tap at the centre bounce, kick it forward, but no mark. He felt a tap would be quicker than a handball, and the next thing, you're kicking a goal. That would take probably eight seconds, so that was his ideal way of playing football. You could, theoretically, kick seven goals a minute.

Yes, I did say to the players they had to handball, but we talked about a lot of other things as well. It was mentioned to them what had occurred at half-time some seven weeks before in a match against Hawthorn, where we hadn't been going so very well. On that day, the players had been told when they went out to play that if they didn't handball, they would be taken off. That was a big threat — particularly in those days when you couldn't replace players if you took them off, but it wasn't an idle threat. Idle threats are useless. When I went to the players at quarter-time we were five goals down and they probably expected a blast, but they didn't get one because they were trying. They had been a bit rusty, some passes had gone astray and I said 'just keep at this thing, it will work'. Now, we won that game by eight goals, so we kicked 13 more goals than them in three quarters.

In the grand final, at half-time, I said to the players, 'If we could get 13 in three quarters, why can't we get eight in two?' We made some positional changes, too, putting on Teddy Hopkins, and he was just brilliant. That was a risk, too, because in those days when you took someone off, you couldn't send them back on.

There was also a feeling we had a chance because Collingwood was also the 'Colliwobble' team of that time. But the discipline shown by the Carlton players in carrying out these additional plans was just terrific.

After reading my history books, I knew a bit about these 'Colliwobbles'. I had even played in a preliminary final with

Richmond when the Tigers came back from six goals down at half-time to beat Collingwood. I didn't know a lot about the Adelaide-wobbles though.

I guess in Ron's explanation of the fight back in the 1970 Grand Final, you can see some of the necessary ingredients. You have to stick to your plan, just do it better. And you have to try something new. When I first became a coach, the three biggest influences on me were Tom Hafey, John Kennedy and Ron Barassi.

From Tom, I got discipline and the need to have your players fit through hard training sessions. From John Kennedy came the knowledge you had to be physical in the way you played the game. You also had to develop a team to win by having a group of young people coming through together. From Barassi, I learned not to be frightened of trying something different.

In 1984, in the grand final against Hawthorn, we had thrown players forward like Billy Duckworth. But we had also engendered in the players a sense of self-belief, as well as the belief that the Hawks were gone. Sometimes you can say all these things and the players don't buy it. Other times — well, who knows why, but they respond.

At half-time in the game against Adelaide, we had to make sure we kept up the confidence of the players, rather than give them a blast of criticism. We knew we were the better side; we *had* been all year. I had become pretty determined we weren't going to let this game get away, for a lot of reasons.

One: I hate losing preliminary finals.

Two: as the Crows took control of the second quarter, their coach, Graham Cornes, began sitting in his coach's box with his feet up on the table.

Some of the Crows were smiling and laughing, obviously thinking: 'How easy is *this*?' That infuriated me. Other teams can always beat Essendon; that's part of football. But they should never show disrespect to our club, and not in such a blatant way from the opposition coach.

I walked among the players, speaking quietly to them all. I reminded them about this great journey they were taking in football. I said how at times it could be easy, while at others they really would have to dig deep, deeper than they even knew they could.

I said that it was that time now; time to find something in themselves that was really special, that would set them apart for the rest of their lives.

I went to Tim Watson. When people ask me about my relationship with Tim, I just smile and say: 'Sometimes you fall in love with players.' I know I said executives shouldn't do it, and coaches shouldn't either. But sometimes you do. Tim's a fascinating character, a man I really like despite the differences we've had over the years. He wrote a book about me. I must get around to reading it one day!

I said to Tim in the quiet of the half-time dressing room, deep in the bowels of the MCG: 'Is this how you want it all to end, Tim? Do you want your whole career to end like this? This might be the last match in your last season, your last 60 minutes of football. Do you want to go out there and end it all? Do you want to look back on your career and know that it ended in defeat — that you never played in one last grand final you should have been in?'

Even after 27 years as a coach, I'm not sure just what are the right and wrong ways to do things. But there must have been a real chemistry between the coach and the players that day because the rest is a glorious piece of black and red history.

Tim kicked the final goal of the match. He got his one last grand final — and we won it.

After all the excitement of the preliminary final, the grand final turned out to be a bit of an anticlimax in terms of the score line. We won pretty comfortably in the end, but the finish of the match was just magnificent. Gavin Wanganeen, one of the first back men in the modern era to win a Brownlow Medal, and the first Aboriginal, kicked the final goal of the game. Often when you win the Brownlow, your grand final preparations get blown away. Gavin never missed a beat in front of 92,862 people.

The game went well for us. Michael Long did his Pele thing, weaving through Carlton defenders like a New York taxi driver through traffic to kick the sort of goal that sets a team alight. Down back, things were nice and tight. Mark Thompson was showing the leadership you want from your captain, taking Fraser Brown right out of the game. Gary O'Donnell was playing the game of his life after missing out on premierships in 1984 and 1985. Mark Harvey was the Rock of Gibraltar at centre-half back. You're never going to completely shut down a player of the class of Greg Williams, but Sean Denham was making him earn every one of his possessions.

Mark Mercuri was doing a super job for us on the half-forward line and James Hird was solid until the last quarter, when he started eyeing off the scoreboard instead of watching the game. I sent the runner out with the clear message that he should keep playing it hard right to the end, or he might find himself on the bench when the final siren went.

As for Longie, he was just running around being Longie. He

got 33 possessions, just about every one of them a little gem. And so the skinny little kid that recruiting officer Noel Judkins had first identified as a potential champion over in Adelaide won the Norm Smith Medal in the United Nations' Year of Indigenous People. Not even Shane Warne's scriptwriter during the 2006/07 Ashes series could have come up with this sort of stuff: he didn't let us down. Who would ever have believed that Michael Long, the shyest person in the world when he came to Essendon, would appear on stage in 2008, singing in an opera? Life's a rich journey if you want it to be.

In 1993, Mark Thompson became a premiership captain as well as a premiership player, setting himself up for the final accolade, premiership coach, 14 years later.

The list of honours we accumulated for the year included the night premiership, the Michael Tuck Medal, the minor premiership, the day flag, the Brownlow Medal and the Norm Smith Medal. We had Mark Harvey and Gavin Wanganeen in the All-Australian side and I was honoured to be named as the All-Australian Coach.

As for Tim Watson, he was named Father of the Year! Though not for teaching young Jobe how to kick. Jobe is a terrific young footballer who has an amazing capacity to find the ball. As he worked on improving his kicking skills, whenever I saw Tim I would say to him: 'Why didn't you do more kick-to-kick work with him in the backyard when he was young?' I hope Jobe Watson gets the chance to become a premiership player like his father. He has worked hard enough to deserve it.

As a coach, I was particularly satisfied by that grand final victory because the opposing coach was David Parkin. I have always admired him, and I always felt challenged by him. I was a tradesman; he was the university-educated man. What he had been taught at university about sports physiology, I had to find out by trial and error. Board members at Essendon would question me about my knowledge of sports science because of what they had heard about David Parkin. That irked me, so I set out to become the best sports physiologist I could, mainly by listening to good fitness people like Peter Power. Peter was just the best person to teach me the things I needed to know. He was also incredibly loyal.

Parkin also brought a whole new language to the game, phrases like 'at the coal face' or 'down the corridor'. He was the innovator's innovator. He was one of the first coaches to break up training into groups. Prior to that, the whole squad trained together. In 1995, he introduced 'empowerment' and 'ownership' into the football dictionary. He gave the players at Carlton greater control over the way they trained and played, even down to crucial issues such as team selection for a grand final. This was delegation without abdication — and then some. It would have taken a lot of courage to go down that path, especially at a club like Carlton. David Parkin has never lacked courage.

He had two eras at Carlton. When we came up against him in 1993, he was a few years into his second stint and pretty much the complete coach. So, winning that grand final against him was a precious personal moment for me. He might claim he has got square over the years, not least in the 1999 preliminary final, but for me just to be considered level with 'The Professor' is an achievement I would be proud of.

Of course, no account of 1993 would be complete without mention of the Derek Kickett story. Everywhere I go in Australia I still get asked: 'Why did you leave Derek out of the side for the grand final after he played every game that year?'

The answer is: 'Blame David Parkin!' I wanted to give him as much as possible to think about in the week leading up to the grand final. A lot of people probably don't realise the amount of work that goes into preparing for *any* game, let alone a grand final. The football department produces files and videos on every player, and they talk about every possible permutation the opposition might try. If you have thought and talked about it before the game, then you have the chance to respond to it more quickly if it actually happens. I really wanted to make David think. I also wanted to try to surprise him. In those first few minutes of a game, if an opponent pulls a surprise, you spend so much time trying to come to grips with it, the rest of the game can slip away from you.

After the last training session before the grand final I named a group of three and a group of four players: only two from each group would play. That meant David had seven players to think about for at least a couple of days, three of whom wouldn't be playing. If he took a hunch and concentrated on the wrong players, then we would have an advantage. These are the things you do in a grand final week. You're after every possible little thing you can get. In the end, the subterfuge probably wasn't necessary. We won pretty easily.

I felt sorry for Derek then, and still do. I have tried to contact him many times since to explain it all to him, but he refuses to talk to me. I doubt there is much more I can do to heal the rift. I just hope people understand that there are decisions that you have to make as a coach that are in the best interests of the team and the club. I also hope there will still be a time when Derek and I can mend our differences, although I doubt it.

That matter aside, 1993 was pretty much the perfect year. You don't get them very often. I told the media after the grand final it was the year the Essendon Football Club stole a premiership, coming eighth the previous year, and after losing so many experienced players.

The big question, though, was all about the infamous premiership hangover. I was of the view we didn't have to have one. I remember saying that early success had come to Royce Hart, Kevin Bartlett and the rest of us at Richmond, so there was no reason why it had to impact negatively on this young Essendon side.

Despite all the assurances, and after another victory in the Ansett Cup Grand Final, we didn't make the finals in 1994, even though it was the year the top eight was introduced. We finished a disappointing tenth. It was Tim Watson's last year. He retired for good this time, and good on him. He has since carved out a wonderful career for himself in the media, and also has a coaching stint at St Kilda to look back on, sandwiched between Stan Alves and Malcolm Blight: some good names there to be part of, even if all three of them got the sack. I'd like to sit down with Tim some time and ask him how those years as coach at Moorabbin changed his thinking about football, about life. I find that a lot of people, when they get to be the senior coach, discover that it's a life-altering experience: that what seemed pretty easy from the outside is a hell of a lot tougher, and lonelier, once you're the person at the top, the person who has to take total responsibility.

There were still good things to come out of the year. James Hird went from being a talented young player to a talented young potential leader of our club.

In 1995, we showed a bit more character. We lost a semi-final to Richmond.

The season to follow was a bitter-sweet one. We narrowly

lost the preliminary final to Sydney, beaten by a Tony Lockett point. But James Hird won the Brownlow Medal, shared with Michael Voss: two of the finest people in footy. Corey McKernan also received 21 votes, but was disqualified after being reported earlier in the year.

A Brownlow Medal is just one of the many awards that have gone James Hird's way. He was a premiership player in 1993, a premiership captain in 2000. He is without doubt the best player I have coached. It was typical James to say, when he got his Brownlow Medal on the Monday night before the grand final, that despite being grateful for the honour he would have preferred to have been playing one more game that season.

I hate losing grand finals — I think I made that pretty obvious in 1983. But losing preliminary finals, and by a point — gee, that's a deep scar, too. It's like getting out in the 90s if you're a cricketer. History remembers grand finalists, even losing grand finalists. We know who Carlton beat in the 1970 Grand Final, who Collingwood beat in 1990 — no, not that old joke again. However, no one remembers teams that lose preliminary finals; well, except at Essendon where we long remember this game.

The SCG was packed to the rafters — 41,731. If nothing else, it was going to be a great night for Australian football in its toughest market.

We got away to a great start, kicking the first four goals. Our second quarter was ordinary, indeed — just two points, while the Swans kicked five goals. They led by two at half-time. You could tell a close one was brewing in the third quarter, especially when we kicked three late goals to trail by one point at the final break. We got the first two goals in the final quarter and looked set to win, even with our growing list of injured players, including Matthew Lloyd, who had ruptured his spleen.

With just three minutes to play, we were two goals up. Sydney kicked a goal through Dale Lewis, then Darren Creswell levelled the scores. With just 18 seconds to go, Tony Lockett took a mark. As he prepared for his kick, the siren went. All he needed to do was kick a point, which he did. It was a gut-wrenching moment.

With so many players injured, I doubt we would have beaten North Melbourne the following week in the grand final. But I would have liked the opportunity to try, even without Lloyd (who was taken from the field straight to hospital), Dean Wallis (hamstring), Sean Denham (back), Gavin Wanganeen (shoulder reconstruction), Darren Bewick (neck) and Damien Hardwick (bruised sternum).

North under Denis Pagan, and with Wayne Carey at centre-half forward and Glenn Archer turning in a monumental performance in the grand final, would have been hard to beat. Thankfully, our performance was considered good enough for me to be reappointed as coach. And if nothing else, well at least Derek Kickett got his chance to play in a grand final — for the Swans.

Adelaide won the next two grand finals under Malcolm Blight, which for Malcolm was icing on a very large cake. One of the best players of his generation, as a coach he had taken Geelong to three grand finals with the simple philosophy of: I don't care how many points they score, we will score more. Sadly, that philosophy didn't quite work on the big day, though it did produce at least one memorable grand final in 1989.

Malcolm had a reputation for being eccentric. He drinks port from a beer glass and sometimes, instead of training, he would send the players to the beach. When he was sacked by St Kilda for apparently behaving erratically, some people, especially those who had worked with him at Geelong and Adelaide, couldn't see what the problem was. He was doing exactly as he did when he took his teams to five grand finals.

I probably have a lot of reasons to thank Malcolm. By being a different sort of Cat — and Bird — he made me look pretty normal. That's because there were a lot of people at Essendon around the time of those Adelaide flags who were not only thinking I had lost the plot, but saying it out loud. There were even people privately campaigning to get on to the board at Windy Hill on the basis that they would get rid of me. In 1997, Brian Donohoe and Lionel Krongold, both good friends and supporters of mine, left the board. They were replaced by Alec Epis, a former player, and Graeme McMahon, my old ruckman from the Prahran premiership days. Graeme, a straight-shooting senior executive with Ansett Airlines, was vice chairman to David Shaw.

11

Seasons of Redemption

I was aware by 1998 that a group of people that included Alec Epis, Tim Watson and Mark Thompson, among a few others, had formed a view that the time had come for me to go. A board member who had played in two premierships, a favourite son and a premiership captain who was now on the staff as an assistant coach — that's a pretty powerful faction within a footy club. I know that Alec was quietly telling his friends that my time was up and he was going to be the man who would ensure that it was. He did, but it took another ten years.

An ambitious man who had long wanted to be chairman of selectors, Alec had never been a fan of mine, pretty much from 1980 when, apparently, he discovered it was my car outside Colin Stubbs's house. The story goes that Alec, who didn't live far from Colin, had been keeping a close eye on just who the club might be talking to as the potential replacement for Barry Davis. When he saw a car he didn't know, he made some phone calls to a few friends who were able to tell him it was mine.

I'm not sure what Alec's original beef was about my appointment. In the mid-1990s, there were a number of criticisms of me being bandied around. One was that after 17 or 18 years I had run out of ideas — that a lot of players who had only known me as their coach were getting tired of the same old stories.

Another claim was that I was never at the club, that I was off attending functions instead of coaching the side. I have always believed that promoting the club and the game was a vital part of my role and I will never apologise for that. I concede now that at that time I could have been a little more organised with the paperwork, particularly working alongside people like Mark Thompson who was absolutely meticulous in his preparations. Sometimes it might not just be enough to have thought about what you might do in the coaching box come match day; you need to have prepared a few notes. It's a balance, really: there are some coaches who are brilliant Monday to Friday but struggle on match day. There are others who are great with magnets, with the off-the-top-of-the head stuff during a game, but whose paperwork leaves a lot to be desired. Probably the most successful coaches are those with the right mix of both skills.

There were a lot of meetings going on, some official, some not so, some around the club, some up among the grapevines which just kept buzzing that I was on the way out. In his book, *Reading the Play*, James Hird described it as the 'most difficult and sensitive period in my 16-year involvement with him', *him* being yours truly. By 1998, when what James called a putsch was set to go, Graeme McMahon was chairman while Hirdie was about six weeks into his captaincy.

Football being football, all this stuff was finding its way to the media. The good ship *Essendon* had sprung more leaks than the *Titanic*. It was getting out of control. Also, by now Peter Jackson was the CEO. He held a meeting with Gary O'Donnell and James in the gym and asked them their views on whether I should remain as coach.

Graeme McMahon was also out and about, sounding people out. He too spoke with James Hird. James wrote in his book that as a newly appointed captain, he didn't feel confident enough to tell those involved to stop the lobbying against me. The position he finally took was that I had coached Essendon footy club well for a long time and he didn't want to hear any more about the matter.

There was another meeting that a lot of people probably don't know about. Graeme McMahon and Neil McKissock, the deputy chairman, had arranged to meet Brian Ward and me at the Hilton Hotel. They had come to give me the news that they didn't think they had the numbers and that my time was up as coach. They outlined the reasons.

I said to Graeme and Neil: 'I know you've got your job to do and I have my job to do, but don't expect me to make your job any bloody easier. I won't be resigning. It's up to you to make the decision and convince the board and the supporters that it's the right one. I don't think you will be able to do that, because you haven't been able to convince me.'

Wardie believes that was a pivotal moment in the whole episode.

Soon after, Graeme McMahon brought the matter to a head. He brought all the main players into a meeting and said: 'Sheedy is the coach. Pull your heads in!'

At the next committee meeting, they went through the usual club business. Then at the end of the night there was a discussion about my future. There are some people who believe that the future of the club coach ought to have been at the top of the agenda, but apparently not then, nor in 2007.

That night, after I had decided I couldn't wait any longer to hear about whether I *still* had a job and turned off my phone, a number of people spoke against me, including, I've been told, Don McKenzie, Kevin Egan and Alec Epis. Alec then moved a motion that I should be replaced. Despite what the others had said, no one seconded the motion, so I was to serve out my contract until the end of 1999. Apparently a lot of people on the committee were reasonably comfortable with that outcome, because they thought 1999 would be my last year, anyway.

James Hird's description — 'the most difficult and sensitive period' — fits with a lot of what I was feeling then. You're trying to do a job, to build a side to win a premiership, to establish your club all over Australia — and back home, people are engaging in serious bouts of negativity. I didn't say too much to people about how I felt at that time. Some of my closest friends would have known that I was hurting a fair bit. But as a coach, with a responsibility to lead your club, you can't let your personal issues get in the way. So, out in public, I just had to get on with the job.

I thank Graeme McMahon for that great show of support, and also James Hird, who wrote in his book: 'We played the preliminary final the next year, 1999, and then two grand finals in a row ... I'd say keeping Sheeds was the right decision.'

I don't hold a grudge against Tim or Mark. When both became senior coaches, I think their view of what I had been trying to do at Essendon changed. But at that time, they probably thought they were supporting a decision in the best interests of their footy club. Despite his involvement in the 'putsch', Mark was allowed to serve out his time at Windy Hill as an assistant coach before moving across to North Melbourne under Denis Pagan and then on to Geelong. Our relationship was a bit wobbly for a while, but I think we got it back on track when I appeared at a fundraising night for Geelong in the Alex Popescu Room at Kardinia Park. There were a range of guest speakers, with the night to finish off with 'Bomber' and me together on the stage. I was running late. As I entered the function, I made a big deal of looking for Mitchell White, who by that time had shifted from the West Coast to Geelong. That got a bit of a laugh to start with. If you watched the body language, 'Bomber' and I were probably leaning away from each other up on the stage. But as the night went on, things lightened up a fair bit. We ended up agreeing that as captain and coach of a premiership team, we had probably spent more time in each other's company than we had with our wives. 'We should probably have a couple of kids,' Mark quipped.

When he went to Geelong, I was keen to see if Mark could be a senior coach. It's not a given, just because you have been a good player and a good assistant coach. I think come 2007 'Bomber' Thompson has passed all the tests, so much so that I was *his* assistant for the Hall of Fame game celebrating 150 years of Australian football. I hope my paperwork was okay, 'Bomber'!

As for Alec Epis, well he would have been a sympathetic ear on the board for Mark and Tim. He was new to the role and probably wanted to create his own identity, to show that he could be as tough in the committee room as he had been as a player alongside the likes of 'Bluey' Shelton in one of the best-ever Essendon backlines.

Thankfully, around this time Brian Donohoe was still doing his bit to keep my stock high with the Essendon public. I had gone to watch a player we were thinking about recruiting, rather than going to the game involving our next opponent, something which coaches are traditionally supposed to do. The *Herald Sun* newspaper in Melbourne made a big deal out of it and called on readers to ring in and vote on which game I should have gone to — the one involving a potential recruit, or the one involving Essendon's next opponents. Using the redial button with great dexterity, Brian was able to achieve an 86–14 vote in favour of the decision to go and watch the new recruit. 'It cost me a few bob, but it was worth it,' he says, whenever that incident comes up for mention.

One of the things that I resolved after the whole blow-up was the issue of organising my diary — I needed to get better at mixing the promotional and coaching aspects of my work. At the recommendation of Brian Ward, I appointed a lifelong friend, Jeanette Curwood, as my personal assistant. Jeanette had worked with Alan Schwab at Richmond and had also been a senior manager with AMP. She has done a great job for me over the past decade or so. I know there are some people who reckon she deserves a premiership medal for her efforts in dealing with my weird requests for statistics or other items before match days, not to mention making my travel arrangements or getting all the memorabilia I promise to people as I travel around the place. Even though I'm no longer coaching, she is still helping me run my business. I believe in saying 'thank you', but I wonder if I've said it often enough to Jeanette? I know she doesn't think I have, so here it is now in black and white, Jeanette: a big THANK YOU.

There's another person I should thank, too, for all her loyal support of me, of the football department and of Essendon Football Club. Her name is Lorna Birney, the football department's administration assistant. I like Lorna for a lot of reasons but mostly because she is highly efficient at her job, and she is Irish, so she understands me.

All over football — sport, probably — there are thousands and thousands of people like Lorna Birney. They work away behind the scenes year in and year out, trying to make sense out of chaos. Outside the club, they get little or no recognition. But without them, our game would cease to exist as we know it today. Thank you, Lorna Birney, and thank you to all the Lornas out there.

In 1998, I passed what to me was a most amazing milestone — Dick Reynolds' record of 416 games as coach of Essendon. He was, quite simply, the King of Windy Hill. Even now, years after his death, you still expect to bump into his ghost as you wander the corridors and laneways around the ground.

Richard Sylvanus Reynolds was more than a footballer at Windy Hill. He was a beacon of hope when times were pretty tough, not unlike Don Bradman during the Depression years. Like his brother Tom, who also played at Essendon, King Richard came from the Woodlands club. He had been knocked back by Carlton before he came to the Bombers. He played his first game for Essendon as an 18-year-old in 1933, the same year that Bradman was battling against England in the Bodyline series. By 1934, when he won the first of three Brownlow Medals, the secretary of Essendon, Frank Reid, was effusing that he was the greatest find of the decade. But which one? He played until 1951, his last game being the grand final the Bombers lost to Geelong. He then stayed on as non-playing coach until 1960, completing 22 years as coach during which he won four premierships, an unbelievable performance.

As great as those achievements are, they are not as great as the man himself. He was humble almost to a fault. When people wanted to talk to him about his genius as a player, he would defer to others, always saying that Bill Hutchison was a better player than he was. The judges of the Champions of Essendon begged to differ. On 30 August 2002, they named Dick Reynolds as the club's greatest ever player, ahead of John Coleman and James Hird, with Hutchison fourth. I am so pleased that Dick got to hear the applause and feel the respect of the club one more time. He died two days later.

I was honoured to be asked to be one of the speakers at his memorial service. When the hearse carrying his coffin made one final lap of Windy Hill, the people broke into a reverential version of the Bombers' theme song. He was, truly, their king.

Dick Reynolds and I were two very different coaches. I once invited him into the coach's box during a game. He said I made more changes in the first ten minutes than he would in a whole match. His advice was to get a second runner before I wore out the first one.

As well as being humble, Dick was a great forgiver, something else that is vital to longevity in football, and particularly coaching. If someone let him down, his attitude was: 'Let's forget about it.' When he retired to the Gold Coast, I would call in whenever I could for a cup of tea and a biscuit. We had the most wonderful conversations about Essendon. As an Essendon supporter, I knew all there was to know about the Dick Reynolds legend before I knew the man himself. Sitting in the same room as one of my heroes, listening to him talking about events at which I had been no more than a spectator, was an enormous thrill. Beating his record that year was a reminder of how privileged I was to be allowed to follow in his giant stud marks at Essendon. The words 'great' and 'legend' can get tossed around like confetti in modern sport. They make a perfect marriage when you put them in the same sentence at 'Dick Reynolds'.

In 1999, we had another close one in a preliminary final, losing to Carlton. It was galling stuff. We had a great team; we should have done more with it. After that game, James Hird came to me and suggested that all the players go to the grand final between Carlton and North Melbourne as a group and watch together the game they all knew in their busted hearts they should have been playing in. That was one of the foundations for what happened the next season.

Another tumultuous experience for me in 1999 was deciding whether to stay on at Essendon or shift to Richmond. I was closer to joining Richmond than many people might believe. Negotiations between my solicitor Brian Ward and Essendon over a new contract had become very difficult. Brian and Graeme McMahon didn't see eye-to-eye on a lot of what I would consider now were small matters. It had become Brian's view that I should go to Richmond, as *The Australian* revealed on 18 August 1999.

> RICHMOND *are believed to have again sounded out one of their favourite sons, Kevin Sheedy, about returning to Punt Road as coach.*
>
> *The approach to Sheedy, understood to have been made through his manager and friend Brian Ward, comes as the Bomber coach is in the middle of delicate negotiations*

with Essendon over a new contract. He has a two-year offer — believed to be worth $500,000 a season — in front of him from the Bombers.

But late yesterday Sheedy had still not signed, fuelling speculation he may be considering the latest offer from the Tigers.

Jeff Gieschen is understood to be on contract to coach Richmond until the end of 2001. But the Tigers may be prepared to pay him out after their disappointing season.

I suddenly found myself being torn in two very different directions. I loved both clubs passionately. I probably wanted to stay at Essendon, but the negotiations between Brian Ward and the club had reached a stalemate. The offer from Richmond was a good one, financially and otherwise. It was the chance, in a lot of people's eyes besides my own, to go 'home'. I think I agonised over what I should do more than just about any other thing in my whole life. Decision time had all but come in the week leading up to the last home-and-away game of the 1999 season. It was at the MCG against Melbourne, a Saturday game.

On the Friday, I had lunch with Michael Duffy, Allan Hird and Brian Donohoe, and told them I was leaving. I now know Michael didn't think I was doing the right thing, but I don't remember him saying a lot at the time. Allan and Brian both tried to talk me out of going. But at that stage, I had pretty much made up my mind — so much so that Brian was arranging for a media conference right after the game the next day. It was going to be across the road at the Hilton Hotel, and I would announce during it my decision to return to Richmond.

Enter Lionel Krongold, another of my very dear and close friends. I had first got to know Lionel when he was a member of the coterie group, the Essendonians. He had then gone on to become a board member and had already played an influential behind-the-scenes part in earlier contract renegotiations, just quietly helping things along here and there. He had also played a significant role in talking me out of going to the Swans back in 1992.

Lionel was even more proactive in 1999.

On the Friday night before that game against Melbourne, I rang him as a courtesy to let him know: 'Tomorrow might be my last game for the Bombers.'

'I don't want to hear that,' he said.

This is how Lionel recalls the events of the next 24 hours, which saw his judicious phone calls and chats manage to change my mind.

'I rang Peter Jackson that Friday night,' Lionel says. 'I told him he had better speak with Graeme McMahon, and that he had better speak with Kevin. On Saturday morning, I got a phone call from Kevin, saying he wanted to come to my home and that he wanted to talk. He told me about the press conference and the announcement that he would be going to Richmond. I asked him why, and how it had come to this, and he told me they had made an offer and what it was. He told me what Essendon had offered him ... they weren't that far apart over a three-year contract, but over a five-year period, they were. I explained to Kevin that, after tax, it wasn't as far apart as he thought it was. I also reminded him of his great love for Essendon, and that he owed it to the club to stay on, especially with the group of young players that was coming through. I said, "I don't think you will get a premiership at Richmond, but you're on the cusp of one at Essendon."'

'I also told him I thought that McMahon and Jackson would come to the party on a new contract. I pointed out that there was a greater surety about his payment from Essendon, which was a very solid club. I wasn't saying that Richmond wasn't a solid club financially, but at least we could be certain about Essendon in that regard. I guess I was trying to plant a seed of doubt in his mind about Richmond's ability to pay. I also asked him to make sure he had one more conversation with the club before the media conference. My son was playing in an Amateurs grand final at Box Hill. I missed the start because of the meeting with Kevin.

'He went straight from my house to the MCG, where he got a message that Jackson and McMahon wanted to speak with him tomorrow morning and that they wanted to do a deal. Kevin was by now so convinced they were serious that the media conference wasn't held and he ended up signing a new contract at Essendon that, I believe, he felt was pretty satisfactory.'

The main thing at Richmond that convinced me their offer was serious was the presence of Leon Daphne. He has been the best person at Richmond for a long time, restructuring the club, working hard to get it back to its glory days. I hope for Leon's sake those days aren't that far away.

There have, in fact, been two occasions when I could have ended up coaching Richmond. The first was when the Tigers were looking for a replacement for Kevin Bartlett. Kevin still hasn't forgiven Richmond for his sacking back in 1991. There was no way I would have seriously considered replacing him, one of my long-time friends. The job then went to Allan Jeans. Allan and I were always looking at the same jobs.

I am extremely grateful to Lionel for what he did that weekend. Over the years, he has been a good friend to me and my family. The son of a Jewish immigrant from Eastern Europe, he has very much become a solid Australian citizen. He is a successful businessman and also a tireless worker in the community.

The story of how he became an Essendon supporter, having come from a family with no footy background, is priceless. He had been a Footscray supporter simply because he had a red, white and blue jumper. That was his logic for picking a team back then. His father had a business associate who played in the Essendon seconds. He offered to take Lionel to the Western Oval to watch the Bombers play the Bulldogs. The deal was: if Essendon won, then Lionel had to become an Essendon supporter and he would get to go to all their games. Essendon won.

I won too with that decision, especially in 1999 when, instead of holding a media conference to announce my departure to Richmond, one was held confirming I would be staying at Essendon. *The Australian* reported on 31 August:

ESSENDON coach Kevin Sheedy revealed yesterday he had fielded lucrative offers from four rival AFL clubs before agreeing to a three-year deal to remain with the Bombers.

Sheedy, who is now destined to join an elite group of four to have coached more than 500 AFL games over 22 seasons, said he came within a whisker of accepting a five-year deal to coach his former club, Richmond.

But after seeking the counsel of his closest friends last weekend, the 51-year-old decided to stay at Windy Hill in a bid to reap the rewards of his recent player rebuilding program.

' ... I've put a fair bit into recruiting and drafting over the last year or two to get back to somewhere near the players we want to run out there every week.'

Sheedy also used yesterday's announcement to launch a stinging attack on club officials who actively campaigned last year for his contract not to be renewed.

Sheedy said it was vital for club success that the senior coach be afforded loyalty and claimed destabilising influences contributed to the Bombers finishing eighth and missing out on the double chance in 1998.

Essendon chairman Graeme McMahon said the club would also move to ensure Sheedy's coaching assistants, who include former Bombers captain Terry Daniher and ex-Fitzroy and Adelaide coach Robert Shaw, were retained.

Every one of us, the head coach and his assistants, were to become very pleased by those decisions. The year of the Sydney Olympics, the first season of the new millennium, turned out to be one of those magical ones, just like 1993, when just about everything we did turned out to be a good decision.

This is how I wrote about it in *The Australian* after the grand final, which came a month earlier that year because of the Olympics.

OTHERS can decide whether the 2000 Essendon team is the best in AFL and VFL history — I believe we have to win the flag again next year before we can lay claim to the title.

What can be said without contradiction is that this team has given its supporters more value than any other in the modern game.

We won the Ansett Cup, lost only one game in the home-and-away series, didn't lose a final, won the premiership and produced the John Coleman Medallist in Matthew Lloyd.

Australia's 900,000 Bombers fans really have a year to celebrate.

I would like to see more of them become club members, as well as supporters. It would be great if our club had 40,000 members, then 50,000.

But you have to thank them, paid up or not, because like the players, coaches and everyone else at Windy Hill, they have had to live with the pain of last year's one-point preliminary final loss to Carlton.

Losing preliminary finals after all the hard work of getting there is bad enough — losing by a point is shattering. Doing it twice in a couple of years — once after the siren — is something that can easily break lesser people than those we are lucky to have at Essendon.

To their credit the boys turned the disappointment of last September into a powerful motivation to win this year.

...

I am happy for them and proud of them. When you get a kick in the guts, sometimes you want to give up. But they didn't — that's something people around Australia should look at.

Our boys had to work hard for redemption, making big sacrifices that impacted on their private lives.

...

People ask me if some moments are more special than others.

When you know every player so intimately, to see them all with premiership medallions is a triumph.

But it must be extra special for James Hird. Not that long ago, people were telling him he might never play again because of a foot injury.

Now he has a second premiership and a Norm Smith Medal to go with his Brownlow. And he has plenty of good football left in him.

Michael Long, the spirit of Windy Hill, has overcome dreadful knee injuries to earn a second premiership. And though plenty were ready to lose faith in Dean Wallis, we didn't — and that was repaid on Saturday.

As for his great mate Johnny Barnes, what a story that is. Last year Barnes was watching the draft on TV, to see if he still had an AFL career. Now he's a premiership player.

So many great thoughts occur at a time like this. You think of all the good people at your club whom you want to thank; the young players who helped through the season but didn't get a game on Saturday, quietly hoping to get their turn next year; the coaching staff and rest of the football department who took last year's loss on the chin and resolved to walk alongside you through the following season; and your family, whose support never wavers.

And you realise how lucky you are to have had the privilege to be involved, for most of your life, in a game which can be both cruel and generous. You hope this win and this great season will help the game grow in Australia.

...

Football has plenty of critics, but let's not lose sight of a few things. The MCG was full with a 96,249 crowd. The grand final was watched around the nation and the world.

And for those who like fairy stories — the yarns which grow into the myths and legends which are the stuff of football — well, we provided them by the truckload this year.

I am proud to have played my part in making them come true.

For the record, John Barnes had been brought back to Essendon from Geelong, the club he had been traded to in 1990. To say the least, Barnsie is an interesting sort of person. He would impose a media ban on himself, but do it while talking to the media, who were dutifully noting down everything he said, both before and after the ban. He can never stop talking. He is also a practical joker and a pest. However, at the time when Geelong was looking to get rid of him as part of a massive cleanout there, he was still a good player of the type we needed, someone who could play in the ruck, then kick a few goals.

But how were we to meld him into the side that, after the 1999 preliminary final, had committed itself to creating a season of redemption? We were lucky that John Barnes was seeking redemption of his own. Geelong lost four grand finals between 1989 and 1995. Barnsie knew that if he was ever going to play in a winning one, it had to be 2000. He came to us as committed as any of the players gutted by the one-point loss to Carlton.

As well as giving young people their chances, I'm a great believer in second chances for older people. In 2001, after John Barnes had retired, we still had a bit of a hole in the ruck while we brought through the talented youngster David Hille. Ruckman are a bit like leg-spinners; they tend to mature a bit later than other players, so you have to be patient. After all, it does take a bit of time to get used to your opponent putting his knee into your ribs 20 or 30 times a match, while at the same time trying to win the ball.

Anyway, I was lying on a beach in Fiji where I was holidaying with my family, pondering the best way to give David Hille some more time to develop. It was one of those moments in life when you can almost see the light bulb come on over the top of your head. I would go fishing.

I rang Jeanette Curwood, who was out on her daily walk around her local suburb, and asked her to get me Paul Salmon's phone number. She hung up, walked around the corner and immediately bumped into 'The Big Fish'.

'Sheeds wants to talk to you,' she said.

When Jeanette got back to her house, she rang me with Paul's number. I got him in his car while he was driving with his wife, Jo. Apparently they couldn't stop laughing to begin with, thinking I was joking.

It was no joke and that's how we got Paul back for the 2002 season, one in which I think he put to rest a lot of ghosts surrounding his unhappy departure from the club to play for Hawthorn. Paul had become disenchanted with Essendon after some supporters had jeered him. Despite his excellent performances with the Hawks, where he played until the 2000 season, in my mind Paul is a true Essendon person. It was wonderful to be able to bring him home.

There have been times since the 2000 premiership when I wondered about the wisdom of bringing Barnsie home. We once had to put him off a bus coming back from a training camp because the players had had enough of his, let's say, organic humour. The bus was still about an hour's drive from Melbourne at the time. I must ask John how he got home that day.

However, during the 2000 season he was magnificent. He has a great leap, making up for the inches that other ruckmen have on him, and he can read the game of football. They weren't quite Billy Goggin and Polly Farmer, but the kids from Cobram, John and Garry Hocking, made an exciting ruck combination at Geelong. Our players learned quickly how to benefit from Barnsie's deft taps the way 'Buddha' Hocking had done.

We only lost one game in 2000, the day of the flood against the Western Bulldogs. It was a sign of things to come as Australian football became dangerously in need of a Noah. The flood, pushing as many people into the one part of the ground as possible, is an ugly thing, but it's not illegal. It can be beaten, but only if you've got a good team. We had one of those in 2000.

We never wanted to get ahead of ourselves, but there was a confidence — never an arrogance — that this was our year.

It wasn't without its traumas, though. Perhaps the most difficult of these was the serious illness that felled James Hird's daughter Stephanie in the week before the preliminary final. I was halfway home in the car, thinking about what the Hird family was going through at the hospital. I knew the doctors would be looking after Stephanie, I knew James would be looking after his wife Tania. Then the thought struck me: who'd be looking after James? I turned the car around on the freeway and went back to the hospital. I don't think we said much, but perhaps words weren't necessary. As a coach, you must never get too close to your players, whether they're the captain and superstar, or the rookie. But that night, I just knew I had to be there with James, *for* James. I made it clear to him that his family came first; that if he didn't want to play in the preliminary final, he didn't have to.

Thankfully, Stephanie made a complete recovery and James made the decision to play in the preliminary final, which we won. Then came the grand final. Who will ever forget the sight of James clutching his Norm Smith Medal and his wife and daughter after the final siren, tears aplenty? A lot of perspective entered his life in that fortnight. Football is everything, but then again, sometimes it isn't.

You'd have to say that 2001 was a disappointing season. We started as we had left off in 2000. In Round 8, we belted Hawthorn, even though we didn't have a full-strength side. If we thought we were invincible, Leigh Matthews, the coach of Brisbane, the man who still hadn't got enough revenge for the 1984 Grand Final, had another take on it when we came to play the Lions. He borrowed a different sort of line from the Arnold Schwarzenegger movie, *The Predator*: 'If it bleeds, you can kill it!'

We were without Michael Long and Dean Wallis for that game, two blokes we really relied upon to impose themselves on the opposition. The Lions won and didn't lose another game that season, including the grand final.

We could still show signs of invincibility, however. In Round 15, we were more than ten goals down at quarter-time against North Melbourne. In the second quarter, they were in front by 69 points. The fact that we came back and won said a lot about the character of our players, though it was a bit of a worry that we could get behind by 69 points. I don't know if we ever actually recovered from that game.

There were other disappointments along the way to the finals, but we still managed to finish on top. At the end of the season we beat Sydney by a point. Steve Alessio kicked a goal after the siren. Now *they* knew how *we* felt in 1996. We then had wins over the West Coast and Collingwood, then beat Richmond and Hawthorn to qualify for the grand final against Brisbane.

James Hird played with an injury in that match. I know he was embarrassed by his performance in that game, when his ability to move the way we know he can was greatly restricted. He shouldn't feel embarrassed, however. Few people have given as much to Essendon as he has over the past two decades.

Grand final week had been highly emotional and that probably had an impact, though it shouldn't have. We already knew it would be John Barnes's last game. Then, on the Monday, Dean Wallis announced he was retiring immediately; that he wouldn't be playing in the grand final.

On Wednesday, Michael Long shredded a hamstring at training, so he couldn't play. The stars that had aligned so sweetly during 2000 were dropping out of the sky all over the place.

Losing a grand final is never easy. This one hurt everyone at the club. It was pretty disappointing to read in the next few days and weeks, however, that Essendon was an under-achieving team and club. Events since have shown the nonsense of that. What other Melbourne-based club has managed a three-year period like we achieved in 1999, 2000 and 2001: a preliminary final, a premiership and then a grand final? The answer is 'none'. Collingwood has lost two grand finals; but until Geelong's victory in 2007, Victorian clubs winning the grand final were a bit thin on the ground.

I think a lot of the critics, some of whom let the fact that they also barracked for Essendon get in the way of their clear thinking, didn't realise just how different a competition the AFL had become. There would right now be a lot of Melbourne clubs who would *love* to under-achieve the way Essendon allegedly did over those three seasons.

12

What Goes Up, Must Come Down

In 2002, we lost to Port Adelaide in a semi-final. We were still a top-eight side, but we had raised the bar of expectations pretty high at Essendon in 2000.

We would have loved to have done better, but by that time Port Adelaide had been in the competition long enough to become a pretty good side. And Port were helped a fair bit in that game by the player we had given them to help get them started, Gavin Wanganeen. Good old Essendon, still helping out the rest of the comp.

Really, though, we had started to reach that situation as a club where you begin to spiral down after a time of a lot of success. It's a time when you know you have to start cutting your losses, get rid of some of the older players who had brought you your success, and then bring in some new ones. That's all pretty good in theory. Managing it is another story altogether. I had seen in 1987 and 1997 how, when you take the rebuilding path and the club isn't as successful as it had been, how administrators and supporters struggle to cope.

A lot of Essendon fans are pretty demanding. They want the ultimate success all the time. That's never going to happen. The draft and the salary cap are there with the theoretical aim that each team will win a premiership every 16 years. There's also the small matter of gravity. What goes up must come down. To win a premiership every seven years, as happened during my time at Essendon, you have to buck the system, even defy gravity. Hawthorn hasn't won a premiership since 1991, while you'd have to go back to 1980 for Richmond's last flag. Geelong went 44 years without a flag. The Bombers had one in 2000. Under the AFL's system, we weren't supposed to have another one until 2016. Under our own record of achievement, we weren't due for another one until at least 2007. However, by about 2002 and 2003, supporters at Windy Hill were already getting pretty restless. They wanted it to be 2000 every year.

It was an impossible dream, even though as a coach you have to accept that in the end you will get measured by your premierships, not your sixths and sevenths. Sometimes, too, you get judged for not making the finals. However, being criticised for missing the finals at Essendon three years in row shouldn't have been the major issue. The major issue should have been: are we getting anywhere towards building for the next premiership?

In 2007, we were on the way back up. We had recruited good young players, we had ten wins and we were climbing away from being a bottom-four side.

However, the Bomber aircraft I was trying to pilot self-destructed around me. When a board loses its nerve and begins interfering with the coach, with the football department, the mould for building a new team has been broken. It may not be fixed for some time.

On Anzac Day in 2008, I watched Essendon get thrashed by Collingwood. The week after, Port Adelaide easily defeated the Bombers. I couldn't help but think that most premierships are won by teams with coaches who have great defensive skills.

After the 2000 premiership, I had been quietly mentally preparing myself to deal with the inevitable years of decline with a sense of grace and understanding for the players who had delivered that success. You just can't wipe out those players who have performed so bravely and loyally for you, for their club and for the supporters.

There's no doubt we had to start trading, and we did. But we weren't helped in that regard by the decision to put Mark Mercuri on a five-year contract. That was one of the biggest mistakes the club made in the post-2000 era. That decision was never run by the football department. I won't say who made the decision. The club did it and we're all part of the club.

In the end, though, that is where a coach starts to lose control of the difficult process of moving out some of the premiership players to refresh the list while keeping the soul of the club. I was trying to present and manage a case of 'Yes, we're going down, but we're going down for the right reasons because we're rebuilding.'

I could have buzzed off in 2002 and said to Essendon, 'Give me a ring if you want me as coach in 2005', after all the tough decisions had been made and implemented. That would have meant that my name wasn't muddied by the results of the seasons of rebuilding.

In 2006, we hit rock bottom, but so did a lot of other clubs who are flying along at the top of the competition now: Geelong, Hawthorn, the Western Bulldogs. The simple fact is that when Essendon went down, went through the rebuilding process, endured some short-term pain for the vital long-term gain, the club couldn't handle it.

There is no doubt in my mind, though, that by 2007 we were over the worst of it. The next year was going to be a good year, with the likes of Paddy Ryder and Alwyn Davey maturing as senior AFL footballers, playing alongside experienced men like Scott Lucas, Dustin Fletcher, Mal Michael and, dare I say it, James Hird and Chris Judd.

Back in 2003 I had embarked on a new path when the AFL asked me if I would help promote the game in America. I set off with David Matthews from the AFL to go and have a look at the USA AFL. I just love saying that: the United States of America Australian Football League.

David and I went to Chicago, New York and California, where we met up with the former Sydney ruckman John Ironmonger who has played a big part in establishing our game on the American west coast.

It was fantastic also to touch base with the thousand or so AFL players in the United States at their annual carnival in Atlanta, Georgia. David and I had a lot of meetings to attend there as well. The first of those was with a mayor from Florida. We sat down with him at 7 am. (Everyone on the east coast of America is on a tight schedule!) David and I were quickly astonished by what we were hearing from this mayor. We couldn't believe that anyone in America could have so much enthusiasm for Australian football. He was going to construct a purpose-built stadium, with the capacity for 30,000 spectators, for cricket and Australian football. We just *had* to ask him, and it was probably me who did: 'Why would an American mayor want to build a ground for cricket and Australian football?'

I can still remember his exact words: 'Because you've got the greatest football game I have ever seen in the world!'

Back in the land of the converted, I had heard that many times. In my wildest dreams up until then, I had never believed I would hear it said with an American accent.

I had been to Florida before. In the 1980s, Essendon and Hawthorn had played an exhibition game at the Joe Robbie Stadium, in Miami, maybe the first planting of the seed that this mayor now wanted to see grow into a huge tree. Essendon had also sent me to DisneyWorld to do a management course. I remembered that Florida wasn't exactly the coldest place on earth, and that there were plenty of opportunities for sports such as swimming, surfing and, of course, tennis and golf. So many of the world's top tennis players and golfers live in Miami. So, why did this mayor think his people would like to play a game that was developed in Melbourne, Australia, to keep cricketers fit in winter?

His answer was: 'They already are.' There was a development league with a strong junior program already in place. Young people in Florida were already playing and enjoying Australian football. He was just going to provide them with a better facility in which to do that.

At the end of this trip, I joined up with my son Sam to do a bit of father/son bonding and to see America together. We watched the Green Bay Packers play — the 'Cheese heads', as they are also known, because of their famous hats shaped like a bit of cheese. The supporters are truly amazing: they turn up to the games in their utes, or 'picks-ups' as they call them, drop the tailgates and have a barbecue before the game. It was like turning up to the MCG for a game before a crowd of around 70,000 people and finding them all out in the parkland around the stadium cooking steaks.

I also saw a marquee with a chandelier and I thought to myself, 'I can't come all this way and not go in there.' It was like a big diamond-shaped star in the sky and, just like the Three Wise Men, I had to follow it.

At that time, Sam perhaps didn't realise just how much his father liked getting out and about and having a good time, meeting new people, learning new things. We were still in the early stages of our father/son bonding process, the first time the two of us were on a major trip together without his mother and his sisters. He was about to embark on a crash course.

Sam said, 'You're not going in there, are you, Dad?'

I said, 'No, Paul Hogan is!'

I walked into the marquee, where there were about 80 people. Up close, the chandelier, my guiding light, my inspiration, was really gleaming. I said to the first person I came across: 'G'day, Kev Sheedy from Australia.'

There was an immediate chorus of people saying, 'Great to have you here!'

Sam and I were in!

It was the best food and wine you could have; the best hospitality possible. There is no doubt that *Crocodile Dundee* was still popular with these Americans. Paul Hogan definitely opened the door for a lot of Australians in the United States.

Sam and I did plenty of other interesting things, including helping to measure the field for the 'Say G'day to LA' game between Sydney and the Kangaroos at UCLA.

On our last days in Los Angeles we thought we would have a good look around Rodeo Drive, do a bit of shopping and stay in the most famous hotel in town, The Beverly Wilshire, where the movie *Pretty Woman* had been filmed. As we were sitting in the restaurant eating our dinner, it was pretty obvious that Sam wasn't really listening to what his dear old dad was trying to get across to him. His eyes were locked on something over my shoulder. Eventually, his eyes wide, he said: 'Don't look now, Dad, but Muhammad Ali is coming towards us.'

Muhammad Ali ... the Greatest! He was walking around the restaurant doing magic tricks for everyone. And do I mean *everyone*. It was a big restaurant, but there he was providing all the diners with a little bit of Ali magic.

I had met Muhammad Ali once before, when he was a guest of the Australian businessman Dick Pratt. But it was all a new and very exciting experience for Sam.

When you meet Muhammad Ali, even these days when he's not in good health, the first thing you notice about him is that he has a charming presence. His eyes speak for him. They are probably the most exciting eyes I have ever seen. When you look at him, you know what he is trying to say, even if his illness makes it hard for him to communicate. Here he was this day, still very much the entertainer, working the room, making people happy. He gave us an autographed photo of himself and moved on.

Then Sam said, 'Dad, do you think he'd mind if I asked him for a photo with me?'

I said 'Son, the only way you're going to get a photo is if you make that decision for yourself. You're going to have to ask him. There are only two things that can happen here: he'll either say "yes" or he'll say "no". Whatever he says, I just want you to have the courage to ask.'

It was a good lesson. Sam went over, asked the question and now has the photo hanging in his room. And it's not just of Ali, but also of his wife. And it's not just three people standing together. The champ grabbed Sam's fist and put it into his face like he was being knocked out by a straight left!

13

Coaching Australia

Following our visit to the United States, I was recharged and excited about what might lie ahead. I wanted to see Essendon be a premiership club again. I was then in my mid-fifties, but in the US I had discovered there were still a lot of things to be learned about football ... and about life.

All this enthusiasm bubbled over, some might say got me into trouble, when I attended the annual AFL coaches conference. One of the speakers from the AFL mentioned that the International Rules series between Australia and Ireland had been a real debacle. International Rules is a mix of Australian and Gaelic football, using a round ball and goal nets.

I couldn't see why, with so many other pressing issues to address, this topic had been brought up at our conference and I said so. No one in the room was involved in the series, I said. I reminded the people from the AFL that they kept appointing people to coach Australia who had never coached. I said it was embarrassing that the AFL had brought this matter up at this conference because it was *their* fault, *their* decision, that had caused all the problems.

'Don't insult us coaches,' I said. 'Lift your own act!'

On this occasion, the AFL listened. It seemed that Mick Malthouse would coach Australia in the next series, but — so the story goes — the Magpies weren't going all that well at the time and Mick had to withdraw. So, the AFL came to me and asked if I could take on the job of Australian coach. I said I could do it, but only if the Essendon board agreed to it. In the 1980s, when Greg Sewell was president, the board members had stopped me coaching the Victorian side because they felt it might take my focus off the Bombers. I could understand that and, as much as I loved coaching my state, I had accepted it. However, I had seen, in rugby league, how someone like Wayne Bennett had been able to coach not just his club, but his state and his country. I knew deep down I would love to be able to coach my country, particularly after having been a player for Australia in a series against Ireland in 1978.

Essendon agreed to my coaching Australia. I then had to put in place the structures I needed to do it successfully. I met with the chairman of the AFL, Ron Evans, and another commissioner, Bill Kelty. I accused Ron of not really being serious about International Rules. He assured me that both he and the AFL *were* serious.

I then put to him a number of things that I believed needed changing. I wanted to sound out Ron and Bill to see their reaction before I put them to Andrew Demetriou, the AFL's CEO, and his football operations manager, Adrian Anderson. I knew that if Ron took them on board first, in that quiet way of his, he would make sure they happened.

We had to have someone who was actually a full-time coach coaching. It ended up being Danny Frawley, who had just left Richmond.

A lot of people who ended up in the Australian camp were of Irish descent — Danny, Kevin Sheahan; passionate people who wanted to get involved because, like me, they appreciated the country from which their forbears had come.

We also had to change the selection process. We had to get rid of the All-Australian team being the basis for the national side for the International Rules. Selection in the All-Australian team was a reward for having an exceptional season playing Australian football. It had nothing to do with picking a team to play a different game called International Rules where speed was more important than having a big ruckman! Gerard Healy reckoned if we got that through the AFL, we were all geniuses. Move over, Einstein.

We made a few other appointments, among them an IT specialist so that, as well as printed documents, we had a lot of information on screen. While I'm not great with computers, I'm well aware of what they can achieve in the coaching box, churning out facts and figures far faster than people can.

I've tried to become more computer literate myself, but with not a lot of success. I remember having to ring Jeanette Curwood one weekend to find out my password. She then got on to the IT person who had helped set up my computer account, who was out doing her weekend shopping. When Jeanette told her what the problem was, they both got to have a laugh at my expense.

'I tried to make it as easy as I could for Kevin,' the kindly IT lady had said. And she had. The easy-to-remember password she had allocated me was … 'password'.

Another important development as we got ready to take on Ireland was the appointment of Jim and Brian Stynes to be our forward scouts, to give us the absolute best report on every Irish player. Basically, we moved all the things that we do at club level on a day-to-day basis into the international sphere.

We also needed to know that the players we were going to pick would be fair dinkum. We wrote a letter to each of them, saying: 'If you want to be considered for selection, you must let us know by the end of July.' The players, and we ended up with somewhere between 100 and 200, had to commit themselves to two years, two series — the same length as my contract to coach Australia.

The turnaround was just amazing. By the time we got to Perth for the first game of the 2005 series, interest was sky-high. The game was a sell-out and it was pretty obvious that we were coaching a group of players who were determined to be a team. Stephen Silvagni, the full-back of the 20th century and a regular performer in International Rules in goal, did a really great job for us in the lead-up when he convinced Dustin Fletcher to play in goal for the Australian side. To be the goalie in this game, you need to be a freak. Dustin was cat-like in front of goal, and he had the courage just to stand there and wait as his opponents sought to kick the round ball straight into him, or through him into the back of the net.

We knew we were going into the series in good shape, because we had picked players who were ready-made for this game. They were players who could have played *any* sport, athletes who had great kicking and passing skills no matter what the shape of the ball. They were also players who could run fast, bounce the ball, draw an opponent, then execute a disposal. For the first time, Australia had picked a team to play

International Rules. And we took the players from wherever we thought we needed them, not just from the All-Australian team. We even picked two players from their clubs' rookie lists — the lightning speed of Andrew Lovett from Essendon and Dale Morris from the Western Bulldogs.

Australia produced its highest score ever in Perth. Despite that resounding performance, ticket sales had been quiet in Melbourne for the second game, but that was about to change.

The AFL asked me if I could ramp things up.

'How high?' I asked. 'Do you want headlines, eight back pages, three back pages? Just let me know the number you want.'

The AFL said, 'If you reckon you can do that, just do it.' At the next pre-match press conference, I told a friend of mine to wait until there was a quiet moment and then ask me how I felt about our game going up against an A-League soccer match involving the Melbourne Victory.

You can see why I'm always suspicious of what goes on at media conferences. That's because I know the sorts of things *I* get up to.

When there was a lull in the proceedings, from the back of the room came the question. 'Nil-all, 1-nil, 1-all ...? Get a *life*,' was my reply.

We got the back pages. We got talk-back radio. Soccer supporters rang up to criticise me. Footy supporters rang up to defend their game. Soon the whole town was talking about round ball footy, International Rules and soccer.

We got a crowd, and so too did the Melbourne Victory. Geoff Miles, their CEO, is a very good friend. We had a chat later about our packed houses, sharing a bottle of champagne to toast our success. He told me a few people in soccer had been upset, but he told them to settle down, that's just the way Kevin Sheedy does things. And so we had it, soccer at one end of the Yarra, footy at the other end. Melbourne will support anything, so long as it's good.

International Rules had become good for Australia. We won both games. The second game wasn't without its moments, especially when Chris Johnson put his elbow out and created the biggest brawl of all time. Nothing like what Chris did had ever happened in Gaelic football. They didn't play their game like that. Chris was suspended, but in his defence, a lot of Irish players had been ankle tackling and raking our players with their feet. I think it's fair to say that as far as our players were concerned, they didn't mind if they were punched, but they took umbrage at being kicked. For Australian footballers, being kicked is a bit like someone coming to your party and knocking over your barbecue. You just don't do it.

We knew the Irish would be waiting for us when we went over there in 2006. And they were, and that was just their media. They have the most enormous press. There would be somewhere between 50 and 70 people at every media conference. Just about every town seemed to have its own newspaper and radio station. The build-up was huge, the tension high. Everyone in Ireland seemed to have heard of Chris Johnson!

The Irish had a new coach; a Ron Barassi type, we were told by Brian Stynes, our forward scout. We had our antenna up for just about anything, but in the first Test in Galway, the Irish still got under our guard, winning the game in the last three or four minutes.

We really had to build ourselves up for the second Test at Croke Park. It was a sell-out. Again, the tension and the expectation were enormous. To win the series, which was decided on aggregates, we had to beat them by more than they beat us at Galway. So, we certainly didn't need Brendan Fevola getting involved in an argument with a barman on the one day off we had on the whole trip.

Up until that ruckus, which led to Brendan being sent home, it had been a pretty good day. We had gone to the races, two bus-loads of us. The tips had been fantastic, and everyone was cashed up when we got to the last race. The final tip was a horse that went into the race somewhere between 15 and 20–1. We weren't all convinced we should back him, but gee, it had already been a good day — so, what the heck, we loaded up.

He was last after 2000 metres, but then he slowly began sneaking around the outside. With 1000 metres to go, he was in the middle of the field, and you could just tell the other horses were starting to falter. They got to the home straight and our tip just took off and won by two lengths. I think the whole grandstand lifted off the ground. So, it was very much a dampener when we discovered that Brendan Fevola wasn't only off the ground, but off the tour.

I was pleased for Fev when, in the 2008 Hall of Fame game, he was named best on the ground, winning the Allen Aylett Medal. I spent a bit of time with him after that match, just reminding him of what he can achieve when he sets his mind to it.

But back in Ireland in 2006, we had to concentrate once more and get down to the business of beating Ireland, and beating them well.

Croke Park was a sell-out, the fulfilment of a dream for people like Harry Beitzel and Ian Law, who had first come up with the idea of International Rules back in the 1960s.

We won — the game and the series — but again, controversy surrounded the match. Daniel Pearce tackled one of the Irish players, their henchman, a bit of a Gaelic version of Leigh Matthews. There was nothing wrong with Daniel's tackle, but the Irishman was knocked unconscious when his head hit the ground and he was taken from the field on a stretcher.

The tension was amazing. There was only a small number of Australians crowded into Croke Park amid all these very angry Irish people. The Windy Hill brawl was nothing compared to this. I had never come across anything like it in my sporting career. There were lots of crisis meetings going on all over the place between Irish and Australian officials, and the series was called off in 2007.

It was back on again in 2008, though, the Irish having agreed to help Australia celebrate 150 years of our game. I didn't think they would be away for too long.

Despite the ruckus just about every time one of our players tackled one of theirs, I really enjoyed my time as Australian coach. It was the best bit of the latter part of my career, which by the start of 2007 was coming to an end at Essendon.

I thought we had started to come up again in 2007. The evidence on the field seemed to be showing that, especially in the middle of the season when, until we were hit by injuries, we looked a good chance of making the final eight. But by now, others had a completely different view of things.

14

The Dismissal

It was during the 2006 finals series that I really sensed I wouldn't be around at Windy Hill after my contract expired at the end of 2007. A senior AFL coach spoke to me about a conversation he had had with Ray Horsburgh, the Essendon chairman. He told me that Ray had said that I wouldn't be coaching the Bombers after my contract ran out. That coach's parting words were something like: 'Trust me, just keep an eye on Ray Horsburgh!'

I was very interested in what this person had to say, because it was very different from the conversations I had been having with Ray about the same time.

Ray had come on to the Essendon board in August 2003. He has a lot of experience in business, if not necessarily in football. He was the CEO of the Smorgon Steel Group, which apparently employs more than 6000 people. If you look at his biography on the Essendon website, he has also been involved in a lot of other important organisations, including the Business Council of Australia. His experience in football as a supporter included helping set up the Diamond Dons Coterie, a supporter group.

The next major indication about my future came in January 2007, when I was having a conversation with Peter Jackson, the Essendon CEO, at Lancemore Hill, a winery and conference centre just out of Kilmore. It was a very hot day and we were sharing a bottle of wine.

Peter asked me how I felt about the way that Glenn McGrath and Shane Warne had retired from Test cricket together, going out at the end of the Ashes series against England. Peter's view was that, as it seemed like it would be James Hird's last year, and as I was coming out of contract in the same year, James and I could go out together. He was probably also thinking that if I were to stay I would ask James to play on in 2008, which was true. Clearly, most people at Essendon in management and board positions thought Hird should retire in 2007. In fact, most of them had wanted him to retire at the end of 2006.

To be fair, Peter was going about things the right way, telling me the truth about his feelings that James and I should go out together. In some ways it wasn't a bad sort of a suggestion, except I didn't agree with it.

Peter and I have disagreed many times in the past. In July 2006, I had been injured at training, struck down by one of the players, Dean Solomon. I managed to coach that weekend, but ended up having to have an operation on my shoulder early the next week. I turned up at training later in the week, sore, but ready to coach, only to be informed that Peter Jackson had held a media conference and announced that Gary O'Donnell would be coach. He had done that without speaking to me. I sat in the coach's box that weekend. Interestingly, the AFL was of the view that I *was* the coach that day, as they counted that match when they celebrated my passing Jock McHale's record 12 months later. That was because I had signed all the match-day sheets as coach.

I knew on that summer's day in Lancemore Hill that Peter had made up his mind that he wouldn't be supporting the continuation of my coaching career at Essendon. That was something my own intuition had been telling me for a while. After being involved in footy clubs for 40 years, watching contracts being negotiated, and negotiating your own, you develop a set of pretty sensitive antennas.

There had been a number of things …

I had been keen to lay the groundwork to get the young Irishman, Martin Clarke, to Essendon. It was going to cost us around $20,000. Peter Jackson had said 'no', the funding wasn't available and the recruiting department was disappointed. We needed an influx of new ideas and new talent. He was on the menu from Gerard Sholly, the person sent by the AFL clubs to Ireland to find out which players might be good enough to play here in Australia. However, we needed an investment in the project. Collingwood won the battle because, when it was put to Eddie McGuire and his board, they said 'yes'.

'Anything to get a better list of players,' was the way Eddie justified the decision.

That was the first 'no'.

There was another clue when we tried to get Neil Balme to the club as manager of the football department. Our team doctors, Bruce Reid and Ian Reynolds, had discussed with me who we thought would be the best person to help us manage our list.

We all came to the same conclusion: it had to be Neil. He was leaving Collingwood where he had been the football manager, he had experience as a coach, and he had also managed a business in South Australia. I thought Neil would be a lot better than Dominic Cato, whom Peter had already appointed to the role, because he was a real football sort of person. Dominic is a wonderful young man who will make it in football, but not as the footy manager. It just takes the right sort of person to do that job and Balmie ticked most of the boxes. This was the biggest no I had ever had in 27 years at Essendon. Well done Geelong.

Neil was interviewed by Peter Jackson and was, I believe, ready to take the job. However, Peter said: 'No, he's not the sort of person I'm looking for.' So Neil went to Geelong, who went on to take out the premiership in 2007!

If Neil had been at Essendon, the club might have been in a really good position to woo back Mark Thompson as my replacement. As it turned out, the club decided not to interview Mark — a premiership player and captain. Instead, Essendon chose to appoint Matthew Knights before the 2007 Grand Final. As I understand it, Mark had been led to believe he would be interviewed after the grand final. As a great servant of the Essendon Football Club, he's entitled to feel disappointed that an interview didn't take place, even though he might never have left Geelong, especially with Neil Balme in his camp.

It was also disappointing that Neale Daniher, another solid Essendon citizen despite all those years at Melbourne, learned that he was out of contention via the media. Either way, they would have been the best two people for the job. That's not being unfair to Matthew Knights, but the Essendon chairman said he wanted Mark Williams or Mark Thompson. I believe Mark Williams was interested in coming but was on contract at Port Adelaide. So, here you had two premiership coaches and a grand final coach. We can only hope that Matthew is the right decision. He's an excellent person and is destined to be a good coach.

Peter making that comment about Neil Balme not being the sort of person he wanted at Essendon marked the start of letting me know what was coming up. He was planning a different sort of set-up at Essendon to the one I felt we needed. Possibly he wanted a younger group of managers, people he thought could better relate to Generation Y. As the CEO, he is entitled to take that view.

In May 2007, Peter and I had another conversation that indicated I would probably not get the votes on the board to stay on as coach. Peter has always told me the truth. I appreciate that, and always felt comfortable with that. Whether he was right or wrong is another issue.

However, Ray Horsburgh was still telling me something different. We had two or three breakfast meetings at the Botanic Hotel, where he told me he thought he could get the votes up and that I should stay on as coach. I had two options to think about then. Is the chairman trying to do what Graeme McMahon and Ron Evans had done in the past, biding his time and hoping to win over the board? Or were things as my senior coach informant had suggested? I just sat and watched and listened.

Interestingly, until July 2007, Ray, Peter and I had never all been in the same room together, so I guess they were all playing off against each other. Peter would have been working to convince the other board members not to back off from the decision to let me go so as to begin the process of renewing the club. Whether Ray was working to rebuild the votes, I don't know. I only hope that is the truth: it concerned me when I was told the final vote was unanimous.

All along, I was probably just celebrating once Balme didn't get the job. I think I realised I had 18 months to go, and that I should enjoy what was left of my time at Essendon. I had to back away from the players, to get out of their minds the idea of Kevin Sheedy staying on.

I also had to give the other coaches a chance to develop themselves, and stand back to see if the full-time assistant coaches O'Donnell, Ayres or Wallis could step up. Matthew Knights was then living in Bendigo as the coach of the Bendigo Bombers. It was pretty similar to David Parkin's experience during his last days at Carlton — seeing who was out there who could take over at Princes Park.

I also had to think about my own future.

The club was trying to work out the next leaders in the playing group, after Peter Jackson had taken them to Japan. I'm not sure that is a successful way to develop leaders. I would rather that money had been spent on getting Clarke and other players from Ireland. It would have been pretty exciting to get a football player of their calibre into the side.

Coaching Australia in the International Rules series against Ireland also hurt my chances of staying on at Essendon. Some people thought that I too should have been in Japan. Coaching Australia was a very important decision for me. It was about learning to coach other young men at a new game, all in a short time, while attempting to revitalise the game of International Rules.

The four matches against Ireland were probably some of the happiest times of my coaching career, particularly when the Bombers were down. I learned an enormous lot about other coaches from other clubs. It was a tremendous experience working with Gerard Healy, Jimmy Stynes, his brother Brian, whom we made forward scout, Robert DiPierdomenico, Stephen Silvagni and Danny Frawley. It sounds like if you weren't Italian or Irish, you wouldn't get into the team! We made Barry Hall and Dustin Fletcher captain in Ireland, while in Australia it was Andrew McLeod and Chris Johnson who were the leaders — two indigenous footballers.

The role was also important to me for another reason. Once you know you can do that at a national level, there is no reason why you can't continue to coach at AFL level.

It was an exciting time. All in all, we had more than 200,000 people attend the games. It was an exciting high for all the young players — well, except for the Irish. Most of the team were Generation Y players. I often wonder why you can't work with Generation Y in your own club, but you can for the national team. I knew, though, that I might have lost some of the players at Essendon because they knew I would have cleared them. This included a few really big names, as we will see very soon.

So, there was a lot of uncertainty around while I was trying to coach Essendon in 2007. It was all being reported in the media, despite Ray Horsburgh banning senior members of the club from talking to the media about my future. Talking to the media *on the record*, at least. (You can never stop all those 'You didn't get this from me, but ...' types of conversations.) I hadn't told anyone about what the senior coach had told me in 2006 apart from a few of my closest friends.

The thing that finally brought everything to a head at Essendon was the sacking of Denis Pagan by Carlton on 22 July 2007. I've had a conversation since then with Denis, in which he joked that he was the one who really cost me my job at Essendon. It seemed that the Blues would sign Michael

Voss, the former Brisbane captain, as coach — and Essendon panicked. There were people at Essendon who wanted Voss as the Bombers' next coach, even though he had no coaching experience. If they were going to get him, they had to move swiftly before Carlton signed him. And again, to be fair, they didn't want to be speaking with him while my future hadn't been decided. So, there was the famous board meeting on Monday, 23 July 2007, where the position of coach was apparently never discussed. Well, that's what Ray Horsburgh told the media straight after the meeting, apparently showing the journalists the agenda, where there was no mention of the coach's position. However, there were so many media people there that Monday night, for what was just a usual training night, I think someone must have let the cat out of the bag.

I was driving out of the car park after giving my coach's report to the board, and the journalists asked me: 'Kevin, how did you go?'

Although my position hadn't been discussed, I said: 'They've given me a ten-year contract!' I was joking, of course, and they all burst out laughing. I drove off into the darkest of nights.

The next day, I got a phone call. Ray and Peter Jackson wanted to meet me. I said to Jeanette Curwood, 'I think this is the biggest meeting I'll ever go to!'

We met at the Sofitel Hotel. Peter said he thought it was a good place to meet, as no one would know us there. It's very much a non-footy hotel. We only spoke for about three or four minutes. I read a report somewhere that we drank a good bottle of wine — a Kennedy's Point sauvignon blanc. Peter and Ray might have, but once they told me the board had voted not to renew my contract, I left. Ray said the board's decision was unanimous. I suppose as chairman, he had to say that, but I know that wasn't right. One person, Daryl Jackson, had voted for me to be retained.

Before I left the meeting, I told Ray and Peter that I wanted to coach until the end of my contract, which I thought was the right thing to do, the loyal thing to do for the fans. I can remember Allan Hird saying to me years ago, 'Whatever happens, don't let a board sack you in the middle of the year, because it causes such disruption in a club.' I thought I could help Essendon avoid some of that disruption if I stayed until the end of my contract and also assisted with getting things ready for the next coach — a seamless takeover.

Nevertheless, it was a pretty tough time. A lot of the players became quite emotional. There were a lot of things being said and written in the media. I tried my best to keep out of them, but you can't always. I still had my media work to do, and everything I said was being forensically analysed to find some clue about how I was feeling. I was disappointed, for sure, but only because I would now never get the chance to coach all the talented young kids I had helped recruit. I never tried to hide that fact. I still don't.

Privately, I was disappointed to learn that a number of people I respected, including some senior journalists, were whispering that I drank too much. I would love to know where that story came from. Nothing could be further from the truth. I drink a lot more tea and coffee than wine, and I don't drink beer at all. However, this issue still came up in discussions when I went for a fireside chat at Melbourne about coaching there.

Maybe people didn't realise I was just focused on enjoying my last 18 months at Essendon. I had been criticised in 2007 for not going to watch a reserves game at Bendigo. Instead,

I was at the Essendon Social Club, having a glass of wine with the members and making notes while watching Collingwood play on television. We were to play them the following week. You don't need to send every selector to a reserves game in Bendigo. We had trained that morning and everyone was going on the one highway. As ever, I was going to go my way — which was to sit down, relax and watch what the other team was going to do to Collingwood. Sometimes sitting and watching matches, whether at the game itself or on television, you see something that you can learn from. Or you might see someone you're prepared to trade for. Some people — board members — don't seem to understand that I was using my time to benefit the club, even if I wasn't at a reserves game.

Additionally, I have some grave concerns about Essendon's partnership with Bendigo. I'm not quite sure if it has worked. Whether it's at the Bendigo end or the Essendon end, I'm not sure, but I don't think it's produced many players. What would be wrong with Essendon having its own team in the VFL, run out of Windy Hill and drawing players from the local district league in the same way Geelong does? Remembering, of course, that in 2007, Geelong won not just the AFL flag, but the VFL flag, too!

As the arguments about the decision not to renew my contract flew around, a player survey was released that indicated the Essendon players weren't happy with me. The trouble with surveys like that is not so much the answers, as the questions. Additionally, I wasn't the only one at Essendon to have been the subject of an unfavourable survey. That one has never been released to the media.

Ray Horsburgh was copping so much of a pounding after the press release that his wife went public to say the decision about my contract wasn't just his, but the whole board's. Mrs Horsburgh was correct.

No doubt Ray himself felt he needed to state his case, too, but in a lot of people's minds he went too far when he said I had become bitter. He then found himself on the back foot again. People who know me know I couldn't ever become bitter about a decision that Essendon had every right to make. I had always known that, sooner or later, the day would come when it would be made. That's why when Peter and Ray told me of the board's decision I wanted to hold a media conference as soon as possible, and said: 'Let's get on with it, so that I can concentrate on coaching.' There were two reasons for that. I think the supporters had a right to know as quickly as possible what was happening at their club. It's too easy in the hurly-burly of football politics to forget about them sometimes.

Additionally, we had a big game against Adelaide coming up that weekend. One we won.

The press conference Peter and I held at Windy Hill was just fantastic. I was asked a lot of questions, including what I thought my greatest achievement was. Looking up into the seats where a few players were sitting, I knew instantly what to say: it was having Adam Ramanauskas back on the field after his battle with cancer. He was a reminder that while we can all take football far too seriously, there are more important things in life, such as health. It had been an absolute privilege to be part of the huge Essendon support crew who, along with some very fine doctors, helped that young man get his health and his life back together. It's in times like those that you find the real spirit of your footy club.

After the media conference, I had a couple of functions to attend, the first at Strathmore footy club, followed by a private function involving the Prahran Football Club. Even though it had been a pretty tumultuous day, to say the least, I thought I should honour those commitments. I'm glad I did. After some pretty serious detective work by James Hird, the players had found out where the Prahran dinner was being held and 12 of them turned up as extra guests, apparently just to make sure their old coach was going okay.

Over the next few days, I picked up that there was a lot of disenchantment among the supporters over my sacking. But a lot of people also agreed with the decision. That, as I'd learned a long time ago, is football.

It all got a bit difficult for the board, however — especially some of the members who hadn't been involved in football all that long — when Michael Voss announced he was no longer looking to become an AFL coach. That put the cat among the pigeons, and not just at Essendon. I think you have to look at your own organisation when those sorts of things happen, when the planning might seem to be getting done on the run. But that was someone else's problem. My role was to coach the Essendon Football Club to the end of my contract and to the best of my ability. After the win over Adelaide, we were still a chance to make the finals, but we lost a few games after that and that hope ended.

We still had a huge crowd at the MCG in Round 21 for what was James Hird's and my last game in Melbourne. It was a surreal occasion: 90,000 people in this great coliseum that had been so much a part of my life for so long. The 'G just seemed to be glistening that afternoon as we tried to respond to the challenge of giving James a winning send-off. However, the Tigers had their own challenge to respond to, that of remaining one of the 'Big Four' Melbourne clubs. Over the years, it has always been Carlton, Collingwood, Essendon and Richmond. But in recent years, the Tigers' performances haven't always matched that reputation.

This night, they won with plenty to spare. Their players, the rest of the club and their supporters were then generous in joining in with the Essendon supporters for a final Melbourne farewell for me and James. You could feel the electricity and the tension of the night, a real piece of football theatre — like the last night of a long-running Broadway show. Instead of Rogers and Hammerstein, it was Hird and Sheedy.

The walk around the MCG, James going in one direction with his wife and children, and me the other way, was a way of saying thanks to all the loyal footy fans who had supported us over our careers. I could just imagine the Hird kids during show-and-tell at school the next week! My wife Gerri was there, too — rock solid as ever — in the members' entrance. It was just like always: 'I'll be here when you get back.' She smiled as I set off on the journey around the boundary. My children were also there. It was wonderful!

Despite the disappointment of the loss, I was determined to savour the moment. Eventually, James and I completed our circuit. It took a long time, but it was wonderful. I can only say 'thank you' to the people who waited right until the end, when there was a presentation from the Richmond Football Club, a jumper signed by all the players honouring my last game against the Tigers.

The other members of the Essendon coaching staff were livid about the performance of their side. It wasn't the way to send off a great player like James Hird. I shared that view. I thought our effort had been deplorable, especially as it was at the MCG in front of our own fan base. Allan Hird was right: getting rid of a coach mid-season creates an erratic performance level. You win one week, you lose the next. You would think that every player would have put their whole heart and soul into this game for James Hird, but it wasn't like that. Driving home, I wondered how to read it. I could cope with losing by a kick, as we would do the next week against West Coast in Perth, but this game against Richmond wasn't that sort of performance. Yes, Allan was right …

At least the big crowd that day would have helped the finances of both Richmond and Essendon, since we share the gate for the Dreamtime games. After 27 years, things like making sure we got a good crowd to help fill the coffers are so ingrained in my thought processes that I can't help but be thinking about them right up until the end, especially as I'm a life member of both these clubs. I really wanted the Tigers back in the top four, and here we had these two suburban clubs attracting approximately 150,000 for our two games in 2007, which was a pleasing sign. I reckoned we'd probably helped the West Coast make a few more bob in the last round too, not that the Eagles ever need much financial help these days. Western Australia is now the most powerful state in Australia. You've only got to sneeze over there and it's gold dust.

The Eagles were also in farewell mode for other reasons that day. They were losing Chris Judd. His manager had told me the year before, at the Spring Racing Carnival, (in the Emirates Airlines marquee) that Judd would probably be coming back to Melbourne. This bit of information had really got me thinking. The conversation took place right in Eddie McGuire's backyard, as Emirates Airlines sponsors Collingwood. Adrian Dodoro and I were there, working, looking for an inkling about whether there was an honest chance that Judd would come back to Melbourne. If that was the case, we needed to get ourselves properly placed to get involved in a deal to bring him to Essendon.

We had a lot of players from Western Australia, so there were plenty to trade. In the 2006 draft we took Scott Gumbleton and Leroy Jetta. I have no hesitation in saying we had all the bases covered for *anyone* wanting to come back from the west — but in particular, Judd.

Even though I won't be involved in the future of Essendon, I still can't help but wonder what a great asset Chris might have been to the club. If I had stayed on as coach, I would have gone all out to get him. With all the young kids around, he would have been the perfect player of experience to have in the mid-field. It fact, it would have been sensational — having the same impact as bringing that other West Coast player, Tim Watson, into the young side of 1993.

To get Chris Judd, we would have had to trade hard, with a bit more than some talented youngsters in the deal. Maybe it would take an established superstar to convince the Eagles to let Judd come to Windy Hill. Matthew Lloyd and I are different sorts of people. He likes everything structured, while I like to try to win games sometimes by simply catching an opponent on the hop, by trying something utterly unexpected such as playing a few players in different positions. I reckon we won two flags with a structured approach to the grand final, and two — 1984 and 1993 — by *not* taking that approach. Anyway, my thinking back in 2007, was moving towards the idea that if we were going to swap a superstar to get Chris Judd, perhaps we could swap Matthew Lloyd. Even now, West Coast still needs a full-forward, so they might have been really interested in the deal.

Going to Perth would have given Matthew the chance to play in his favourite position all the time. He wasn't always happy when I switched him to centre-half forward. It can be a hard thing in a footy club if the captain doesn't agree with what the coach believes is best for the team.

History tells you good trading can also be highly beneficial for the team. When we let Paul Salmon go to Hawthorn, the deal meant we got Paul Barnard and Sean Wellman, who were important players in a premiership. Paul Salmon needed to go to Hawthorn to play in his preferred position in the ruck. At Essendon, I had been playing Peter Somerville there ahead of him. So, everyone benefited from that trade.

Exchanging Lloyd for Judd would have been a bigger call than letting 'The Big Fish' go to Glenferrie Road. It would have been right up there with the Billy Barrot/Ian Stewart swap between Richmond and St Kilda. But I would have had the balls to do it. In fact before being told my contract would not be renewed I had pretty much decided to do it. I'd seen what had happened at Richmond when Alan Schwab and Graeme Richmond were booed for trading Barrot: when Richmond won two premierships, Schwabbie and GR were suddenly geniuses. If a person of lesser strength had been in charge, then perhaps the deal wouldn't have been done, and Richmond might not have won those two flags.

When you look at Lloyd and Judd, their contracts wouldn't have been far apart. They were the marquee players and captains at their club. Essendon would have had to throw in another player and/or draft choice, and I would have done that, just like Carlton did.

The Bombers had to get Judd. He is the best player to have come up for many years. He had the leadership qualities that

Essendon needed, and he's in the right age-group for a five year plan. It wasn't about Sheedy, Lloyd, Carlton, West Coast or Judd; it was simply time that Essendon got a great player back after having lost so many great players. There is a lot of gold in Western Australia and this was a golden nugget opportunity. Essendon was lucky to be on Judd's selection menu. Once again, Carlton won, just like they did with Bradley, just like they did with Justin Madden. Not getting Judd was a huge loss for the Bombers.

When you look at some of the top full-forwards who have been traded, did it really hurt their club that much? We had Kelvin Templeton at Footscray, Lockett and Barry Hall at St Kilda, and Salmon at Essendon. It never seemed to upset those clubs that much to lose a champion full-forward. A deal like this with the Eagles would have helped make it up to the Essendon supporters for the loss of players over the years for which we got little compensation in the way of good players.

- Craig Bradley to Carlton: He committed to the Bombers by signing a Form 4, but football headquarters changed the rules.
- Roger Merrett and Geoff Raines to the Brisbane Bears: The Bears needed players; Essendon needed money.
- Merv Neagle to Sydney: To support the dream of a Swans' premiership one day.
- Greg Anderson to Adelaide: The Crows needed help in their first year.
- Gavin Wanganeen to Port: One of our superstars goes back to Adelaide to start off another franchise.

To top it all off, in the 2006 draft, headquarters changed the rules again. You now don't get to pick two and pick four as your second choice. The second choice now becomes a much later pick. Our choice would have been Joel Selwood, who went to Geelong and won a Rising Star award and a premiership in his first year.

Even if Essendon got Judd, the club was still minus seven in the trading stakes when you look back over the years. Essendon has been too generous to other clubs. It gets worse when you take into account that, at the end of 2007, Essendon let Kepler Bradley go — for nothing. I would never have done that. He's 200 centimetres, just 21 years of age. It took Cameron Mooney, after being cleared after the 1999 premiership he won at North Melbourne, until 2007 to really prove himself as a top-class player. Big men take time. Patience is so important in football.

Kepler Bradley was played in positions in the backline to find out if he was any good there. Clearly, he is a tall half-forward flanker who can run all day but who could also pinch hit in various positions. One day, if he believes in himself, he'll be a very good player like Kevin Walsh and Dean Wallis were. For players like Bradley and their coaches — and the management, and the fans — it's all about tolerance in the first 50 to 100 games!

As an exercise in what might have been, this is the side that Mark Thompson, or Neale Daniher, or whoever else Essendon interviewed, could have put on the field in 2008:

B: Dempsey, Michael, Fletcher
HB: Lovett-Murray, Ryder, McPhee/Welsh
C: Stanton, Judd, Winderlich
HF: Hird (Best and Fairest 2007), Gumbleton, Lovett
F: Davey, Lucas, Neagle
R: Hille, McVeigh, Monfries

Bench: Laycock, Nash, Riemers, Jetta
Emergencies: Bradley, Houli, Slattery

The logic of doing a Judd/Lloyd swap became more overwhelming the more I thought about it, especially if the captain didn't want to play where the coach asked him to. Also, with Judd, Essendon might have a few more chances to win a premiership before the retirement of Dustin Fletcher, Scott Lucas and Mal Michael. If another champion player was included in that mix, particularly a midfielder, with all the young kids coming through, then that chance might be just a bit closer.

I think Geelong showed in 2007 that if you have a good midfield, the rest can fall into place for you. I have a lot of respect for what Cam Mooney achieved in 2007 playing at full-forward for Geelong, but I'm sure he would be the first to admit the service he was getting from the midfield — from Gary Ablett, James Bartel and co. — was an important part of that. Not many 100-goal goal-kickers play in premierships in the year they make the ton.

Essendon has a lot of good young players who could carry out the Mooney role at full-forward if the ball was coming laces out from a Chris Judd-led midfield.

I know that if we had been able to put together a deal to get Chris Judd to Essendon, James Hird would have played another year. He told me that himself. And I'm sure I would have been able to persuade James to have played on for less money, easing any salary cap problems.

James Hird and Chris Judd in the same side! Coaches all around Australia would have been going to bed having nightmares about hearing Denis Cometti saying: 'Hird kicks to Judd who takes the mark, plays on, handpasses back to the running Hird who kicks the goal and hugs the supporter in the front row ... centimetre perfect!'

As it turned out, Essendon didn't have a coach at the time that Judd was making his visits to prospective Melbourne-based clubs. The Bombers' sales pitch was done by a panel including Peter Jackson and Matthew Lloyd. He went on radio in Melbourne to say that all the young West Australians at Windy Hill were up for trade, then had to clarify his statement pretty quickly.

It will be interesting to watch what happens over the next few seasons; how things play out at Essendon and especially at Carlton, the club to which Judd went in the end.

I must admit that, in addition to not being able to coach all the young kids at Essendon, there is one other thing about my departure that saddens me just a little. I had one more board meeting to attend to finish my time at Essendon. It was held during the finals in 2007. Not one person came up to me at that meeting to say 'thanks' for the job I had done coaching Essendon for the past 27 years. To be honest, I don't know why I went to the meeting in the end, though I thought the board might want to discuss some things about the list as part of the hand-over process.

I ate my meal, then after about 20 minutes the board members all got up and started to leave. I thought we could have been a lot more intelligent about things that night. As I write this chapter, in June 2008, I am yet to receive a letter from the Essendon board thanking me for being the coach for close on three decades.

Despite all that, I will always be a very strong supporter of the club. I have friendships and memories that stretch back not just for the 27 years I was coach, but right back to the time when I was a kid in South Yarra barracking for the Bombers, hero-worshipping 'Bluey' Shelton. I'll go to Bombers' matches, and I'll also go to watch Richmond play, and I shall enjoy watching them both without having the pressures of being coach.

I will certainly enjoy the Dreamtime Games between Essendon and Richmond a bit more from the neutral perspective; reflecting on the great contribution that Aboriginal people have made to our game, rather than worrying too much about who's on Matthew Richardson.

And if my mind starts to wander in that direction, I will just have to try and resist the temptation to wonder what the result might have been if Essendon had James Hird and Chris Judd playing together with the Bombers in 2008 — and maybe beyond!

15

Facing the Media

On Wednesday, 25 July 2007, notice went out from Essendon about a media conference at Windy Hill. Word spread around Melbourne like wildfire. I don't think people in the footy world needed to be Einstein to know what was coming.

Even though Ray Horsburgh had denied after the board meeting on the Monday that the coaching position had been on the agenda, a lot of people had seen through that. When the media's on your trail, you've got to be pretty good at deflecting. I don't think at that time Ray was very good at deflecting. So, he said that the position of coach hadn't been discussed and produced a copy of the agenda to prove it.

Apparently the position of coach was raised in general business by Peter Jackson. Some people might think that such an important decision would have its own agenda item, but maybe things had moved too quickly for Essendon. The subject wasn't on the agenda until Denis Pagan, by leaving Carlton, and Michael Voss, by putting his hand up to coach, had put it on.

Anyway, Ray and Peter told me of the decision on the Tuesday. I went to a function that night at the Racing Museum where I danced around the subject pretty delicately. I know a few people there that night reckoned they had worked it out, because apparently I was being pretty philosophical about my coaching future. Generally, though, I thought I did a pretty good job of deflecting. You learn to do that when you've had a bit of experience in footy. You don't have to lie when you get asked a question you don't want to answer. Sometimes you ask a question of your own. Our new prime minister, another Kevin who had a better 07 than me, does that pretty well. Sometimes, you can even change the subject. I know a lot of the media in Melbourne — around Australia, in fact — reckoned they had worked me out over the years, but I can still break even with them, or do even better, most days.

After the racing function, I went to see my solicitor, Brian Ward, and spent a couple of hours chatting with him. He has been a remarkable friend to me over the years, more usually in times of crisis than in the good times. He is an excellent dispenser of wisdom.

I found out during the course of writing this book that Brian had made some notes about our meeting after I left. This is what he wrote in the early hours of 25 July 2007:

Kevin rang me late yesterday afternoon to see if it was OK to call in at about 9.15 pm. He arrived about 10.30 pm.

He told me that Ray Horsburgh and Peter Jackson met with him earlier in the evening and told him that the club would not be offering him another contract. He said that Jackson favoured a press conference on Wednesday,

25 July 2007 because as he put it there would be leaks from the Board ...

We talked about Kevin's situation until about 11.30 pm. We had a cup of tea and I cooked him some crumpets with cheese and chutney as we had done numerous times in the past. Comfort food when comfort was called for.

I reminded Kevin of the time in my office in Round 5 of 1979 when he retired as a player. Graeme Richmond said he was the slowest of Hart, Bartlett and Bourke so he had to go. I remember tears welling up in Kevin's eyes. In a moment he was on to the next phase of his life ... and what a phase it was — 27 years at Essendon after a year and a half working at Richmond.

This time Kevin seems a bit more frail. He asked me how old I thought Norm Smith was when he died. He told me he was 58; two years younger than us. He made the point that we both were lucky to be alive.

He said Jackson wanted him to play the kids and asked what I thought of that. I said it was his business how to coach the team and in my opinion he should coach to win and maybe Essendon could make the finals and then who knows?

Kevin said the club had Adelaide that week and he doubted Essendon would win with its injuries.

We talked about what was wrong with the team. We both agreed it was a lack of pace in the midfield. He gave Jobe Watson as an example, he was too slow and there was nowhere he could play. He told me that Jackson was putting pressure on him to play Watson. He also said his other midfielders were 'one paced' and lacked the acceleration required. His midfielders also lacked the 'hardness' of Chapman and co. at Geelong.

We talked about what's next. He asked me if he should consider coaching again and I said 'yes'. He doubted if he could work for the AFL full-time and thought the media was an obvious choice.

He then talked of further publications. He mentioned a quarterly publication which I called 'The Sheedy Papers' providing his unique insight into the season.

I knew he would be all right. He asked me to think of some dot points to use for the media conference. I said I would call him at 9.30 am in the morning.

An important moment in time.

Brian Ward

25/7/07

Brian made that call at 9.30 am, to give me a lot of commonsense dot points for the media conference. By the time Peter Jackson and I walked into the room at Windy Hill, it seemed like half of Melbourne was there. Certainly most of the football media was along, with more cameras than you'd find in all the duty free shops at Melbourne Airport. It was nice, even if I joked about there being a funeral.

I have transcribed the question time that followed Peter Jackson's confirmation of what they had pretty well guessed anyway: Essendon wouldn't be renewing my contract. I think it captures the flavour of the occasion:

Kevin Sheedy: Any questions?

Q: Do you feel gutted that the board has lost faith in you going forward?

KS: No. The way I sort of run my line of thought is that they have been a great client to myself, the Essendon footy club, and you don't get a 27-year client that often and that is probably the way I have looked at it, giving valued added to the club as well as a coach and I think that is the best way I looked at it. I have been very lucky to have had this opportunity. Peter and I have been discussing it since about probably late January. We discussed it up at the seminar about the 31st of January. We discussed about whether Hirdie and I should really go out at the same time. It is probably similar to the boys in the Test side like Warnie and that. So that was the first discussion we had. The next discussion was probably about in late May and we were in the middle of a few wins and we thought we just have to be careful about how you do it then, because it can affect the team at times. The later you leave it then, the better.

I think I made a comment to most of you I would like to keep coaching for as long as I can. And in the end that's what I have done.

Q: So, you have known for a while …

KS: That probably I would not coach at Essendon next year? Yeah.

Q: Do you feel ready to go?

KS: Do I feel ready to go? When you look at the number of players that we've brought into the team this year … it is very hard when you have won eight and lost eight and are sitting just outside the eight. So, it is a very difficult question to answer. But I think the club has made a decision and you move on. I think the

305

club has been fantastic as a club. You don't often, as I have said in the past, get the chance to coach the team you barracked for. So many people wouldn't get that opportunity. I have had it, so I am very lucky like that.

Q: Kevin, who told you and when was it?

KS: Basically, probably in January. Peter and I just about had that conversation in January.

Q: So you have played the entire year knowing that this would be your last year?

KS: I would say just about that, yeah.

Q: Are you going to coach elsewhere, Kevin?

KS: I will take that on board when it comes up, if it comes up.

Q: Would you have preferred for the club to have waited?

KS: No, I think it is the right time now because there would be four jobs on the market for a start off. And I think this club has got to get on with making the next decision. It is a pretty important decision for the club to make, being in a position of replacing a president, which was last year; replacing a coach, which is this year; and obviously, Peter probably may stay at Essendon for another year or so. We are transferring people in this club and moving on, so from that point of view it is a difficult period. And then obviously James Hird, and you know that Fletcher Lloyd and Lucas are going to go.

Peter Jackson: Did you just sack me?

KS: In other words, I probably did. We have had that discussion.

Q: Do you think this decision was a mistake?

KS: I don't necessarily think it is the correct decision *or* a mistake. It is just one of the difficult decisions in footy. The other guy isn't alive, is he, so from that point of view I am pretty fortunate. I would like to stay alive a lot longer than what Jock McHale did after he left Collingwood, because I think he died within two years. The same with Norm Smith ... so I am probably looking for a bit of health.

PJ: Can I just respond to that? Whether it is the correct decision is hard to answer. Come back here in three to five years. Apparently I won't be here, but come back here in three to five years.

KS: I will be on the board by then. I know you won't be here ... [LAUGHTER].

PJ: I don't know what to say after that. You probably will be, as long as you're not president, that's all. But we don't know. You've got a great man here. We'll probably try and appoint a very good coach. In three years' time we will know if it is right or not.

Q: Half of your life has been spent here. I know you're always up, but you don't seem like this is a big deal?

KS: Well, I don't think it is. It is footy, it is sport. I have spoken at conferences around the world. Two years ago they just couldn't believe that any coach ... in Great Britain, they were flabbergasted you could coach for 25 years. So from that point of view you have to realise, in that moment of time, you are a very fortunate person to be allowed to coach for such a long time at one place. If another opportunity comes up I will look at it if it is right. If it's not, well I have got to plan the next ten years of my life.

PJ: Guys, can I just say: I don't think a lot of people understand what Kevin's like. The best way I can answer is that two weeks ago he broke the record. And I got the whole staff down in the gym to make a big deal about the momentous nature of this record. I asked him to respond and he began to address the players about beating the Western Bulldogs, to the point that everyone started to have a little bit of a giggle and a laugh. To the extent I had to interrupt and tell him, 'This isn't a coach's address, Kevin. It's about you.' 'Well, it's not about me; it's about the club and the team.' We said to him last night, 'This is where it's at.' Well, he said to me this morning: 'Let's get this over and done with, because we have to beat Adelaide.'

I mean, he is an extraordinary person ...

Q: Kevin, do you think it is the 27 years, or the results?

KS: I think more the 27 years than anything else. I think that is an honest, realistic evaluation. Why wouldn't it be? How long do you stay? You see other people move from different sorts of organisations — say, in the press. It is a long time to stay at a club. There is my association with Richmond, and I also love my club Prahran. When you lock up 43 years of my life, you have got to be realistic.

...

Q: You must have had some thought about what you will do next year.

KS: I will be in footy somewhere and enjoying myself. I might be assisting in areas of football. I might be writing. I might have an exciting website! I mean, everything is going that way, isn't it?

Q: Would you like to coach Richmond?

KS: We play them very soon. It will be my last match in Melbourne. I would like to get a big crowd there. So, can I think about that?

Q: Would you entertain the job?

KS: That is a hard call, not only because Terry [Wallace] has got a two-year contract.

...

Q: Have you taken counsel from anyone ... advice, mentors from over the years?

KS: I have had ongoing discussions with a lot of people, the likes of Neville Gay and Brian Donohoe and Lionel Krongold ... former board members of this club. I am actually virtually saying 'thank you' to all the presidents and all the board people that have been in charge of this club in my time. I was allowed to coach Essendon after a very awkward period for the Bombers. You come and go and you'll leave them in better shape. And that is really what the important issue about being a coach is. Some may win a premiership. Some may win more than one. Some don't win any, but have you grown that organisation? That is an important issue to relate with Peter, to you people, and to our fans out there, footy fans in general. That is the big issue: did a person come into your club and make it a better club?

Q: Did you talk to Ron Evans before he passed away about this?

KS: Of course I did.

Q: Was he aware of this situation?

KS: He's nearly planning my exit ... Are you there, pal? I think there was a lot of work done over the past 12 months or so making sure my next period in footy would be very exciting somewhere.

Q: Have you found it difficult to maintain this secret since January?

KS: Well, it is very difficult because you just have to keep your nose down and try to win as many games as you can and get to somewhere near the last three or four or five rounds, and say, 'Look, there's a fair chance Hirdie and I will go out together.'

Q: You were still hoping you would stay?

KS: Well, what do you do if you get to the finals? That's the awkward result. Just imagine if ... Hird and Davey don't go down and we beat Geelong. It is a very difficult position to be in after 27 years ... What is the nicest way to exit?

...

Q: What is your proudest achievement?

KS: He is standing up there, Ramanauskas, the best story in footy this year. What he has gone through ... He is an absolute superstar.

Q: Do you think that the perception of what the media have created around you over these years has been an accurate one?

KS: What, that you don't know who I am?

Q: *Do* we know who you are?

KS: No, and I don't want you to know. We can talk about that when my career is over.

Q: Did the players and assistant coaches know in January?

PJ: No, the players and assistant coaches knew at 10 o'clock this morning.

Q: And what did you say, Kevin?

KS: 'Well, fellas, you'd better get good.' That's what Jack Gibson would say. I just told them that is where the situation is, really. I think a few of the boys had been in other clubs and seen it happen before. Obviously, Gary Ayres has. So, you must move on. We've got training coming up today; we've got to prepare for Adelaide.

Q: Did you decide at the board meeting on Monday night it had to be done this week?

PJ: Yes.

Q: When was Kevin told? Monday night at the board meeting?

PJ: Tuesday.

Q: Who told him?

PJ: Oh, the chairman and I spoke with him.

Q: Is Ray Horsburgh behind this decision, and why isn't he here today?

PJ: Well, we run the club as a board of governance. I am the appointed managing director and spokesman. I suppose it is the same way as Andrew Demetriou fronts the AFL.

Q: But still, symbolically, Kevin has been here 27 years. Would it be an unfair expectation for the chairman to be here, and is he behind the decision?

PJ: He's not behind the decision. There are 11 people on the board and, as I said to you before, it was a vast majority confirmation of the decision and all the board are now united behind it.

Q: Ray Horsburgh wasn't one of those, was he?

PJ: Wasn't one of what?

Q: One of the people supporting the decision, or not?

PJ: Yes.

...

Q: Peter, can I get some clarification here? You said a significant number of people on the board were in agreement. Are you saying it wasn't unanimous? But then the club had a meeting ...

PJ: Some of these things are never unanimous. Cabinet decisions aren't necessarily unanimous. I am telling you, it was the vast, vast majority. It wasn't even close. I am not going to tell you what the numbers were. It wasn't even close.

Q: Was the chairman for Kevin? Did he want him to continue?

PJ: I am not sure what is behind that question.

Q: Was there a vote held on Monday night ...? Did the chairman, Ray Horsburgh, suggest that Kevin continue, or did he not?

PJ: You want to know the chairman's individual vote? I can see it is important to you, so I will tell you the chairman's individual vote was that the contract not be renewed. But that is as far as I am going to say about what individual directors said and I am not going to tell you any more.

Q: Why did you come out and issue a statement saying it wasn't discussed on Monday night when the decision was made on Monday night?

PJ: The decision, the whole matter, wasn't finalised on Monday night. The loop was closed on Tuesday morning and communicated to Kevin. I think it was just an attempt to keep the media at bay. Put that down to learning.

KS: To keep you wolves from the door.

Q: How would you have felt having to fend that off for the next six weeks or so?

KS: That is why we are here today.

PJ: That's exactly right. That's the whole point.

Q: You are an expert in handling the media. Would it be too much even for you?

...

KS: I think it is about the right time. Personally, I think we have waited as long as we could. You could have been another two weeks, but who cares; it doesn't matter. Make the decision and get on with life.

Q: A lot of fans have emailed saying how gutted they are. Did you expect this announcement would provoke that?

KS: I don't know. I get on pretty well with the fans. I am probably a fans sort of footy coach. When I talk to the media it is about talking to the fans, not just the media. You people relay that message, whether it is from me or the board. It is a tough call after 27 years. Some people may feel gutted. I am going to cop a fair bit of that myself coming through my PA. The decision is, let's get the team right over the next six weeks, have a great time playing footy and move on.

Q: The ones that are angry, what do you say to them?

KS: I will just tell them I love them.

Q: Would you like an ongoing role at the club?

KS: No, you can't be here and coaching somewhere else.

Q: Did you discuss with James leaving at the same time?

KS: No, that is a hard call. But Hirdie would probably have said 'no'.

Q: So, he never discussed doing it at the same time?

KS: No, that was between Peter and myself in January.

Q: There's a position going over in the West. Would you consider going over there?

KS: What, as assistant to Mark Harvey? [LAUGHTER] That would be a very hard call, that one. I would have to think about that. Taking orders off Mark Harvey would be very difficult. He would just say, 'You're right' or 'You're not'.

Q: Would you consider moving over there?

KS: Look, you would consider moving if you thought ... We play them in a couple of weeks. I will see Harvs when I get over there. The one thing about the coaches association is that we're trying to get a lot of great young coaches and senior coaches together so that if you get hit over the head with a baseball bat, or you retire, you all look after each other. I think that is important that we get that. Then I have to go back and see Woosha in Round 22. That's going to be exciting. We will zip it over the next sort of month or so. There will be a line in the mud, not the sand — the mud against Hawthorn.

Q: Have you spoken to Denis Pagan at all?

KS: I rang him up and said, 'Denis, how are you doing?' We are heading out to dinner with our wives. That was yesterday morning.

Q: Did you tell him what your future will be?

KS: No, I wasn't going to tell him at the time because he

has had enough disappointments. [LAUGHTER]

Q: You've told us your proudest moment; what is your *least* proudest moment?

KS: Just getting beaten by one kick in finals ... It is just frustrating. We missed two grand finals by a kick and maybe six or seven finals by a kick. When you work all year with a group of people together and get rolled ... I think up in Brisbane, Wanganeen hit the post. There is a lot of effort by boards and CEOs and players and presidents, who give up their lives and a heap of time, and you get beaten by a kick. It is frustrating, but I can't complain about seven grand finals and three preliminary finals.

Q: Is 60 too old to go on coaching? There has been a lot of talk about you and Denis Pagan, and also about John Howard as prime minister?

KS: Well, Johnny won't be prime minister, because he keeps getting older. If I got a job next year, I would enjoy it. It is probably an opportunity for Kevin Sheedy and Essendon to live without each other, to give it a go — and that is exciting, energising.

Q: Were there any tears this morning among the players?

KS: I didn't see any of the players.

Q: You told them, though?

KS: No. Peter told them.

PJ: I spoke with the players this morning, and Kevin will see them at the normal meeting this afternoon.

Q: Talking about a three- to five-year plan, are you suggesting the next coach might have a five-year contract?

PJ: No, I am not suggesting that at all.

KS: I want to hear this one!

PJ: We need to talk to someone with the potential to do that, but we wouldn't offer a five-year contract.

Q: What about people in the football department, people like Doc Reid who have been here as long as Kevin? Does this mean the club has to overhaul the football department?

KS: I think that the whole club has to look at itself.

...

Q: Is the club going to overhaul the football department?

PJ: I wouldn't use that word. A new coach won't come in here and clean everyone out. That just won't happen. We appoint the high performance manager, the fitness people, the conditioning people, the list managers, the doctors and the physios. We had the AFL medical officers in here on Monday talking to us about the drug codes, and they acknowledge we have some of the best medical people in the competition. So, will they feel a bit unusual if Kevin's not around? Well, yeah, probably. Will they think about their own decisions? Yeah, possibly. Have they been here long enough, too long? Will we overhaul them? No, not necessarily. We will take each one on their merits.

Q: Have you been close to pulling the pin before?

KS: I think the one time was going to coach Richmond.

Q: Is this a retirement or a sacking?

KS: To me, it is the finishing of a contract. I am honouring that until Round 22 plus, if we get there. That is the way I look at it. I think this is the beauty of this.

I don't think a lot of people understand that sort of thing ... I am happy that I will actually coach to Round 22 or our last game with the team, and you move on and do whatever you want to do in your life. So, I don't care what you want to call it. As far as I am concerned, I have never asked Essendon for a coaching job — and the fans have got to understand that. They will either offer you a job, or they don't.

Q: How emotional do you think the next six weeks will be for you personally?

KS: Ah, not emotional, no. The job is to coach, to get it done.

Q: Kevin, how are you feeling today?

KS: I didn't realise I had so many friends. It is pretty good. I am pretty good, yeah, pretty good.

...

Q: Peter, thank you for Ray Horsburgh's thoughts. What were your thoughts? You've worked with him for 12 years.

KS: Oh, don't start that.

PJ: I have found this a very difficult process because I have spent so much time with him and I have a lot of admiration for him. Conducting himself the way he is conducting himself today, for example, you just can't help but admire the guy. He has had a more profound impact on this club than anyone else. I have enjoyed the opportunity of working with him for 12 years. He is unique, he is challenging, he is frustrating, he is stimulating — he is all those sorts of things. But at the end of the day, one of the most important things

317

is that he … has got the opportunity for phase three of his footy life. The first two have been fantastic as a Richmond player and an Essendon coach. I personally believe it is time for Kevin to go out on phase three of his football life. And that is what the conversation in January was about.

Q: You told him then that you thought his time was up?

PJ: I think it is important that he sets out on phase three of his life. And I will throw some words back at him. He will talk to the players up there, he will talk to James Hird and say, 'You've got six hours of football left.' Well, I will say to him: 'What's a year or two, Kevin? I mean, you taught me that lesson with your players. Why do you want to hang on for the sake of it if you can go into phase three and phase three could be more exciting than the first two phases? You may not be aware of it right now, just as players aren't when they're playing, but James Hird is going to have his whole life ahead of him after this year. Michael Long had his whole life ahead of him when he retired, and look at the contribution Michael has made.' This bloke can make a bigger and broader contribution to football in the third phase of his life. And I think that is the important thing, so all I did was throw his own advice back to him.

KS: That is dangerous.

…

Q: Peter, as a national football club, Essendon and Kevin have pretty much been synonymous throughout the life of the AFL. How much of a vacuum is he going to leave in terms of the Essendon name, the brand

The best player I ever coached … James Hird. When you're coaching legendary players you almost end up having some sort of bout, if only with their intelligence. Mostly though, we got on pretty well. I am always very thankful for James being the player he was at the club. He could make things happen in a game, just like Tim Watson and Michael Long.

Left: Gerri has a couple of favourite sayings: 'I will be waiting when you get back' and 'No more books from overseas'. It's a bit of a joke between us.

Below: Me in my library. As you can see from the bookshelves, I always come back from overseas with a lot of books.

Left: Daughter Chelsea and me at the Brownlow Medal. I share the Brownlow night with each of my daughters.

Below: Jessica, Renee, Chelsea and Sam Sheedy. The four amigos get on pretty well together and have done well to live with their surname.

Right: Andrew Lovett and James Hird ... two exciting players. And great to see Aboriginal people and non-indigenous people getting on so well ... with AFL footy leading the way.

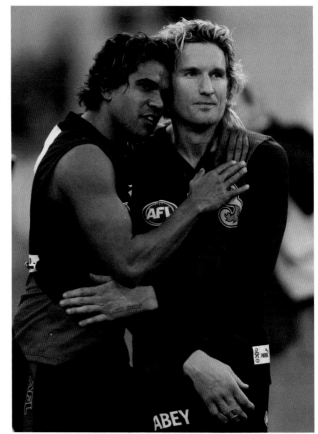

Below: Sometimes you're just thinking about training drills, working out what to do better, so you always need a pen in hand.

Left: The best time in a match is when you have the chance to be pensive ... how can we win the game, how can we keep ahead? You need a lot of thinking time. It's crucial time.

Left: Just cool it guys! It was great to be at ground level on the bench because you get to feel what the players do. Adam Ramanauskas and Mal Michael are the players on the bench.

Above: David Parkin *(left)*, me, Leigh Matthews and Peter Knights out for dinner. I always try to keep Leigh's arms away from me.

Below: A fantastic gift for a record-breaking match after playing for and coaching the only two clubs with sashes in the VFL/AFL. *Inset:* The medal that goes with it.

Above: Peter Jackson on tour in Japan with the Essendon leadership group. Peter was with the new Baby Bombers while I was overseas in Ireland with the Australian team. Probably not a good move politically.

Below: One of the best times of my life, coaching Australia against Ireland. To coach your own country is a dream come true and I don't think people understand how much the players like it, either.

Above: Facing the media in July 2007. It was a fantastic opportunity to be in front of the media throng. This was the biggest crowd I'd ever had to front so I put on a show and had a bit of fun. No one knew that I had known this would happen for 12 months. It probably came a few weeks earlier than I expected it. When Michael Voss put his hand up, the boss went for Voss.

Left: At the media conference at Windy Hill in July 2007. I am looking up to thank my angels ... 27 years ... I was very lucky to have that.

Left: Ray Horsburgh being attacked by the press. Great to see John Coleman taking a mark over Caroline Wilson.

Right: I sidestepped Caroline by sneaking out the back door, leaving all the pressure to Ray.

Above and below: See the Bombers fly up … singing the club song. This was after beating Adelaide. The mood among the board wasn't quite so happy.

Above and below: See the girl *(above right)* on the left hand stick? She's a Tigers' girl. A Tiger and a Bomber, you couldn't have it any better way. The forgotten heroes in football clubs are the people who make great banners.

Above: Brian Rogers and me. Brian served me for more than 20 years at Essendon. His ability to concentrate is just so important.

Below: With James Hird at the end of our last game at the MCG; 90,000 people came along ... a fantastic crowd. One wonders whether it was set up that way before the start of the season.

The ghost that hangs over us all, the wonderful Jock McHale. He has been the best coach ever. It was the performance of an absolute superstar to work through the Depression and keep his club together the way he did. He died shortly after finishing up as a coach … I am trying to avoid that.

Left: Andrew Demetriou and me: 'Come on Kevin, come and work for the AFL. We have a job called Ambassador for the 150th year of the game. No, you don't need a holiday, just keep on working.'

Below: Just working out what can be done with footy, player-wise, AFL-wise and in my role as ambassador ... Brendan Gale, head of the Players Association, Andrew Demetriou and me.

Right: In 2008, it was great to get up to Moyston where Tom Wills went to live, and have a kick with the local kids on the AFL and NAB Roadshow.

Below: Me, Aaron Davey and Nathan Buckley just doing a bit of a fun shot for the 150th year.

Above: Entering the AFL Hall of Fame alongside some amazing people. Back row: Des Tuddenham, me, Glen Jakovich, Noel Teasdale, Gavin Brown, Garry Hocking. Front row: Geoff Motley, Alex Jesaulenko and umpire Tom McArthur.

Left: Entering the Australian Football of Fame via a 44-year journey over 1000 games ... with Mike Fitzpatrick, head of the AFL.

— whatever you want to call it — next season and onwards?

PJ: I walked into this club in 1996 after the Boston Consulting Group had done a review of the club, and the board had decided to appoint a CEO. I sat down with the two guys at that time and they said, 'You only have one person in this club who knows anything about marketing, and unfortunately he is the head coach.' He put this club's brand out nationally, there's no argument about that.

KS: What's a marketing manager get in an AFL club?

PJ: Not as much as a head coach.

KS: Okay.

PJ: Not even as much as an assistant coach, sometimes.

KS: See you later, Mark.

PJ: So, I think we have been conscious over the last four or five years that we can't remain totally and utterly dependent on Kevin's brand. Yeah, look, he is still very, very important, but I don't think the football club is dependent on him, on his brand and his own marketing. And you know, Kevin just said a few minutes ago we've got to go our own way a bit, and we will. And part of that is growing up and being independent. He will be a loss in that sense, but I don't think it will be a vacuum.

As we walked out, we got a round of applause from all the journalists. It must have been quite a show.

I understand that Peter was pretty happy I hadn't trashed the brand. I would never have done that, Peter.

319

16

The Class Act from Canberra

James Hird dedicated a chapter to me in his book. It's an honour I am more than happy to repay. James called that chapter 'The Plumber from Prahran'. Thinking about what to call this chapter, I am reminded of a drought relief fundraising night I attended near Geelong in 2007. The MC asked me to do some word associations and listed various incidents and people. When he said 'James Hird', my reply was instant, just one word: 'class'. So, 'The Class Act from Canberra' it is.

James Hird grew up in Canberra, far from the Melbourne suburb he came to represent so brilliantly all over Australia. However, his Essendon pedigree is one of the best. His grandfather was a premiership player, a long-serving club official and a man who helped me to shape my career in coaching. His father, Allan Hird Junior, played four games for Essendon.

James came to Essendon via the draft, November 1990, pick number 79. Back then, I don't believe anyone at Essendon believed we had picked a winner, let alone a premiership winner (twice), a best and fairest winner, Brownlow winner or a Norm

Smith winner. We had selected a kid with raw courage, a bit of an ability to read a game, and a proud Essendon name. How many players walk into their footy club and see a grandstand with their surname on it?

Certainly with that name, he shouldn't have been playing at another club. It's one of the reasons we recruited Joel Reynolds, grandson of Dick, from the little village of Ceres, near Geelong. If Joel was going to have an AFL career, then commonsense demanded he have it at Essendon. Sadly, injury has prevented that from happening, so far.

Injury plenty of times tried to interfere with the career of James Hird. Having spent my two years in the army and served alongside men who had fought in Vietnam, I always use the word 'courage' cautiously in the context of sport. However, as well as displaying class, James has shown an enormous amount of courage — both on the field, and off it — when fighting to come back from any number of serious injuries. There can't be too many bits of his body that, at some time, haven't been damaged, bruised or broken. When it came to contesting the ball, he was fearless. In that way, he made my job as coach much easier because I could point him out to other players and say, 'That's what you've got to do if you want to succeed at this level.'

I have also long admired James's commitment to having a life outside of football. He completed a degree in civil engineering at RMIT, and he is one of the most dedicated husbands and fathers you will ever meet. All of that has allowed him to keep his football in perspective, especially when first his daughter Stephanie and then his son Tom fell ill.

In the end, it was a pretty simple decision to make James captain of Essendon, a position he took over from Gary

O'Donnell in 1998. James is a natural leader on the field, the sort of bloke whose lead you want the other players to follow.

However, it was what he came to do off the field that really set him apart, especially after we lost the preliminary final to Carlton in 1999. He suggested that all the team attend the grand final. He wanted that moment to be the start of season 2000 for us, sitting and watching together a game we all knew we should have been playing in.

You can't coach that. That's instinctive.

That's one of the great joys of my near 20-year working relationship with James Hird, treading that fine line between coaching someone with class, and just letting them do what comes naturally. I had watched the way Tom Hafey had dealt with people like Royce Hart and Kevin Bartlett. By the time they had become champions, there wasn't a lot Tom could teach them about football. It was much the same with James. When he was playing at his best, well, no one could coach that. He was out there on a different level to everybody else, and up in the coach's box I had to be careful not to become a spectator.

Sometimes I might give James a technical hint here and there, but generally, he was the sort of player you'd leave alone, fully confident he would give you 100 per cent while at the same time obeying all the team rules, often even setting them. There were times when I would give him a fearful bake in front of the rest of the team. I know that would upset him, but I had to do that just to let the rest of the team know that no one was above criticism. In the end, he accepted that, just as he has come to accept a lot of other things about me.

People have called James and me 'The Odd Couple'. I'm not entirely sure just what they mean by that. I don't think the relationship we have had since 1990 is all that odd. To me, it is pretty much what you would expect between a coach and his genius player who happen to have been born 26 years apart. There are things about which James and I have a pretty solid understanding — football, the importance of football, the importance of a life outside football. We don't live in each other's back pockets. He's too classy for a back-pocket. I tried him at full-back one day on Gary Ablett Senior. It didn't last long. It was on the day Ablett kicked 14 goals and beat six players. I immediately got the feeling James thought this full-back position wasn't for him.

As to be expected, there is also a generation gap. James grew up in Canberra in the 1970s and 1980s; I grew up on the streets of South Yarra in the 1950s and 1960s. Hirdie was just four years old when Elvis Presley died. James could have celebrated his first birthday watching colour television at home. My first sighting of television was of a fuzzy, black-and-white image through a shop window.

I have already said a number of times in this book that I believe James could and should have played on in 2008. After all, he won the best and fairest in 2007, so he was still the best player at Essendon. Most players at Essendon loved playing footy with James Hird. There are times when great players such as Bartlett, Greg Williams and Ian Stewart struggle to pick up their opponent, because Hird is two steps ahead of them. This can always catch champions out. Most team-mates normally put up with the back-up, moving off their opponent to help a champion move to where he thinks the game can be won. They back up the champion in case there is a turnover. The way players move these days, everyone does that, so most of the players would take up the slack for James.

Recent history tells us, though, that it wasn't to be, so we both have to move on to the next phase in our lives. There have been some indications that James would like to coach. There was a theory doing the rounds in 2007 that he would take a year off in 2008, while I would be reappointed as coach for three years. He would come back as an assistant in 2009 and 2010, and then take over from me. Again, recent history tells us that wasn't to be. This theory was proposed by some Sheedy supporters who felt the change-over could have been done differently. That's a lovely thought, but they don't always come to fruition in football.

Some great players don't make it as coaches; others, like Leigh Matthews, Malcolm Blight and Ron Barassi, do — to the extent of winning multiple premierships. None of them played in the back line. Most long-serving coaches come out of defence, but not these three.

I believe James Hird would make an excellent coach. While he was blessed with so much natural talent, he also had to work very hard to get it out of himself, mostly in overcoming injury. That will make him more understanding of people who don't have a lot of talent, but have a lot of dedication and a willingness to learn. As he showed in 1999 after the preliminary final loss to Carlton, he has the ability to find a reason for persisting when times are tough, when people are at their lowest. As for reading the game on match-day: few did it better than James Hird the player. Even when he was injured and sitting in the coach's box, he was always on the button when offering advice about how set-ups should be around stoppages. Now, with rotations, most coaches struggle to know who is who at a stoppage because some are blocking, some are stopping, and that is rotated on the ground. If you have a dumb midfield, you're in trouble; if you don't have a physical midfield, you're in trouble. If you lack speed ... well, forget about it.

In my view, if he does become a coach, James Hird will be shifting the magnets three moves ahead of the bounce of the ball.

As professionals, James and I had to keep a little distance between us at Essendon. In any business or organisation, you can't afford to have your senior people so close that judgments can be impaired by personal relationships. Now that we are both retired, at least from Essendon, I believe our friendship will move into a different dimension. I know I have frustrated James at times with some of the things I have done, or not done, as coach. With those out of the way, we can just be friends, sitting and watching the footy, talking about family, life, whatever we please, whenever we want to.

I shall always vividly recall two moments from his times as a player. One was in 2002, when after that awful collision with Mark McVeigh that literally rearranged his face, in his first game back he was exactly the same James Hird as before — straight into the contest. You can't coach that.

The other moment was when he kicked the winning goal against the West Coast in 2004 after 'the umpire incident' and then ran and hugged a spectator. You can't coach that, either. It had been a horrendous time for James. He had made some ill-judged remarks about umpire Scott McLaren and all hell had broken loose, as it can do in footy in Melbourne. I'd had some private views on the umpiring of 'The Chemist', as I called Scott, but I had never mentioned them to James. What I heard him say that night knocked me off the couch. There I was sitting down to watch *The Footy Show* with a nice glass of red, relaxing, wondering what nonsense Sam Newman would get up to, and next thing Jimbo has spoken and I'm on the floor.

I think, in the end, James got through that with his reputation intact. It was probably up there with my comment back in 1984 about Hawthorn and what they were sniffing; when you say it, it seems harmless enough. Then, all of a sudden, the magnitude gets pretty terrifying.

By hugging that spectator, James Hird revealed his true spirit and character. He would never intentionally do anything to harm his club or his game. Rather, he always wants to embrace both and the good things for which they stand.

Most people think James is stand-offish. In some ways, they are right. He doesn't suffer fools. He is an extremely intelligent young man. He is wary about opening himself up to people, which we all are. But he is also shy. I think a lot of his family have been like that. When you ask Jim to do something, though — to help the community, a school, or someone with an illness — he is never backward in helping.

It would be fair to say that the most important step in his development has been his family. You only have to watch him have a game of footy with his kids. My sister Barbara works at the same school where Jim's kids have gone, and she thinks they are fantastic.

It has always made me smile that Anzac Day was always among James's greatest days at Essendon. If you looked outside his front door in Canberra, there was the War Memorial. The place across the road from James wasn't any ordinary home; it housed memories of Australians at war. Every Anzac Day as a kid he would have witnessed the Dawn Service and heard the playing of 'The Last Post' and worked out pretty early what it all meant. Little wonder he had three Anzac Day medals before he was 30.

I will always be grateful to have had a class act like James Hird as a player and as a friend. He is the best player I ever coached, and is up there with the likes of Kevin Bartlett, Leigh Matthews, Michael Voss, Wayne Carey and Gary Ablett as one of the greatest players in the history of the game. He is also high among the best people I have met in football.

17

In the Long Run

If we apply the same word association game to Michael Long as we did to James Hird, my response would have to be: 'a beautiful person'.

One of the great privileges of being a long-serving coach is that you get to see people develop in all sorts of ways. Gee, have we been lucky with the way Longie has come on. The shy, skinny young kid with the potential to be footy's Pele that we recruited has grown into more than just a great player. He's become a sort of beacon for not just his people, but for Australia.

I've never been able to understand discrimination. When I was a kid, I knew there were people who were different and some of the adults around me didn't like them very much. I eventually learned, and it wasn't all that easy in South Yarra, that we had these other people living in Australia called Aboriginals. As I got older, I found I could get on with many of them pretty well. Most of them seemed to have the same sort of outlook on life as I do. They just wanted to do the best for their families and for their communities. If their skin was a different colour, or they prayed to a different god than I did, that shouldn't matter. If your child needed an operation and the only person who could save him or her was a black Muslim, or a Jewish person, or Japanese, you wouldn't care. So, where is the problem with not caring about a person's race or religion the rest of the time? You don't have to be a white Christian to be a wonderful and kind sort of person. They come in all sorts of packages, as life has shown me many times.

Michael Long is one of the best of those packages. He has endured discrimination and risen above it. That takes a special sort of courage. He has used that courage to challenge a prime minister about what we had to do in Australia to make Aboriginal people feel more a part of our country and what it has to offer. As Michael said, he was going to too many funerals. Too many of his friends from the Northern Territory were dying prematurely. Something had to change. Michael wanted to do what he could to change things. You learn very quickly that you can't change things too quickly in this country, in *any* country. But the longest journey always starts with the first steps.

So Longie walked from Melbourne to Canberra: 650 kilometres. He set off on 21 November 2004. He had the support of a lot of people, both from the Aboriginal and the white communities — and the Essendon Football Club community. A lot of staff members travelled with him on the early part of the walk, attending to his blisters. Some people wanted Michael to call it off when those blisters became pretty painful, but he persisted and with the persistence came even more public support.

He was cheered as he walked through country towns in Victoria. His website garnered him even more support.

Encouraged by this, Michael and a few of the other walkers composed a letter while on the road for the prime minister of the time, John Howard. It's a beautiful letter.

The Hon J.W. Howard
Prime Minister of Australia
Parliament House
Canberra ACT 2060   *December 2004*

Dear Prime Minister
I would like the opportunity for Paul Briggs, John Cusack, Alan Thorpe, Pat Dodson and myself to meet with you, the Prime Minister of this nation, to discuss some of the problems that continue to trouble the indigenous communities of Australia.

If there is one thing I have learned in my years on the sporting field, it's that Australians believe in fair play. I believe that you now have the opportunity to show good sportsmanship by acknowledging that us Aboriginals are important players in the make up of the national team.

As indigenous Australians, we want nothing more than any other Australian citizen wants: a safe place to live, the fair opportunity to work for a decent living and for our children to be guaranteed health, education and a secure future. We ask you to go back to the scoreboard to look at Aboriginal life expectancy and unemployment and to work with us to kick some goals on these issues.

In football, many different teams make up the code. They each have their own identity and traditions. There will always be differences between clubs and this is celebrated and respected. We share a common bond that unites all Australians.

As the first Australians, however, we are unique on the Australian landscape and wish to preserve our identity as such.

As the leader of this country, Prime Minister, you are the only person who can give permission to the Australian people in communities across Australia to embrace us. We believe that the Australian people will follow your example and embrace our culture and concerns when they are guided by the strong leadership that only you and your government can provide.

We all wish to see the appalling conditions of Aboriginal people improve and want to play our role in achieving outcomes through self-determination.

Like our walk to Canberra, we are all on a very long and hard journey, but a journey that we are prepared to overcome and achieve. Prime Minister, we'd like to sit down with you to determine a way forward for our people.
Yours sincerely,

Michael Long

He might be softly spoken, he might be shy, but I learned over a long period of time that Michael Long is a very hard person to say 'no' to. And he is very genuine. I think a lot of other people saw this as the walk went on. He was cheered through the streets of Canberra when he got there. Then he got to meet the prime minister on 2 December.

It hasn't stopped there, though. The Long Walk has grown into a foundation to try to help get things changed in Australia for Aboriginal people by holding events that raise awareness about what Aboriginal people can achieve if given the chance.

Last year I went to a function in Melbourne where there were a whole range of young Aboriginal people who had been given a chance. At the end, a young girl, probably only 11 or 12, got up and played the violin. She was fantastic.

We have got to look at all the ways we can provide young people with opportunities. As Michael says on his website: 'This isn't about Indigenous Australia and White Australia — This is about ALL Australia.'

I have no doubt that what Michael has been doing for Aboriginal people has helped put a lot of their issues out there, especially in the political area. And that's terrific, because I believe that there is in our country a spirit of cooperation, a willingness to listen on both sides.

One of the reasons Australian football has been so successful in building bridges with Aboriginal people is because it has always been a partnership. We provide young Aboriginal men with an opportunity to play in an elite competition and to earn a lot of money. In return, they provide us with a whole new recruiting zone. And what a recruiting zone it is. They play the game in the most artistic way. They are the best disposers of the football.

Recently, with David Matthews from the AFL and Martin Flanagan of *The Age*, I went to the Tiwi Islands, Bathurst and Melville, which are just north of Darwin. Melville is the second-largest island in Australia, after Tasmania, and ahead of Kangaroo Island. I was Michael Long's guest. I enjoyed his hospitality immensely: 'Another cup of tea, Sheeds?'

The visit and, of course, the footy match were full of amazing stats and events from start to finish. There are just 2600 people living on Bathurst and Melville Islands. They share 30 surnames among the whole of that population. About 35 per cent of them play Australian football. There are seven teams playing on the islands. The grand finalists were the Tapalinga Superstars and the Imalu Tigers. This is the club of Michael's family, from Melville Island. About 3000 people turned up to watch the game. Yes, I know I said the population was 2600. Around 500 people flew in from Darwin, or came across on charter boats.

There were so many things to make you smile about the way this game was played. The crowd changes ends with the teams as each quarter finishes. It was just like the John Coleman days at Essendon, when the crowd would use the breaks to go to the end to which he would be kicking.

The goal-posts were wider at one end than at the other.

It seemed there was a rule that there had to be at least one dog on the playing arena throughout the game. When the two teams came on to the ground, there was music, balloons, streamers, lots of kids and, of course, lots of dogs.

I heard one of the best pre-match addresses ever from the coach of the Superstars: 'Be disciplined, but don't be too serious.' Whether they were disciplined or serious, the players were certainly keen. They were back on the field after half-time five minutes before the umpires were ready.

All this magical stuff was going on even before I got to talk about the football, which was simply amazing. I believe it should be compulsory for every one of the AFL Rules Committee either to come to watch the next grand final on the Tiwi Islands, or at least watch a video of this one.

The game was so free flowing, there were only three stoppages for the whole match. They all came in the last quarter; after it had rained. There were no reports of players hitting each other. That's probably not surprising; they're playing against their own family members. Also, they only have eyes for the ball. Their love of the Australian game and of the heroes of Australian football is everywhere to be seen. Three players presented to the crowd were called 'Ablett', 'Paul Salmon' and 'Silvagni'. I asked another kid what his name was and he said, 'My name is Jack Burke.' It wasn't Wirrpunda or another of those delightfully sing-songy Aboriginal names; it was an Irish/ Celtic sort of name, like 'Kev Sheedy'.

These islands have probably unearthed another superstar in Cyril Rioli, a relative of both Maurice Rioli and Michael Long, who played his first game with Hawthorn in 2007.

So far in this book, I have quoted *The Australian* and the *Herald Sun*. To keep things balanced, I will include the pieces Martin Flanagan wrote for *The Age* about our trip to the Tiwi Islands. Martin is a beautiful writer and he can tell the story of that trip probably a lot better than I can.

Kevin Sheedy is Australian football's ambassador in this, its 150th year. I spent last weekend with him in Darwin, going with him to Bathurst Island for the Tiwi Islands Grand Final. I don't know how well I knew Kevin Sheedy beforehand. I don't know how well I know him now. But I do know that he excites me in some way. There's something alive about him in a way that in the rest of us, if not dead, is in semi-permanent retirement from an early age.

Walking with him through Darwin, it seems as if he engages the whole street. It's like the opening scene in a movie in which Sheedy is played by Robin Williams. An old woman stops him and asks him if he's 'off the ship'.

That gets his imagination going about the ship. Later, he and I will have to go and find the ship. By then another woman will have approached who is also off the ship. Her name is Vera, she's Welsh (this causes him to digress about Celtic culture) and she lives in Queensland. Vera says she won $50 on Sheedy in 1984 when the Bombers won their first premiership.

This happens in the pub where we have lunch. All the time, he's engaged with Vera, he's also talking to the blokes at the next table. When he entered the pub, he picked up a glass ashtray and ran it under their noses, saying, 'Tips, please'. It's a joke about what a man might do for a dollar which the men get. He's also watching the races and having bets and talking to me, telling me stories I should write like one on former umpire Harry Beitzel who suffered the fate of going to prison when a business in which he was involved was held to have taken money fraudulently.

'Harry did something wrong,' says Sheedy. 'But what about all the good things he did?' I say I'm not sure the newspaper will pay for me to go to Sydney to write about Harry. 'I'll pay,' he says, one eye on the screen, watching the horses. He's a mile ahead. He whacks a big note on the table. He's shouting.

When he leaves the pub we're going to the Darwin Grand Final but first we detour and look for the ship. We drive up and down the Darwin waterfront but in the end he goes, 'Look.' He says it with some pride like the father of a new baby. The search has been worth it. He's found what he was looking for. A white ocean liner. We sit and look at the ship as he muses aloud. 'How many people on that boat? Two thousand? Imagine if someone told them there was a game of Australian football on in town with Aboriginal players?'

And the point is — he's right. Of course, it would interest people from other places. They're here to see what's special about Australia. This is an example of how Kevin Sheedy thinks: We drive back towards town, he gets out and takes a photo of the ship. He takes photos of everything like he writes everything down. In the pub, he kept writing out instructions for me on betting slips.

'Harry,' reads the first (that is, do the story on Harry Beitzel). 'Look Up Bel Esprit,' says the next. That's the name of a horse in which he has an interest. The third betting slip lists three games I should see this year — Dreamtime at the G, the Eureka game and the International Cup. He has something to do with each of them. Dreamtime at the G is a consequence of him making Essendon, if not an Aboriginal club, a club at which Aboriginal people feel welcome. The Eureka game between Richmond and North Melbourne honours 'working people' and he is conscious of his working class origins. And the International Cup — well, Sheedy says, 'we have to keep talking about this great game of ours'.

Briefly, the subject of the recent international series in Ireland arises, the one in which he coached and the Irish complained of Australian violence. 'I'd like to coach Ireland,' he says. Once you've agreed on a set of rules, he tells me, you do what you can within those rules. To his mind, I gather, the Irish are too classical in their approach.

We go to the Darwin Grand Final. The last one of these I saw, between Buffaloes and St Mary's, was as good a game as I had seen in a very long time. For sheer viewing enjoyment, I put it up with some of the Cats' performances in 2007. This one, alas, was disappointing. The great regret is that the newly formed Tiwi Bombers didn't make the final. Having won eight straight, the skilful islanders fell away but the big news from the Top End is that next year the Tiwis are doing something they've never done before. A pre-season.

I'm ten years younger than Kevin Sheedy but I can't go at his pace. He's flown up the night before, given a speech, got up early, given another speech. The time in the pub is his first time off in days. We go to the footy, meet up with the AFL and NTFL people, are joined by the Longs — Michael, his wife, his son, two of his brothers, since the Longs seldom go anywhere alone, that not being the Aboriginal way. And there is this lively interaction going on, lots of talk and laughter and, yes, some alcohol is being consumed and after a day and half a night of this I am nearly gone when Sheedy suggests a group of us, including two AFL officials, leave for a meeting. In the pool at his hotel. Brian Wilson of the Beach Boys did this — held meetings in pools — and people say he was a genius.

The second article of the series, 'Travelling with the Ambassador', starts in the pool of a hotel near Darwin airport.

'How good is this?' Kevin Sheedy keeps chortling. For a man of 60 the AFL's Ambassador in its 150th season is in good shape, still solid and strong. To see him in bathers is to be reminded of him as a player — how fierce he was, how hard, yet also skilful.

To see myself in bathers is also to see Kevin Sheedy because the bathers I am wearing are his. So are the bathers of everyone at the meeting he has convened. For some reason, Kevin Sheedy travels Australia with a bagful of bathers. Presumably, so he can hold meetings such as this. 'The water's exactly the right temperature,' he keeps saying, like a connoisseur might say about wine. And so we splash about and talk.

Sheedy is dismissive of the idea of tanking. 'I tanked in 1993 — I played all my young players — and I won a premiership.'

He's been going since six o'clock in the morning. In the course of the day we have watched and celebrated a grand final. But this is not the day's end. When Sheedy and the others get out of the pool, it's to go to the St Mary's club house, St Mary's being the club of the Long family, where Sheedy is taken into the special circle out the back where a seat is saved for him beside Jack Long, the elder. They sing all night. St Mary's has just won its 26th flag. Sheedy gets home hours after I am in bed. The next day I judge him to be a little less ebullient but then it's an altogether different day.

We fly out to Bathurst Island, landing in Nguiu. This is where the purest form of our game is played. There will not be a single ball-up in the first half of the Tiwi Grand Final and only two or three thereafter. There will also be cyclonic rain during the second and third quarters but the Tiwis continue to play the ball, always the ball.

Sheedy's arrival on the island is something I am anxious to witness. Last year, when Essendon played the Aboriginal All-Stars in Darwin, I was amazed to see the bulk of the largely black audience of 10,000 barracked, silently or otherwise, for Essendon. That single fact says who and what Kevin Sheedy is in Aboriginal Australia. At the ground where the Tiwi Island Grand Final is to be played several old women approach him smiling and touch his arm.

Then he disappeared and I can't find him — he's backstage talking to some locals and I'm reminded of the previous day, when Waratahs got belted by 96 points in the Darwin Grand Final.

Having awarded the premiership cup to the winning coach and captain, Sheedy left the podium and walked over to the losers who were sitting slumped upon the ground, got them standing and spoke to them for a some minutes.

Someone in the grandstand said: 'I wonder what he's saying to them?' I knew. He was telling them he'd been where they were at the moment. After the '83 grand final when Essendon got belted all over the park by Hawthorn. Back the next year, the Bombers wrought a terrible vengeance.

I don't mind losing him for two quarters because I understand certain things aren't going to happen if I am standing beside him. I've watched him as he's walked around the boundary on our arrival. When you walk on Aboriginal land it is wise to walk quietly. Sheedy does. He knows how to be among Aboriginal people. You have to be quiet so things come to you like birds come to a tree.

An AFL scout at the Tiwi Grand Final gives me his assessment of Sheedy relative to locals. 'The only difference is the colour,' he says.

I watch the final quarter with Sheedy on the boundary. He's into it. He sees hard play penalised and doesn't like it. There's also a moment when the wet ball goes forward, a pack rises to meet it and he says: 'It's going over the back boys.' There is nothing remarkable in the words, but there is in the earliness with which he makes the call. The ball was still metres from the pack. I hadn't anticipated it, hadn't seen it. Maybe a fraction later I would have — but not then.

Do you remember when you played footy and the other bloke knew better than you where the ball was going? He's got that gift, as well as others. He knows something about people. He has an idea about how to get the best out of them. And if you ask him a serious question — as distinct from a boring routine one which he's fielded so often over the years from the press — he'll give you a serious answer.

And he still has his fire. I thought he'd lost it, but, no, at our pool meeting on the second night, to which he summons any lonely people he finds in the bar, the subject arises of cricket and the trouble this summer between India and Australia. He roars his defiance about what he would do. 'When someone puts it on you in sport, you put it straight back on them,' he shouts, and you see exactly what he brought to the playing field in the old days when footy was a tough, tough game. The meeting is also around 10 o'clock at night after a very long day. At midnight he flies out on a red-eye special to Sydney where he is talking about the game.

I think I had better explain those bathers. You are always having a dip in a pool when you are in Darwin because it's hot. I always take two pairs of bathers and I also have two pairs of Essendon training shorts. What Martin also probably didn't realise is that I had already been to Perth for a week for a West Australian Hall of Fame opening. I had also been to two colleges to take training, spoken at the AFL Ambassadors program in Perth, talked to the Australian team going to Africa, and attended three other functions. And I was ready to zoom off to South Africa once the two grand finals in Darwin had finished, so I had a decent amount of luggage. When you're on the road these days, you've got to take more than Willie Nelson's backpack.

People who meet me at my car are always amazed to see it looking like a walk-in — or drive-in — wardrobe. But when you're visiting different people all day, driving all over town, you owe it to them to turn up looking your best, not in the clothes you've been wearing all day.

I like Martin Flanagan a lot. It's probably the Irish connection. But he also has his own deep connection with Aboriginal Australia, and a great passion for Australian football, which I admire. He wrote a book about Tom Wills, the father of Australian football, and a play. We all come at our game from different angles, but so long as we all love football, we can accept that.

I think the acceptance now of Aboriginal people in our game is something that we can be so proud of. It wasn't that long ago that Michael Long had to take the huge and difficult step of reporting Damien Monkhorst for racial vilification. And what was said on the field was nothing compared to what was said about Michael off the field after the incident in the 1995 Anzac Day match.

Can you believe it, there were a lot of people in football who reckoned that Longie should be prepared to cop a bit of racial abuse on the field and just get on with it. And these were people who you would think were a pretty decent type of person.

The matter went to mediation with a resolution that I don't think entirely pleased Michael. But the ramifications have rolled on, with the AFL really leading the way in setting up education programs about racial and religious vilification.

Football has moved far more quickly — much further — than governments on this matter. The rewards to our game have been fantastic people like Paddy Ryder and Alwyn Davey at Essendon, and Buddy Franklin and Cyril Rioli at Hawthorn. And the best thing is there are still more of them to come.

What Michael did, and what the AFL followed up with, just had to be done. We had to realise that whatever we might have thought we could get away with in the past, it couldn't continue in the future if Aboriginal people were going to feel welcome. Michael's courage, and also that of Nicky Winmar, the St Kilda player who took a stand against racial abuse from the Collingwood crowd, have been part of a whole process of change in football. There were some clubs in the past that wouldn't recruit Aboriginal players. Now, a club that doesn't go looking for Aboriginal players is considered behind the eight-ball.

When the next generations of young Aboriginal kids come through, they should occasionally find a spare moment to remember what Michael Long has done for them. I think all Australians should be thankful.

I know what he did for me. Michael Long showed such an array of talents that he actually taught us a different way of playing football by the way he played. He and his family and friends have also shown me a different Australia that was way beyond my imagination as a young bloke in South Yarra. They have taught me: 'Kevin, it is not all about you; it's about us, too.'

I was also happy to remind Michael that a lot of my people, the Irish, didn't come to Australia freely. They came in chains. I think that helped give him a better understanding of Australia, too.

When you have those sorts of exchanges, and you hear from Michael's friends and family that all they want is the same things we do — education, health services, a fair go for their kids — then the stereotypes and the prejudices just disappear.

From an AFL perspective, hopefully our loyalty to the Northern Territory and to the indigenous people of Australia will pay off. It's a very important part of this game that it can bring in the great young talent of the indigenous players. And they are getting taller! You can now pick a whole team of them, not just 'smalls' like Michael.

From what I see every time I go back to Darwin, to the Tiwi Islands, whatever their size, there are many more Michael Longs out there, many more beautiful people.

18

King of the Coaches

In 2007, I reached a milestone in my football life that was a bit like climbing Mt Everest without oxygen maybe; but, when I think about it, with a lot of Sherpa Tenzing Norgays — people who had been loyal and brave colleagues who helped me on the way up.

In the game against the Western Bulldogs at Telstra Dome on 14 July 2007, I broke the record set by the wonderful Jock McHale for most games in the VFL/AFL as a player or coach. Jock's record had been 878, all with Collingwood. I am proud of my effort, which was spread over two clubs — 251 games as a player with Richmond and 635 as coach of Essendon. However, all I could think of that day, apart from how to beat the Bulldogs, was what an amazing person Jock McHale must have been. How committed must he have been to Collingwood to have given so much of his life to it? And it wasn't a life without setbacks, both on and off the field. He and his wife Violet lost two sons while they were still infants. They also lost their daughter Jean, aged just 16, to meningitis.

Things like that can break lesser men. Jock McHale was never a lesser man.

The loss of so many children did impact on his relationships with his surviving son, Jock McHale Junior. Jock Senior didn't want his son to play football, but he did — for Collingwood, with his father as coach. Apparently, things could get a bit tense around the dinner table when this matter came up.

In my book *The 500 Club*, I paid tribute to Jock, calling him 'the ghost of coaching. No matter what anyone else achieves, he is there, floating above us.'

It is flattering, I wrote then, to hear two Collingwood stalwarts — Lou Richards and Gordon Carlyon, the club's former secretary/manager — say that I am the closest coach to Jock McHale they have seen. Flattering, but not true. Even as I passed this record in July 2007, I knew that he would remain the towering presence for coaches — 714 games as either a player–coach, or coach. And all for the one club.

I never underestimate the challenges of being a player–coach. I tried it in the army and learned then how tough it is. Sure, you're out on the field and have direct contact with your team. Against that, though, you don't have the panoramic view from the coach's box from which to dictate play. And the view gets worse if you're on the ground, in thick mud, trying to win possession of the ball.

I would have loved to have been able to sit down and have a cup of tea and a biscuit with Jock, to talk about footy, and life. Sadly, he died in 1953, felled — so it is said — by the strain of watching Collingwood win the grand final that year. He was the epitome of the 'Kill for Collingwood' spirit.

His ideas and mine would have been a lot different on a lot of issues. He would probably have shared with Dick Reynolds the view that I should get a second runner before I wore out the first one. Well I did get that second runner, eventually. But I reckon we would have had similar views on a lot of other things.

On 2 May 1925, he shared his views on coaching with readers of *The Sporting Globe*. They make fascinating reading:

It is an easy task for me to put methods of coaching into operation when the players are on the field. It is a different matter altogether to endeavour to write an article explaining the coaching business.

Coaching is the most important thing for a footballer and his team, provided the coach is a good one. He should be an experienced man with mature judgment and plenty of tact. A coach should be a man who has played the game and knows exactly what is required of a player. Always he should be on the lookout for rote weaknesses.

The success of a coach depends greatly on the material at his disposal. It may be good or weak. If a coach has natural talent at his disposal he will be a poor mentor if he cannot get his team into a high place. A good coach also should be able to bring along a weak side, and to improve the form of the players. Coaching has many aspects, and it is only considerable experience that teaches what is mostly required.

I had the good fortune to learn football in a particularly good school. By playing and mingling with some of the best known figures that the game has produced I have gleaned many useful points which other young players probably would not be able to pick up. I was particularly lucky to be under the charge of the large Dick Condon.

*He was a master mind as far as football was concerned,
and it can be said of him that what he did not know
about the game was not worth knowing. Condon was a
man who believed in the players practising and training
assiduously. He realised that fitness was the first equipment
a footballer should possess.*

...

*Fifteen years' coaching of the Magpies has convinced
me that a young player who wants to make good must
have keenness, determination, anticipation and he must
not be selfish. Keenness is essential. Any player who is
careless or slovenly in his methods is not of much use in
a team, and should not be in demand. A player must be
keen to razor-sharpness.*

*Determination is also wanted. Determination generally
means success in any sphere or walk of life, for if a
fellow makes up his mind that he cannot be beaten in a
certain thing, it is seldom that he fails. Unselfishness or
combination comes in where a player has to be an assistant
to his team mates. Football is all combination work, and a
player has to fit into his team's work and style.*

*Anticipation is necessary for the footballer. You cannot
go hot-headed after the ball. One must be cool, watchful,
and be able to gauge the flight of the ball. Keep your eyes
on the ball, and you begin to study its peculiarities and
note how it will travel faster and lower with a drop kick,
and higher and slower with a punt kick.*

*Any player, particularly a youngster, who enters into
a senior club's rooms for the first time must be made at
home. It is the object of the committee at Collingwood to
make the players happy, and any new member is accorded*

a warm welcome. Collingwood has become renowned for its hospitality, because the officials have treated the players well — not like a lot of schoolboys, or persons who are paid just for their services as players. A little kindness will work wonders anywhere, and if a player is made happy in a club room, he soon wants to make his neighbours happy.

On the other hand if a player is ignored, he soon commences to growl to the other players. Thus dissension is created and it is not long before certain players and officials are at loggerheads. While they are unfriendly a club cannot hope to compete successfully against other teams on the field. A happy spirit, fostered in the dressing room from the start of the season, goes a long way toward the winning of the premiership.

This happiness I attribute in a big way to the past successes of Collingwood teams. The players have been taught to pull together, and they have done so with a will. One can point to a few other clubs and reveal how their sides have failed, though gifted with excellent material.

At Collingwood we have also encouraged the old players to come round and have a talk with the present players. It is a common sight to see a young player benefiting by the hints of an old player. Those old players will not refer disparagingly to the game nowadays, and laud the heroes of the past. One will always strike a few cranks in this respect, but the men desired are those who will have a friendly chat with a player. A player never likes to talk to anyone who knows nothing about the game.

...

I try to induce every player to take as keen an interest in practice as he does in a match. Probably an indifferent action in practice will be responsible for a careless action in a match.

On Tuesday evening the players should have some match practice, and be kept moving for a solid half an hour or more.

About 20 minutes should be devoted to marking practice and stab kicking. The marking of stab kicks is also important, and plenty of this work will get the players in good fettle. A man playing in the centre wants plenty of twisting about and short, nippy work. The half back man wants dash and should be taught to come through a pack fearlessly.

A half forward needs to be a man who will mark well, and can turn quickly on either foot. By practising a player can become fairly proficient in quick turning. It is excellent practice for a big man. Ruck men need plenty of work that will improve their stamina.

Of all the forwards I have had anything to do with, I consider there is none to equal Dick Lee. He was a truly marvellous player. With all his wonderful ability as a kick and a mark, his play was made of greater value by his pluck and his coolness.

On a Thursday evening I consider that training should be lighter, but while the players are on the field, they should put plenty of vim into their work, and have a good perspiration running from them. It must be remembered however, that a hard match is to be played on Saturday. Therefore too much energy should not be wasted by players in practice.

...

Nearly every footballer has a different temperament. Some players are easily upset. Others do not worry over anything. A coach should make it his business to study the feelings of every man, and to learn his views on various things. It is wonderfully helpful to a coach if he hopes to achieve the best results, if he knows exactly the temperament of each player.

I have studied the men under my charge at Collingwood, and know fairly well their good points, and any weaknesses that they may have. Some players are unduly anxious. Some are pessimistic and others too confident. Numerous other little faults are common.

I do not believe in too much bellowing at players. A quiet word spoken in place will generally do far more than a sharp, insolently delivered command. Sometimes the voice has to be raised when discipline is required, and some players are a little too fresh.

A moody man does not want bullying. He wants to be built up in hope, and quiet, well-spoken words of encouragement will often make him a force to be reckoned with.

Players should eat well and have plenty of rest. They should look after themselves. Very few players can last long if they dissipate. In regard to drinking, a teetotaller is not the only man who makes a good footballer. A player may have an occasional drink. Beer is the best drink in moderation. Spirits are not good at all. On a Friday, however, a player should leave the drink alone.

There is a lot of poetry in those words of Jock's from 80 years ago, and there is a lot of that magic ingredient — commonsense.

A lot of practices have changed since 1925, but essentially the template is the same today. Here's a guy coaching in the early 20th century, talking about 'anticipation', and being 'cool, watchful' and 'able to gauge the flight of the ball' or the peculiarities of a kick. We talk about these things today; they just have different names. I love his comment 'A little kindness will work wonders anywhere', and his use of the word 'growl'.

Other terms that stick out for me are 'pull together', 'will' and 'gifted'. No one is 'gifted' these days; they are automatically 'superstars'.

He calls past players 'old players'. And what about the line, 'One will always strike a few cranks'? I've met a few of them, too, Jock.

What was called 'having a friendly chat' back then would be called a 'one-on-one' today. And what about getting the players 'in good fettle'? And 'plenty of twisting about and short, nippy work'? That's music to the ears of this baby boomer. I love the Twist.

Jock made only one comment about a forward, Dick Lee: 'there is none to equal' him. This is a man who coached in 17 grand finals, yet he reckoned he had only one really good forward.

His preference for beer over spirits might, these days, be regarded as a bit of a conflict of interest. He worked at the brewery in Carlton, from which he walked to training at Victoria Park in Collingwood. He never got a licence to drive.

Lou Richards played a lot of football with Jock McHale and his observations of him are truly noteworthy. They go back to 1940 when he played in the Collingwood reserves side that won the flag. 'I was 17 and Jock came up to me after the grand final and said, "Son, you'll be playing for Collingwood next year." It was the greatest thrill of my life. I couldn't get home quick enough to tell Mum and Dad. The next year, somehow, I ended up with the locker next to his. I remember just staring at him the first time. He must have thought I was an idiot.'

Lou reckons that McHale had a charisma about him that was not unlike that of the Hollywood actor George Burns, whom he met.

'I used to love being with him. I loved him. He was a grumpy old bugger, bit like Lionel Barrymore. He could have got a fortune at other clubs, but he never took anything more than what the players got, which was three pounds a week plus one pound in the provident fund.

'He never told you much. Everything he did was really basic, but he wouldn't hesitate to make a move. He'd swap the wings over if they were playing badly, or move the centre-half forward to centre-half back. He'd never can an umpire, either. He'd say, "If you play well enough, you'll beat the umpire, too."

'One of the other things he used to say was, "Watch the top players and do what they do."

'He had three great loves, the family, the Collingwood Football Club and the brewery. If you played a good game he'd say, "Young Richards, you'd better come with me." He'd take you down to the brewery and pour you a great big pot. It was one of the biggest thrills of my life.'

As good as he was at dispensing the prized ale, Lou reckons Jock wasn't real big when it came to dispensing sympathy.

'I was lying on the table in the medical room, really crook, when Jock came in and said, "Come on, get up. You're all right." I just got up because he told me to. I took Edna to the pictures that night and was that crook I had to go to the doctor.

I had a depressed fracture of the cheekbone. I played the next week, too. Old Jock could have sympathy, but he didn't want to mollycoddle you!'

One of Jock's more fascinating claims to fame is that he has been named as the coach of a NSW Australian football Team of the Century. He was born in Botany in Sydney, not far from where James Cook landed in 1770. What an amazing story for Australian football to have these pioneers of our history linked in this way, hundreds of years apart. McHale's family didn't move to Victoria until he was five. So, not only did the original rule makers, Harrison and Wills, come from New South Wales, but so too did the game's greatest coach.

Ungarie, with a population considerably less than that of Botany, managed to produce two members of that NSW Team of the Century — Anthony and Terry Daniher. Paul Kelly, Shane Crawford and Wayne Carey were also in that side, a reminder that not all of New South Wales was rugby mad before the Swans arrived in Sydney in the early 1980s.

I can't believe that Neale and Chris Daniher weren't picked. Even though Neale didn't get to play 100 senior games because of injury, he probably deserves to be in ahead of Troy Luff, who came from Traralgon in Victoria. Chris Daniher could feel aggrieved to have missed out, too, after having played 124 games, including a premiership in 1993, coming off the bench from a seat that a lot of people thought Derek Kickett should have been sitting on.

I am pleased, however, to see that the selectors of this NSW Team of the Century were on to the fact that McHale was born in their state. I think we should make even more of it than that. Perhaps Collingwood and Sydney could play for the McHale Trophy, or Sydney and the new team in the Western Suburbs.

What a way to show to the new audiences in Sydney that they, too, are part of the history of Australian football.

Jock was a great believer in assistant coaches way before they became the modern fashion. He would have specialists to teach players how to kick or mark, leaving him to concentrate on overall strategies and team selection.

I really do think Jock McHale and I would have had a great conversation over that cup of tea. Just like with Norm and Len Smith, I would love to know what he would do about the flood. Given some of the playing conditions he had to endure, when grounds would be covered in water, I reckon he might be a lot closer to the answer than modern-day coaches!

As part of writing *The 500 Club*, I met Jock's daughter-in-law, June, and gained a wonderful insight into this great man for whom family, club and work were all equally important. I may have passed him statistically, but that's all. He remains the towering figure in the game for all coaches to look up to, as his nomination for the Collingwood Hall of Fame, written in April 2004, confirms:

More than 50 years after his death, Jock McHale remains the most iconic figure in the club's history. First as a player and then as coach he set remarkable records in longevity and commitment that inspired all around him. His 261 games as a player are often overlooked. But he had an outstanding playing career, mainly in the centre and across half-back, and strung together a record 191 games in succession.

But his playing achievements were dwarfed by what he did as coach, 38 years, 714 matches, eight Premierships, nine times runners-up. It's a record that, even today, still beggars belief. McHale's strengths as coach lay in his ability to prepare and inspire players, and instil discipline into the team's game plan. No-one dared question him, or his tactics. And he had a hatred of defeat that was legendary. Fortunately, he didn't have to suffer defeats too often. As his record shows, he was truly 'the King of Coaches'.

19

A Little Horse Called Bel Esprit

Ever since my father took me along as a youngster, I have always loved horse-racing. I don't mind a punt; in fact, concentrating on the form guide, trying to pick a few winners here and there, has always been a good mental holiday for me from some of the pressures of coaching. If you think about football all the time, you'll end up mad. Horses became a nice diversion because I could never be just a fan at the football, but I could be at the races. The night I was told by Ray Horsburgh and Peter Jackson that I wouldn't be coaching at Essendon after 2007 I had a lovely diversion. I went to the Racing Museum in Melbourne to talk about Bel Esprit, this beautiful little horse that — and in the most extraordinary way, too — had come into my life.

I can talk for hours about how I came to end up owning a champion runner, and now one of the best breeding sires in Australia. There was a fair bit of luck in it, but it also happened because of a couple of friendships with people that have been important to me for a long time — Brian Donohoe and Michael Duffy.

Brian has put together two books on the life and times of Bel Esprit, made up of cuttings from the newspapers and other bits of memorabilia. In my camera, I carry around some footage of Bel Esprit rolling around in the dust at his home at Eliza Park, just out of Melbourne.

Michael says that introducing Brian, then me, to owning racehorses was a bit like the pair of us discovering sex. Yes, we do get pretty excited. But gee, for me Bel Esprit is really worth getting excited about. When he ran in The Golden Slipper at Rosehill in 2002, I took the whole family up for the experience. It was a special moment to be able to share with Geraldine and the children; a 'thank you', perhaps, to my own father for having taken me to the races. As we get older, they say we all become our fathers. I would be proud if that has happened.

Having lost my father at a young age, I have come to rely on a number of good people for advice — Tom Hafey first and foremost probably, Neville Gay, Brian Donohoe, Lionel Krongold, Ron Evans, Brian Ward ... All good people I could ring up for a chat, or to ask them to come around for a cup of tea and to talk me through an issue.

Michael Duffy was someone I listened to a lot. He was part of the lunch party that convinced me to allow Mark Thompson to stay on at Essendon until the end of the 1998 season despite his involvement in the push to get rid of me. It was good advice as sacking a coach, even an assistant coach, always disrupts a club, especially mid-season.

Michael is a former minister in the Hawke government. He once, rather famously, took on media tycoon Kerry Packer over the rights and responsibilities of people who owned television stations. Michael thought he was doing a pretty good job of sticking up for the ordinary people in the street who wanted to have access to the best possible media services, until he realised that he'd managed to upset not just Kerry Packer, but also Rupert Murdoch. Apparently that quinella didn't go down all that well with his Cabinet colleagues, particularly the prime minister. Despite that, he managed to have a decent career as a politician. He was Minister for Communications, Minister for Trade Negotiations and Attorney-General in the Hawke government. In December 2007, he was appointed chairman of Racing Victoria Limited's new independent board.

There are a lot of things I admire about Michael, mostly to do with the fact that he's always been a straight shooter, a bloke with no pretensions. Even after he was elected to federal parliament in the early 1980s, he still went to watch Essendon play from the outer; standing on a little platform he made for himself out of two beer cans and a bit of wood.

When you're sitting in your comfortable seats at Telstra Dome you should remember it wasn't all that long ago that going to the footy was a lot less salubrious than it is today. Thankfully, people like Ron Evans at Essendon could see the need to change and convinced the members to move to the MCG.

It was Ron who, one day at Moorabbin in the early 1980s, saw Michael Duffy standing on his cans. With Noel Allanson, the treasurer, he wandered over and introduced himself to the new federal Member for Holt. Apparently, Ron's words to Noel were: 'I told you it was him.'

Ron invited Michael to a number of Essendon functions after that and it was at one of those that he met Brian Donohoe, another straight shooter. They hit it off pretty much from the start, and their friendship has lasted to today — to the point that Michael invited Brian to be part of a small syndicate to own this horse called Bel Esprit. I'll let Michael tell the story from here.

'An accountant by the name of Martin O'Connor had asked me on various occasions to go and have a look at Macedon Lodge, which is a world-class thoroughbred training facility close to the Macedon Ranges. For all sorts of reasons, for a long time there had been no time to go. However, he rang me one day and said he was going up with Brian Martin, the race-caller, and could I come. I was free and I said, "Yes, I will."

'So we went up there and I looked around all the fantastic facilities and then we came back to the entertainment area and we were having a drink. While I was doing that I picked up a *Sydney Classic* sale catalogue. I was flicking through it, and the Macedon Lodge people asked me if I would like to look at any of the horses they had purchased at the sale.

'I said, "Not really," because the only one I liked was the colt by Royal Academy out of Bespoken and I thought it would be a bit dear. But John Symons, who was the resident trainer, told me they had bought the horse for just $9500.

'I said, "What's wrong with him?"

'John replied: "Not much, expect he has got a splint."

' "That could put a few people off." However, I thought back very carefully to when I was a kid in 1951. My father bred a horse and he sent it off to the yearling sales in Melbourne and didn't get a bid for it. The reason was, it had a splint. However, it raced from when it was three years old to when it was seven, when it was killed in a fall in the Albury Cup, and was always sound and didn't have any leg problems.

'So, at that price, I said I wouldn't mind getting involved.

'Kurt Stern, who owned Macedon Lodge, said he wanted to keep a few shares, and I said I would get rid of the rest.

'So I made a few phone calls and very quickly had a syndicate that involved myself, Kurt Stern, Brian Forrest, a very dear friend of mind, David Cox, the bookmaker, and Brian Donohoe. I was happy enough with those numbers, but then Brian rang me and said: "Do you mind if my son Peter comes in?"

'I said, "No."

'Then he went into a spiel about how I had forgotten someone who should be offered a share.

'I said, "Who?"

'He said, "Kevin."

'I said, "Kevin who?" I didn't relate to Kevin buying a horse.

'Brian replied, "Kevin Sheedy! Who do you think?"

'I said, "Would Kevin like a share?" and he said, "Yes."

'I told Brian there had already been a closure on the deal, but I would ring the other people and see if they were happy and they were.

'I've got to say, given how things turned out, Kevin was pretty bloody lucky and his great mate Brian Donohoe had done him another good turn.

'By that stage, the horse had been broken in and he was spelling and the total cost was closer to $13,000, which was to be divided by seven.

'A bit later, John Symons rang me and said the horse was very smart and he thought he should run him at Moonee Valley on W.S. Cox Plate day in October 2001. I said, "There is a good two-year-old race at Wangaratta at that time. Why not there?"

'John said, "I think he is better than that."

'I was incredulous, and thought, "Yeah, I've heard all that before about horses."

'But Bel Esprit went straight into a listed race as a first-up run and won, so the trainer was right.

'He then won his next four races as a two-year-old and then

was a very unlucky in the Golden Slipper. He drew the inside barrier and the inside was off after rain.

'He went on and won two Group One races, the Blue Diamond Stakes and the Doomben 10,000 and was placed in four Group Ones, winning prize money of $2,073,600. So, even before he went to stud, he had become a pretty good return on investment for all of us. In fact, my son Patrick reckons we should have a small monument to Bel Esprit out in the garden.

'We then sold him to stud for a substantial amount, but we retained 14 shares in him.

'The stud was Eliza Park, which is at Kerrie, just out of Melbourne. I had received a phone call from Shane McGrath, who is the general manager there. I thought at first his call might just have been a feeler, but he was genuine about wanting to take Bel Esprit to Eliza Park and we got a good deal. And that was even before the Equine Influenza situation, which meant that no stallions could be brought into Victoria. Bel Esprit already had a good book before the EI situation, but suddenly he became very busy.'

He was indeed. Bel Esprit covered 264 mares.

This is what Ric Chapman wrote about Bel Esprit's efforts in the magazine *The Blood Horse*:

With many leading stallions locked-down in quarantine for the initial part of the season, and travel throughout Australia suspended for the first three months of the breeding season (especially those headed for the horse rich population in the New South Wales Hunter Valley), Victoria's Eliza Park-based sire, former champion Australian two year old and multiple grade one winner Bel Esprit (Royal Academy-Bespoken, by

Vain) covered an Australian record of 264 mares. Read that again — 264 mares in a five months period from one barn in one country. No shuttling — although given his debut crop is outstanding and that his future gallopers will stamp themselves through sheer force of numbers, connections are open to the prospect of shuttling. His prodigious powers in the barn surpassed the 245 set by Coolmore champion sire Encosta de Lago in 2005. Bel Esprit (whose previous high mark was 210 mares in 2006) stood this season for $20,000.

Racing's a pretty tough industry and while there have been good results already among Bel Esprit's offspring, that will have to continue if he is to remain in good demand as a stud horse.

But gee, I have already had my fun from him. The horse owes me absolutely nothing. He also completes one of the amazing journeys in my life, the one that started when Mal Brown took me overseas and we ended up in Kentucky, where we saw the super-sire Nijinsky. As Michael Duffy put it, I was probably more impressed about seeing him than he was about seeing me, but all these years on, there's something a bit romantic about owning a horse that has the name Nijinsky in his pedigree.

Nijinsky and Bel Esprit have a bit in common. Michael Duffy reckons if you look at photos of Nijinsky, the likeness is quite extraordinary. They both have a similar temperament — not nasty, but stubborn. They both could, at times, require a bit of cajoling going into the starting barriers. Perhaps that's another reason to like him. Certainly, as the years pass and Bel Esprit's progeny make their mark in Australian racing, I shall always have a great fondness for this beaut little horse and those visits to Eliza Park just to watch him roll around in the dust.

20

Exploring the New World

These days, I feel I am a cross between Davy Crockett and Christopher Columbus, moving around the world and my country looking at different opportunities to build the future of the game of Australian football.

Since I left Essendon in October 2007, I have been to Canada, the United States, Europe and South Africa. I have travelled to Perth for Western Australia's Hall of Fame festivities, to Darwin for their grand final, and to Townsville to open a new stadium.

I also had the most marvellous honour of being inducted into the AFL Hall of Fame in May 2008, a couple of days before the game between Victoria and the Dream Team held to celebrate 150 years of Australian football. It was one of the best nights of my life, sitting there among all the greats of the game. I enjoyed catching up with a whole lot of my former team-mates and being in the company of a lot of the people who have made Australian football the success it already is, including the great administrators. My wife and children were also there and it was probably their best night in footy as well.

We are all lucky to be involved in this great game in this great country. There are still a lot of things we Australians need to keep working on, such as ensuring that we have the Barrier Reef in the future and other important environmental issues, and social issues such as embracing the Aboriginal people. Responsibility for doing those things will fall on the working people of Australia, the ones we are honouring in the new iconic game to go up alongside Anzac Day and Dreamtime — the Eureka Game.

It is a celebration of the people who have literally built this great nation: working people!

Whether you drive or fly around Australia, there is so much to feel good about. I fly into Perth and I can't help but think, 'What a beautiful city.' How pretty is Tasmania? If you arrived on earth and asked yourself, 'Where is the best country to live over the next 50 years?', you would have to consider Australia. If you picked somewhere else, I would like to know where it is because I haven't heard of people trying to catch boats with holes in them to get there. Australia is mightily attractive to people from all over the world ... the Middle East, Indo-China, Europe.

Per head of population, we just have to be the best sporting nation in the world, too. We are the only country with four great football codes. On top of that, we came third in the Olympic Games. We also have a pretty good cricket team, and we go all right in basketball and netball.

Wherever I go now, after 27 years as coach of Essendon, people want to know what I will be doing in the future. I know I will want to spend a lot more time in the garden. Like my solicitor and friend Brian Ward, I really enjoy gardening. It's peaceful and you can think about anything you want to: where to put the petunias, what to make the next iconic football game. It's amazing the things that can come into your mind when you have a bit of peace.

Most importantly, whatever else happens, I want to enjoy life. I want to enjoy my wonderful country, and I want to enjoy helping develop the game of Australian football.

When I look back over my life and career so far, I would have to say I have always been a development officer. The young boy from South Yarra was doing all he could to develop himself to play in the VFL. When I got to Richmond, I was developing myself to move from the back-pocket to be on the ball. My first full-time job in footy had the title 'development officer'.

Over the years I have had the privilege of developing ideas, people, teams and, for 27 wonderful years, the club that I barracked for as a kid — Essendon. Now I have the honour of being asked to develop the whole game of Australian football, not just here in Australia but overseas as well. I really do believe that Australian football can succeed overseas. I know that a lot of people say, 'There goes Sheeds again', whenever I start talking about it. But I have been to America and I have seen the sort of enthusiasm that is growing there for our game. As that mayor in Florida said: '… you've got the greatest football game I have ever seen in the world!' You've only got to get a few more mayors and governors, maybe even a president, talking like that and it's amazing how things can snowball.

Back in 1891, would the person who created basketball, the Reverend James Naismith, have believed that in the 21st century, his game would be one of the most popular in the world? Born in Canada, Naismith was teaching physical education at Springfield College in the United States — no, Homer Simpson wasn't there — and wanted to have a sport that young Christian men could play indoors during the cold winters in North America.

In 1892, he drew up some formal rules but in the early days, it was all pretty basic. The players used a soccer ball, which they dribbled up and down the court. The iron hoops and basket didn't come until 1893. In the first years, points were scored by putting the ball into a peach basket.

In 1903, they got really clever and cut the bottom out of the basket, so that they didn't have to stop the game to get it out manually every time someone scored. Now just about every garage in Australia has one of these nets hanging off it.

As I'm thinking about all this, I'm hearing the words to that song by Paul Kelly and Kev Carmody: 'From little things, big things grow'. It's about Aboriginal reconciliation. It can also be about one of the things that is really trying to help Aboriginal reconciliation, Australian football. Australian football is not a little thing in Australia, but in global terms it still is. But who knows what it will be like in 100 years from now, or even 50? My first game of senior football was in 1967, 41 years ago. When I look back at how the game has changed in that time, how could you safely predict just about *anything* about the next 41 years?

The next generation of aeroplanes, the supersonic Airbuses, might be able to take us to Los Angeles in four hours, instead of 14. It was advances in transport that made it easier for the Victorian Football Association and the Victorian Football League to spread out into the suburbs, and for the Australian Football League to spread out across a continent.

What about the people who started the VFA? Could they have ever conceived that it would become the VFL, then the AFL, and be played not just in the suburbs of Melbourne, but all over Australia?

I wrote a book called *Follow Your Dreams*. The title, and a lot of the stories it contained were a way of encouraging people to get out and do their best, to find out what they wanted to do with their lives and then go after it full pelt.

I had a dream to play VFL footy and I got to fulfil that. I had a dream to coach, and I got to do that for 27 years. I have a dream that my game, your game, our Australian game, will make its mark on the world just as so many other Australians have done, whether they are performers like Paul Hogan or Nicole Kidman, sportsmen like Ian Thorpe or Cathy Freeman, or scientists like Professor Peter Doherty, who shared the 1996 Nobel Prize.

We are an amazing lot of people, we Australians, drawn from all over the world to this massive island, where we have created a democracy, an economy, a community that is the envy of the world. I believe that, in time, the game of football — Australian football — we created will also become the envy of the world.

Whatever else happens in the future, I want to be involved in footy. I want to help develop the game here in Australia from being the national competition to the national winter game. That will happen. It's already started.

When the great day comes — and it will — when we're playing for four premiership points overseas, I will know that we are really starting to move it forward.

Hello.

Stand your ground.

Thanks.

List of Appendices

Appendix A

KEVIN SHEEDY THE PLAYER: 1967–1979

DATE	SEASON	RND	SESSION	VENUE	KEVIN'S CLUB	G	B	PTS	OPPONENT	G	B	PTS	MARGIN	ATTENDANCE	K	M	HB	FF	FA	GLS	BEH	BEST 6	RESERVES MATCHES
15/4/1967	1967	1		MCG	RICHMOND	15	20	110	ESSENDON	11	9	75	35	56,387									
22/4/1967	1967	2		Whitten Oval	RICHMOND RES	15	9	99	WSTRN BLDGS RES	7	7	49	50										0 GOALS
29/4/1967	1967	3		MCG	RICHMOND	11	12	78	FITZROY	7	11	53	25	20,938	16	3	2	3	2	0	0		
6/5/1967	1967	4		Arden St Oval	RICHMOND	11	22	88	KANGAROOS	10	8	68	20	12,750	18	6	3	5	3	1	0	1	
13/5/1967	1967	5		MCG	RICHMOND	16	22	118	HAWTHORN	5	13	43	75	27,175	10	4	2	1	4	0	1		
20/5/1967	1967	6		Moorabbin	RICHMOND	14	15	99	ST KILDA	9	4	58	41	32,342	16	3	6	5	1	0	0		
27/5/1967	1967	7		MCG	RICHMOND	18	11	119	GEELONG	12	9	81	38	50,348	19	6	5	5	2	1	0	1	
3/6/1967	1967	8		MCG	RICHMOND	13	5	83	COLLINGWOOD	13	12	90	-7	71,946	4	1	3	0	3	0	0		
12/6/1967	1967	9		Optus Oval	RICHMOND RES	23	12	150	CARLTON RES	10	13	73	77										0 GOALS
24/6/1967	1967	10		MCG	RICHMOND RES	14	20	104	MELBOURNE RES	8	9	57	47										0 GOALS
1/7/1967	1967	11		Lake Oval	RICHMOND RES	15	19	109	STH MLB/SYD RES	8	5	53	56										1 GOAL
8/7/1967	1967	12		Windy Hill	RICHMOND RES	19	14	128	ESSENDON RES	13	7	85	43										0 GOALS
22/7/1967	1967	13		MCG	RICHMOND	19	16	130	WSTRN BLDGS	8	10	58	72	20,827									
29/7/1967	1967	14		Optus Oval	RICHMOND	8	19	67	FITZROY	8	10	58	9	13,684									
5/8/1967	1967	15		MCG	RICHMOND	14	21	105	KANGAROOS	13	7	85	20	34,447									
12/8/1967	1967	16		Glenferrie Oval	RICHMOND	23	30	168	HAWTHORN	7	12	54	114	19,441									
19/8/1967	1967	17		MCG	RICHMOND	12	13	85	ST KILDA	7	11	53	32	48,209									
26/8/1967	1967	18		Skilled Stadium	RICHMOND	18	9	117	GEELONG	15	15	105	12	34,616									
9/9/1967	1967		SS	MCG	RICHMOND	20	21	141	CARLTON	14	17	101	40	99,051									
23/9/1967	1967		GF	MCG	RICHMOND	16	18	114	GEELONG	15	15	105	9	109,396									
15/4/1968	1968	1		Victoria Park	RICHMOND RES	16	11	107	COLLINGWOOD RES	11	13	79	28										5 GOALS
20/4/1968	1968	2		MCG	RICHMOND	17	16	118	CARLTON	10	12	72	46	51,887	1	0	0	0	0	0	0		
25/4/1968	1968	3		MCG	RICHMOND RES	17	7	109	GEELONG RES	9	9	63	46										0 GOALS
4/5/1968	1968	4		Moorabbin	RICHMOND	7	18	60	ST KILDA	12	12	84	-24	30,606	16	1	10	4	2	0	1		
11/5/1968	1968	5		Lake Oval	RICHMOND	13	25	103	STH MLB/SYDNEY	8	10	58	45	17,783	19	4	6	4	2	0	1		

Appendix A

DATE	SEASON	RND	SESSION	VENUE	KEVIN'S CLUB	G	B	PTS	OPPONENT	G	B	PTS	MARGIN	ATTENDANCE	K	M	HB	FF	FA	GLS	BEH	BEST 6 MATCHES	RESERVES
18/5/1968	1968	6		MCG	RICHMOND	14	17	101	KANGAROOS	4	7	31	70	24,317	3	1	0	1	1	0	0		0 GOALS
25/5/1968	1968	7		Windy Hill	RICHMOND RES	14	10	94	ESSENDON RES	6	17	53	41										
10/6/1968	1968	8		MCG	RICHMOND RES	23	20	158	HAWTHORN RES	7	8	50	108										3 GOALS
15/6/1968	1968	9		MCG	RICHMOND	17	17	119	MELBOURNE	9	9	63	56	39,609	17	1	5	1	0	1	0		
22/6/1968	1968	10		Optus Oval	RICHMOND	15	15	105	FITZROY	12	12	84	21	11,204	19	3	7	6	4	0	2		
29/6/1968	1968	11		MCG	RICHMOND	17	20	122	WSTRN BLDGS	16	8	104	18	17,844	25	5	6	5	1	0	1	1	
6/7/1968	1968	12		MCG	RICHMOND	17	12	114	COLLINGWOOD	17	15	117	-3	43,165	13	2	3	2	2	0	1		
13/7/1968	1968	13		Optus Oval	RICHMOND	10	14	74	CARLTON	11	14	80	-6	24,245	17	6	0	5	2	0	0	1	
20/7/1968	1968	14		Skilled Stadium	RICHMOND	9	16	70	GEELONG	13	11	89	-19	23,932	17	4	4	7	1	0	0	1	
27/7/1968	1968	15		MCG	RICHMOND	13	16	94	ST KILDA	9	10	64	30	42,740	9	2	2	3	0	0	0		
3/8/1968	1968	16		MCG	RICHMOND	15	21	111	STH MLB/SYDNEY	10	11	71	40	22,404	8	3	2	3	0	0	0		
10/8/1968	1968	17		Arden St Oval	RICHMOND	11	19	85	KANGAROOS	7	9	51	34	9,374	21	5	0	2	1	0	0	1	
17/8/1968	1968	18		MCG	RICHMOND	10	14	74	ESSENDON	7	12	54	20	68,529	13	4	5	2	1	0	0	1	
24/8/1968	1968	19		Glenferrie Oval	RICHMOND	11	22	88	HAWTHORN	11	13	79	9	21,772	11	5	3	0	1	0	0		
31/8/1968	1968	20		MCG	RICHMOND	18	21	129	MELBOURNE	12	8	80	49	34,546	8	5	7	0	1	0	0		
7/4/1969	1969	1		MCG	RICHMOND	15	21	111	ESSENDON	12	10	82	29	62,152	10	3	1	4	1	0	0	1	
12/4/1969	1969	2		Victoria Park	RICHMOND	14	15	99	COLLINGWOOD	11	16	82	17	27,353	11	1	6	4	0	0	0		
19/4/1969	1969	3		MCG	RICHMOND	13	28	106	KANGAROOS	16	15	111	-5	26,884	18	4	2	6	0	0	0		
26/4/1969	1969	4		Lake Oval	RICHMOND	19	22	136	STH MLB/SYDNEY	13	13	91	45	16,663	21	7	2	3	1	0	0	1	
3/5/1969	1969	5		MCG	RICHMOND	18	12	120	FITZROY	6	19	55	65	22,991	19	5	1	3	1	0	0		
10/5/1969	1969	6		MCG	RICHMOND	16	25	121	MELBOURNE	13	15	93	28	26,848	8	3	4	2	2	0	0	1	
17/5/1969	1969	7		MCG	RICHMOND	7	10	52	HAWTHORN	8	13	61	-9	35,933	19	5	5	2	3	0	0		
24/5/1969	1969	8		MCG	RICHMOND	12	14	86	CARLTON	17	13	115	-29	48,656	12	1	3	5	1	0	0	1	
31/5/1969	1969	9		Whitten Oval	RICHMOND	7	8	50	WSTRN BLDGS	8	13	61	-11	8,529	22	6	0	7	2	0	0	1	
7/6/1969	1969	10		MCG	RICHMOND	14	10	94	ST KILDA	11	14	80	14	44,710	23	2	1	4	1	1	0	1	
21/6/1969	1969	11		Skilled Stadium	RICHMOND	12	14	86	GEELONG	17	11	113	-27	24,278	10	2	5	1	2	0	0		
28/6/1969	1969	12		Windy Hill	RICHMOND	7	12	54	ESSENDON	8	15	63	-9	16,957	8	1	0	3	4	0	0		
5/7/1969	1969	13		MCG	RICHMOND	13	15	93	COLLINGWOOD	12	19	91	2	45,546	11	2	1	4	0	0	0		
12/7/1969	1969	14		Arden St Oval	RICHMOND	17	15	117	KANGAROOS	6	12	48	69	10,597	14	6	4	2	2	0	0		
19/7/1969	1969	15		MCG	RICHMOND	22	12	144	STH MLB/SYDNEY	11	11	77	67	21,959	24	9	2	2	3	0	0	1	

Appendix A

DATE	SEASON	RND	SESSION	VENUE	KEVIN'S CLUB	G	B	PTS	OPPONENT	G	B	PTS	MARGIN	ATTENDANCE	K	M	HB	FF	FA	GLS	BEH	BEST 6	RESERVES MATCHES
2/8/1969	1969	16		Optus Oval	RICHMOND	8	9	57	FITZROY	9	12	66	-9	16,211	20	6	1	6	3	0	0		
9/8/1969	1969	17		MCG	RICHMOND	19	11	125	MELBOURNE	12	13	85	40	23,519	23	9	3	6	1	0	0	1	
16/8/1969	1969	18		Glenferrie Oval	RICHMOND	13	21	99	HAWTHORN	13	10	88	11	19,480	23	6	0	5	4	0	0	1	
23/8/1969	1969	19		Optus Oval	RICHMOND	24	12	156	CARLTON	20	7	127	29	27,657	12	3	1	4	1	0	0	1	
30/8/1969	1969	20		MCG	RICHMOND	23	16	154	WSTRN BLDGS	9	10	64	90	33,591	24	5	4	6	6	0	1	1	
6/9/1969	1969	FS		MCG	RICHMOND	25	17	167	GEELONG	7	7	49	118	101,233	19	4	2	6	0	0	1	1	
20/9/1969	1969	PF		MCG	RICHMOND	15	17	107	COLLINGWOOD	12	9	81	26	108,279	13	3	3	6	2	0	0		
27/9/1969	1969	GF		MCG	RICHMOND	12	13	85	CARLTON	8	12	60	25	119,165	17	8	0	4	4	0	0		
5/4/1970	1970	1		MCG	RICHMOND	14	12	96	FITZROY	16	20	116	-20	38,617	12	1	1	2	1	0	0	1	
11/4/1970	1970	2		Victoria Park	RICHMOND	13	16	94	COLLINGWOOD	19	19	133	-39	35,318	18	4	3	5	2	0	0	1	
18/4/1970	1970	3		MCG	RICHMOND	17	12	114	CARLTON	15	11	101	13	46,373	18	9	5	4	1	0	0		
25/4/1970	1970	4		Moorabbin	RICHMOND	7	12	54	ST KILDA	15	19	109	-55	32,147	14	5	3	3	0	0	0		
2/5/1970	1970	5		MCG	RICHMOND	6	13	49	STH MLB/SYDNEY	10	11	71	-22	23,084	11	3	3	3	0	0	0		
9/5/1970	1970	6		Waverley Park	RICHMOND	21	11	137	HAWTHORN	20	10	130	7	26,138	14	3	4	4	2	0	0	1	
16/5/1970	1970	7		MCG	RICHMOND	16	20	116	GEELONG	15	2	92	24	43,435	12	4	8	2	1	0	0		
23/5/1970	1970	8		MCG	RICHMOND	18	19	127	MELBOURNE	15	10	100	27	36,064	12	5	4	4	0	0	0		
30/5/1970	1970	9		MCG	RICHMOND	10	17	77	KANGAROOS	15	7	97	-20	22,284	17	2	3	3	2	0	0		
6/6/1970	1970	10		Windy Hill	RICHMOND	15	14	104	ESSENDON	14	13	97	7	20,650	12	2	3	3	0	0	0		
15/6/1970	1970	11		MCG	RICHMOND	22	15	147	WSTRN BLDGS	13	12	90	57	41,866	21	11	4	3	1	0	0	1	
20/6/1970	1970	12		Junction Oval	RICHMOND	8	9	57	FITZROY	12	11	83	-26	14,541	8	4	1	2	0	0	0		
27/6/1970	1970	13		Waverley Park	RICHMOND	11	13	79	COLLINGWOOD	9	13	67	12	23,939									
4/7/1970	1970	14		Optus Oval	RICHMOND	7	7	49	CARLTON	11	12	78	-29	26,895									
11/7/1970	1970	15		MCG	RICHMOND	11	15	81	ST KILDA	7	21	63	18	38,037	18	9	9	1	1	1	1	1	
18/7/1970	1970	16		Lake Oval	RICHMOND	12	17	89	STH MLB/SYDNEY	11	9	75	14	25,051	12	1	2	2	3	0	1		
25/7/1970	1970	17		MCG	RICHMOND	15	15	105	HAWTHORN	11	17	83	22	55,740	14	3	1	1	1	1	1		
1/8/1970	1970	18		Waverley Park	RICHMOND	8	13	61	GEELONG	13	10	88	-27	26,378	17	4	3	2	2	0	0		
8/8/1970	1970	19		MCG	RICHMOND	9	10	64	MELBOURNE	18	10	118	-54	25,158	12	3	3	3	1	1	0		
15/8/1970	1970	20		Arden St Oval	RICHMOND	16	10	106	KANGAROOS	7	6	48	58	8,837	26	12	5	5	3	2	0		
22/8/1970	1970	21		MCG	RICHMOND	23	13	151	ESSENDON	11	11	77	74	25,862	8	1	1	2	0	0	0		
29/8/1970	1970	22		Whitten Oval	RICHMOND	10	12	72	WSTRN BLDGS	12	10	82	-10	16,672	17	7	3	5	4	0	0		
3/4/1971	1971	1		Junction Oval	RICHMOND	22	18	150	FITZROY	14	15	99	51	18,386	10	1	1	3	0	1	1		
12/4/1971	1971	2		MCG	RICHMOND	10	9	69	COLLINGWOOD	16	10	106	-37	82,172	15	3	1	4	3	0	0		
17/4/1971	1971	3		Waverley Park	RICHMOND	10	8	68	ST KILDA	6	13	49	19	33,489	17	6	0	3	1	0	0	1	

Appendix A

DATE	SEASON	RND	SESSION	VENUE	KEVIN'S CLUB	G	B	PTS	OPPONENT	G	B	PTS	MARGIN	ATTENDANCE	K	M	HB	FF	FA	GLS	BEH	BEST 6	RESERVES MATCHES
24/4/1971	1971	4		Lake Oval	RICHMOND	20	13	133	STH MLB/SYDNEY	5	9	39	94	18,895	15	6	1	6	0	0	0		
1/5/1971	1971	5		MCG	RICHMOND	14	17	101	WSTRN BLDGS	17	19	121	-20	23,758	5	1	1	1	1	0	0		
8/5/1971	1971	6		Arden St Oval	RICHMOND	22	14	146	KANGAROOS	12	12	84	62	13,047	12	2	3	3	2	0	0	1	
15/5/1971	1971	7		Glenferrie Oval	RICHMOND	12	6	78	HAWTHORN	21	19	145	-67	22,956	6	2	2	0	3	2	0	1	
22/5/1971	1971	8		MCG	RICHMOND	16	26	122	CARLTON	9	16	70	52	52,783	7	2	3	2	0	0	0		
29/5/1971	1971	9		Waverley Park	RICHMOND	17	11	113	ESSENDON	13	11	89	24	16,300	6	1	3	3	3	0	0		
5/6/1971	1971	10		MCG	RICHMOND	15	16	106	MELBOURNE	11	9	75	31	48,708	11	1	2	3	2	0	1		
14/6/1971	1971	11		Skilled Stadium	RICHMOND	20	13	133	GEELONG	12	11	83	50	23,388	10	3	0	2	2	0	0		
19/6/1971	1971	12		MCG	RICHMOND	6	11	47	FITZROY	8	17	65	-18	24,831	15	6	5	1	1	0	0		
26/6/1971	1971	13		Victoria Park	RICHMOND	12	12	84	COLLINGWOOD	18	16	124	-40	33,338	21	6	1	7	4	0	0	1	
3/7/1971	1971	14		Moorabbin	RICHMOND	13	12	90	ST KILDA	13	9	87	3	28,825	15	6	0	1	1	0	0	1	
10/7/1971	1971	15		MCG	RICHMOND	12	18	90	STH MLB/SYDNEY	11	13	79	11	22,870	13	6	3	3	1	0	0		
17/7/1971	1971	16		Whitten Oval	RICHMOND	6	15	51	WSTRN BLDGS	13	8	86	-35	17,826	8	3	3	0	1	0	0		
24/7/1971	1971	17		Waverley Park	RICHMOND	25	19	169	KANGAROOS	12	7	79	90	11,416	15	4	6	6	3	0	0		
31/7/1971	1971	18		MCG	RICHMOND	16	12	108	HAWTHORN	11	10	76	32	47,951	5	1	3	2	0	0	0		
7/8/1971	1971	19		Optus Oval	RICHMOND	14	17	101	CARLTON	8	10	58	43	34,224	13	1	5	4	0	0	0		
14/8/1971	1971	20		MCG	RICHMOND	18	18	126	ESSENDON	10	12	72	54	28,388	9	2	1	3	1	0	0		
21/8/1971	1971	21		MCG	RICHMOND	19	9	123	MELBOURNE	15	12	102	21	37,732	9	3	6	2	2	0	0		
28/8/1971	1971	22		MCG	RICHMOND	16	14	110	GEELONG	14	18	102	8	36,423	14	4	1	4	3	0	0		
4/9/1971	1971	FS		MCG	RICHMOND	18	13	121	COLLINGWOOD	11	11	77	44	99,771	14	4	1	4	3	0	0	1	
18/9/1971	1971	PF		MCG	RICHMOND	12	6	78	ST KILDA	16	12	108	-30	102,494	12	3	0	4	3	0	0		
3/4/1972	1972	1		MCG	RICHMOND	16	9	105	COLLINGWOOD	14	17	101	4	72,714	12	5	5	1	0	0	0	1	
8/4/1972	1972	2		Skilled Stadium	RICHMOND	22	17	149	GEELONG	10	3	63	86	18,494	13	5	3	2	1	0	0		
25/4/1972	1972	3		MCG	RICHMOND	16	15	111	ESSENDON	19	17	131	-20	55,823	12	4	1	3	1	0	0		
22/4/1972	1972	4		Optus Oval	RICHMOND	15	19	109	CARLTON	15	14	104	5	28,536	22	8	0	2	0	0	0		
25/4/1972	1972	5		MCG	RICHMOND	13	11	89	MELBOURNE	12	12	84	5	38,154	15	2	4	6	1	0	0	1	
6/5/1972	1972	6		Moorabbin	RICHMOND	10	16	76	ST KILDA	24	21	165	-89	34,055	9	4	4	1	4	0	0		
13/5/1972	1972	7		MCG	RICHMOND	17	19	121	KANGAROOS	13	16	94	27	17,331	13	5	9	2	0	0	0		
20/5/1972	1972	8		Waverley Park	RICHMOND	11	25	91	HAWTHORN	13	6	84	7	25,845	13	4	2	4	0	0	0		
27/5/1972	1972	9		Junction Oval	RICHMOND	16	9	105	FITZROY	12	25	97	8	21,753	21	3	0	8	1	0	0	1	
3/6/1972	1972	10		MCG	RICHMOND	15	14	104	WSTRN BLDGS	12	14	86	18	36,985	11	4	3	1	1	0	0		

Appendix A

DATE	SEASON	RND	SESSION	VENUE	KEVIN'S CLUB	G	B	PTS	OPPONENT	G	B	PTS	MARGIN	ATTENDANCE	K	M	HB	FF	FA	GLS	BEH	BEST 6	RESERVES MATCHES
10/6/1972	1972	11		MCG	RICHMOND	14	11	95	STH MLB/SYDNEY	2	19	31	64	18,692									1
17/6/1972	1972	12		Victoria Park	RICHMOND	12	13	85	COLLINGWOOD	11	24	90	-5	28,188									
1/7/1972	1972	13		MCG	RICHMOND	14	8	92	GEELONG	25	18	168	-76	22,595									
8/7/1972	1972	14		MCG	RICHMOND	17	17	119	CARLTON	13	10	88	31	46,471	18	5	1	4	0	0	1	1	
15/7/1972	1972	15		Windy Hill	RICHMOND	17	9	111	ESSENDON	13	12	90	21	22,251	12	2	0	5	1	0	0		
22/7/1972	1972	16		MCG	RICHMOND	19	9	123	MELBOURNE	11	18	84	39	32,416	17	7	1	1	2	0	0		
29/7/1972	1972	17		MCG	RICHMOND	23	15	153	ST KILDA	11	15	81	72	44,348	14	4	3	5	1	1	0		
5/8/1972	1972	18		Waverley Park	RICHMOND	13	20	98	KANGAROOS	6	14	50	48	11,393	16	7	2	1	1	0	0		
12/8/1972	1972	19		Glenferrie Oval	RICHMOND	17	11	113	HAWTHORN	15	12	102	11	18,103									
19/8/1972	1972	20		MCG	RICHMOND	20	17	137	FITZROY	13	22	100	37	27,651	16	4	2	5	0	0	0		
26/8/1972	1972	21		Whitten Oval	RICHMOND	18	17	125	WSTRN BLDGS	17	21	123	2	18,117	6	1	7	0	4	0	0		
2/9/1972	1972	22		Waverley Park	RICHMOND	23	20	158	STH MLB/SYDNEY	12	10	82	76	16,541	13	6	1	3	1	0	0		
9/9/1972	1972	QF		MCG	RICHMOND	25	14	164	COLLINGWOOD	18	12	120	44	91,900	14	4	1	2	3	0	0		
16/9/1972	1972	SS		Waverley Park	RICHMOND	8	13	61	CARLTON	8	13	61	0	54,338	16	2	5	2	2	0	0	1	
23/9/1972	1972	SSR		MCG	RICHMOND	15	20	110	CARLTON	9	15	69	41	92,670	2	0	2	1	1	0	0		
7/10/1972	1972	GF		MCG	RICHMOND	22	18	150	CARLTON	28	9	177	-27	112,393	9	1	4	3	2	3	2		
7/4/1973	1973	1		Windy Hill	RICHMOND	19	15	129	ESSENDON	19	13	127	2	27,959	9	2	0	3	3	2	0		
14/4/1973	1973	2		MCG	RICHMOND	18	19	127	GEELONG	16	14	110	17	29,665	21	5	3	5	1	0	1		
21/4/1973	1973	3		Moorabbin	RICHMOND	17	8	110	ST KILDA	12	9	81	29	30,000	11	3	0	1	2	0	0		
25/4/1973	1973	4		MCG	RICHMOND	11	18	84	KANGAROOS	14	20	104	-20	48,923	13	4	3	2	5	0	0		
5/5/1973	1973	5		MCG	RICHMOND	16	14	110	MELBOURNE	13	13	91	19	37,667	7	1	1	1	3	0	0		
12/5/1973	1973	6		MCG	RICHMOND	18	20	128	CARLTON	15	12	102	26	54,139	12	4	1	0	1	0	0		
19/5/1973	1973	7		Waverley Park	RICHMOND	16	21	117	FITZROY	12	8	80	37	19,539	15	5	10	3	0	0	2		
26/5/1973	1973	8		MCG	RICHMOND	10	22	82	HAWTHORN	16	23	119	-37	32,613	18	5	5	1	1	1	0	1	
4/6/1973	1973	9		Waverley Park	RICHMOND	10	6	66	COLLINGWOOD	15	15	105	-39	55,827	11	3	10	2	2	0	1		
9/6/1973	1973	10		Lake Oval	RICHMOND	13	14	92	STH MLB/SYDNEY	9	8	62	30	10,726	20	4	6	3	2	0	1	1	
16/6/1973	1973	11		Whitten Oval	RICHMOND	17	7	109	WSTRN BLDGS	7	16	58	51	16,733	19	10	2	3	3	1	1		
23/6/1973	1973	12		MCG	RICHMOND	15	21	111	ESSENDON	13	17	95	16	43,892	21	4	7	6	4	1	1		
30/6/1973	1973	13		Waverley Park	RICHMOND	21	7	133	GEELONG	13	11	89	44	13,219	18	5	4	1	1	2	1		
7/7/1973	1973	14		Arden St Oval	RICHMOND	17	15	117	KANGAROOS	11	12	78	39	19,114	20	4	4	3	2	2	1		
14/7/1973	1973	15		Waverley Park	RICHMOND	13	12	90	ST KILDA	11	11	77	13	31,502	19	1	4	3	1	2	1		
21/7/1973	1973	16		MCG	RICHMOND	16	14	110	MELBOURNE	9	19	73	37	30,492	16	5	8	5	1	3	1		

Appendix A

DATE	SEASON	RND	SESSION	VENUE	KEVIN'S CLUB	G	B	PTS	OPPONENT	G	B	PTS	MARGIN	ATTENDANCE	K	M	HB	FF	FA	GLS	BEH	BEST 6	RESERVES MATCHES
28/7/1973	1973	17		Optus Oval	RICHMOND	10	21	81	CARLTON	15	17	107	-26	28,592	14	3	4	5	1	0	2		
4/8/1973	1973	18		MCG	RICHMOND	15	14	104	FITZROY	13	14	92	12	20,278	15	2	5	5	4	1	0		
11/8/1973	1973	19		Glenferrie Oval	RICHMOND	12	10	82	HAWTHORN	11	11	77	5	20,286	6	0	5	2	1	1	1		
18/8/1973	1973	20		Victoria Park	RICHMOND	14	16	100	COLLINGWOOD	8	11	59	41	28,286	7	0	6	2	1	1	0	1	
25/8/1973	1973	21		MCG	RICHMOND	22	11	143	STH MLB/SYDNEY	13	16	94	49	24,307	19	5	4	5	2	0	0		
1/9/1973	1973	22		MCG	RICHMOND	10	16	76	WSTRN BLDGS	11	11	77	-1	24,671	15	3	1	6	2	0	0		
8/9/1973	1973	QF		MCG	RICHMOND	10	11	71	CARLTON	13	13	91	-20	86,386	13	3	8	3	3	0	0	1	
15/9/1973	1973	FS		MCG	RICHMOND	15	18	108	ST KILDA	9	14	68	40	86,483	16	5	9	3	3	0	0	1	
22/9/1973	1973	PF		MCG	RICHMOND	15	15	105	COLLINGWOOD	14	14	98	7	98,652	16	5	7	5	6	3	3	1	
29/9/1973	1973	GF		MCG	RICHMOND	16	20	116	CARLTON	12	14	86	30	116,956	17	1	2	1	2	2	1	1	
6/4/1974	1974	1		MCG	RICHMOND	12	16	88	HAWTHORN	15	14	104	-16	38,735	16	5	6	4	2	1	1	1	
13/4/1974	1974	2		Junction Oval	RICHMOND	15	26	116	FITZROY	9	13	67	49	17,040	18	2	6	5	2	3	1	1	
20/4/1974	1974	3		Optus Oval	RICHMOND	18	11	119	CARLTON	11	15	81	38	33,050	16	4	6	6	1	1	1	1	
27/4/1974	1974	4		MCG	RICHMOND	13	16	94	MELBOURNE	9	15	69	25	28,080	18	2	5	4	0	1	1	1	
4/5/1974	1974	5		Moorabbin	RICHMOND	15	20	110	ST KILDA	13	12	90	20	30,673	16	7	8	5	0	1	1		
11/5/1974	1974	6		MCG	RICHMOND	17	11	113	GEELONG	18	15	123	-10	31,483	23	2	4	3	2	3	3	1	
18/5/1974	1974	7		Windy Hill	RICHMOND	16	19	115	ESSENDON	15	15	105	10	24,376	15	7	8	5	3	0	3		
25/5/1974	1974	8		Arden St Oval	RICHMOND	13	17	95	KANGAROOS	9	16	70	25	22,841	23	2	8	5	3	0	1		
1/6/1974	1974	9		Lake Oval	RICHMOND	9	20	74	COLLINGWOOD	21	17	143	-69	66,829									
8/6/1974	1974	10		MCG	RICHMOND	23	9	147	STH MLB/SYDNEY	9	13	67	80	12,054	12	4	8	3	4	2	0	1	
17/6/1974	1974	11		Optus Oval	RICHMOND	19	19	133	WSTRN BLDGS	15	11	101	32	68,446	8	2	8	4	4	2	1		
22/6/1974	1974	12		Waverley Park	RICHMOND	15	18	108	HAWTHORN	19	17	131	-23	15,710	16	5	8	3	1	1	1	1	
29/6/1974	1974	13		MCG	RICHMOND	29	21	195	FITZROY	9	12	66	129	16,455	20	3	11	2	0	2	1		
6/7/1974	1974	14		MCG	RICHMOND	23	15	153	MELBOURNE	11	24	90	63	21,146	16	5	9	1	1	0	1	1	
13/7/1974	1974	15		MCG	RICHMOND	15	15	105	CARLTON	11	9	75	30	36,417	9	3	4	1	0	0	1		
20/7/1974	1974	16		MCG	RICHMOND	15	24	114	ST KILDA	11	13	79	35	28,045	21	5	8	2	3	1	5	1	
27/7/1974	1974	17		Waverley Park	RICHMOND	13	15	93	GEELONG	8	9	57	36	15,578	19	4	3	4	2	0	3	1	
3/8/1974	1974	18		MCG	RICHMOND	20	15	135	ESSENDON	12	16	88	47	34,011	22	2	8	4	3	4	1	1	
10/8/1974	1974	19		Waverley Park	RICHMOND	15	12	102	KANGAROOS	11	11	77	25	40,399	18	1	3	2	1	1	0		
17/8/1974	1974	20		Victoria Park	RICHMOND	16	11	107	COLLINGWOOD	10	20	80	27	36,729	15	2	7	0	5	2	1		
24/8/1974	1974	21		MCG	RICHMOND	23	24	162	STH MLB/SYDNEY	17	27	129	33	32,651	15	2	5	0	1	3	3		
31/8/1974	1974	22		Whitten Oval	RICHMOND	11	14	80	WSTRN BLDGS	13	9	87	-7	25,190	13	3	5	0	1	1	1		
14/9/1974	1974	SS		Waverley Park	RICHMOND	10	13	73	KANGAROOS	6	16	52	21	57,569	24	1	0	3	3	0	1	1	

Appendix A

DATE	SEASON	RND	SESSION	VENUE	KEVIN'S CLUB	G	B	PTS	OPPONENT	G	B	PTS	MARGIN	ATTENDANCE	K	M	HB	FF	FA	GLS	BEH	BEST 6	RESERVES MATCHES
28/9/1974	1974	GF		MCG	RICHMOND	18	20	128	KANGAROOS	13	9	87	41	113,839	21	6	12	5	2	2	1		
5/4/1975	1975	1		Junction Oval	RICHMOND	15	13	103	FITZROY	14	14	98	5	14,442	20	3	7	3	3	1	0	1	
12/4/1975	1975	2		MCG	RICHMOND	15	22	112	GEELONG	10	12	72	40	33,600	15	1	8	1	2	1	0		
19/4/1975	1975	3		Waverley Park	RICHMOND	12	15	87	HAWTHORN	17	14	116	-29	39,496	11	2	2	3	1	1	1		
26/4/1975	1975	4		Whitten Oval	RICHMOND	4	19	43	WSTRN BLDGS	16	13	109	-66	25,388	15	5	3	1	2	0	0		
3/5/1975	1975	5		MCG	RICHMOND	19	23	137	STH MLB/SYDNEY	12	14	86	51	25,296	5	2	3	2	3	0	0		
10/5/1975	1975	6		Victoria Park	RICHMOND	22	14	146	COLLINGWOOD	14	12	96	50	27,729	14	2	7	3	1	3	1		
17/5/1975	1975	7		MCG	RICHMOND	19	18	132	MELBOURNE	10	18	78	54	29,131	14	2	8	3	1	1	2	1	
24/5/1975	1975	8		Arden St Oval	RICHMOND	9	12	66	KANGAROOS	11	8	74	-8	20,257	14	2	6	2	3	0	0	1	
31/5/1975	1975	9		Optus Oval	RICHMOND	9	13	67	CARLTON	16	19	115	-48	32,576	9	3	3	1	4	0	0		
7/6/1975	1975	10		MCG	RICHMOND	19	14	128	ESSENDON	12	9	81	47	49,469	11	2	3	3	1	0	0		
16/6/1975	1975	11		Waverley Park	RICHMOND	13	12	90	ST KILDA	14	18	102	-12	33,653	9	3	9	1	2	0	0		
21/6/1975	1975	12		MCG	RICHMOND	13	18	96	FITZROY	13	20	98	-2	21,049	3	0	2	1	1	0	0		
28/6/1975	1975	13		Skilled Stadium	RICHMOND	13	14	92	GEELONG	8	13	61	31	14,747									
5/7/1975	1975	14		MCG	RICHMOND	17	18	120	WSTRN BLDGS	12	10	82	38	29,501									
12/7/1975	1975	15		Optus Oval	RICHMOND	2	20	32	HAWTHORN	14	10	94	-62	17,115									
19/7/1975	1975	16		Lake Oval	RICHMOND	26	11	167	STH MLB/SYDNEY	8	12	60	107	13,411	11	3	8	4	3	0	0		
26/7/1975	1975	17		MCG	RICHMOND	16	19	115	COLLINGWOOD	10	9	69	46	56,846	3	0	2	1	1	0	0		
2/8/1975	1975	18		MCG	RICHMOND	12	18	90	MELBOURNE	19	13	127	-37	25,211	19	7	10	3	2	2	0	1	
9/8/1975	1975	19		MCG	RICHMOND	13	18	96	KANGAROOS	13	23	101	-5	39,664	18	3	8	4	3	0	0		
16/8/1975	1975	20		MCG	RICHMOND	13	20	98	CARLTON	14	11	95	3	49,756	16	1	8	2	5	0	1		
23/8/1975	1975	21		Waverley Park	RICHMOND	20	16	136	ESSENDON	17	15	117	19	23,601	12	1	6	2	2	0	1		
30/8/1975	1975	22		MCG	RICHMOND	17	14	116	ST KILDA	8	20	68	48	39,275	8	2	3	1	2	1	1		
6/9/1975	1975	EF		Waverley Park	RICHMOND	11	11	77	COLLINGWOOD	10	13	73	4	65,512		3	2	0	4	0	1		
13/9/1975	1975	FS		MCG	RICHMOND	9	17	71	CARLTON	9	8	62	9	76,967	12	3	6	6	3	1	0	1	
20/9/1975	1975	PF		Waverley Park	RICHMOND	8	11	59	KANGAROOS	10	16	76	-17	71,130	5	0	4	1	2	0	0		
3/4/1976	1976	1		MCG	RICHMOND	16	21	117	FITZROY	14	14	98	19	28,834	2	1	1	0	0	0	0		
10/4/1976	1976	2		Skilled Stadium	RICHMOND	14	11	95	GEELONG	22	11	143	-48	20,443	10	2	6	1	3	1	0		
19/4/1976	1976	3		MCG	RICHMOND	14	18	102	KANGAROOS	12	11	83	19	41,413	7	4	3	0	0	0	0		
24/4/1976	1976	4		Victoria Park	RICHMOND	15	9	99	COLLINGWOOD	16	18	114	-15	27,009	14	2	5	3	0	0	0		
1/5/1976	1976	5		MCG	RICHMOND	12	17	89	WSTRN BLDGS	15	20	110	-21	31,434	6	4	8	3	0	0	0		
8/5/1976	1976	6		Waverley Park	RICHMOND	17	17	119	ESSENDON	9	10	64	55	27,631	14	5	8	3	3	0	0	1	

Appendix A

DATE	SEASON	RND	SESSION	VENUE	KEVIN'S CLUB	G	B	PTS	OPPONENT	G	B	PTS	MARGIN	ATTENDANCE	K	M	HB	FF	FA	GLS	BEH	BEST 6	RESERVES MATCHES
15/5/1976	1976	7		Optus Oval	RICHMOND	9	15	69	CARLTON	21	14	140	-71	30,395	12	3	4	7	0	0	0	1	
22/5/1976	1976	8		MCG	RICHMOND	14	11	95	MELBOURNE	9	15	69	26	22,145	16	4	4	7	1	0	0	1	
29/5/1976	1976	9		Lake Oval	RICHMOND	13	10	88	STH MLB/SYDNEY	13	18	96	-8	14,222	16	2	3	7	0	0	0	1	
5/6/1976	1976	10		MCG	RICHMOND	13	10	88	HAWTHORN	15	10	100	-12	29,608	17	1	5	5	2	0	0	1	
12/6/1976	1976	11		Moorabbin	RICHMOND	15	6	96	ST KILDA	19	13	127	-31	21,681	13	3	3	3	0	0	0	1	
19/6/1976	1976	12		Junction Oval	RICHMOND	13	12	90	FITZROY	22	14	146	-56	12,644	6	3	3	2	0	0	0	1	
26/6/1976	1976	13		MCG	RICHMOND	15	12	102	GEELONG	14	14	98	4	28,608	12	4	12	0	2	0	0	1	
3/7/1976	1976	14		MCG	RICHMOND	23	13	151	COLLINGWOOD	7	14	56	95	36,477	11	4	5	3	1	0	0	1	
10/7/1976	1976	15		Arden St Oval	RICHMOND	11	11	77	KANGAROOS	12	10	82	-5	18,421	5	0	3	3	2	0	0		
17/7/1976	1976	16		Waverley Park	RICHMOND	12	19	91	WSTRN BLDGS	15	6	96	-5	22,795	13	7	10	4	2	0	0	1	
24/7/1976	1976	17		Windy Hill	RICHMOND	15	16	106	ESSENDON	8	15	63	43	21,585	15	12	12	5	2	0	0	1	
31/7/1976	1976	18		MCG	RICHMOND	8	17	65	CARLTON	22	16	148	-83	39,744	13	2	5	2	2	0	0	1	
7/8/1976	1976	19		MCG	RICHMOND	13	11	89	MELBOURNE	17	17	119	-30	16,585	10	1	8	4	4	0	0	1	
14/8/1976	1976	20		MCG	RICHMOND	16	14	110	STH MLB/SYDNEY	12	12	84	26	20,817	20	6	5	2	2	1	0	1	
21/8/1976	1976	21		Optus Oval	RICHMOND	17	12	114	HAWTHORN	11	16	82	32	13,574	8	3	5	4	6	0	0		
28/8/1976	1976	22		Waverley Park	RICHMOND	21	14	140	ST KILDA	14	22	106	34	27,429	8	1	1	1	0	0	0		
2/4/1977	1977	1		Junction Oval	RICHMOND	18	21	129	FITZROY	21	17	143	-14	17,740	6	2	3	1	1	0	0		
11/4/1977	1977	2		MCG	RICHMOND	19	6	120	HAWTHORN	17	17	119	1	42,192	10	1	5	0	0	0	0		
16/4/1977	1977	3		Lake Oval	RICHMOND	13	13	91	STH MLB/SYDNEY	11	13	79	12	25,768	14	5	3	4	2	0	0	1	
25/4/1977	1977	4		MCG	RICHMOND	14	16	100	COLLINGWOOD	17	24	126	-26	91,936	7	0	4	0	0	0	0		
30/4/1977	1977	5		MCG	RICHMOND	19	17	131	MELBOURNE	13	24	102	29	22,272	15	6	4	4	0	0	0	1	
7/5/1977	1977	6		Waverley Park	RICHMOND	19	15	129	KANGAROOS	14	12	96	33	34,408	20	3	8	6	3	2	0	1	
14/5/1977	1977	7		MCG	RICHMOND	14	15	99	ESSENDON	15	9	99	0	32,326	24	7	7	4	0	2	1	1	
21/5/1977	1977	8		MCG	RICHMOND	16	18	114	WSTRN BLDGS	13	17	95	19	21,519	6	5	12	1	3	0	0	1	
28/5/1977	1977	9		Waverley Park	RICHMOND	18	13	121	GEELONG	10	11	71	50	26,007	12	3	12	0	3	0	0	1	
4/6/1977	1977	10		Optus Oval	RICHMOND	19	11	125	CARLTON	16	9	105	20	28,556	20	4	8	6	3	3	1	1	
13/6/1977	1977	11		Moorabbin	RICHMOND	16	5	101	ST KILDA	13	10	88	13	23,979	10	2	5	2	1	1	0	1	
18/6/1977	1977	12		MCG	RICHMOND	13	15	93	FITZROY	6	5	41	52	12,877	10	4	2	2	1	2	0	1	
25/6/1977	1977	13		Waverley Park	RICHMOND	7	10	52	HAWTHORN	9	12	66	-14	34,820	13	0	13	6	2	0	0	1	
2/7/1977	1977	14		Victoria Park	RICHMOND	11	12	78	COLLINGWOOD	22	9	141	-63	32,833	11	3	8	4	3	0	0	1	
9/7/1977	1977	15		Waverley Park	RICHMOND	14	16	100	STH MLB/SYDNEY	10	11	71	29	34,291	14	9	9	9	1	0	0	1	
16/7/1977	1977	16		MCG	RICHMOND	10	11	71	MELBOURNE	13	12	90	-19	19,075	13	5	8	4	2	0	0	1	
23/7/1977	1977	17		Arden St Oval	RICHMOND	14	14	98	KANGAROOS	15	11	101	-3	15,359	10	3	10	5	5	0	0	1	

Appendix A

DATE	SEASON	RND	SESSION	VENUE	KEVIN'S CLUB	G	B	PTS	OPPONENT	G	B	PTS	MARGIN	ATTENDANCE	K	M	HB	FF	FA	GLS	BEH	BEST 6	RESERVES MATCHES
30/7/1977	1977	18		MCG	RICHMOND	16	15	111	ESSENDON	9	11	65	46	33,085	18	5	18	3	3	0	0	3	
6/8/1977	1977	19		Whitten Oval	RICHMOND	15	11	101	WSTRN BLDGS	19	15	129	-28	16,897	9	3	11	0	4	0	0		
13/8/1977	1977	20		Skilled Stadium	RICHMOND	19	18	132	GEELONG	5	16	46	86	17,081	14	5	7	2	2	2	0		
20/8/1977	1977	21		MCG	RICHMOND	15	13	103	CARLTON	14	16	100	3	49,134	13	0	6	5	3	0	0	1	
27/8/1977	1977	22		MCG	RICHMOND	25	21	171	ST KILDA	17	10	112	59	24,122	11	5	7	5	4	0	0	1	
3/9/1977	1977	EF		Waverley Park	RICHMOND	13	10	88	STH MLB/SYDNEY	7	12	54	34	63,663	12	2	6	5	2	0	0		
10/9/1977	1977	FS		Waverley Park	RICHMOND	9	9	63	KANGAROOS	16	14	110	-47	48,105	29	4	5	5	2	0	0	1	
1/4/1978	1978	1		MCG	RICHMOND	25	24	174	CARLTON	14	13	97	77	49,031	13	3	5	5	1	0	0	1	
8/4/1978	1978	2		Arden St Oval	RICHMOND	14	9	93	KANGAROOS	25	16	166	-73	22,505	8	0	3	3	2	0	0		
15/4/1978	1978	3		MCG	RICHMOND	16	14	110	ST KILDA	15	20	110	0	35,602									
22/4/1978	1978	4		Skilled Stadium	RICHMOND	15	8	98	GEELONG	18	17	125	-27	20,566	14	2	4	2	1	0	0	1	
25/4/1978	1978	5		MCG	RICHMOND	19	16	130	MELBOURNE	8	11	59	71	34,212	14	1	7	2	2	0	0	1	
6/5/1978	1978	6		Windy Hill	RICHMOND	19	15	129	ESSENDON	22	18	150	-21	21,946	8	2	2	1	3	0	0		
13/5/1978	1978	7		MCG	RICHMOND	14	14	98	STH MLB/SYDNEY	19	11	125	-27	25,904	10	0	6	4	2	0	0		
20/5/1978	1978	8		Waverley Park	RICHMOND	9	16	70	HAWTHORN	14	15	99	-29	27,224	14	2	6	5	2	0	0	1	
27/5/1978	1978	9		Victoria Park	RICHMOND	10	16	76	COLLINGWOOD	12	20	92	-16	28,651	15	5	9	5	2	0	0	1	
3/6/1978	1978	10		MCG	RICHMOND	12	14	86	FITZROY	11	14	80	6	21,122	7	5	6	2	4	0	0		
17/6/1978	1978	11		MCG	RICHMOND	23	17	155	WSTRN BLDGS	14	13	97	58	22,764	5	1	9	2	2	0	0	1	
24/6/1978	1978	12		Optus Oval	RICHMOND	13	16	94	CARLTON	20	17	137	-43	28,266	17	5	10	2	2	0	0		
1/7/1978	1978	13		MCG	RICHMOND	21	16	142	KANGAROOS	17	15	117	25	27,156	12	4	5	2	2	0	0		
8/7/1978	1978	14		MCG	RICHMOND	17	20	122	GEELONG	18	9	117	5	24,417	10	4	8	4	0	0	0		
15/7/1978	1978	15		Moorabbin	RICHMOND	19	11	125	ST KILDA	10	11	71	54	18,958	9	1	5	5	1	0	0	1	
22/7/1978	1978	16		MCG	RICHMOND	17	19	121	MELBOURNE	14	9	93	28	18,416	8	0	2	2	4	0	0		
29/7/1978	1978	17		MCG	RICHMOND	20	16	136	ESSENDON	13	18	96	40	41,878									
5/8/1978	1978	18		Waverley Park	RICHMOND	9	16	70	STH MLB/SYDNEY	14	9	93	-23	31,717	8	3	10	3	1	0	0	1	
12/8/1978	1978	19		Optus Oval	RICHMOND	10	10	70	HAWTHORN	18	19	127	-57	15,980									
19/8/1978	1978	20		MCG	RICHMOND	16	13	109	COLLINGWOOD	19	9	123	-14	59,580	6	1	6	2	2	1	0		
16/8/1978	1978	21		Junction Oval	RICHMOND	17	15	117	FITZROY	20	14	134	-17	11,200	11	2	8	4	3	2	0		
2/9/1978	1978	22		Waverley Park	RICHMOND	19	20	134	WSTRN BLDGS	11	15	81	53	17,768	14	5	11	5	1	1	0	1	
7/4/1979	1979	1		Lake Oval	RICHMOND	19	11	125	STH MLB/SYDNEY	15	21	111	14	18,603	11	4	9	3	2	0	0		
16/4/1979	1979	2		MCG	RICHMOND	13	18	96	CARLTON	23	9	147	-51	59,942	13	0	5	6	0	0	0	1	
21/4/1979	1979	3		MCG	RICHMOND	20	12	132	FITZROY	16	16	112	20	24,635	20								

Appendix A

DATE	SEASON	RND	SESSION	VENUE	KEVIN'S CLUB	G	B	PTS	OPPONENT	G	B	PTS	MARGIN	ATTENDANCE	K	M	HB	FF	FA	GLS	BEH	BEST 6 MATCHES	RESERVES
25/4/1979	1979	4		MCG	RICHMOND	15	19	109	MELBOURNE	16	23	119	-10	44,708	6	1	3	1	1	0	1		
5/5/1979	1979	5		MCG	RICHMOND	11	16	82	HAWTHORN	24	17	161	-79	31,448	3	0	1	0	2	0	0		
12/5/1979	1979	6		Waverley Park	RICHMOND	13	16	94	KANGAROOS	14	15	99	-5	22,626									
19/5/1979	1979	7		Moorabbin	RICHMOND	14	15	99	ST KILDA	16	15	111	-12	18,087									
26/5/1979	1979	8		MCG	RICHMOND	22	26	158	WSTRN BLDGS	12	13	85	73	21,672									
2/6/1979	1979	9		Victoria Park	RICHMOND	10	20	80	COLLINGWOOD	19	18	132	-52	31,474									
9/6/1979	1979	10		MCG	RICHMOND	14	17	101	GEELONG	18	19	127	-26	24,824									
18/6/1979	1979	11		Waverley Park	RICHMOND	16	12	108	ESSENDON	20	12	132	-24	53,116									
23/6/1979	1979	12		MCG	RICHMOND	25	16	166	STH MLB/SYDNEY	16	14	110	56	21,216									
30/6/1979	1979	13		Optus Oval	RICHMOND	12	10	82	CARLTON	21	12	138	-56	21,792									
7/7/1979	1979	14		MCG	RICHMOND	17	18	120	MELBOURNE	10	16	76	44	19,879									
15/7/1979	1979	15		SCG	RICHMOND	22	20	152	FITZROY	20	15	135	17	17,140									
21/7/1979	1979	16		Optus Oval	RICHMOND	18	11	119	HAWTHORN	14	20	104	15	13,557									
28/7/1979	1979	17		MCG	RICHMOND	16	15	111	KANGAROOS	19	10	124	-13	38,111									
4/8/1979	1979	18		Waverley Park	RICHMOND	28	22	190	ST KILDA	18	11	119	71	24,651									
11/8/1979	1979	19		Whitten Oval	RICHMOND	6	5	41	WSTRN BLDGS	13	19	97	-56	12,557									
18/8/1979	1979	20		MCG	RICHMOND	10	15	75	COLLINGWOOD	13	17	95	-20	61,624									
25/8/1979	1979	21		Skilled Stadium	RICHMOND	12	17	89	GEELONG	17	13	115	-26	18,039									
9/1/1979	1979	22		Windy Hill	RICHMOND	18	14	122	ESSENDON	8	15	63	59	22,589									

Appendix B

KEVIN SHEEDY'S LEAGUE PLAYING CAREER HONOURS

SEASON	PREMIERSHIP MATCHES MTCHS	K	M	HB	FF	FA	GLS	BEH	BEST 6	BROWNLOW MEDAL VOTES	PRE-SEAS NIGHT SERIES MTCHS	INTERSTATE GLS	INTERSTATE MTCHS	RESERVES GLS	RESERVES MTCHS	RESERVES GLS	RESERVES BEST 6	HONOURS
1967	6	83	23	21	19	15	2	1	2	3	0	0	0	0	5	1	1	
1968	16	217	51	60	45	19	1	6	5	1	2	0	0	0	4	8	1	
1969	23	381	101	51	96	45	1	2	16	11	0	0	1	0	0	0		Runner-up in Best and Fairest count
1970	19	281	91	66	54	24	2	2	10	2	1	0	1	0	0	0		Special Service trophy
1971	23	263	73	51	65	39	2	2	5	3	0	0	1	0	0	0		Third in Best and Fairest count/ Best Player in Finals award
1972	23	294	87	60	62	27	4	3	8	6	0	0	3	0	0	0		Fourth in Best and Fairest count
1973	25	372	91	117	80	52	20	24	13	4	0	0	0	0	0	0		Third in Best and Fairest count/ Most Determined Player award
1974	23	393	78	144	67	45	34	34	14	0	0	0	1	1	0	0		
1975	23	240	50	118	47	51	9	8	7	0	0	0	0	0	0	0		
1976	22	254	74	119	66	32	2	0	13	18	0	0	0	0	0	0		Best and Fairest award/Most Determined Player award/ RFC Life Membership
1977	*24	321	86	81	73	45	10	5	14	13	3	0	1	0	0	0		Fifth in Best and Fairest count/ Outstanding Service award
1978	20	203	42	122	61	33	3	0	8	1	1	0	0	0	0	0		Club captain
1979	4	33	5	18	10	5	0	1	1	0	0	0	0	0	0	0		Appointed skills coach after early retirement
TOTALS	251	3335	852	1028	745	432	90	88	116	62	7	0	8	1	9	9	2	

Some match statistics are unavailable

KEVIN SHEEDY THE COACH: 1981–2007

DATE	SEASON	RND	SESSION	VENUE	KEVIN'S CLUB	G	B	PTS	OPPONENT	G	B	PTS	MARGIN	ATTENDANCE	FIELD UMPIRE ONE	FIELD UMPIRE TWO	FIELD UMPIRE THREE
28/3/1981	1981	1		Skilled Stadium	ESSENDON	10	11	71	GEELONG	10	17	77	-6	17,783	P.G. Saville	I.G.A. Robinson	
4/4/1981	1981	2		Windy Hill	ESSENDON	16	15	111	KANGAROOS	15	9	99	12	26,443	N.R. Nash	P.R. Cameron	
11/4/1981	1981	3		MCG	ESSENDON	16	18	114	RICHMOND	17	16	118	-4	61,908	G.F. Dore	G.G. Vernon	
20/4/1981	1981	4		Windy Hill	ESSENDON	11	13	79	HAWTHORN	13	16	94	-15	29,597	I.G.A. Robinson	K.F. Smith	
25/4/1981	1981	5		Waverley Park	ESSENDON	15	14	104	FITZROY	19	11	125	-21	33,465	N.R. Nash	I.G.A. Robinson	
2/5/1981	1981	6		Whitten Oval	ESSENDON	12	11	83	WSTRN BLDGS	13	13	91	-8	19,624	P.R. Cameron	G.T.D. Morrow	
9/5/1981	1981	7		Windy Hill	ESSENDON	14	17	101	ST KILDA	11	10	76	25	16,828	I.G.A. Robinson	J.J. Russo	
16/5/1981	1981	8		Waverley Park	ESSENDON	21	18	144	COLLINGWOOD	14	3	87	57	79,326	A.P. Coates	M.W. Prince	A.M. Panozzo
23/5/1981	1981	9		MCG	ESSENDON	14	20	104	MELBOURNE	10	10	70	34	31,769	J. Harvey	C. Mitchell	R. Williams
30/5/1981	1981	10		Windy Hill	ESSENDON	11	13	79	CARLTON	6	8	44	35	30,574	D.G. Rich	P.R. Cameron	
8/6/1981	1981	11		Lake Oval	ESSENDON	15	18	108	STH MLB/SYDNEY	12	8	80	28	28,588	N.R. Nash	J. Chapman	
13/6/1981	1981	12		Arden St Oval	ESSENDON	18	29	137	KANGAROOS	13	12	90	47	22,526	J.E. Morgan	I.G.A. Robinson	
20/6/1981	1981	13		Windy Hill	ESSENDON	12	22	94	RICHMOND	13	12	90	4	30,718	S.R. Carbines	I.G.A. Robinson	
28/6/1981	1981	14		Gabba	ESSENDON	22	19	151	HAWTHORN	20	13	133	18	20,351	R. Kelsey	J. Schmitt	M. Nash
4/7/1981	1981	15		Junction Oval	ESSENDON	11	14	80	FITZROY	8	13	61	19	18,374	J. Chapman	K.F. Smith	
18/7/1981	1981	16		Windy Hill	ESSENDON	22	21	153	WSTRN BLDGS	8	12	60	93	21,588	M.D. Ball	M.W. Viney	
25/7/1981	1981	17		Moorabbin	ESSENDON	12	21	93	ST KILDA	12	4	76	17	23,126	A.C. Bryant	J.R. Sutcliffe	
2/8/1981	1981	18		MCG	ESSENDON	12	16	88	COLLINGWOOD	9	15	69	19	64,149	B.J. Allen	S.A. McInerney	A. Lewis
8/8/1981	1981	19		Windy Hill	ESSENDON	14	20	104	MELBOURNE	9	6	60	44	15,411	R.A. Castle	S.D. McDonald	
15/8/1981	1981	20		Optus Oval	ESSENDON	14	15	99	CARLTON	15	8	98	1	36,736	J.J. Russo	B.J. Garland	
22/8/1981	1981	21		Windy Hill	ESSENDON	26	23	179	STH MLB/SYDNEY	10	8	68	111	18,773	J.J. Russo	G.G. Vernon	
29/8/1981	1981	22		Waverley Park	ESSENDON	6	11	47	GEELONG	7	13	55	-8	75,221	I.W. Clayton	D.A. Howlett	
5/9/1981	1981	EF		Waverley Park	ESSENDON	13	16	94	FITZROY	16	13	109	-15	58,598	B.J. Bulluss	G.J. Sidebottom	
27/3/1982	1982	1		Windy Hill	ESSENDON	29	16	190	WSTRN BLDGS	11	15	81	109	26,456	G.J. Fallet	B.K. Sheehan	
3/04/1982	1982	2		Waverley Park	ESSENDON	13	13	91	CARLTON	8	17	65	26	60,208	R.C. Sawers	J.S. Harvey	
12/4/1982	1982	3		MCG	ESSENDON	16	14	110	RICHMOND	25	22	172	-62	90,564	R.C. Sawers	G.J. Sidebottom	
17/4/1982	1982	4		Windy Hill	ESSENDON	12	19	91	KANGAROOS	14	24	108	-17	27,190	J.E. Morgan	N.R. Nash	
24/4/1982	1982	5		Junction Oval	ESSENDON	15	12	102	FITZROY	18	19	127	-25	18,268	D.G. Rich	R.C. Sawers	
2/5/1982	1982	6		SCG	ESSENDON	18	9	117	STH MLB/SYDNEY	15	21	111	6	15,461	M.G. Bird	G.F. Dore	
8/5/1982	1982	7		Windy Hill	ESSENDON	17	20	122	COLLINGWOOD	9	13	67	55	27,001	P.R. Carey	R.C. Sawers	

Appendix C

DATE	SEASON	RND	SESSION	VENUE	KEVIN'S CLUB	G	B	PTS	OPPONENT	G	B	PTS	MARGIN	ATTENDANCE	FIELD UMPIRE ONE	FIELD UMPIRE TWO	FIELD UMPIRE THREE
15/5/1982	1982	8		Optus Oval	ESSENDON	16	15	111	HAWTHORN	15	15	105	6	26,875	B.J. Allen	B.J. Carland	
22/5/1982	1982	9		Windy Hill	ESSENDON	19	19	133	MELBOURNE	12	13	85	48	22,437	R.A. Castle	P.R. Carey	
29/5/1982	1982	10		Waverley Park	ESSENDON	22	17	149	ST KILDA	18	11	119	30	36,736	D.R. Goldspink	B.K. Sheehan	
5/6/1982	1982	11		Skilled Stadium	ESSENDON	17	9	111	GEELONG	10	11	71	40	31,096	B.K. Sheehan	H.D. Kennedy	
14/6/1982	1982	12		Windy Hill	ESSENDON	19	12	126	CARLTON	8	18	66	60	33,792	J.J. Russo	G.W. Forster	
19/6/1982	1982	13		Waverley Park	ESSENDON	10	5	65	RICHMOND	12	10	82	-17	64,319	I.G.A. Robinson	J.J. Russo	
26/6/1982	1982	14		MCG	ESSENDON	15	15	105	KANGAROOS	14	13	97	8	47,656	D.R. Goldspink	G.F Dore	G.G. Vernon
3/7/1982	1982	15		Windy Hill	ESSENDON	21	13	139	FITZROY	7	12	54	85	20,059	B.K. Sheehan	G.G. Vernon	
17/7/1982	1982	16		Windy Hill	ESSENDON	12	10	82	STH MLB/SYDNEY	17	13	115	-33	22,359	W.R. Deller	J.R. Sutcliffe	
24/7/1982	1982	17		Victoria Park	ESSENDON	17	17	119	COLLINGWOOD	15	18	108	11	21,875	P.R. James	I.G.A. Robinson	
31/7/1982	1982	18		Windy Hill	ESSENDON	12	10	82	HAWTHORN	15	10	100	-18	22,993	G.R. James	R.C. Sawers	
7/8/1982	1982	19		Waverley Park	ESSENDON	20	17	137	MELBOURNE	14	17	101	36	28,379	D.R. Goldspink	J.J. Russo	
14/8/1982	1982	20		Moorabbin	ESSENDON	13	12	90	ST KILDA	10	16	76	14	16,705	K.R. Dargavel	V. Vasilou	
21/8/1982	1982	21		Windy Hill	ESSENDON	14	12	96	GEELONG	12	13	85	11	17,596	P.R. Cameron	G.R. James	
28/8/1982	1982	22		Whitten Oval	ESSENDON	32	16	208	WSTRN BLDGS	9	8	62	146	21,575	C.B. Mitchell	M.A. Nash	A.M. Panozzo
4/9/1982	1982	EF		Waverley Park	ESSENDON	16	19	115	KANGAROOS	19	14	128	-13	50,537	A.C. Bryant	P.R. Cameron	
27/3/1983	1983	1		SCG	ESSENDON	15	20	110	STH MLB/SYDNEY	17	9	111	-1	11,916	D.A. Howlett	P.G. Saville	
4/4/1983	1983	2		Windy Hill	ESSENDON	20	11	131	ST KILDA	10	10	70	61	28,071	P.R. Carey	S.D. McDonald	
9/4/1983	1983	3		Junction Oval	ESSENDON	7	14	56	FITZROY	14	13	97	-41	21,478	I.G.A. Robinson	D.G. Rich	
16/4/1983	1983	4		Windy Hill	ESSENDON	20	21	141	COLLINGWOOD	17	15	117	24	28,250	D.A. Howlett	G.J. Gale	
25/4/1983	1983	5		Waverley Park	ESSENDON	20	8	128	KANGAROOS	17	21	123	5	47,722	I.W. Clayton	B.K. Sheehan	
30/4/1983	1983	6		Windy Hill	ESSENDON	27	19	181	WSTRN BLDGS	7	7	49	132	26,387	P.R. Carey	G.W. Forster	
7/5/1983	1983	7		MCG	ESSENDON	21	11	137	RICHMOND	16	16	112	25	49,707	S.A. McLaren	D.A. Howlett	M. Sexton
14/5/1983	1983	8		Optus Oval	ESSENDON	14	11	95	HAWTHORN	20	17	137	-42	21,835	P.J. Howe	P.R. Carey	
21/5/1983	1983	9		Windy Hill	ESSENDON	22	17	149	MELBOURNE	17	13	115	34	19,955	P.R. Cameron	G.T.D. Morrow	
28/5/1983	1983	10		Windy Hill	ESSENDON	15	19	109	GEELONG	15	7	97	12	20,793	G.J. Sidebottom	N.R. Nash	
4/6/1983	1983	11		Waverley Park	ESSENDON	19	12	126	CARLTON	15	11	101	25	60,619	D.G. Rich	P.R. Carey	
11/6/1983	1983	12		Windy Hill	ESSENDON	23	18	156	STH MLB/SYDNEY	13	5	83	73	20,012	R.C. Sawers	I.W. Clayton	
18/6/1983	1983	13		Waverley Park	ESSENDON	21	12	138	ST KILDA	13	13	91	47	30,616	H.D. Kennedy	J.J. Russo	
25/6/1983	1983	14		Windy Hill	ESSENDON	8	10	58	FITZROY	9	11	65	-7	22,947	R.C. Sawers	V. Vasilou	
2/7/1983	1983	15		Victoria Park	ESSENDON	13	9	87	COLLINGWOOD	16	8	104	-17	33,641	R.C. Sawers	K.F. Smith	
9/7/1983	1983	16		Arden St Oval	ESSENDON	16	11	107	KANGAROOS	19	14	128	-21	22,345	G.R. James	D.G. Rich	
23/7/1983	1983	17		Whitten Oval	ESSENDON	18	17	125	WSTRN BLDGS	16	11	107	18	20,708	S.V. Luckman	P.R. Carey	

Appendix C

DATE	SEASON	RND	SESSION	VENUE	KEVIN'S CLUB	G	B	PTS	OPPONENT	G	B	PTS	MARGIN	ATTENDANCE	FIELD UMPIRE ONE	FIELD UMPIRE TWO	FIELD UMPIRE THREE
30/7/1983	1983	18		Windy Hill	ESSENDON	6	14	50	RICHMOND	19	10	124	-74	18,067	K.F. Smith	W.R. Deller	
6/8/1983	1983	19		Windy Hill	ESSENDON	23	18	156	HAWTHORN	16	14	110	46	19,237	S.D. McDonald	P.G. Saville	
13/8/1983	1983	20		MCG	ESSENDON	21	15	141	MELBOURNE	19	10	124	17	38,620	A.P. Coates	T. Pfeiffer	D. McCauley
20/8/1983	1983	21		Skilled Stadium	ESSENDON	26	9	165	GEELONG	12	11	83	82	32,808	D.A. Howlett	R.C. Sawers	
27/8/1983	1983	22		Waverley Park	ESSENDON	18	10	118	CARLTON	8	19	67	51	64,232	D.R. Goldspink	J.J. Russo	
3/9/1983	1983	EF		Waverley Park	ESSENDON	17	12	114	CARLTON	12	9	81	33	65,881	D.A. Howlett	R.C. Sawers	D. McCauley
10/9/1983	1983	FS		MCG	ESSENDON	16	13	109	FITZROY	12	14	86	23	81,090	D.G. Rich	H.D. Kennedy	
17/9/1983	1983	PF		Waverley Park	ESSENDON	25	14	164	KANGAROOS	12	6	78	86	63,785	H. Kennedy	S. McBurney	D. McCauley
24/9/1983	1983	GF		MCG	ESSENDON	8	9	57	HAWTHORN	20	20	140	-83	110,332	A.C. Bryant	K.J. Quinn	S. Wenn
31/3/1984	1984	1		Moorabbin	ESSENDON	19	20	134	ST KILDA	14	13	97	37	26,019	S.R. Carbines	G.J. Sidebottom	
7/4/1984	1984	2		Windy Hill	ESSENDON	16	14	110	HAWTHORN	17	14	116	-6	22,841	G.R. James	J.J. Russo	
14/4/1984	1984	3		Windy Hill	ESSENDON	26	13	169	COLLINGWOOD	16	10	106	63	28,120	B.M. Trezise	M.D. Ball	
21/4/1984	1984	4		Waverley Park	ESSENDON	17	24	126	MELBOURNE	14	7	91	35	31,535	P.R. Cameron	G.G. Vernon	
25/4/1984	1984	5		MCG	ESSENDON	20	15	135	RICHMOND	12	14	86	49	55,141	D. Goldspink	S. Hanley	C. Rowe
5/5/1984	1984	6		Junction Oval	ESSENDON	22	12	144	FITZROY	13	15	93	51	20,274	A.C. Bryant	P.J. Howe	
12/5/1984	1984	7		Windy Hill	ESSENDON	12	10	82	WSTRN BLDGS	16	8	104	-22	21,196	P.R. Cameron	K.R. Dargavel	
19/5/1984	1984	8		Waverley Park	ESSENDON	19	19	133	GEELONG	14	6	90	43	39,926	H.D. Kennedy	D.G. Rich	
26/5/1984	1984	9		Windy Hill	ESSENDON	16	17	113	CARLTON	9	12	66	47	27,346	G.W. Forster	D.G. Rich	
2/6/1984	1984	10		Arden St Oval	ESSENDON	16	12	108	KANGAROOS	15	16	106	2	17,290	C.B. Mitchell	P.J. Howe	
9/6/1984	1984	11		Windy Hill	ESSENDON	20	15	135	STH MLB/SYDNEY	14	10	94	41	21,740	P.R. Cameron	I.G.A. Robinson	
16/6/1984	1984	12		Optus Oval	ESSENDON	6	10	46	HAWTHORN	12	21	93	-47	25,726	R.C. Sawers	I.G.A. Robinson	
23/6/1984	1984	13		Victoria Park	ESSENDON	19	9	123	COLLINGWOOD	12	17	89	34	32,701	G.R. Rich	I.G.A. Robinson	
30/6/1984	1984	14		Waverley Park	ESSENDON	14	15	99	MELBOURNE	7	14	56	43	46,753	B.J. Garland	D.A. Howlett	
7/7/1984	1984	15		Windy Hill	ESSENDON	14	10	94	RICHMOND	7	19	61	33	16,934	I.G.A. Robinson	A.C. Bryant	
14/7/1984	1984	16		Windy Hill	ESSENDON	20	7	127	FITZROY	9	12	66	61	17,749	D.A. Howlett	D.R. Goldspink	
28/7/1984	1984	17		Whitten Oval	ESSENDON	4	10	34	WSTRN BLDGS	3	14	32	2	16,771	G.R. James	R.C. Sawers	
4/8/1984	1984	18		Waverley Park	ESSENDON	19	22	136	GEELONG	12	17	89	47	31,675	B.J. Allen	B.K. Sheehan	
11/8/1984	1984	19		Optus Oval	ESSENDON	15	12	102	CARLTON	12	18	90	12	26,876	P.R. Cameron	B.K. Sheehan	
18/8/1984	1984	20		Windy Hill	ESSENDON	22	6	138	ST KILDA	13	5	83	55	13,842	I.W. Clayton	B.K. Sheehan	
26/8/1984	1984	21		SCG	ESSENDON	14	15	99	STH MLB/SYDNEY	23	17	155	-56	12,173	B.J. Bulluss	I.W. Clayton	
1/9/1984	1984	22		Windy Hill	ESSENDON	27	7	169	KANGAROOS	19	17	131	38	21,002	G.F. Dore	D.A. Howlett	
16/9/1984	1984	SS		MCG	ESSENDON	15	15	105	HAWTHORN	16	17	113	-8	76,514	G.F. Dore	A.G. McKernan	

Appendix C

DATE	SEASON	RND	SESSION	VENUE	KEVIN'S CLUB	G	B	PTS	OPPONENT	G	B	PTS	MARGIN	ATTENDANCE	FIELD UMPIRE ONE	FIELD UMPIRE TWO	FIELD UMPIRE THREE
22/9/1984	1984	PF		Waverley Park	ESSENDON	28	6	174	COLLINGWOOD	5	11	41	133	73,550	B. Allen	A. Coates	M. Vozzo
29/9/1984	1984	GF		MCG	ESSENDON	14	21	105	HAWTHORN	12	9	81	24	92,685	B.K. Sheehan	K.C. Callaghan	C. Durham
23/3/1985	1985	1		Waverley Park	ESSENDON	17	12	114	HAWTHORN	15	10	100	14	41,694	J.J. Russo	S.B. Harris	
30/3/1985	1985	2		Windy Hill	ESSENDON	21	11	137	RICHMOND	18	12	120	17	22,838	C.B. Mitchell	P.R. Cameron	
8/4/1985	1985	3		Victoria Park	ESSENDON	24	22	166	FITZROY	8	15	63	103	17,093	G.R. Howe	I.W. Clayton	
20/4/1985	1985	4		Windy Hill	ESSENDON	13	8	86	COLLINGWOOD	12	10	82	4	26,521	I.G.A. Robinson	M.R. Westgarth	
27/4/1985	1985	5		Whitten Oval	ESSENDON	11	18	84	WSTRN BLDGS	18	17	125	-41	33,697	S.R. Carbines	G.J. Sidebottom	
4/5/1985	1985	6		Windy Hill	ESSENDON	27	14	176	CARLTON	8	19	67	109	22,928	D.R. Goldspink	S.B. Harris	
11/5/1985	1985	7		Waverley Park	ESSENDON	14	9	93	KANGAROOS	22	20	152	-59	32,125	K.F. Smith	N.R. Nash	
18/5/1985	1985	8		Skilled Stadium	ESSENDON	10	15	75	GEELONG	8	11	59	16	21,796	A.P. Coates	M.S. Sneddon	
25/5/1985	1985	9		Windy Hill	ESSENDON	23	15	153	MELBOURNE	9	17	71	82	19,985	P.R. Carey	J.J. Russo	
1/6/1985	1985	10		Moorabbin	ESSENDON	21	20	146	ST KILDA	18	12	120	26	16,736	I.G.A. Robinson	G.T.D. Morrow	
8/6/1985	1985	11		Windy Hill	ESSENDON	17	11	113	STH MLB/SYDNEY	11	5	71	42	17,652	J.J. Russo	R.C. Sawers	
15/6/1985	1985	12		MCG	ESSENDON	23	12	150	RICHMOND	10	9	69	81	36,851	C. Mitchell	S. McLaren	S. Jeffery
22/6/1985	1985	13		Windy Hill	ESSENDON	21	14	140	FITZROY	16	17	113	27	18,353	R.A. Castle	B.G. Woodhead	
29/6/1985	1985	14		Waverley Park	ESSENDON	21	11	137	HAWTHORN	15	11	101	36	48,880	B.K. Sheehan	G.G. Vernon	
6/7/1985	1985	15		Victoria Park	ESSENDON	13	11	89	COLLINGWOOD	11	12	78	11	26,014	D.G. James	R.C. Sawers	
20/7/1985	1985	16		Windy Hill	ESSENDON	17	10	112	WSTRN BLDGS	13	10	88	24	28,270	P.J. Howe	P.R. Cameron	
27/7/1985	1985	17		Optus Oval	ESSENDON	10	8	68	CARLTON	18	12	120	-52	28,777	I.G.A. Robinson	R.C. Sawers	
3/8/1985	1985	18		Windy Hill	ESSENDON	25	16	166	KANGAROOS	8	14	62	104	18,741	P.R. Carey	J.J. Russo	
10/8/1985	1985	19		Waverley Park	ESSENDON	13	11	89	GEELONG	8	16	64	25	34,614	J.J. Russo	C.B. Mitchell	
17/8/1985	1985	20		MCG	ESSENDON	17	10	112	MELBOURNE	15	7	97	15	22,193	D.A. Howlett	M.A. Nash	G.F. Dore
24/8/1985	1985	21		Windy Hill	ESSENDON	27	22	184	ST KILDA	14	7	91	93	14,133	P.R. Carey	C.B. Mitchell	
1/9/1985	1985	22		SCG	ESSENDON	24	21	165	STH MLB/SYDNEY	11	12	78	87	12,180	D. Howlett	M. Ellis	K. Nicholls
15/9/1985	1985	SS		Waverley Park	ESSENDON	14	18	102	HAWTHORN	9	8	62	40	67,063	M.D. Abbott	G.F. Dore	
28/9/1985	1985	GF		MCG	ESSENDON	26	14	170	HAWTHORN	14	8	92	78	100,042	H. Kennedy	B. Allen	M. Head
29/3/1986	1986	1		Victoria Park	ESSENDON	19	19	133	COLLINGWOOD	10	8	68	65	28,634	P.J. Howe	M.R. Westgarth	
5/4/1986	1986	2		Windy Hill	ESSENDON	21	22	148	GEELONG	7	9	51	97	19,387	P.R. Cameron	C.B. Mitchell	D.A. Howlett
12/4/1986	1986	3		Waverley Park	ESSENDON	13	11	89	WSTRN BLDGS	11	15	81	8	33,546	I.W. Clayton	R.A. Castle	
19/4/1986	1986	4		Windy Hill	ESSENDON	27	8	170	MELBOURNE	17	6	108	62	18,265	D.A. Howlett	P. O'Rilley	
25/4/1986	1986	5		Waverley Park	ESSENDON	8	7	55	CARLTON	10	11	71	-16	68,151	G.J. Sidebottom	K.F. Smith	
3/5/1986	1986	6		Waverley Park	ESSENDON	15	12	102	HAWTHORN	19	12	126	-24	38,381	P.R. Cameron	N.R. Nash	
10/5/1986	1986	7		MCG	ESSENDON	21	19	145	RICHMOND	16	9	105	40	38,456	D. Howlett	D. Humphery-Smith	R. Kelsey

Appendix C

DATE	SEASON	RND	SESSION	VENUE	KEVIN'S CLUB	G	B	PTS	OPPONENT	G	B	PTS	MARGIN	ATTENDANCE	FIELD UMPIRE ONE	FIELD UMPIRE TWO	FIELD UMPIRE THREE
17/5/1986	1986	8		Windy Hill	ESSENDON	22	14	146	ST KILDA	12	12	84	62	15,132	J.J. Russo	G.J. Fallet	
24/5/1986	1986	9		Victoria Park	ESSENDON	10	10	70	FITZROY	18	7	115	-45	14,979	P.J. Cameron	M.R. Westgarth	
30/5/1986	1986	10	N	MCG	ESSENDON	18	13	121	KANGAROOS	21	11	137	-16	40,531	J.J. Russo	M.W. Viney	
9/6/1986	1986	11		Windy Hill	ESSENDON	9	4	58	STH MLB/SYDNEY	10	18	78	-20	27,267	A.C. Bryant	K.R. Dargavel	
14/6/1986	1986	12		Waverley Park	ESSENDON	13	16	94	COLLINGWOOD	18	12	120	-26	49,022	N.R. Nash	I.G.A. Robinson	
21/6/1986	1986	13		Skilled Stadium	ESSENDON	12	17	89	GEELONG	11	11	77	12	23,840	D.G. Rich	B.J. Carland	
28/6/1986	1986	14		Windy Hill	ESSENDON	8	8	56	WSTRN BLDGS	12	13	85	-29	21,312	G.W. Marcy	N.R. Nash	
5/7/1986	1986	15		MCG	ESSENDON	27	20	182	MELBOURNE	8	12	60	122	21,560	M. James	C. Rowe	S. McInerney
13/7/1986	1986	16		SCG	ESSENDON	15	13	103	STH MLB/SYDNEY	24	18	162	-59	33,192	G.T.D. Morrow	K.F. Smith	
20/7/1986	1986	17		MCG	ESSENDON	15	15	105	CARLTON	11	14	80	25	51,646	B.K. Sheehan	C.B. Mitchell	A. Malcolm
2/8/1986	1986	18		Windy Hill	ESSENDON	21	11	137	HAWTHORN	6	14	50	87	21,223	D.G. Rich	M.D. Ball	
9/8/1986	1986	19		Waverley Park	ESSENDON	23	16	154	RICHMOND	11	9	75	79	30,349	B. Sheehan	M. McKenzie	S. Wenn
16/8/1986	1986	20		Moorabbin	ESSENDON	11	16	82	ST KILDA	6	12	48	34	13,171	G.L. Walsh	R.A. Castle	
23/8/1986	1986	21		Windy Hill	ESSENDON	8	13	61	FITZROY	14	12	96	-35	18,882	P.R. Cameron	M.J. Dye	
30/8/1986	1986	22		Windy Hill	ESSENDON	10	19	79	KANGAROOS	15	11	101	-22	17,982	G.T.D. Morrow	A.C. Bryant	
6/9/1986	1986	EF		Waverley Park	ESSENDON	8	9	57	FITZROY	8	10	58	-1	59,420	J.J. Russo	R.A. Castle	
28/3/1987	1987	1		Waverley Park	ESSENDON	19	7	121	WSTRN BLDGS	9	8	62	59	22,550	G.G. Vernon	J.J. Russo	H.D. Kennedy
4/4/1987	1987	2		Windy Hill	ESSENDON	17	17	119	WEST COAST	17	12	114	5	19,845	G.R. James	K.F. Smith	
11/4/1987	1987	3		MCG	ESSENDON	12	12	84	RICHMOND	19	16	130	-46	27,528	A.C. Bryant	P.J. Waight	
20/4/1987	1987	4		Windy Hill	ESSENDON	17	11	113	STH MLB/SYDNEY	9	12	66	47	24,207	P.R. Cameron	G.G. Vernon	
25/4/1987	1987	5		Waverley Park	ESSENDON	9	8	62	CARLTON	17	14	116	-54	56,124	J.E. Morgan	N.R. Nash	
2/5/1987	1987	6		Windy Hill	ESSENDON	14	12	96	GEELONG	13	18	96	0	16,042	R.C. Sawers	D.G. Rich	
9/5/1987	1987	7		Optus Oval	ESSENDON	21	8	134	FITZROY	25	9	159	-25	14,103	P.R. Cameron	R.A. Castle	
16/5/1987	1987	8		Waverley Park	ESSENDON	14	10	94	COLLINGWOOD	10	8	68	26	28,085	D.G. Rich	P.R. Carey	
23/5/1987	1987	9		Waverley Park	ESSENDON	7	9	51	HAWTHORN	25	15	165	-114	32,634	P.J. Howe	J.R. Sutcliffe	
30/5/1987	1987	10		Windy Hill	ESSENDON	11	14	80	MELBOURNE	15	12	102	-22	13,796	P.R. Cameron	K.R. Dargavel	
6/6/1987	1987	11		Moorabbin	ESSENDON	18	13	121	ST KILDA	16	10	106	15	23,725	G.F. Dore	B.G. Woodhead	
12/6/1987	1987	12	N	MCG	ESSENDON	9	10	64	KANGAROOS	15	10	100	-36	23,944	B.K. Sheehan	R.A. Castle	
20/6/1987	1987	13		Windy Hill	ESSENDON	9	10	64	BRISBANE	3	9	27	37	8,724	M.R. Westgarth	P.R. Cameron	
27/6/1987	1987	14		Windy Hill	ESSENDON	7	10	52	WSTRN BLDGS	9	10	64	-12	17,364	G.T.D. Morrow	I.G.A. Robinson	
3/7/1987	1987	15	N	WACA	ESSENDON	21	20	146	WEST COAST	18	10	118	28	15,740	G.G. Vernon	I.W. Clayton	
11/7/1987	1987	16		Windy Hill	ESSENDON	21	11	137	RICHMOND	12	11	83	54	13,593	B.K. Sheehan	B.J. Carland	
26/7/1987	1987	17		SCG	ESSENDON	11	7	73	STH MLB/SYDNEY	36	20	236	-163	23,009	J.E. Morgan	V. Vasiou	

Appendix C

DATE	SEASON	RND	SESSION	VENUE	KEVIN'S CLUB	G	B	PTS	OPPONENT	G	B	PTS	MARGIN	ATTENDANCE	FIELD UMPIRE ONE	FIELD UMPIRE TWO	FIELD UMPIRE THREE
1/8/1987	1987	18		Waverley Park	ESSENDON	10	9	69	CARLTON	10	10	70	-1	29,761	B.K. Sheehan	P.R. Carey	
8/8/1987	1987	19		Skilled Stadium	ESSENDON	9	11	65	GEELONG	12	20	92	-27	29,884	M.J. Dye	N.R. Nash	
15/8/1987	1987	20		Windy Hill	ESSENDON	20	7	127	FITZROY	11	20	86	41	12,466	R.A. Castle	J.J. Russo	
22/8/1987	1987	21		Waverley Park	ESSENDON	9	10	64	HAWTHORN	17	12	114	-50	27,046	P.R. Cameron	G.T.D. Morrow	
30/8/1987	1987	22		MCG	ESSENDON	21	13	139	COLLINGWOOD	23	6	144	-5	28,887	D.R. Goldspink	R.C. Sawers	
2/4/1988	1988	1		Windy Hill	ESSENDON	25	14	164	KANGAROOS	12	10	82	82	18,410	R.C. Sawers	G.F. Dore	
8/4/1988	1988	2	N	WACA	ESSENDON	11	10	76	WEST COAST	26	19	175	-99	24,886	D.G. Rich	R.C. Sawers	
16/4/1988	1988	3		Windy Hill	ESSENDON	11	13	79	CARLTON	23	13	151	-72	21,472	P.R. Cameron	R.C. Sawers	
25/4/1988	1988	4		Moorabbin	ESSENDON	14	7	91	ST KILDA	10	9	69	22	31,679	R.C. Sawers	M.S. Sneddon	
30/4/1988	1988	5		Skilled Stadium	ESSENDON	13	14	92	GEELONG	17	14	116	-24	20,110	S.R. Carbines	B.S. Hood	
7/5/1988	1988	6		MCG	ESSENDON	16	5	101	MELBOURNE	9	14	68	33	34,697	H. Kennedy	S. McBurney	S. McInerney
14/5/1988	1988	7		Windy Hill	ESSENDON	17	17	119	COLLINGWOOD	11	9	75	44	24,224	G.F. Dore	C.B. Mitchell	
21/5/1988	1988	8		Windy Hill	ESSENDON	20	17	137	RICHMOND	13	11	89	48	14,568	P.R. Cameron	S.B. Harris	
27/5/1988	1988	9	N	MCG	ESSENDON	29	20	194	BRISBANE	8	6	54	140	26,653	M. Nicholls	J. Schmitt	M. Avon
3/6/1988	1988	10	N	SCG	ESSENDON	8	7	55	STH MLB/SYDNEY	11	11	77	-22	14,753	P.R. Carey	P.J. Howe	
13/6/1988	1988	11		Optus Oval	ESSENDON	10	8	68	HAWTHORN	17	16	118	-50	27,642	A.C. Bryant	K.F. Smith	
18/6/1988	1988	12		Waverley Park	ESSENDON	4	9	33	FITZROY	7	9	51	-18	18,854	R.C. Sawers	B.G. Woodhead	
25/6/1988	1988	13		Windy Hill	ESSENDON	10	15	75	WSTRN BLDGS	15	9	99	-24	15,861	S. Fisher	G. Ryan	
2/7/1988	1988	14		Windy Hill	ESSENDON	16	16	112	WEST COAST	13	7	85	27	10,298	D.A. Howlett	R.C. Sawers	
10/7/1988	1988	15		MCG	ESSENDON	21	14	140	KANGAROOS	14	10	94	46	26,755	M. Ellis	C. Mitchell	D. Morris
16/7/1988	1988	16		Windy Hill	ESSENDON	16	14	110	FITZROY	9	12	66	44	14,477	P.R. Cameron	S.D. McDonald	
24/7/1988	1988	17		Carrara	ESSENDON	16	7	103	BRISBANE	10	14	74	29	15,950	P.J. Howe	I.A. Bedford	
30/7/1988	1988	18		Waverley Park	ESSENDON	9	8	62	HAWTHORN	12	16	88	-26	35,662	D.A. Howlett	G.R. James	
6/8/1988	1988	19		Windy Hill	ESSENDON	12	18	90	GEELONG	24	13	157	-67	15,636	G.R. James	R.C. Sawers	
13/8/1988	1988	20		Waverley Park	ESSENDON	10	13	73	COLLINGWOOD	10	14	74	-1	52,719	P.R. Cameron	J.J. Russo	
20/8/1988	1988	21		Windy Hill	ESSENDON	19	14	128	MELBOURNE	13	12	90	38	19,163	I.G.A. Robinson	P.R. Cameron	
27/8/1988	1988	22		Waverley Park	ESSENDON	12	12	84	ST KILDA	8	17	65	19	26,134	P.R. Cameron	M.S. Sneddon	
31/3/1989	1989	1	N	WACA	ESSENDON	17	10	112	WEST COAST	14	12	96	16	25,664	R.A. Castle	G.G. Vernon	
8/4/1989	1989	2		Windy Hill	ESSENDON	14	10	94	MELBOURNE	9	14	68	26	20,431	G.R. James	P.J. Waight	
15/4/1989	1989	3		Optus Oval	ESSENDON	13	13	91	HAWTHORN	20	15	135	-44	23,922	D.A. Howlett	J.J. Russo	
25/4/1989	1989	4		Optus Oval	ESSENDON	21	12	138	CARLTON	15	20	110	28	33,074	M.G. Bird	P.R. Carey	
29/4/1989	1989	5		Windy Hill	ESSENDON	20	18	138	ST KILDA	12	12	84	54	18,542	D.A. Howlett	S.B. Harris	
7/5/1989	1989	6		MCG	ESSENDON	16	9	105	KANGAROOS	17	19	121	-16	34,379	D.G. Rich	J.J. Russo	

Appendix C

DATE	SEASON	RND	SESSION	VENUE	KEVIN'S CLUB	G	B	PTS	OPPONENT	G	B	PTS	MARGIN	ATTENDANCE	FIELD UMPIRE ONE	FIELD UMPIRE TWO	FIELD UMPIRE THREE
14/5/1989	1989	7		Carrara	ESSENDON	17	10	112	BRISBANE	12	9	81	31	12,034	B.J. Carland	G.W. Forster	
20/5/1989	1989	8		Windy Hill	ESSENDON	21	19	145	RICHMOND	12	15	87	58	18,030	B.K. Sheehan	I.W. Clayton	
27/5/1989	1989	9		Waverley Park	ESSENDON	19	11	125	COLLINGWOOD	7	16	58	67	71,390	D.A. Howlett	C.B. Mitchell	J Love
3/6/1989	1989	10		Windy Hill	ESSENDON	18	14	122	FITZROY	10	9	69	53	15,556	P.G. Saville	B.K. Sheehan	
12/6/1989	1989	11		MCG	ESSENDON	4	11	35	GEELONG	12	17	89	-54	87,653	N.R. Nash	K.F. Smith	
17/6/1989	1989	12		Windy Hill	ESSENDON	7	8	50	STH MLB/SYDNEY	7	13	55	-5	13,351	P.R. Cameron	S.M.P. Nolan	
24/6/1989	1989	13		Windy Hill	ESSENDON	3	10	28	WSTRN BLDGS	3	5	23	5	13,429	A.C. Bryant	P.R. Cameron	
8/7/1989	1989	14		Waverley Park	ESSENDON	9	7	61	CARLTON	8	10	58	3	34,617	I.G.A. Robinson	P.R. Cameron	
15/7/1989	1989	15		Windy Hill	ESSENDON	25	10	160	WEST COAST	1	12	18	142	11,452	D.B. Anthony	T.N. Garrett	
22/7/1989	1989	16		MCG	ESSENDON	14	15	99	RICHMOND	9	12	66	33	23,964	D. Howlett	V. Sercia	T. Shearer
29/7/1989	1989	17		Moorabbin	ESSENDON	20	13	133	ST KILDA	16	10	106	27	17,008	R.C. Sawers	G.J. Fallet	
6/8/1989	1989	18		Whitten Oval	ESSENDON	7	9	51	WSTRN BLDGS	3	5	23	28	16,005	C.B. Mitchell	B.J. Carland	
12/8/1989	1989	19		Windy Hill	ESSENDON	15	11	101	BRISBANE	7	5	47	54	11,915	S.B. Harris	B.J. Carland	
19/8/1989	1989	20		Windy Hill	ESSENDON	19	14	128	KANGAROOS	17	10	112	16	15,794	R.A. Castle	R.C. Sawers	
25/8/1989	1989	21	N	SCG	ESSENDON	15	14	104	STH MLB/SYDNEY	15	20	110	-6	12,042	I.G.A. Robinson	S.D. McDonald	
2/9/1989	1989	22		MCG	ESSENDON	16	12	108	MELBOURNE	13	11	89	19	41,080	R.C. Sawers	A.P. Coates	G.G. Vernon
10/9/1989	1989	QF		MCG	ESSENDON	24	13	157	GEELONG	11	15	81	76	75,861	D. Woodcock	M. McKenzie	C. Mitchell
16/9/1989	1989	SS		Waverley Park	ESSENDON	11	10	76	HAWTHORN	16	16	112	-36	66,003	R.C. Sawers	G.R. James	
23/9/1989	1989	PF		Waverley Park	ESSENDON	10	10	70	GEELONG	24	20	164	-94	67,892	J.E. Morgan	N.R. Nash	
31/3/1990	1990	1		Windy Hill	ESSENDON	20	21	141	FITZROY	8	12	60	81	18,960	D.G. Rich	B.J. Carland	
8/4/1990	1990	2		MCG	ESSENDON	24	15	159	HAWTHORN	14	13	97	62	55,311	B. Sheehan	C. Rowe	S. McBurney
16/4/1990	1990	3		MCG	ESSENDON	14	11	95	MELBOURNE	18	14	122	-27	59,894	H.D. Kennedy	D.G. Rich	
21/4/1990	1990	4		MCG	ESSENDON	18	19	127	RICHMOND	6	13	49	78	17,975	S. McBurney	S. McLaren	S. Jeffery
28/4/1990	1990	5		Waverley Park	ESSENDON	11	15	81	GEELONG	12	17	89	-8	42,097	P.J. Howe	R.C. Sawers	
5/5/1990	1990	6		MCG	ESSENDON	15	11	101	COLLINGWOOD	10	15	75	26	63,318	S. McLaren	D. Goldspink	M. Ellis
12/5/1990	1990	7		Windy Hill	ESSENDON	13	13	91	CARLTON	17	9	111	-20	22,198	I.G.A. Robinson	V. Vasilou	
20/5/1990	1990	8		Whitten Oval	ESSENDON	14	13	97	WSTRN BLDGS	11	12	78	19	25,255	G.F. Dore	R.C. Sawers	
26/5/1990	1990	9		Windy Hill	ESSENDON	18	16	124	ST KILDA	17	11	113	11	21,251	P.R. Cameron	K.F. Smith	
3/6/1990	1990	10		SCG	ESSENDON	25	14	164	STH MLB/SYDNEY	11	8	74	90	12,551	D. Howlett	M. Vozzo	S. McBurney
9/6/1990	1990	11		Windy Hill	ESSENDON	15	9	99	WEST COAST	8	12	60	39	19,427	P.R. Cameron	R.C. Sawers	
16/6/1990	1990	12		Windy Hill	ESSENDON	18	16	124	KANGAROOS	13	16	94	30	16,311	G.T.D. Morrow	R.C. Sawers	
23/6/1990	1990	13	N	Carrara	ESSENDON	15	19	109	BRISBANE	7	13	55	54	10,105	D.R. Goldspink	S.B. Harris	
7/7/1990	1990	14		Optus Oval	ESSENDON	20	24	144	FITZROY	9	7	61	83	13,339	G.F. Dore	S.A. McLaren	T. Shearer

Appendix C

DATE	SEASON	RND	SESSION	VENUE	KEVIN'S CLUB	G	B	PTS	OPPONENT	G	B	PTS	MARGIN	ATTENDANCE	FIELD UMPIRE ONE	FIELD UMPIRE TWO	FIELD UMPIRE THREE
14/7/1990	1990	15		Optus Oval	ESSENDON	21	16	142	HAWTHORN	10	7	67	75	25,159	M. Ellis	B.K. Sheehan	C. Durham
21/7/1990	1990	16		Windy Hill	ESSENDON	15	16	106	MELBOURNE	17	12	114	-8	19,945	P.R. Cameron	J.E. Morgan	D. Humphery-Smith
28/7/1990	1990	17		Waverley Park	ESSENDON	18	17	125	RICHMOND	6	10	46	79	24,436	S. McBurney	T. Burton	
4/8/1990	1990	18		Skilled Stadium	ESSENDON	13	16	94	GEELONG	14	8	92	2	19,103	I.G.A. Robinson	B.J. Carland	
12/8/1990	1990	19		Waverley Park	ESSENDON	13	6	84	COLLINGWOOD	11	12	78	6	65,293	P.R. Carey	P.R. Cameron	
18/8/1990	1990	20		Optus Oval	ESSENDON	12	15	87	CARLTON	16	11	107	-20	25,455	J.J. Russo	C.B. Mitchell	
25/8/1990	1990	21		Windy Hill	ESSENDON	15	14	104	WSTRN BLDGS	11	14	80	24	17,258	P.R. Cameron	B.G. Woodhead	
1/9/1990	1990	22		Moorabbin	ESSENDON	19	14	128	ST KILDA	13	15	93	35	26,661	H.D. Kennedy	G.R. Scroop	
23/9/1990	1990	SS		MCG	ESSENDON	7	12	54	COLLINGWOOD	17	15	117	-63	91,555	G.T.D. Morrow	A.C. Bryant	
29/9/1990	1990	PF		Waverley Park	ESSENDON	18	13	121	WEST COAST	8	10	58	63	55,813	R.C. Sawers	D.G. Rich	H.D. Kennedy
6/10/1990	1990	GF		MCG	ESSENDON	5	11	41	COLLINGWOOD	13	11	89	-48	98,944	G.R. James	R.C. Sawers	
1/4/1991	1991	1		MCG	ESSENDON	16	17	113	RICHMOND	17	7	109	4	31,793	M.R. Westgarth	T.N. Garrett	K.C. Callaghan
6/4/1991	1991	2		MCG	ESSENDON	25	17	167	KANGAROOS	13	16	94	73	24,961	M. James	M. Ellis	S. McLaren
13/4/1991	1991	3		Windy Hill	ESSENDON	12	20	92	ADELAIDE	6	11	47	45	20,197	S.B. Harris	G.W. Forster	
19/4/1991	1991	4	N	SCG	ESSENDON	24	17	161	STH MLB/SYDNEY	19	16	130	31	13,140	G.F. Dore	B.K. Sheehan	D.R. Goldspink
27/4/1991	1991	5	N	Carrara	ESSENDON	16	18	114	BRISBANE	12	11	83	31	9,253	H.D. Kennedy	M.W. Viney	
4/5/1991	1991	6		Waverley Park	ESSENDON	17	13	115	CARLTON	13	16	94	21	47,651	D.G. Rich	R.C. Sawers	
11/5/1991	1991	7		Windy Hill	ESSENDON	13	9	87	WEST COAST	14	10	94	-7	21,438	I.G.A. Robinson	N.R. Nash	
18/5/1991	1991	8		Waverley Park	ESSENDON	13	9	87	HAWTHORN	15	13	103	-16	40,537	R.C. Sawers	P.R. Cameron	
25/5/1991	1991	9		Moorabbin	ESSENDON	16	13	109	ST KILDA	11	15	81	28	33,832	G.F. Dore	H.D. Kennedy	
1/6/1991	1991	10		Windy Hill	ESSENDON	12	14	86	MELBOURNE	12	8	80	6	21,635	N.R. Nash	I.G.A. Robinson	
16/6/1991	1991	11		Waverley Park	ESSENDON	10	14	74	COLLINGWOOD	11	10	76	-2	41,948	P.R. Cameron	J.J. Russo	
23/6/1991	1991	12		Windy Hill	ESSENDON	17	20	122	FITZROY	12	11	83	39	16,519	I.W. Clayton	P.J. Howe	
30/6/1991	1991	13		Whitten Oval	ESSENDON	6	7	43	WSTRN BLDGS	11	23	89	-46	17,536	J. Chapman	M.J. Dye	
8/7/1991	1991	14		Skilled Stadium	ESSENDON	10	15	75	GEELONG	13	21	99	-24	23,102	A.C. Bryant	D.A. Howlett	
14/7/1991	1991	15		Windy Hill	ESSENDON	6	7	43	RICHMOND	7	18	60	-17	13,501	K.R. Dargavel	G.R. James	
21/7/1991	1991	16		Windy Hill	ESSENDON	19	9	123	KANGAROOS	5	19	49	74	19,322	S.D. McDonald	G.W. Forster	
28/7/1991	1991	17	N	AAMI Stadium	ESSENDON	9	11	65	ADELAIDE	23	23	161	-96	41,716	C.B. Mitchell	R.C. Sawers	
3/8/1991	1991	18		Windy Hill	ESSENDON	22	19	151	STH MLB/SYDNEY	12	12	84	67	14,341	I.W. Clayton	R.A. Castle	
10/8/1991	1991	19		Windy Hill	ESSENDON	23	19	157	BRISBANE	17	10	112	45	12,970	C.B. Mitchell	P.J. Howe	
17/8/1991	1991	20		Waverley Park	ESSENDON	13	10	88	CARLTON	12	12	84	4	34,588	R.C. Sawers	G.F. Dore	
25/8/1991	1991	21		Subiaco	ESSENDON	7	10	52	WEST COAST	16	19	115	-63	38,990	R.C. Sawers	C.B. Mitchell	
31/8/1991	1991	22		Waverley Park	ESSENDON	9	9	63	HAWTHORN	21	17	143	-80	48,311	M.J. Dye	N.R. Nash	A.G. McKernan

Appendix C

DATE	SEASON	RND	SESSION	VENUE	KEVIN'S CLUB	G	B	PTS	OPPONENT	G	B	PTS	MARGIN	ATTENDANCE	FIELD UMPIRE ONE	FIELD UMPIRE TWO	FIELD UMPIRE THREE
7/9/1991	1991	1EF		Waverley Park	ESSENDON	11	9	75	MELBOURNE	17	11	113	-38	46,032	G.T.D. Morrow	N.R. Nash	
22/3/1992	1992	1		Waverley Park	ESSENDON	17	9	111	ST KILDA	18	20	128	-17	44,520	R.C. Sawers	G.T.D. Morrow	
29/3/1992	1992	2		MCG	ESSENDON	15	8	98	FITZROY	22	18	150	-52	29,206	I.G.A. Robinson	K.F. Smith	
5/4/1992	1992	3		Whitten Oval	ESSENDON	13	13	91	WSTRN BLDGS	9	15	69	22	21,569	P.R. Cameron	T.N. Garrett	
11/4/1992	1992	4		Waverley Park	ESSENDON	17	13	115	COLLINGWOOD	19	10	124	-9	54,984	P.R. Cameron	A.C. Bryant	
18/4/1992	1992	5		Waverley Park	ESSENDON	22	9	141	HAWTHORN	16	18	114	27	32,509	B.K. Sheehan	P.R. Carey	
25/4/1992	1992	6		MCG	ESSENDON	18	16	124	MELBOURNE	19	9	123	1	41,405	D.R. Goldspink	P.R. Carey	
9/5/1992	1992	8		Optus Oval	ESSENDON	11	14	80	KANGAROOS	19	18	132	-52	15,911	J.E. Morgan	K.F. Smith	
16/5/1992	1992	9		MCG	ESSENDON	17	22	124	GEELONG	28	13	181	-57	41,244	R.C. Sawers	K.F. Smith	
23/5/1992	1992	10		Optus Oval	ESSENDON	7	22	64	CARLTON	18	8	116	-52	27,993	R.C. Sawers	K.F. Smith	
31/5/1992	1992	11		MCG	ESSENDON	16	20	116	STH MLB/SYDNEY	10	13	73	43	20,476	J. Harvey	A. Coates	J. Love
6/6/1992	1992	12		MCG	ESSENDON	19	16	130	RICHMOND	11	13	79	51	35,967	D. Goldspink	S. McLaren	S. McBurney
14/6/1992	1992	13		Carrara	ESSENDON	18	11	119	BRISBANE	12	13	85	34	6,442	D.R. Goldspink	J.S. Harvey	
27/6/1992	1992	15		MCG	ESSENDON	9	8	62	WEST COAST	20	17	137	-75	32,849	K.R. Dargavel	P.J. Howe	
4/7/1992	1992	16		MCG	ESSENDON	16	15	111	ST KILDA	11	17	83	28	42,461	B. Sheehan	T. Burton	D. Humphery-Smith
12/7/1992	1992	17		North Hobart	ESSENDON	11	14	80	FITZROY	10	17	77	3	10,265	B.J. Allen	D.G. Rich	
18/7/1992	1992	18		MCG	ESSENDON	13	15	93	WSTRN BLDGS	10	17	77	16	44,142	P.R. Carey	S.A. McLaren	D. Ackland
24/7/1992	1992	19	N	MCG	ESSENDON	8	13	61	COLLINGWOOD	10	23	83	-22	88,066	D.G. Rich	R.C. Sawers	
1/8/1992	1992	20		MCG	ESSENDON	8	8	56	HAWTHORN	32	24	216	-160	41,070	G.R. James	K.J. Quinn	
8/8/1992	1992	21		MCG	ESSENDON	19	12	126	MELBOURNE	13	16	94	32	25,508	A. Coates	V. Sercia	C. Durham
21/6/1992	1994	23	N	AAMI Stadium	ESSENDON	8	10	58	ADELAIDE	17	13	115	-57	43,163	C.B. Mitchell	G.G. Vernon	
22/8/1992	1992	23		MCG	ESSENDON	20	19	139	KANGAROOS	10	11	71	68	21,044	B. Allen	B. Sheehan	S. McBurney
29/8/1992	1992	24		Waverley Park	ESSENDON	9	10	64	GEELONG	16	14	110	-46	42,968	J.E. Morgan	I.G.A. Robinson	
28/3/1993	1993	1		Subiaco	ESSENDON	17	8	110	WEST COAST	17	21	123	-13	34,361	H. Kennedy	S. McBurney	G. Scroop
3/4/1993	1993	2		MCG	ESSENDON	20	12	132	CARLTON	19	18	132	0	49,856	P.R. Carey	A.P. Coates	
12/4/1993	1993	3		MCG	ESSENDON	16	13	109	COLLINGWOOD	21	13	139	-30	87,638	R.A. Castle	S.B. Harris	
18/4/1993	1993	4		SCG	ESSENDON	28	13	181	STH MLB/SYDNEY	14	11	95	86	9,023	D. Goldspink	J. Harvey	J. Love
24/4/1993	1993	5		Whitten Oval	ESSENDON	11	15	81	WSTRN BLDGS	20	7	127	-46	26,923	V. Vasilou	P.R. Cameron	
1/5/1993	1993	6		MCG	ESSENDON	23	18	156	GEELONG	19	18	132	24	46,588	D.A. Howlett	G.G. Vernon	S Kronja
15/5/1993	1993	8		Waverley Park	ESSENDON	19	11	125	ST KILDA	9	13	67	58	43,886	P.R. Carey	B.K. Sheehan	M.A. Nash
22/5/1993	1993	9		MCG	ESSENDON	16	15	111	ADELAIDE	10	5	65	46	34,372	S. McLaren	D. Goldspink	G. Dore
28/5/1993	1993	10	N	MCG	ESSENDON	19	15	129	FITZROY	19	11	125	4	50,567	M.G. Bird	D.A. Howlett	K. Chambers

Appendix C

DATE	SEASON	RND	SESSION	VENUE	KEVIN'S CLUB	G	B	PTS	OPPONENT	G	B	PTS	MARGIN	ATTENDANCE	FIELD UMPIRE ONE	FIELD UMPIRE TWO	FIELD UMPIRE THREE
14/6/1993	1993	11		Waverley Park	ESSENDON	17	14	116	HAWTHORN	12	14	86	30	47,295	R.C. Sawers	G.G. Vernon	
19/6/1993	1993	12		MCG	ESSENDON	10	11	71	MELBOURNE	15	15	105	-34	44,094	P.R. Cameron	D.A. Howlett	
26/6/1993	1993	13		Optus Oval	ESSENDON	21	15	141	RICHMOND	8	15	63	78	19,105	D.G. Rich	S.A. McInerney	R. Williams
3/7/1993	1993	14		MCG	ESSENDON	23	17	155	BRISBANE	4	15	39	116	20,453	S. McBurney	M. James	B. Allen
9/7/1993	1993	15	N	MCG	ESSENDON	13	13	91	KANGAROOS	19	15	129	-38	55,693	S.D. McDonald	R.C. Sawers	
18/7/1993	1993	16		MCG	ESSENDON	12	17	89	WEST COAST	13	9	87	2	44,507	R.C. Sawers	G.F. Dore	M.R. Westgarth
24/7/1993	1993	17		MCG	ESSENDON	15	14	104	CARLTON	12	11	83	21	67,035	D.A. Howlett	G.F. Dore	G. Deller
30/7/1993	1993	18	N	MCG	ESSENDON	18	15	123	COLLINGWOOD	7	13	55	68	87,573	B. Allen	M. Ellis	H. Kennedy
6/8/1993	1993	19	N	MCG	ESSENDON	18	9	117	STH MLB/SYDNEY	13	18	96	21	22,813	P.R. Carey	V. Sercia	M. Sexton
14/8/1993	1993	20		MCG	ESSENDON	14	14	98	WSTRN BLDGS	12	13	85	13	40,229	R.C. Sawers	G.R. Scroop	B.K. Sheehan
21/8/1993	1993	21		Skilled Stadium	ESSENDON	14	10	94	GEELONG	19	12	126	-32	37,303	N.R. Nash	I.G.A. Robinson	
4/9/1993	1993	QF	N	MCG	ESSENDON	14	14	98	CARLTON	15	10	100	-2	79,739	K. Chambers	D.A. Howlett	M. McKenzie
12/9/1993	1993	FS		MCG	ESSENDON	16	12	108	WEST COAST	11	10	76	32	75,453	P. Carey	B. Allen	G.R. Scroop
18/9/1993	1993	PF		MCG	ESSENDON	17	9	111	ADELAIDE	14	16	100	11	76,380	D.R. Goldspink	M.W. Prince	M. Norden
25/9/1993	1993	GF		MCG	ESSENDON	20	13	133	CARLTON	13	11	89	44	96,862	H. Kennedy	D. Howlett	K. Chambers
26/3/1994	1994	1		MCG	ESSENDON	12	10	82	WEST COAST	11	13	79	3	39,492	G.N. Caulfield	A.G. McKernan	
2/4/1994	1994	2		Optus Oval	ESSENDON	14	15	99	FITZROY	17	10	112	-13	24,872	P.R. Cameron	P.R. Carey	
9/4/1994	1994	3		Waverley Park	ESSENDON	14	10	94	ST KILDA	16	12	108	-14	30,454	P.R. Cameron	P.R. Carey	
16/4/1994	1994	4		MCG	ESSENDON	9	12	66	MELBOURNE	12	12	84	-18	61,193	G.F. Dore	J.J. Russo	
23/4/1994	1994	5		MCG	ESSENDON	14	14	98	COLLINGWOOD	14	10	94	4	74,330	G.G. Vernon	P.R. Carey	J.S. Harvey
7/5/1994	1994	7		Waverley Park	ESSENDON	11	9	75	HAWTHORN	12	16	88	-13	33,927	K.F. Smith	R.C. Sawers	M.G. Bird
15/5/1994	1994	8		Optus Oval	ESSENDON	20	11	131	ADELAIDE	13	10	88	43	28,626	B.K. Sheehan	T.N. Garrett	
21/5/1994	1994	9		Waverley Park	ESSENDON	9	9	63	CARLTON	7	20	62	1	40,080	I.G.A. Robinson	G.L. Walsh	
28/5/1994	1994	10		MCG	ESSENDON	16	16	112	GEELONG	15	11	101	11	75,129	A.P. Coates	H.D. Kennedy	R.C. Sawers
4/6/1994	1994	11		Optus Oval	ESSENDON	24	10	154	RICHMOND	17	6	108	46	22,547	A.M. Panozzo	G.F. Dore	B.K. Sheehan
13/6/1994	1994	12		Waverley Park	ESSENDON	9	10	64	WSTRN BLDGS	13	14	92	-28	39,181	A.C. Bryant	G.T.D. Morrow	
19/6/1994	1994	13		Gabba	ESSENDON	11	15	81	BRISBANE	17	12	114	-33	18,484	D.R. Goldspink	C.B. Mitchell	S.A. McLaren
26/6/1994	1994	14		MCG	ESSENDON	19	15	129	STH MLB/SYDNEY	14	11	95	34	27,094	S. McBurney	P. Carey	M. Nash
2/7/1994	1994	15		MCG	ESSENDON	14	8	92	KANGAROOS	11	19	85	7	50,141	A.P. Coates	T. Pfeiffer	R.C. Sawers
10/7/1994	1994	16		Subiaco	ESSENDON	5	14	44	WEST COAST	11	14	80	-36	29,723	A.P. Coates	G.F. Dore	D.R. Goldspink
17/7/1994	1994	17		MCG	ESSENDON	24	9	153	FITZROY	12	17	89	64	33,265	G. Dore	M. James	S. McLaren
23/7/1994	1994	18		MCG	ESSENDON	15	10	100	ST KILDA	18	2	110	-10	38,858	P.W. Repper	T.N. Garrett	
30/7/1994	1994	19		MCG	ESSENDON	8	10	58	MELBOURNE	21	9	135	-77	43,132	R.C. Sawers	K.F. Smith	

Appendix C

DATE	SEASON	RND	SESSION	VENUE	KEVIN'S CLUB	G	B	PTS	OPPONENT	G	B	PTS	MARGIN	ATTENDANCE	FIELD UMPIRE ONE	FIELD UMPIRE TWO	FIELD UMPIRE THREE
5/8/1994	1994	20	N	MCG	ESSENDON	17	4	106	COLLINGWOOD	19	20	134	-28	76,565	J.J. Russo	P.R. Carey	D. Humphery-Smith
21/8/1994	1994	22		MCG	ESSENDON	20	16	136	HAWTHORN	12	12	84	52	49,354	H. Kennedy	M. McKenzie	J.J. Russo
28/8/1994	1994	23		AAMI Stadium	ESSENDON	8	10	58	ADELAIDE	17	13	115	-57	41,669	C.B. Mitchell	T.N. Garrett	G.R. Scroop
3/9/1994	1994	24		MCG	ESSENDON	12	8	80	CARLTON	9	8	62	18	61,231	H.D. Kennedy	G.G. Vernon	
1/4/1995	1995	1		Whitten Oval	ESSENDON	16	16	112	FITZROY	6	2	38	74	17,869	D.R. Goldspink	G.G. Vernon	
7/4/1995	1995	2	N	WACA	ESSENDON	12	19	91	FREMANTLE	11	16	82	9	23,688	M. McKenzie	G.R. Scroop	G.G. Vernon
17/4/1995	1995	3		MCG	ESSENDON	14	14	98	MELBOURNE	12	10	82	16	60,057	R.C. Sawers	M. McKenzie	M. Norden
25/4/1995	1995	4		MCG	ESSENDON	16	15	111	COLLINGWOOD	17	9	111	0	94,825	A.P. Coates	B.K. Sheehan	
30/4/1995	1995	5		Optus Oval	ESSENDON	24	10	154	ST KILDA	5	8	38	116	17,930	M. Nash	C. Mitchell	A. Malcolm
7/5/1995	1995	6		Optus Oval	ESSENDON	19	14	128	BRISBANE	14	16	100	28	17,646	G.G. Vernon	D.R. Agnew	B.J. Allen
13/5/1995	1995	7		MCG	ESSENDON	9	13	67	CARLTON	10	15	75	-8	73,753	M.D. Abbott	C.B. Mitchell	
21/5/1995	1995	8		Subiaco	ESSENDON	16	12	108	WEST COAST	13	12	90	18	34,731	C. Mitchell	K. Nicholls	J. Schmitt
27/5/1995	1995	9		MCG	ESSENDON	15	11	101	WSTRN BLDGS	9	13	67	34	38,719	G. Vernon	D. Howlett	J. Harvey
2/6/1995	1995	10	N	MCG	ESSENDON	15	9	99	KANGAROOS	19	12	126	-27	59,354	B.K. Sheehan	C.B. Mitchell	
10/6/1995	1995	11		MCG	ESSENDON	17	10	112	GEELONG	19	9	123	-11	77,643	H.D. Kennedy	J.J. Russo	
23/6/1995	1995	12	N	MCG	ESSENDON	10	18	78	HAWTHORN	8	12	60	18	47,237	D.A. Howlett	D.R. Goldspink	R.C. Sawers
2/7/1995	1995	13		SCG	ESSENDON	17	17	119	STH MLB/SYDNEY	21	12	138	-19	21,853	I.W. Clayton	S.D. McDonald	
8/7/1995	1995	14		MCG	ESSENDON	27	20	182	ADELAIDE	8	12	60	122	40,269	S. McLaren	D. Morris	S. Wenn
14/7/1995	1995	15	N	MCG	ESSENDON	15	11	101	RICHMOND	15	11	101	0	76,628	D.R. Goldspink	B.K Sheehan	
22/7/1995	1995	16		MCG	ESSENDON	22	18	150	FITZROY	12	7	79	71	25,295	M. Vozzo	M. Ellis	D. Goldspink
29/7/1995	1995	17		MCG	ESSENDON	21	9	135	FREMANTLE	13	9	87	48	29,102	A. Coates	B. Allen	J. Harvey
5/8/1995	1995	18		MCG	ESSENDON	15	16	106	MELBOURNE	11	7	73	33	52,523	D. Goldspink	M. Ellis	C. Durham
12/8/1995	1995	19		MCG	ESSENDON	16	14	110	COLLINGWOOD	15	12	102	8	77,448	A.P. Coates	R.C. Sawers	B.K. Sheehan
19/8/1995	1995	20		Waverley Park	ESSENDON	23	13	151	ST KILDA	10	15	75	76	34,121	B.K Sheehan	D.G Rich	A.M. Panozzo
26/8/1995	1995	21	N	Gabba	ESSENDON	12	12	84	BRISBANE	17	14	116	-32	12,657	B.K. Sheehan	D.G. Rich	G.F. Dore
2/9/1995	1995	22		MCG	ESSENDON	9	13	67	CARLTON	16	12	108	-41	87,984	G.J. Sidebottom	S.D. McDonald	
9/9/1995	1995	1QF		Waverley Park	ESSENDON	11	8	74	WEST COAST	8	7	55	19	36,102	B.K. Sheehan	C.B. Mitchell	
16/9/1995	1995	2SF		MCG	ESSENDON	11	7	73	RICHMOND	12	14	86	-13	88,308	D.A. Howlett	G.R. Scroop	P.R. Carey
30/3/1996	1996	1		MCG	ESSENDON	19	8	122	RICHMOND	15	14	104	18	52,271	M.A. Nash	S.A. McLaren	
7/4/1996	1996	2		MCG	ESSENDON	10	12	72	CARLTON	15	11	101	-29	62,207	R.C. Sawers	P.R. Carey	
14/4/1996	1996	3		Waverley Park	ESSENDON	16	13	109	WEST COAST	6	14	50	59	20,852	D.R. Agnew	R.C. Sawers	B.J. Allen
20/4/1996	1996	4		AAMI Stadium	ESSENDON	23	23	161	ADELAIDE	9	11	65	96	45,266	M. McKenzie	S. McLaren	D. Rich
25/4/1996	1996	5	N	MCG	ESSENDON	16	9	105	COLLINGWOOD	17	15	117	-12	87,549	D.A. Howlett	B.K. Sheehan	

Appendix C

DATE	SEASON	RND	SESSION	VENUE	KEVIN'S CLUB	G	B	PTS	OPPONENT	G	B	PTS	MARGIN	ATTENDANCE	FIELD UMPIRE ONE	FIELD UMPIRE TWO	FIELD UMPIRE THREE
3/5/1996	1996	6	N	SCG	ESSENDON	12	18	90	STH MLB/SYDNEY	14	6	90	0	22,088	B.J. Carland	J.R. Van Beek	D. McCauley
8/5/1996	1996	7	N	MCG	ESSENDON	22	11	143	GEELONG	17	12	114	29	75,632	H. Kennedy	A. Malcolm	
19/5/1996	1996	8		MCG	ESSENDON	23	13	151	WSTRN BLDGS	13	6	84	67	36,766	K. Nicholls	S. McLaren	G. Dore
25/5/1996	1996	9		MCG	ESSENDON	11	23	89	MELBOURNE	12	5	77	12	37,288	P.R. Carey	J.J. Russo	B.K. Sheehan
8/6/1996	1996	10	N	Waverley Park	ESSENDON	13	11	89	ST KILDA	9	13	67	22	43,925	I.W Clayton	P.R. Cameron	
16/6/1996	1996	11		MCG	ESSENDON	13	12	90	FREMANTLE	12	17	89	1	31,383	H.D. Kennedy	A.P. Coates	A.G. McKernan
23/6/1996	1996	12		MCG	ESSENDON	14	11	95	KANGAROOS	16	11	107	-12	39,515	P.R. Carey	S.B. Harris	
29/6/1996	1996	13		MCG	ESSENDON	18	13	121	HAWTHORN	15	10	100	21	43,481	S. Hanley	D.A. Howlett	S. Wenn
30/6/1996	1996	14		Optus Oval	ESSENDON	17	16	118	FITZROY	7	10	52	66	12,748	S.A. McLaren	G.R. Scroop	M.R. Westgarth
14/7/1996	1996	15		Gabba	ESSENDON	10	8	68	BRISBANE	15	13	103	-35	20,378	K.C. Callaghan	G.N. Caulfield	G.F. Dore
20/7/1996	1996	16		MCG	ESSENDON	15	18	108	RICHMOND	13	10	88	20	58,768	R.C. Sawers	M.A. Nash	B.J. Allen
27/7/1996	1996	17		MCG	ESSENDON	11	16	82	CARLTON	13	13	91	-9	65,420	P.R. Cameron	J.J. Russo	
4/8/1996	1996	18		Subiaco	ESSENDON	14	9	93	WEST COAST	14	15	99	-6	37,669	B. Sheehan	M. James	D. Morris
10/8/1996	1996	19		Optus Oval	ESSENDON	21	17	143	ADELAIDE	16	11	107	36	15,794	D.G. Rich	B.J. Allen	C.B. Mitchell
18/8/1996	1996	20		MCG	ESSENDON	11	11	77	COLLINGWOOD	9	10	64	13	51,057	B.J. Allen	P.R. Carey	M.A. Nash
24/8/1996	1996	21		MCG	ESSENDON	14	16	100	STH MLB/SYDNEY	12	10	82	18	69,237	C.B. Mitchell	B.K. Sheehan	S. McBurney
30/8/1996	1996	22		MCG	ESSENDON	11	13	79	WSTRN BLDGS	11	10	76	3	42,598	G.F. Dore	J.S. Harvey	J.J. Russo
6/9/1996	1996	2QF	N	Gabba	ESSENDON	15	10	100	BRISBANE	15	11	101	-1	22,003	G. Dore	D. Goldspink	B. Sheehan
14/9/1996	1996	1SF	N	MCG	ESSENDON	22	12	144	WEST COAST	8	19	67	77	85,656	M. James	B. Allen	S. McLaren
21/9/1996	1996	2PF	N	SCG	ESSENDON	10	9	69	STH MLB/SYDNEY	10	10	70	-1	41,731	B.K. Sheehan	R.A. Castle	
31/3/1997	1997	1		MCG	ESSENDON	16	10	106	CARLTON	15	9	99	7	82,363	B.J. Allen	P.R. Carey	R.C. Sawers
6/4/1997	1997	2		AAMI Stadium	ESSENDON	14	9	93	PORT ADEL	8	12	60	33	43,720	C. Mitchell	A. Coates	M. Avon
13/4/1997	1997	3		MCG	ESSENDON	18	14	122	KANGAROOS	12	8	80	42	57,978	D. Howlett	S. Hanley	M. Norden
20/4/1997	1997	4		MCG	ESSENDON	11	12	78	GEELONG	11	19	85	-7	54,922	A.P. Coates	D.G Rich	
25/4/1997	1997	5		MCG	ESSENDON	10	10	70	COLLINGWOOD	14	15	99	-29	83,271	P.J. Howe	M.S. Sneddon	
3/5/1997	1997	6		MCG	ESSENDON	15	12	102	BRISBANE	9	17	71	31	37,642	G. Dore	G. Deller	
11/5/1997	1997	7		AAMI Stadium	ESSENDON	11	7	73	ADELAIDE	18	18	126	-53	39,275			S. McInerney
18/5/1997	1997	8		MCG	ESSENDON	14	16	100	ST KILDA	18	16	124	-24	51,928	C.B. Mitchell	P.R. Cameron	
25/5/1997	1997	9		Subiaco	ESSENDON	13	7	85	WEST COAST	16	14	110	-25	38,984	H. Kennedy	S. McBurney	S. Wenn
1/6/1997	1997	10		MCG	ESSENDON	17	12	114	WSTRN BLDGS	20	16	136	-22	50,138	P.R. Carey	C.B. Mitchell	
7/6/1997	1997	11		MCG	ESSENDON	13	13	91	HAWTHORN	17	22	124	-33	60,594	P.J. Howe	M.S. Sneddon	
15/6/1997	1997	12		Subiaco	ESSENDON	9	6	60	FREMANTLE	24	13	157	-97	21,956	R.C. Sawers	B.K. Sheehan	
29/6/1997	1997	13		MCG	ESSENDON	19	13	127	RICHMOND	4	10	34	93	58,812	H. Kennedy	S. McInerney	D. Woodcock

Appendix C

DATE	SEASON	RND	SESSION	VENUE	KEVIN'S CLUB	G	B	PTS	OPPONENT	G	B	PTS	MARGIN	ATTENDANCE	FIELD UMPIRE ONE	FIELD UMPIRE TWO	FIELD UMPIRE THREE
6/7/1997	1997	14		MCG	ESSENDON	18	12	120	MELBOURNE	8	9	57	63	44,803	B. Allen	M. McKenzie	D. Goldspink
13/7/1997	1997	15		SCG	ESSENDON	11	12	78	STH MLB/SYDNEY	11	13	79	-1	36,077	D.R. Goldspink	C.B. Mitchell	C.B. Mitchell
19/7/1997	1997	16		MCG	ESSENDON	13	9	87	CARLTON	25	15	165	-78	58,512	P.R. Cameron	M.J. Dye	
25/7/1997	1997	17	N	MCG	ESSENDON	10	12	72	PORT ADEL	18	14	122	-50	33,076	J.J. Russo	I.G.A. Robinson	
1/8/1997	1997	18	N	MCG	ESSENDON	8	16	64	KANGAROOS	11	17	83	-19	38,614	R.C. Sawers	D.G. Rich	
10/8/1997	1997	19		MCG	ESSENDON	11	7	73	GEELONG	9	14	68	5	53,901	B.K. Sheehan	A.G. McKernan	G.G. Vernon
16/8/1997	1997	20		MCG	ESSENDON	12	9	81	COLLINGWOOD	13	13	91	-10	50,944	P.R. Cameron	H.D. Kennedy	
23/8/1997	1997	21	N	Gabba	ESSENDON	16	10	106	BRISBANE	15	12	102	4	21,065	R. Kelsey	B. Allen	S Hanley
30/8/1997	1997	22		Optus Oval	ESSENDON	16	6	102	ADELAIDE	14	14	98	4	25,636	C.B. Mitchell	H.D. Kennedy	
29/3/1998	1998	1		MCG	ESSENDON	13	11	89	RICHMOND	14	19	103	-14	70,200	B.J. Allen	A.P. Coates	D. Margetts
5/4/1998	1998	2		MCG	ESSENDON	28	14	182	ST KILDA	13	15	93	89	53,905	S. McBurney	M. McKenzie	
13/4/1998	1998	3		Waverley Park	ESSENDON	14	15	99	CARLTON	14	14	98	1	68,177	D.G. Rich	G.L. Walsh	C.B. Mitchell
19/4/1998	1998	4		MCG	ESSENDON	11	10	76	FREMANTLE	14	16	100	-24	26,241	K.F. Smith	I.G.A. Robinson	
25/4/1998	1998	5	T	MCG	ESSENDON	12	16	88	COLLINGWOOD	15	18	108	-20	81,542	P.R. Carey	B.K. Sheehan	
2/5/1998	1998	6		Optus Oval	ESSENDON	13	11	89	WSTRN BLDGS	13	19	97	-8	24,813	B.K. Sheehan	M.W. Viney	
9/5/1998	1998	7		MCG	ESSENDON	11	4	70	GEELONG	12	7	79	-9	56,093	A.P. Coates	D.G. Rich	
15/5/1998	1998	8	N	MCG	ESSENDON	12	12	84	BRISBANE	8	22	70	14	35,384	D.R. Goldspink	J.S. Harvey	H.D. Kennedy
23/5/1998	1998	9	T	MCG	ESSENDON	18	14	122	MELBOURNE	12	12	84	38	49,580	B. Sheehan	J. Schmitt	D. Humphery-Smith
30/5/1998	1998	10	T	Waverley Park	ESSENDON	13	15	93	HAWTHORN	13	9	87	6	41,780	J.J. Russo	R.C. Sawers	
5/6/1998	1998	11	N	MCG	ESSENDON	24	16	160	STH MLB/SYDNEY	15	10	100	60	62,866	B. Allen	M. McKenzie	D. Goldspink
13/6/1998	1998	12	N	AAMI Stadium	ESSENDON	15	16	106	ADELAIDE	18	18	108	-2	40,700	J. Harvey	R. Williams	B. Allen
19/6/1998	1998	13	N	MCG	ESSENDON	11	6	72	WEST COAST	11	17	83	-11	45,277	C.B. Mitchell	G.G. Vernon	
26/6/1998	1998	14	N	MCG	ESSENDON	16	13	109	KANGAROOS	19	13	127	-18	48,618	S.D. McDonald	B.K. Sheehan	
4/7/1998	1998	15		MCG	ESSENDON	16	12	108	PORT ADEL	12	9	81	27	37,685	J. Harvey	G. Vernon	S. McInerney
19/7/1998	1998	16		MCG	ESSENDON	14	10	94	RICHMOND	10	15	75	19	83,773	H.D. Kennedy	A.P. Coates	K.C. Callaghan
25/7/1998	1998	17		Waverley Park	ESSENDON	14	6	90	ST KILDA	13	9	87	3	50,778	P.D. Lawlor	I.G.A. Robinson	
8/2/1998	1998	18		MCG	ESSENDON	12	12	84	CARLTON	11	12	78	6	70,969	B.J. Allen	P.R. Carey	M.A. Nash
8/8/1998	1998	19		Subiaco	ESSENDON	18	11	119	FREMANTLE	12	14	86	33	28,135	G. Dore	S. McInerney	D. Margetts
15/8/1998	1998	20		MCG	ESSENDON	16	13	109	COLLINGWOOD	14	15	99	10	64,480	P.R. Carey	D. McCauley	T. Pfeiffer
20/8/1998	1998	21	N	MCG	ESSENDON	13	12	90	WSTRN BLDGS	14	17	101	-11	67,157	D.R. Goldspink	B.K. Sheehan	
29/8/1998	1998	22		MCG	ESSENDON	18	9	117	GEELONG	19	13	127	-10	61,089	D.A. Howlett	B.K. Sheehan	
4/9/1998	1998	4QF	N	MCG	ESSENDON	8	12	60	KANGAROOS	11	16	82	-22	71,154	D.R. Goldspink	S.B. Harris	V. Sercia
25/3/1999	1999	1	N	MCG	ESSENDON	16	14	110	CARLTON	9	17	71	39	71,501	J. Harvey	S. McBurney	

Appendix C

DATE	SEASON	RND	SESSION	VENUE	KEVIN'S CLUB	G	B	PTS	OPPONENT	G	B	PTS	MARGIN	ATTENDANCE	FIELD UMPIRE ONE	FIELD UMPIRE TWO	FIELD UMPIRE THREE
1/4/1999	1999	2	N	MCG	ESSENDON	22	9	141	KANGAROOS	15	16	106	35	48,383	C. Mitchell	S. Hanley	R. Williams
10/4/1999	1999	3		MCG	ESSENDON	22	17	149	STH MLB/SYDNEY	9	14	68	81	50,324	B. Allen	M. Avon	S. Jeffery
18/4/1999	1999	4		Subiaco	ESSENDON	3	5	23	WEST COAST	15	7	97	-74	32,893	P.R. Carey	D.G. Rich	
25/4/1999	1999	5		MCG	ESSENDON	15	18	108	COLLINGWOOD	15	10	100	8	73,118	P.R. Carey	H.D. Kennedy	S. McBurney
1/5/1999	1999	6		MCG	ESSENDON	17	11	113	RICHMOND	11	12	78	35	59,458	B. Sheehan	J. Harvey	J. Schmitt
8/5/1999	1999	7		MCG	ESSENDON	17	11	113	MELBOURNE	20	14	134	-21	51,722	B.K. Sheehan	M.D. Ball	
14/5/1999	1999	8	N	MCG	ESSENDON	7	9	51	ST KILDA	13	16	94	-43	62,928	P.J. Howe	M.R. Westgarth	
22/5/1999	1999	9		Waverley Park	ESSENDON	15	17	107	HAWTHORN	7	5	47	60	46,479	D.A. Howlett	S.A. McInerney	M. Norden
4/6/1999	1999	10	N	AAMI Stadium	ESSENDON	16	13	109	ADELAIDE	8	13	61	48	39,389			
11/6/1999	1999	11	N	MCG	ESSENDON	21	11	137	GEELONG	15	14	104	33	61,783	D. Goldspink	M. Ellis	S. Wenn
19/6/1999	1999	12	N	Gabba	ESSENDON	13	11	89	BRISBANE	9	17	71	18	24,989	B. Allen	R. Kelsey	K. Nicholls
25/6/1999	1999	13	N	MCG	ESSENDON	10	20	80	WSTRN BLDGS	11	10	76	4	55,230	B.J. Allen	A.P. Coates	H.D. Kennedy
4/7/1999	1999	14		MCG	ESSENDON	16	12	108	FREMANTLE	10	12	72	36	35,273	D. Goldspink	D. McCauley	R. Kelsey
11/7/1999	1999	15		AAMI Stadium	ESSENDON	9	8	62	PORT ADEL	14	15	99	-37	34,671			
18/7/1999	1999	16		MCG	ESSENDON	23	8	146	CARLTON	9	16	70	76	66,207	M. Vozzo	M. Ellis	M. James
24/7/1999	1999	17		MCG	ESSENDON	24	14	158	KANGAROOS	20	12	132	26	68,831	D. Goldspink	S. McLaren	J. Love
31/7/1999	1999	18	N	SCG	ESSENDON	15	3	93	STH MLB/SYDNEY	11	13	79	14	31,776	B.J. Allen	C.B. Mitchell	J Love
6/8/1999	1999	19	N	MCG	ESSENDON	23	15	153	WEST COAST	15	3	93	60	55,096	D. Goldspink	B. Allen	H. Kennedy
13/8/1999	1999	20	N	MCG	ESSENDON	12	15	87	COLLINGWOOD	10	5	65	22	56,129	H.D. Kennedy	M. Ellis	B.J. Allen
20/8/1999	1999	21	N	MCG	ESSENDON	22	15	147	RICHMOND	13	11	89	58	48,835	H. Kennedy	A. Coates	J. Schmitt
28/8/1999	1999	22		MCG	ESSENDON	17	14	116	MELBOURNE	15	9	99	17	47,480	B.J. Allen	G.R. Scroop	H.D. Kennedy
5/9/1999	1999	4QF		MCG	ESSENDON	18	15	123	STH MLB/SYDNEY	7	12	54	69	57,687	D. Goldspink	M. James	S. McLaren
18/9/1999	1999	2PF		MCG	ESSENDON	14	19	103	CARLTON	16	8	104	-1	80,519	B.J. Allen	A.P. Coates	D. McCauley
9/3/2000	2000	1	N	Telstra Dome	ESSENDON	24	12	156	PORT ADEL	8	14	62	94	43,012	B. Allen	C. Rowe	D. Goldspink
16/3/2000	2000	2	N	MCG	ESSENDON	20	10	130	RICHMOND	12	15	87	43	49,521	J. Harvey	A. Coates	J. Love
26/3/2000	2000	3	N	Subiaco	ESSENDON	19	10	124	FREMANTLE	12	16	88	36	26,993	C. Mitchell	G. Coates	K. Nicholls
1/4/2000	2000	4		MCG	ESSENDON	20	17	137	HAWTHORN	14	6	90	47	46,889	B. Sheehan	P. Carey	G. Dore
8/4/2000	2000	5		MCG	ESSENDON	18	15	123	CARLTON	15	9	99	24	64,458	S Wenn	G Deller	A.P. Coates
14/4/2000	2000	6	N	Telstra Dome	ESSENDON	22	12	144	WSTRN BLDGS	12	9	81	63	42,029	J. Schmitt	D. Morris	D. Goldspink
25/4/2000	2000	7		MCG	ESSENDON	21	14	140	COLLINGWOOD	15	10	100	40	88,390	B. Allen	A. Coates	M. McKenzie
1/5/2000	2000	8	N	Gabba	ESSENDON	19	13	127	BRISBANE	9	9	63	64	31,887	S. Wenn	S. McBurney	M. Vozzo
7/5/2000	2000	9		MCG	ESSENDON	15	16	106	MELBOURNE	13	15	93	13	62,608	K.C. Callaghan	D.R. Goldspink	G.F. Dore
14/5/2000	2000	10		Telstra Dome	ESSENDON	20	12	132	ADELAIDE	12	12	84	48	34,626	B. Allen	M. Ellis	D. Woodcock

Appendix C

DATE	SEASON	RND	SESSION	VENUE	KEVIN'S CLUB	G	B	PTS	OPPONENT	G	B	PTS	MARGIN	ATTENDANCE	FIELD UMPIRE ONE	FIELD UMPIRE TWO	FIELD UMPIRE THREE
20/5/2000	2000	11	N	Telstra Dome	ESSENDON	22	13	145	GEELONG	13	9	87	58	47,071	M. James	M. Ellis	S. Jeffery
26/5/2000	2000	12	N	Telstra Dome	ESSENDON	25	19	169	ST KILDA	13	5	83	86	39,836	M. Vozzo	S. McBurney	S. Wenn
4/6/2000	2000	13		MCG	ESSENDON	17	17	119	KANGAROOS	11	4	70	49	67,162	H. Kennedy	M. James	M. Nash
11/6/2000	2000	14		SCG	ESSENDON	12	17	89	STH MLB/SYDNEY	11	10	76	13	29,199	D.A. Howlett	J.R. Van Beek	R Williams
17/6/2000	2000	15	N	Telstra Dome	ESSENDON	15	18	108	WEST COAST	11	10	76	32	39,694	A. Coates	M. Head	B. Rosebury
24/6/2000	2000	16	N	AAMI Stadium	ESSENDON	12	17	89	PORT ADEL	7	16	58	31	37,930	G. Dore	D. Goldspink	M. James
1/7/2000	2000	17		MCG	ESSENDON	24	23	167	RICHMOND	10	6	66	101	73,465	S. McBurney	B. Allen	D. Morris
7/7/2000	2000	18	N	Telstra Dome	ESSENDON	24	15	159	FREMANTLE	11	6	72	87	34,567	M. James	M. Ellis	S. Jeffery
15/7/2000	2000	19	N	Telstra Dome	ESSENDON	25	15	165	HAWTHORN	13	4	82	83	46,956	B. Sheehan	B. Allen	M. Avon
21/7/2000	2000	20	N	MCG	ESSENDON	16	13	109	CARLTON	12	11	83	26	91,571	H. Kennedy	D. Ackland	R. Williams
28/7/2000	2000	21	N	Telstra Dome	ESSENDON	12	9	81	WSTRN BLDGS	14	8	92	-11	45,725	H. Kennedy	T. Burton	M Avon
5/8/2000	2000	22		MCG	ESSENDON	13	19	97	COLLINGWOOD	11	12	78	19	66,608	D.G. Rich	B.K. Sheehan	M.W. Prince
12/8/2000	2000	1QF		MCG	ESSENDON	31	12	198	KANGAROOS	11	7	73	125	68,443	J. Baldwin	B. Allen	S. Jeffery
27/8/2000	2000	1PF		MCG	ESSENDON	18	17	125	CARLTON	12	8	80	45	84,778	H. Kennedy	D. Howlett	M. Norden
2/9/2000	2000	GF		MCG	ESSENDON	19	21	135	MELBOURNE	11	9	75	60	96,249	C. Mitchell	D. Howlett	A. Coates
29/3/2001	2001	1	N	Telstra Dome	ESSENDON	23	8	146	KANGAROOS	9	7	61	85	56,028	B. Sheehan	G. Dore	K. Nicholls
5/4/2001	2001	2	N	Telstra Dome	ESSENDON	23	7	145	PORT ADEL	16	11	107	38	34,918	G. Dore	H. Kennedy	S. Wenn
11/4/2001	2001	3	N	MCG	ESSENDON	11	10	76	CARLTON	14	9	93	-17	63,088	P.R. Cameron	J.S. Harvey	A. Lewis
19/4/2001	2001	4	N	SCG	ESSENDON	15	12	102	STH MLB/SYDNEY	6	19	55	47	40,131	A.P. Coates	D.G. Rich	G.G.Vernon
25/4/2001	2001	5		MCG	ESSENDON	15	13	103	COLLINGWOOD	14	11	95	8	83,905	D.R. Goldspink	S. McBurney	M. Avon
5/5/2001	2001	6		Telstra Dome	ESSENDON	24	14	158	WEST COAST	10	10	70	88	33,841	S. McBurney	H. Kennedy	D. McCauley
11/5/2001	2001	7		MCG	ESSENDON	16	24	120	RICHMOND	10	14	74	46	77,576	M. Norden	S. McInerney	J.R. Van Beek
19/5/2001	2001	8		MCG	ESSENDON	12	13	85	MELBOURNE	11	13	79	6	47,452	D.G. Rich	T.N. Garrett	M. Ellis
25/5/2001	2001	9	N	Telstra Dome	ESSENDON	18	14	122	HAWTHORN	8	9	57	65	50,701	S. McBurney	M. James	D. Humphery-Smith
2/6/2001	2001	10	N	Gabba	ESSENDON	10	14	74	BRISBANE	15	12	102	-28	36,149	D.A. Howlett	J.S. Harvey	R. Kelsey
6/6/2001	2001	11	N	Telstra Dome	ESSENDON	19	14	128	ST KILDA	13	8	86	42	40,075	D. Humphery-Smith	D. Corcoran	
14/6/2001	2001	12	N	Telstra Dome	ESSENDON	18	14	122	ADELAIDE	11	7	73	49	38,816	S. McBurney	B. Sheehan	S. McInerney
29/6/2001	2001	13		Telstra Dome	ESSENDON	18	10	118	FREMANTLE	10	12	72	46	29,528	M. James	G. Dore	M. Ellis
6/7/2001	2001	14	N	Telstra Dome	ESSENDON	24	10	154	WSTRN BLDGS	11	10	76	78	48,728	S. Jeffery	K. Nicholls	S. McInerney
14/7/2001	2001	15		Telstra Dome	ESSENDON	19	13	127	GEELONG	17	10	112	15	48,152	D. Morris	H. Kennedy	S. Jeffery
21/7/2001	2001	16		MCG	ESSENDON	27	9	171	KANGAROOS	25	9	159	12	51,878	D.R. Goldspink	G.R. Scroop	G.G. Vernon
29/7/2001	2001	17		AAMI Stadium	ESSENDON	14	13	97	PORT ADEL	15	14	104	-7	34,671	M. Nash	S. Wenn	S. McInerney

Appendix C

DATE	SEASON	RND	SESSION	VENUE	KEVIN'S CLUB	G	B	PTS	OPPONENT	G	B	PTS	MARGIN	ATTENDANCE	FIELD UMPIRE ONE	FIELD UMPIRE TWO	FIELD UMPIRE THREE
4/8/2001	2001	18		MCG	ESSENDON	14	11	95	CARLTON	16	6	102	-7	75,873	D.A Howlett	C.B. Mitchell	M. Avon
11/8/2001	2001	19	N	Telstra Dome	ESSENDON	11	13	79	STH MLB/SYDNEY	11	11	77	2	45,057	H. Kennedy	S. Hanley	D.G. Rich
17/8/2001	2001	20	N	MCG	ESSENDON	15	17	107	COLLINGWOOD	13	9	87	20	71,518	D.R. Goldspink	J.S. Harvey	D.G. Rich
24/8/2001	2001	21	N	Subiaco	ESSENDON	21	10	136	WEST COAST	6	11	47	89	36,445	M. Vozzo	D. Margetts	D. Goldspink
30/8/2001	2001	22	N	MCG	ESSENDON	12	11	83	RICHMOND	17	5	107	-24	77,024	D.G. Rich	C.B. Mitchell	
6/9/2001	2001	1PF	N	MCG	ESSENDON	11	10	76	HAWTHORN	9	13	67	9	86,468	M.A. Nash	D.G. Rich	J.J. Russo
22/9/2001	2001	1QF		MCG	ESSENDON	17	11	113	RICHMOND	5	13	43	70	78,253	D. Goldspink	M. James	S. McLaren
28/9/2001	2001	GF		MCG	ESSENDON	12	10	82	BRISBANE	15	18	108	-26	91,482	S.V. Luckman	C.B. Mitchell	
30/3/2002	2002	1	N	MCG	ESSENDON	18	18	126	GEELONG	11	10	76	50	42,740	B. Allen	M. McKenzie	S. Hanley
5/4/2002	2002	2	N	MCG	ESSENDON	16	16	112	RICHMOND	8	12	60	52	67,453	S. McLaren	A. Coates	M. Ellis
13/4/2002	2002	3	N	Gabba	ESSENDON	9	13	67	BRISBANE	17	15	117	-50	35,898	M.J. Dye	P.R. Cameron	
19/4/2002	2002	4	N	Telstra Dome	ESSENDON	19	8	122	ADELAIDE	11	15	81	41	40,322	B. Sheehan	J. Schmitt	M. McKenzie
25/4/2002	2002	5	N	MCG	ESSENDON	4	9	33	COLLINGWOOD	9	12	66	-33	84,894	I.G.A. Robinson	D.G. Rich	G.G. Vernon
4/5/2002	2002	6		Subiaco	ESSENDON	9	8	62	FREMANTLE	13	11	89	-27	25,319	K. Nicholls	D.G. Rich	S. Wenn
10/5/2002	2002	7	N	MCG	ESSENDON	12	15	87	CARLTON	9	8	62	25	55,633	M.A. Nash	J. Love	B. Rosebury
19/5/2002	2002	8		Telstra Dome	ESSENDON	26	15	171	ST KILDA	11	6	72	99	34,262	M. Vozzo	A. Coates	M. Head
25/5/2002	2002	9		Telstra Stadium	ESSENDON	12	13	85	STH MLB/SYDNEY	11	17	83	2	54,129	M. James	B. Allen	
31/5/2002	2002	10	N	MCG	ESSENDON	12	12	84	KANGAROOS	12	20	92	-8	34,352	J.S. Harvey	H.D. Kennedy	
8/6/2002	2002	11	N	Telstra Dome	ESSENDON	7	7	40	PORT ADEL	16	12	108	-59	40,044	B. Allen	S. McLaren	M. Nash
14/6/2002	2002	12	N	MCG	ESSENDON	10	12	72	HAWTHORN	10	5	65	7	40,470	H.D. Kennedy	M.W. Prince	J.J. Russo
28/6/2002	2002	13	N	Telstra Dome	ESSENDON	18	12	120	MELBOURNE	16	12	108	12	41,817	D. Goldspink	D. Morris	J. Schmitt
6/7/2002	2002	14	N	Telstra Dome	ESSENDON	17	16	118	WSTRN BLDGS	18	10	118	0	44,864	G. Dore	V. Sercia	K. Nicholls
14/7/2002	2002	15		Subiaco	ESSENDON	8	15	63	WEST COAST	13	12	90	-27	37,600	T. Shearer	G.R. Scroop	G.G. Vernon
20/7/2002	2002	16	N	Telstra Dome	ESSENDON	8	8	56	GEELONG	14	11	95	-39	47,778	G. Dore	D. Morris	V. Sercia
26/7/2002	2002	17	N	MCG	ESSENDON	7	12	54	RICHMOND	7	11	53	1	39,650	R.C. Sawers	D.A. Howlett	T.N. Garrett
3/8/2002	2002	18	N	Telstra Dome	ESSENDON	11	5	71	BRISBANE	16	12	108	-37	43,036	G. Dore	S. McLaren	S. McBurney
11/8/2002	2002	19	N	AAMI Stadium	ESSENDON	11	10	76	ADELAIDE	18	16	124	-48	45,266	M. McKenzie	S.A. McLaren	D.G. Rich
17/8/2002	2002	20	N	MCG	ESSENDON	19	12	126	COLLINGWOOD	10	11	71	55	69,613	D. Goldspink	B. Allen	M. McKenzie
25/8/2002	2002	21		Telstra Dome	ESSENDON	13	15	93	FREMANTLE	10	12	72	21	32,667	S. McLaren	D. Woodcock	S. McBurney
1/9/2002	2002	22		MCG	ESSENDON	12	20	92	CARLTON	5	7	37	55	46,649	D. Humphrey-Smith	M. James	V. Sercia
7/9/2002	2002	1EF		Telstra Dome	ESSENDON	17	9	111	WEST COAST	11	12	78	33	37,475	M. Ellis	D. Goldspink	B. Sheehan
13/9/2002	2002	1SF	N	AAMI Stadium	ESSENDON	8	11	59	PORT ADEL	11	17	83	-24	39,389	S. Hanley	M. Nash	S. McInerney

Appendix C

DATE	SEASON	RND	SESSION	VENUE	KEVIN'S CLUB	G	B	PTS	OPPONENT	G	B	PTS	MARGIN	ATTENDANCE	FIELD UMPIRE ONE	FIELD UMPIRE TWO	FIELD UMPIRE THREE
29/3/2003	2003	1	N	Gabba	ESSENDON	8	13	61	BRISBANE	14	20	104	-43	36,197	D.A. Howlett	K.C. Callaghan	J.R. Van Beek
5/4/2003	2003	2		MCG	ESSENDON	17	10	112	MELBOURNE	10	15	75	37	43,448	A. Coates	M. Norden	V. Sercia
11/4/2003	2003	3	N	MCG	ESSENDON	13	16	94	CARLTON	15	15	105	-11	44,268	J.R. Van Beek	D.G. Rich	D. Goldspink
19/4/2003	2003	4	N	Telstra Dome	ESSENDON	20	9	129	WSTRN BLDGS	16	14	110	19	35,238	B. Sheehan	M. McKenzie	C. Mitchell
25/4/2003	2003	5		MCG	ESSENDON	23	9	147	COLLINGWOOD	12	9	81	66	62,589	A. Coates	M. Vozzo	M. McKenzie
4/5/2003	2003	6		Subiaco	ESSENDON	15	10	100	FREMANTLE	20	11	131	-31	28,492	M.A. Nash	G.R. Scroop	
10/5/2003	2003	7		MCG	ESSENDON	5	12	42	RICHMOND	11	18	84	-42	52,196	P.R. Cameron	I.G.A. Robinson	
16/5/2003	2003	8		MCG	ESSENDON	15	16	106	HAWTHORN	8	5	53	53	48,006	D. Goldspink	M. Ellis	S. McBurney
23/5/2003	2003	9	N	Telstra Dome	ESSENDON	14	12	96	PORT ADEL	23	8	146	-50	35,390	S. McLaren	M. Ellis	G. Dore
1/6/2003	2003	10	N	Telstra Dome	ESSENDON	19	14	128	WEST COAST	16	10	106	22	32,715	D. Goldspink	D. Morris	D. Woodcock
7/6/2003	2003	11	N	Telstra Stadium	ESSENDON	12	7	79	STH MLB/SYDNEY	21	7	133	-54	45,917	M. James	B. Allen	M. Avon
13/6/2003	2003	12	N	Telstra Dome	ESSENDON	13	10	88	KANGAROOS	14	12	96	-8	45,331	D. Mitchell	D. Howlett	T. Burton
27/6/2003	2003	13	N	Telstra Dome	ESSENDON	20	9	129	GEELONG	15	3	93	36	48,374	M. McKenzie	M. James	M. Vozzo
4/7/2003	2003	14	N	Telstra Dome	ESSENDON	17	17	119	ST KILDA	7	9	51	68	49,148	C. Mitchell	M. James	K. Nicholls
11/7/2003	2003	15	N	AAMI Stadium	ESSENDON	7	7	49	ADELAIDE	13	12	90	41	41,758	C. Rowston	S. McLaren	S. McInerney
19/7/2003	2003	16	N	Telstra Dome	ESSENDON	14	10	94	BRISBANE	12	14	86	8	47,744	B. Sheehan	S. McLaren	S. McBurney
26/7/2003	2003	17		MCG	ESSENDON	13	10	88	MELBOURNE	10	11	71	17	33,368	P.R. Carey	R.C. Sawers	R. Williams
2/8/2003	2003	18		MCG	ESSENDON	13	12	90	CARLTON	7	14	56	34	40,497	H. Kennedy	S. McBurney	D. Howlett
10/8/2003	2003	19		Telstra Dome	ESSENDON	22	15	147	WSTRN BLDGS	12	8	80	67	36,138	M. Ellis	S. Ryan	D. Woodcock
17/8/2003	2003	20		MCG	ESSENDON	13	14	92	RICHMOND	7	11	53	39	40,846	D. Goldspink	S. Jeffery	S. McBurney
23/8/2003	2003	21		Telstra Dome	ESSENDON	20	13	133	FREMANTLE	11	7	73	60	42,256	B. Allen	C. Rowe	S. McInerney
29/8/2003	2003	22	N	MCG	ESSENDON	9	13	67	COLLINGWOOD	12	11	83	-16	68,381	S. McBurney	S. Wenn	D. Goldspink
5/9/2003	2003	1EF	N	Subiaco	ESSENDON	15	11	101	FREMANTLE	8	9	57	44	42,770	S. McLaren	M. James	S. Wenn
13/9/2003	2003	1SF	N	AAMI Stadium	ESSENDON	6	8	44	PORT ADEL	12	11	83	-39	36,557	S. McLaren	M. James	C. Rowe
28/3/2004	2004	1		AAMI Stadium	ESSENDON	8	14	62	PORT ADEL	23	20	158	-96	28,413	S. McBurney	M. James	S. Ryan
3/4/2004	2004	2		Telstra Dome	ESSENDON	8	12	60	ST KILDA	13	16	94	-34	44,876	S. McLaren	M. Nicholls	M. Ellis
10/4/2004	2004	3	N	Telstra Dome	ESSENDON	22	5	137	WEST COAST	20	11	131	6	33,195			
16/4/2004	2004	4	N	MCG	ESSENDON	17	15	117	CARLTON	12	8	80	37	60,864			
25/4/2004	2004	5	N	MCG	ESSENDON	17	10	111	COLLINGWOOD	11	13	79	32	57,294			
1/5/2004	2004	6		MCG	ESSENDON	16	12	108	SYDNEY	15	8	98	10	38,946			
7/5/2004	2004	7	N	Telstra Dome	ESSENDON	18	13	121	WSTRN BLDGS	14	11	95	26	45,119			
14/5/2004	2004	8	N	AAMI Stadium	ESSENDON	20	15	135	ADELAIDE	12	12	84	51	46,309			
22/5/2004	2004	9	N	Telstra Dome	ESSENDON	14	13	97	GEELONG	18	12	120	-23	51,400			

Appendix C

DATE	SEASON	RND	SESSION	VENUE	KEVIN'S CLUB	G	B	PTS	OPPONENT	G	B	PTS	MARGIN	ATTENDANCE	FIELD UMPIRE ONE	FIELD UMPIRE TWO	FIELD UMPIRE THREE
4/29/2004	2004	10	N	Telstra Dome	ESSENDON	17	13	115	FREMANTLE	12	13	85	30	38,411			
5/6/2004	2004	11		MCG	ESSENDON	24	10	154	HAWTHORN	12	8	80	74	42,682			
12/6/2004	2004	12	N	Telstra Dome	ESSENDON	14	12	96	BRISBANE	25	12	162	-66	50,003			
20/6/2004	2004	13		MCG	ESSENDON	10	9	69	MELBOURNE	13	17	95	-26	47,314			
2/7/2004	2004	14	N	Telstra Dome	ESSENDON	12	7	79	KANGAROOS	14	16	100	-21	49,419			
10/7/2004	2004	15		MCG	ESSENDON	24	11	155	RICHMOND	11	11	77	78	48,286			
16/7/2004	2004	16	N	Subiaco	ESSENDON	10	13	73	WEST COAST	18	9	117	-44	40,674			
23/7/2004	2004	17	N	Telstra Dome	ESSENDON	14	8	92	ST KILDA	20	7	127	-35	50,392			
31/7/2004	2004	18	N	Telstra Dome	ESSENDON	18	11	119	PORT ADEL	11	13	79	40	35,711			
7/8/2004	2004	19		MCG	ESSENDON	8	9	57	CARLTON	10	14	74	-17	45,083			
13/8/2004	2004	20	N	MCG	ESSENDON	18	13	121	COLLINGWOOD	13	9	87	34	52,983			
21/8/2004	2004	21	N	Telstra Stadium	ESSENDON	12	18	90	SYDNEY	17	8	110	-20	46,440			
29/8/2004	2004	22		Telstra Dome	ESSENDON	17	11	113	WSTRN BLDGS	14	12	96	17	39,894			
4/9/2004	2004	1EF	N	MCG	ESSENDON	15	14	104	MELBOURNE	15	9	99	5	60,903			
11/9/2004	2004	1SF	N	MCG	ESSENDON	9	10	64	GEELONG	10	14	74	-10	53,356			
26/3/2005	2005	1	N	MCG	ESSENDON	8	9	57	MELBOURNE	15	13	103	-46	47,283			
1/4/2005	2005	2	N	MCG	ESSENDON	17	4	106	CARLTON	16	14	110	-4	56,446			
10/4/2005	2005	3		MCG	ESSENDON	10	17	77	HAWTHORN	11	9	75	2	44,971			
16/4/2005	2005	4	N	Telstra Dome	ESSENDON	11	9	75	GEELONG	19	17	131	-56	48,653			
25/4/2005	2005	5		MCG	ESSENDON	11	17	83	COLLINGWOOD	10	9	69	14	70,033			
30/4/2005	2005	6	N	Telstra Dome	ESSENDON	12	16	88	BRISBANE	21	10	136	-48	44,033			
7/5/2005	2005	7	N	Telstra Stadium	ESSENDON	14	4	88	SYDNEY	13	16	94	-6	31,688			
15/5/2005	2005	8	N	Telstra Dome	ESSENDON	17	15	117	FREMANTLE	11	16	82	35	30,383			
21/5/2005	2005	9	N	AAMI Stadium	ESSENDON	9	12	66	PORT ADEL	12	13	85	-19	33,648			
29/5/2005	2005	10	N	Telstra Dome	ESSENDON	21	11	137	WSTRN BLDGS	17	8	110	27	40,454			
4/6/2005	2005	11	N	AAMI Stadium	ESSENDON	9	9	63	ADELAIDE	24	7	151	-88	43,486			
10/6/2005	2005	12	N	Subiaco	ESSENDON	12	10	82	WEST COAST	15	16	106	-24	38,558			
24/6/2005	2005	13	N	Telstra Dome	ESSENDON	19	5	119	ST KILDA	16	8	104	15	48,342			
2/7/2005	2005	14	N	Telstra Dome	ESSENDON	13	8	86	KANGAROOS	19	14	128	-42	48,696			
9/7/2005	2005	15		MCG	ESSENDON	9	12	66	RICHMOND	14	8	92	-26	49,975			
15/7/2005	2005	16	N	MCG	ESSENDON	21	5	131	COLLINGWOOD	15	15	105	26	52,507			
23/7/2005	2005	17	N	Gabba	ESSENDON	14	17	101	BRISBANE	17	12	114	-13	36,077			
29/7/2005	2005	18	N	Telstra Dome	ESSENDON	16	11	107	GEELONG	13	16	94	13	47,122			

Appendix C

DATE	SEASON	RND	SESSION	VENUE	KEVIN'S CLUB	G	B	PTS	OPPONENT	G	B	PTS	MARGIN	ATTENDANCE	FIELD UMPIRE ONE	FIELD UMPIRE TWO	FIELD UMPIRE THREE
6/8/2005	2005	19	N	Telstra Dome	ESSENDON	15	8	98	SYDNEY	18	10	118	-20	41,629			
14/8/2005	2005	20		MCG	ESSENDON	16	8	104	HAWTHORN	17	15	117	-13	32,052			
21/8/2005	2005	21		MCG	ESSENDON	28	14	182	CARLTON	11	17	83	99	37,481			
28/8/2005	2005	22		MCG	ESSENDON	12	13	85	MELBOURNE	13	17	95	-10	55,016			
1/4/2006	2006	1	Night	Telstra Dome	ESSENDON	17	6	108	STH M-SYD	12	9	81	27	45,355		S. Ryan	
8/4/2006	2006	2	Night	Gabba	ESSENDON	15	7	97	BRISBANE	17	13	115	-18	34,357	M. Stevic	S. Wenn	
16/4/2006	2006	3		Telstra Dome	ESSENDON	13	15	93	WSTRN BLDGS	15	14	104	-11	43,947	H. Kennedy	D. Woodcock	
25/4/2006	2006	4		MCG	ESSENDON	12	17	89	COLLINGWOOD	15	16	106	-17	91,234	S. McBurney	S. Ryan	
30/4/2006	2006	5		MCG	ESSENDON	12	11	83	HAWTHORN	12	12	84	-1	40,179	B. Allen	C. Kamolins	
6/5/2006	2006	6	Night	MCG	ESSENDON	13	17	95	RICHMOND	13	19	97	-2	58,439	M. James	M. Nicholls	
14/5/2006	2006	7		MCG	ESSENDON	11	12	78	CARLTON	17	9	111	-33	32,976	M. Head	M. Ellis	
21/5/2006	2006	8		Telstra Dome	ESSENDON	14	8	92	WEST COAST	16	17	113	-21	31,434	H. Kennedy	C. Hendrie	
27/5/2006	2006	9	Night	Telstra Dome	ESSENDON	9	15	69	PORT ADEL	20	9	129	-60	29,232	B. Allen	S. Jeffery	
2/6/2006	2006	10	Night	AAMI Stadium	ESSENDON	6	14	50	ADELAIDE	30	8	188	-138	42,025	D. Woodcock	R. Chamberlain	
9/6/2006	2006	11	Night	Telstra Dome	ESSENDON	13	10	88	GEELONG	20	10	130	-42	43,600	B. Allen	S. Wenn	
18/6/2006	2006	12	Night	Telstra Dome	ESSENDON	10	15	75	MELBOURNE	16	15	111	-36	35,019	M. Ellis	C. Hendrie	
30/6/2006	2006	13	Night	Telstra Dome	ESSENDON	13	11	89	KANGAROOS	14	12	96	-7	33,747	S. Jeffery	S. McBurney	
7/7/2006	2006	14	Night	Subiaco	ESSENDON	12	16	88	FREMANTLE	19	11	125	-37	34,608	S. Meredith	D. Woodcock	
15/7/2006	2006	15		MCG	ESSENDON	10	11	71	ST KILDA	11	8	74	-3	33,082	H. Kennedy	M. Nicholls	
22/7/2006	2006	16		10:50 AM	ESSENDON	16	9	105	CARLTON	15	15	105	0	49,181	J. Schmitt	D. Margetts	
29/7/2006	2006	17	Night	Telstra Dome	ESSENDON	25	10	160	BRISBANE	18	15	123	37	32,761	D. Margetts	S. McLaren	
5/8/2006	2006	18	Night	SCG	ESSENDON	11	7	73	STH M-SYD	17	14	116	-43	25,465	M. Vozzo	J. Schmitt	
11/8/2006	2006	19	Night	MCG	ESSENDON	10	14	74	COLLINGWOOD	9	7	61	13	62,940	M. Vozzo	D. Woodcock	
19/8/2006	2006	20	Night	Telstra Dome	ESSENDON	15	16	106	HAWTHORN	19	10	124	-18	44,275	H. Kennedy	M. Stevic	
26/8/2006	2006	21	Night	MCG	ESSENDON	16	17	113	RICHMOND	20	9	129	-16	48,710	M. Head	C. Hendrie	
1/9/2006	2006	22	Night	Telstra Dome	ESSENDON	18	17	125	WSTRN BLDGS	22	15	147	-22	42,956	R. Chamberlain	M. Ellis	
1/4/2007	2007	1	Early	AAMI Stadium	ESSENDON	16	9	105	ADELAIDE	10	14	74	31	43,064	L. Farmer	H. Kennedy	
8/4/2007	2007	2		Telstra Dome	ESSENDON	19	8	122	FREMANTLE	17	10	112	10	32,623	C. Donlon	S. McBurney	
14/4/2007	2007	3		MCG	ESSENDON	17	20	122	CARLTON	18	17	125	-3	64,710	M. Vozzo	D. Sully	
21/4/2007	2007	4		Telstra Dome	ESSENDON	15	9	99	ST KILDA	9	14	68	31	47,605	S. Jeffery	H. Kennedy	
25/4/2007	2007	5		MCG	ESSENDON	11	13	79	COLLINGWOOD	12	23	95	-16	90,508	S. Jeffery	S. McInerney	
5/5/2007	2007	6		MCG	ESSENDON	15	6	96	HAWTHORN	20	11	131	-35	52,047	S. McBurney	M. Stevic	

Appendix C

DATE	SEASON	RND	SESSION	VENUE	KEVIN'S CLUB	G	B	PTS	OPPONENT	G	B	PTS	MARGIN	ATTENDANCE	FIELD UMPIRE ONE	FIELD UMPIRE TWO	FIELD UMPIRE THREE
11/5/2007	2007	7	Night	Telstra Dome	ESSENDON	13	17	95	KANGAROOS	18	9	117	-22	42,730	M. Vozzo	D. Margetts	
19/5/2007	2007	8		Telstra Dome	ESSENDON	18	19	127	BRISBANE	8	15	63	64	35,034	H. Kennedy	K. Nicholls	
26/5/2007	2007	9	Night	MCG	ESSENDON	12	20	92	RICHMOND	12	12	84	8	61,837	L. Farmer	B. Allen	
2/6/2007	2007	10	Night	SCG	ESSENDON	11	8	74	STH M-SYD	11	7	73	1	26,647	C. Donlon	S. McLaren	
8/6/2007	2007	11	Night	Telstra Dome	ESSENDON	15	5	95	WEST COAST	14	10	94	1	48,913	M. Vozzo	H. Kennedy	
17/6/2007	2007	12	Twilight	AAMI Stadium	ESSENDON	13	17	95	PORT ADEL	19	12	126	-31	25,242	S. Grun	S. Wenn	
29/6/2007	2007	13	Night	Telstra Dome	ESSENDON	19	11	125	MELBOURNE	18	15	123	2	47,552	D. Margetts	S. Grun	
7/7/2007	2007	14	Night	Telstra Dome	ESSENDON	12	11	83	GEELONG	19	19	133	-50	51,156	M. Vozzo	S. McBurney	
15/7/2007	2007	15	Night	Telstra Dome	ESSENDON	14	14	98	WSTRN BLDGS	20	11	131	-33	45,283			
22/7/2007	2007	16		MCG	ESSENDON	14	9	93	COLLINGWOOD	18	14	122	-29	65,531			
30/7/2007	2007	17		Telstra Dome	ESSENDON	18	9	117	ADELAIDE	16	9	105	12	35,010			
6/8/2007	2007	18		MCG	ESSENDON	7	14	56	HAWTHORN	17	17	119	-63	55,019			
13/8/2007	2007	19		Subiaco	ESSENDON	11	11	77	FREMANTLE	21	14	140	-63	38,274			
20/8/2007	2007	20		MCG	ESSENDON	18	10	118	CARLTON	16	12	108	10	48,638			
27/8/2007	2007	21	Twilight	MCG	ESSENDON	13	14	92	RICHMOND	17	17	119	-27	88,468			
2/9/2007	2007	22		Subiaco	ESSENDON	19	10	124	WEST COAST	21	6	132	-8	42,761			

Appendix D
KEVIN SHEEDY'S AFL COACHING CAREER HONOURS

SEASON	PREMIERSHIP MATCHES		TIES	MTCHS	FINALS	FINALS WINS	GF	PREM	PLACE	SUCCESS RATE	PRE-SEAS/NIGHT SERIES		STATE OF ORIGIN		HONOURS
	W	L									W	L	W	L	
1981	16	7	0	23	1	0	0	0	5	70%	5	0			Pre-Seas/Night Premiership
1982	16	7	0	23	1	0	0	0	5	70%	0	1			
1983	18	8	0	26	4	3	1	0	2	69%	0	1			Premiership/Pre-Seas/Night Premiership
1984	20	5	0	25	3	2	1	1	Prem	80%	4	0			Premiership/Pre-Seas/Night Premiership
1985	21	3	0	24	2	2	1	1	Prem	88%	3	1	2	1	
1986	12	11	0	23	1	0	0	0	5	52%	1	1	0	1	
1987	9	12	1	22	0	0	0	0	9	43%	4	0			
1988	12	10	0	22	0	0	0	0	6	55%	1	1			
1989	18	7	0	25	3	1	0	0	3	72%	1	1			Pre-Seas/Night Premiership
1990	18	7	0	25	3	1	1	0	2	72%	4	0			
1991	13	10	0	23	1	0	0	0	6	57%	1	1			
1992	12	10	0	22	0	0	0	0	8	55%	0	1			
1993	16	7	1	24	4	3	1	1	Prem	69%	4	0			Premiership/Pre-Seas/Night Premiership/All Australian Coach
1994	11	11	0	22	0	0	0	0	10	50%	3	0			Pre-Seas/Night Premiership
1995	15	7	2	24	2	1	0	0	5	67%	1	1			
1996	15	9	1	25	3	1	0	0	4	62%	0	1			
1997	9	13	0	22	0	0	0	0	14	41%	0	1			
1998	12	11	0	23	1	0	0	0	8	52%	1	1			
1999	19	5	0	24	2	1	0	0	3	79%	1	0			
2000	24	1	0	25	3	3	1	1	Prem	96%	5	5			Premiership/Pre-Seas/Night Premiership/All Australian Coach
2001	19	6	0	25	3	2	1	0	2	76%	0	3			
2002	13	10	1	24	2	1	0	0	5	56%	0	3			

Appendix D

SEASON	PREMIERSHIP MATCHES				FINALS	FINALS WINS	GF	PREM	PLACE	SUCCESS RATE	PRE-SEAS/NIGHT SERIES		STATE OF ORIGIN		HONORS
	W	L	TIES	MTCHS							W	L	W	L	
2003	14	10	0	24	2	1	0	0	6	58%	0	1			
2004	13	11	0	24	2	1	0	0	6	54%	2	1			
2005	8	14	0	22	0	0	0	0	13	36%	0	1			
2006	3	18	1	22	0	0	0	0	15	16%	0	1			
2007	10	12	0	22	0	0	0	0		45%	0	1			
TOTALS	386	242	7	635	43	23	7	4		61%	41	28	2	2	

Appendix E

KEVIN SHEEDY'S PLAYING ANALYSIS 1967–1979

	WINS	LOSSES	TIES	TOTAL	SUCCESS RATE
Carlton	18	10	1	29	64%
Collingwood	12	10	0	22	55%
Essendon	16	3	1	20	83%
Fitzroy	14	8	0	22	64%
Footscray	11	9	0	20	55%
Geelong	15	7	0	22	68%
Hawthorn	10	11	0	21	48%
Melbourne	18	5	0	23	78%
North Melb	16	10	0	26	62%
St Kilda	16	6	0	22	73%
South Melb	21	4	0	25	84%
TOTALS	167	83	2	252	67%

VENUE	WINS	LOSSES	TIES	TOTAL	SUCCESS RATE
Arden St Oval	7	4	0	11	64%
Glenferrie Oval	3	1	0	4	75%
Junction Oval	4	4	0	8	50%
Kardinia Park	4	4	0	8	50%
Lake Oval	9	1	0	10	90%
MCG	96	36	0	132	73%
Moorabbin	6	4	0	10	60%
Princes Park	7	8	0	15	47%
Victoria Park	3	4	0	7	43%
Waverley Park	20	10	2	32	66%
Whitten Oval	2	5	0	7	29%
Windy Hill	5	2	0	7	71%
TOTALS	166	83	2	251	67%

KEVIN SHEEDY'S COACHING ANALYSIS 1981–2007

	WINS	LOSSES	TIES	TOTAL	SUCCESS RATE
Adelaide	15	9	0	24	63%
Brisbane	19	13	0	32	59%
Carlton	33	22	2	57	60%
Collingwood	34	20	1	55	63%
Fitzroy	19	12	0	31	61%
Fremantle	14	6	0	20	70%
Geelong	22	22	1	45	50%
Hawthorn	26	24	0	50	52%
Kangaroos	23	21	0	44	52%
Melbourne	33	12	0	45	73%
Port Adel	6	11	0	17	35%
Richmond	33	14	1	48	70%
St Kilda	33	8	0	41	80%
Sydney	27	17	1	45	61%
West Coast	22	15	0	37	59%
Western Bulldogs	27	16	1	44	63%
TOTALS	386	242	7	635	61%

	WINS	LOSSES	TIES	TOTAL	SUCCESS RATE
AAMI Stadium	6	16	0	22	27%
Arden St Oval	2	1	0	3	67%
Carrara	5	0	0	5	100%
Gabba	4	9	0	13	31%
Junction Oval	2	2	0	4	50%
Lake Oval	1	0	0	1	100%
MCG	148	84	4	236	64%
Moorabbin	10	0	0	10	100%
North Hobart	1	0	0	1	100%
Optus Oval	14	11	0	25	56%
SCG	9	10	1	20	48%
Skilled Stadium	5	5	0	10	50%
Subiaco	5	15	0	20	25%
Telstra Dome	46	26	1	73	64%
Telstra Stadium	1	3	0	4	25%
Victoria Park	5	2	0	7	71%
WACA	3	1	0	4	75%
Waverley Park	42	31	0	73	58%
Whitten Oval	7	4	0	11	64%
Windy Hill	70	22	1	93	76%
TOTALS	386	242	7	635	61%

Index

INDEX